INTO THE EGYPTIAN MIND

FREDERICK MONDERSON

SUMON PUBLISHERS

SUMON PUBLISHERS
PO Box 160586
Brooklyn, New York 11216

ISBN - 978-1-61023-055-1
LCCN - 2017907786

In the "Tribute to Professor George Simmonds," "Unsung Hero," Dr. Fred Monderson "sat at the feet of his heroes," Brother X, Michael Carter, Dr. Leonard Jeffries, Elombe Brathe, Dr. Lewis, Prof. George Simmonds, Dr. ben-Jochannan, Sister Camille Yarbrough, among others.

ABOUT THE AUTHOR

Dr. Frederick Monderson is a retired African-American college professor and public-school teacher who taught **African History** in the City University of New York and **American History and Government** in the New York public schools. He has written some 1000 articles in the "New York Black Press," *Daily Challenge, Afro Times* and *New American* newspapers. In this venture, Monderson lends his expertise as a historian, Egyptologist, journalist and author of several books including *Ladies in the House*; *Michael Jackson: The Last Dance*; *50 on Point*; *Barack Obama: Ready, Fit to Lead*; *Barack Obama: Master of Washington D.C.*; *Obama: Master and Commander* and *Obama: The Journey*

Completed; *Sonny Carson: The Final Triumph* (5 Volumes); *Black Nationalism: Alive and Well*; *Black Nationalism: Still Alive and Well*; *African Nationalist: Poetry and Prose*; *Guyana: Land of Beauty and Many Waters*; and on Ancient Egypt, *Seven Letters to Mike Tyson on Egyptian Temples*; *10 Poems Praising Great Blacks for Mike Tyson*; *Research Essays on Ancient Egypt*; *Temple of Karnak: The Majestic Architecture of Ancient Kemet*; *Where are the Kamite Kings?*; *Abydos and Osiris*; *Temple of Luxor*; *Medinet Habu: Mortuary Temple of Rameses III*; *The Quintessential Book on Ancient Egypt*: "*Holy Land*" (A Tour Guide Novel on Egypt); *Hatshepsut's Temple at Deir el Bahari*; *Intrigue Through Time*; *An Egyptian Resurrection*, (a Novel on Ancient Egypt); *The Majesty of Egyptian Gods and Temples* (a book of Egyptian Poems); *Egypt Essays on Ancient Kemet*; *The Ramesseum: Mortuary Temple of Rameses II*; *The Colonnade: Then and Now*; *Reflections on Ancient Kemet*; *The Hypostyle Hall*; *Grassroots View of Ancient Egypt*; *Glory of the Ancestors: 19 Letters to O.J. Simpson on Ancient African History*; *Celebrating Dr. Ben-Jochannan*; *Black History Extravaganza: Honoring Dr. Ben Jochannan*; *Let's Liberate the Temple*; *More Woman, More Power*; *Reflections on Ancient Egypt - Book One*; *Reflections on Ancient Egypt - Book Two*; *Black History Everyday - Part One*; *Black History Everyday - Part Two*; *Ancient Egypt: Synthesis*; *Ethiopians in Egypt*: and more. A student of the esteemed Dr. Yosef ben-Jochannan, Dr. Monderson conducts tours to Egypt.

For Tour information, Contact Orleane Brooks-Williams at Nostrand Travel, 730 Nostrand Avenue, Brooklyn, New York 11216. Phone Number 718-756-5300. Next Tour of Egypt is July 27-August 10, 2018.

fredsegypt.com@fredsegypt.com
sumonpublishers.com@sumonpublishers.com
blackegyptbooks.com@blackegyptbooks.com
blackfolksbooks.com@blackfolksbooks.com

Into the Egyptian Mind. Double Temple of Horus and Sobek. Upper frame of the temple's left side entrance of the God Horus Heru) showing the varied capitals, uraei on the cornice and a row of uraei in the rear.

Into the Egyptian Mind. Double Temple of Horus and Sobek. Upper frame of the temple's right-side entrance of the God Sobek showing the varied capitals, uraei on the cornice and a row of uraei in the front.

Very often the issue of names arises regarding modern man's description of the ancient Egyptians and this seems a predetermined pattern. As such, one has to wonder whether this has been part of the systematic attempt to estrange Egypt from Africa and solidify Egypt's place in Europe. After all, today practically every book dealing with the foundations of contemporary European civilization begins with a chapter on Egypt, whereas in earlier times the history began with Greece and Rome. However, and nonetheless, while assessing contemporary arguments as to who were the ancient Egyptians, we cannot ignore the persistent insistence, and must dismiss claims, of a "Caucasian Egypt!" That is, the theory of a migrating people originating in Southwest Asia, who, for "some unknown reason" left their homeland to settle in Egypt is a falsity not founded on fact. Still, the purported view holds, arriving there perhaps sometime during the Old Kingdom these people brought a "superior mental attitude" which "added an impetus to the existing indigenous culture." As a result, Egyptian civilization was able to achieve the great glory the world is so familiar with. Such a late 18th and 19th Century view begun in Europe by German scholars beginning with Hegel and others predominated throughout the 20th Century, stubbornly persists into the 21st Century. However, while not generally challenged by objective scholarship particularly from that epicenter, because there are problems with such a "model," the falsity is being vigorously and systematically challenged by Afrocentrists and others searching for and exposing truth.

The interesting thing is, the anti-Afrocentrists and proponents of this falsity are vehemently fighting back, particularly from an ad hominem perspective, dismissing critical and credible scholarship, even ignoring the contradictions in the Egyptian corpus that nonetheless, mitigates especially against a "Caucasian Egypt." Notwithstanding, this latter view, remains stubbornly consistent with the "Hamitic Hypothesis" position that argued essentially, "Any evidence of a high culture found in Africa was brought there by people of a white morphology."

Naturally, this now discredited theory was and is racist in its intent for it sought to project "White over Black" intellectual, cultural, social and even scientific frames of endowment in human capability and development. Biblical lore was also used to justify this falsity. Still, some of the contradictions as pointed out below, exposes the realities of the situation and asks to what extent could intellectual and lay minds in face of credible evidence that argued against such positions, still allow the perpetuation of the myth of a "White Egypt?"

1. Though similar arguments were put forward by others especially Van Luschan, the theory of a "migrating superior race" gained particular credence through the "migration theory" efforts of W. Flinders Petrie, "the father of modern archaeology." Nonetheless, this approach was dismissed upon critical scrutiny because racist machinations drove Petrie's model! That migrating peoples populated the earth and helped assist in the diffusion and development of culture and ultimately civilization is not altogether far-fetched. Still, to outright argue from a purported superior-inferior, white over black frame of reference, relationship questions the validity of such reasoning in an age when the Slave Trade perpetuated under "naked imperialism," Europe was undergoing its nationalist assertion and consolidation and thereby projecting the superior white man! A classic example of this insane view was representative of Germans seeking to foster Nordic-Aryan superiority over other peoples, white and non-white. Such harsh realities essentially, notwithstanding other regions and peoples being conquered and oppressed, resulted in African people being subjugated and more especially victimized by the horrible institution of slavery, colonization and imperialism!

2. Since man originated in Africa and migrated to people the earth, it is not inconceivable to associate Africans with migration. Brophy and Bauval in their *Black Genesis* (2011) argue a Black African people from a region Southwest of Upper Egypt, Nabta Playa, were the earliest astronomers who

created a calendar based on observations of movements of the heavenly bodies. In scientific ground-breaking, they mapped the heavens, initiated a religious "bovine mother goddess" worship and were farmers who practiced pastoralism and rudimentary forms of agriculture. They, like so many other ancients did artwork utilizing the "predominant red" to represent people and animals. They even traveled great distances in the inhospitable desert navigating by star positioning. All this occurred thousands of years ago from approximately 20,000, but more nearly 7500 to 3,500 years Before Christ. By the latter age, this area was no longer regularly watered by torrential rains which gathered in catch basins allowing practices of farming and cattle rearing or pastoralism. Thus, about 3,500 B.C. as the rains became sparse, these peoples migrated east towards the Nile River in the vicinity south of the Aswan area where they settled. They may very well be associated with what emerged as the Kingdom of Ta-Seti in this region. However, as a result of their extensive travels in the desert, they knew of the existence of the Nile; much unlike the Southwest Asians who probably did not know of the Nile, yet "for some unknown reason" left their homeland and found their way to Egypt.

Possessing millennia of accumulated scientific knowledge developed in observation and charting movements in the heavens, as Bauval and Brophy argued, the inhabitants of Nabta Playa laid the foundation for pharaonic Egypt! Their arrival in Upper Egypt at about 3500 B.C. is very contemporary with evidence in Bruce Williams' discovery, reported in *The New York Times*, of the earliest monarchy at Qustol, in Nubia, dated c. 3400 B.C. Evidently not the entire Nabta Playa community migrated for at least one Old Kingdom cartouche has been found in the original vicinity, perhaps indicating pharaonic attempts to establish contacts with "ancestral beginnings."

3. Many arguments were advanced to support the "Caucasian Egypt" theory particularly those explaining how

the "Dynastic Race" arrived in Egypt, even though these visitors are credited with arriving during the Old Kingdom. That is, after a thriving southern kingdom had galvanized a powerful fighting force, employing the wherewithal of military logistics and ordinance ramifications, mastered the descent of the river, conquered an equally viable northern kingdom, began building temples and initiating religious practices, established a monarchical form of government, possessed a numerical system numbering in the millions, even establishing a calendar and begun the orientation and construction of the "Step," then "True Pyramid" and so much more. Dr. ben-Jochannan argued the "Silt Pyramid" of Nubia predated these two forms. Still, these mountains of stone were antedated by the wind-shaped phenomenon that created the natural pyramids over millennia in the hostile desert environment. Surprisingly still, much of this was predated by the "Negro features of the Sphinx."

Nevertheless, as the story goes, after all of these accomplishments, the Caucasian, "for some unknown reason" who left his native Southwest Asia environment and migrated to Egypt, arrived with his "superior mental attitude" after the native African had done all of the above. There was slight or no evidence of contemporary or comparative accomplishments in the Caucasian home base, and he arrived with nothing but a "white skin and superior intellect," just as "for some unknown" reason he left. No one knows if he actually knew where his final destination would be! Since the route is generally desert-like, we could well imagine the hardships of the journey this early in time; "a struggle for existence;" arriving thirsty, weary, desert whipped but with that "superior mental attitude," looking upon the accomplishments they encountered, they immediately set about reinventing Narmer's wheel! Much more significant, they arrived at a time when the Egyptians were a powerful military state capable of repelling any such invasions as demonstrated in the conquest of Lower Egypt by the Thebans of Upper Egypt who ushered in Unification and dynastic rule.

Into the Egyptian Mind. Double Temple of Horus and Sobek. Classic view of columns of the Peristyle Court, screened panels and the magnificent remains of this Graeco-Roman Temple.

4.   The ancient Egyptians often painted themselves red and as the many theories of Egyptian origins collapsed, those leading the charge of a "Caucasian Egypt" offered the Egyptians were a Caucasian red race! Thus, there were "White Caucasian Egyptians," even "Black Caucasian" Egyptians and now "Red Caucasian" Egyptians. Nevertheless, filterings or survivals of Egyptians painted black in statuary, paintings and even papyrus demanded examination of other possibilities. As it turned out, in his tremendously erudite *African Origins of Civilization: Myth or Reality* Cheikh Anta Diop argued the ancient Egyptians painted themselves red to be distinguished from other Africans! Dr. Yosef ben-Jochannan equally affirmed the ancient Egyptians painted themselves red and also pointed out, today young Nubian brides were colored red with the Henna plant. He sees this as a continuation of the ancient culture. Emile Brugsch-Bey his *History of Egypt* (1901), on the other hand, argued, "Egyptians painted themselves red to create illumination in the dark passage of

the Afterlife" on way to the "Psychostasia" in the Hall of Judgment.

Into the Egyptian Mind. Hatshepsut's Mortuary Temple at Deir el Bahari. From the "Bird's Eye View," the Second Ramp in the Second Court before the Middle Colonnade and Upper Terrace with surviving statues of the Queen and further inward, the Upper Court with Porch entrancing the Sanctuary. All with the mountain as a backdrop. Further on in the upper left, the ruins of Mentuhotep's 11th Dynasty Temple.

Into the Egyptian Mind. Luxor Temple of Amenhotep III and Rameses II. The 14 massive columns of the Processional Colonnade as the waning sun reflects back on its magnificence.

As a young student of ancient history this writer's professor, now seen as misguided, once stated the ancient Egyptians were painted red because they went into the sun and that their women who were painted a lighter color did not go in the sun but stayed at home. Yet, during the 20th Dynasty, Rameses III reported how safe he had made the country that women could come and go as they pleased and not be assaulted or molested in the street! Thus, the various arguments fall apart upon close scrutiny.

The Frenchman Henri L'Hote in his "Tassili Frescoes" discovered in the Sahara and Mary Leakey in "Bushman Art" of East and Southern Africa and who chronicled some 2000 Stone Age sites in the region mention the "predominant red" used by the artists. Recently in 2011, *The New York Times* reported finding a "paint factory" wherein a "paint pot containing red paint and brush" discovered in Southern Africa was dated at 107,000 years old. This factory "find" provided evidence of mixing paint from extracted iron ore particles. Similar sites dated to 150,000 years have also been found but in those instances the clear evidence of "predominant red" had not been evident. However, a previous find in South Africa, dated to 43,000 Before Present (41,000 B.C.) is known. Therefore, the newest Southern African "paint factory" provided clear-cut evidence of the process of extraction and mixing which not only indicated red was a form of cultural coloring but seems to push back the age of early man's thinking by several millennia before the time its generally believed complex social thought processes had actually begun! Again, with this "find" we could also associate the 1973 *New York Times* article chronicling discovery of said iron ore mine in South Africa carbon dated at 43,000 Before Present. As such, it is reasonable to assume iron ore extracts were available and could have been mixed and used by those local artists though evidence of paint had not survived.

Dr. Ivan Van Sertima argued in a lecture, a prevailing view entertained in Europe for much of the 19th Century is that while scientists accept man originated in Africa; the belief is, after migrating to people the world, the African yet stagnated. The Caucasian man, after he had conquered the harsh realities of the ice environment, returned to Africa to civilize the African. This is purely ridiculous Hamitic Hypothesis balls of dung. Now, the paint factory discovery with evidence of paint extraction process that extended man's thinking practices beyond accepted time frames, certainly makes obsolete the above claim.

Understanding what is at stake in the "Egyptian origin argument" and its significance for African history and correcting the putative record, Dr. Diop insisted, "the African who evades the issue of Egypt is either an educated fool or a neurotic person." Prof. John H. Clarke who pointed out "the people who preached racism colonized history" and "when Europe colonized the world it colonized the world's knowledge," admonished, "African history must be written by African historians and scholars!" Maulana Karenga in his work *Maat* (2006: 16) reiterates Diop's contention "that enduring attempts to deny the African character of ancient Egypt and recent claims that the racial or ethnic identity of the ancient Egyptians is irrelevant (Yurco 1989), although it is relevant for the rest of Africa and the world, are both products of an ideological 'scholarship' which grew out of an age of racism and imperialist expansion and the resultant 'need' for a justificatory ideology." This, he states, "led to a concerted effort to discredit dominated peoples through the manipulation of science and the falsification of human history, a falsification which in Africa's case involved depriving it of its most important classical civilization. The thrust seemed to have been one of taking Africans out of Egypt, Egypt out of Africa, and then Africa out of human history. Such a project and view reaffirmed Hegel's and others' Eurocentric claims that Africa was a non-historical continent aided in justifying centuries of oppression and denial of African history and humanity. (Mudimbe 1988; Amin 1989)"

Further, Karenga reinforces the significance of the task ahead by revisiting Diop's "necessary condition" to achieve his "three basic goals" which are: 1) "to reconcile African civilization and history;" 2) "to build a (new) body of modern human sciences;" and 3) "to renew African culture." Thus, he insists, in a new and systematic study of new paradigms posed by the body of knowledge, "Egypt will play in a reconceived and renewed African culture the same role that the Greco-Roman ancient past plays in western culture."

These admonitions mean we must vigorously challenge falsity and misconceptions and strongly aid African historiographic reconstruction so that the record is corrected through systematic correction of distortions and inclusion of omissions of African history and culture systematically implanted by racist Western, European and American historiography. This then will properly reflect the role of Africans in Egypt and in human progress. In this iconoclastic approach, we recognize, as Dr. Leonard James has for the longest emphasized in Egypt, "The existential data contradicts the symbolic representation."

Into the Egyptian Mind. Karnak Temple of God Amon. The "Girdle Wall" of Rameses II. Drama of the Ritual.

Into the Egyptian Mind. Karnak Temple of God Amon. The "Girdle Wall" of Rameses II. Drama of the Ritual.

Into the Egyptian Mind. Karnak Temple of God Amon. The "Girdle Wall" of Rameses II. Drama of the Ritual.

TABLE OF CONTENTS

1. INTRODUCTION — 18
2. LECTURE AT KARNAK — 41
3. EXISTENIALISM AND SYMBOLISM — 132
4. ANCIENT EGYPT: THE STRUGGLE CONTINUES — 142
5. GOD in Ancient Egypt! — 156
6. EGYPTIAN RELIGION — 170
7. RIGHTEOUSNESS — 239
8. THE SANCTUARY — 289
9. THE QUINTESSENTIAL FACE — 313
10. THE PYLON — 324
11. THE ARCHITECTURE OF ANCIENT EGYPT — 341
12. THE KIOSK — 392
13. SALVATION — 400
14. THE EGYPTIAN MYSTERIES — 418
15. CIRCUMCISION — 434
16. THE MUMMY MYSTIQUE — 452

17. LAND OF MANY　　　　464
　　　WATERS
18. PUTTING THEM AWAY　470
　　　NICELY
19. ETERNAL HOUSE　　　477
20. "FESTIVAL"　　　　　514
21. ANCIENT FOUNDATIONS　517
　　　OF HEALTH
22. WALLS IN ANCIENT　　553
　　　EGYPTIAN TEMPLES
　　　AND TOMBS
23. BAPTISM　　　　　　　564
24. INCENSE　　　　　　　569
25. THE APRON　　　　　　575
26. THE HANDS　　　　　　578
27. THE BULL　　　　　　　534
28. THE AVENUE　　　　　587
　　　OF SPHINXES
29. THE COURT　　　　　　592
30. THE COLONNADE　　　597
31. THE PROCESSIONAL　604
　　　COLONNADE
32. THE SACRED LAKE　　610

33. THE "CACHE" 617
34. THE PRIESTHOOD 625
35. PURITY AND PURIFICATION IN ANCIENT EGYPTIAN TEMPLES 652
36. TEMPLE ORIENTATION AND DIVINE WORSHIP 674
37. CONCLUDING POTPOURRI 693

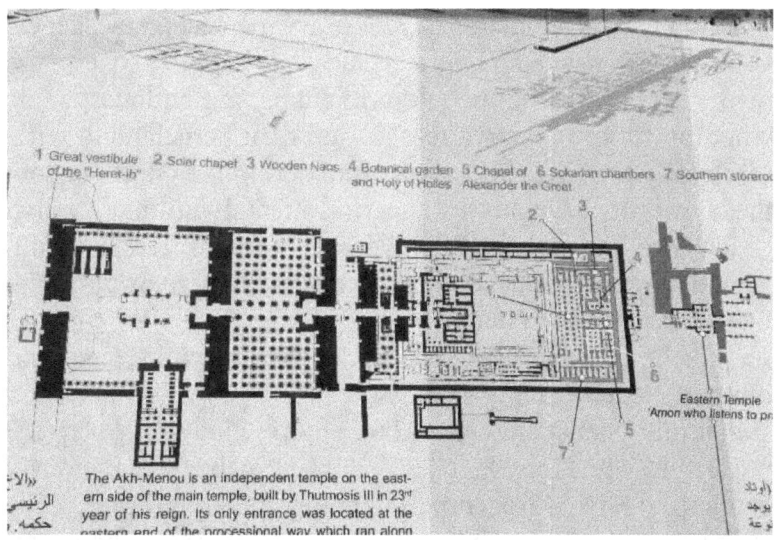

Into the Egyptian Mind. Karnak Temple of God Amon. Plan of the Temple with Thutmose III's Festival Temple the *Akh Menu* highlighted.

1. INTRODUCTION
By
Dr. Fred Monderson

Very often the issue of names arises regarding modern man's description of the ancient Egyptians and this seems a predetermined pattern. As such, one has to remind oneself this has been part of the systematic attempt to estrange Egypt from Africa and solidify Egypt's place in Europe. After all, today practically every book on contemporary European civilization begins with a chapter on Egypt, whereas in earlier times such books on history began with Greece and Rome. Even more important, we cannot today ignore the persistent insistence, yet must dismiss claims of a "Caucasian Egypt!" That is, the theory of a migrating people originating in Southwest Asia, who, for "some unknown reason" left their homeland to settle in Egypt. Arriving there, sometime during the Old Kingdom these people brought a "superior mental attitude" which "added an impetus to the indigenous culture." As a result, Egyptian civilization was able to achieve the great glory the world is so familiar with. Such a late 18th and 19th Century view begun by German scholars beginning with Hegel and others predominated throughout the 20th Century and stubbornly persists into the 21st Century. However, there are problems with this "model" and it is being vigorously challenged by Afrocentrists among other peoples. The interesting thing is, the anti-Afrocentrists are vehemently fighting back, particularly from an *ad hominem* perspective, dismissing credible scholarship, even ignoring the contradictions in the Egyptian corpus that mitigate especially against a "Caucasian Egypt." Pernicious minds attack the "mote in Afrocentric scholarship but ignore the beam of falsity and contradiction in presentation of a white supremacy model." In this regard, they blatantly ignore that the existential data contradicts the symbolic representation. Significantly, not only is new research shedding fresh light but within the "Ancient Records of the Ancient Records," mistakes are being pointed out as made by early scholars, their tremendous efforts in reclaiming the culture, notwithstanding.

Into the Egyptian Mind. Ghizeh Plateau. Close-up of the Great Sphinx.

Into the Egyptian Mind. Ghizeh Plateau. Close-up of the Great Pyramid of Khufu.

More importantly, however, the now sternly criticized perspective is seen as stubbornly consistent with the "Hamitic Hypothesis" position of falsity that argued essentially and espousing, "Any evidence of a high culture found in Africa was brought there by people of a white morphology." Naturally, this now discredited theory was racist in its intent for it sought to project "White over Black" intellectual, cultural, moral, social, and even scientific frames of endowment in human development. Nevertheless, even though some of the contradictions as pointed out below, exposes the realities of the situation one wonders how intellectual and lay minds in face of credible evidence could that argue against such positions, still allow the perpetuation of the myth of a "White Egypt?"

Into the Egyptian Mind. Egyptian Art. Vulture with outstretched wings among the grapes on a ceiling.

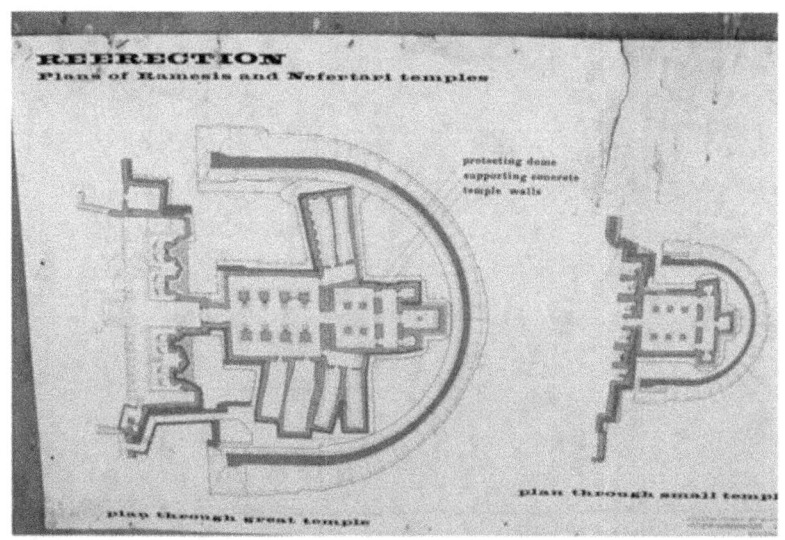

Into the Egyptian Mind. Plan of the Twin Temples of Abu Simbel. The Great Temple of Rameses II (left) and the lesser temple of his wife, Queen Nefertari (right).

Into the Egyptian Mind. Horus Temple at Edfu. Pharaoh stands before enthroned Horus (Heru) wearing the White and Red Double Crown.

Into the Egyptian Mind. Horus Temple at Edfu.
In Double Crown Pharaoh presents a platter of 4 Obelisks.

1. Though similar arguments were put forward by others, the theory of a "migrating superior race" gained credence through the efforts of W. Flinders Petrie, "the father of modern archaeology," but was dismissed upon critical scrutiny because "racist machinations drove the model!" That migrating peoples populated the earth and helped assist in the diffusion and development of culture and ultimately

civilization is not altogether far-fetched but to outright argue from a fostered superior-inferior, white over black, relationship questions the validity of this line of reasoning propagated in an age when the Slave Trade was perpetuated under "naked imperialism." During that time, Europe was undergoing its nationalist assertion and consolidation and the Germans especially sought to foster Nordic-Aryan superiority over other peoples, white and non-white, particularly Africans being victimized by the horrible institution of slavery!

Into the Egyptian Mind. Ghizeh Plateau. View of the Sphinx between Khufu's Pyramid (left) and Khafra's Pyramid (right).

Into the Egyptian Mind. Ghizeh Plateau. From the southeast, side profile of the Sphinx in all its majesty.

Into the Egyptian Mind. Ghizeh Plateau. Thoth (Tehuti) preceding the Red Crown.

Into the Egyptian Mind. Horus Temple at Edfu. Isis (Auset) as Hathor wearing the vulture headdress with Horns and disk surmounted on a mortar.

2. Since man originated in Africa and migrated to people the earth, it is not inconceivable to associate Africans with migration. Brophy and Bauval in their work *Black Genesis* (2011) argue, a black African people from a region Southwest

of Upper Egypt, Nabta Playa, were the earliest astronomers who created a calendar based on observations of movements of the heavenly bodies. These early enquiring and inventive minds mapped the heavens, initiated a religious "bovine mother goddess" worship and were farmers who practiced pastoralism. They did artwork utilizing the "predominant red" to represent people and animals. They even traveled great distances moving cattle to pasture over inhospitable desert navigating, by star positioning, as they migrated to find water and foliage for their cattle. All this occurred thousands of years ago from approximately 20,000-3,500 years Before Christ. By the latter age, this area was no longer regularly watered by torrential rains which gathered in catch basins allowing practices of farming and cattle rearing or pastoralism. Thus, about 3,500 B.C. as the rains became sparse, desiccating the land, these peoples migrated east towards the Nile River in the vicinity of Qustol between Aswan and Abu Simbel, where they settled. As a result of their extensive travels in the desert, they knew of the existence of the Nile; much unlike the Southwest Asians who "for some unknown reason" left their homeland and more than likely did not know of the Nile's whereabouts. Are we to assume they actually knew of the Nile and how to cross the desert to reach it?

Into the Egytpian Mind. Erik Mondersons beside the Sphinx at Memphis in 2018.

Into the Egyptian Mind. Egyptian Art. Workers in various attitudes being supervised by the larger figure to the right.

Into the Egyptian Mind. Egyptian Art. Deceased and wife raise hands in salute to Ra-Horakhty (top) and consort Hathor (bottom) wearing Horns and Disk.

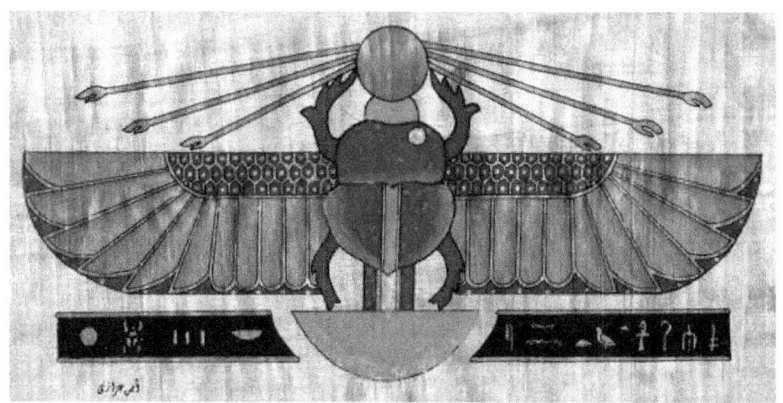

Into the Egyptian Mind. Egyptian Art. Papyrus.
A winged Khepre standing on Heb pushes the ball of the sun.

Into the Egyptian Mind. Erik Monderson on the Ghizeh Plateau with the Sphinx and Khafre's Pyramid at his rear.

Into the Egyptian Mind. Horus Temple at Edfu.
Colossal image of Horus (Heru) enthroned and defaced.

Into the Egyptian Mind. Horus Temple at Edfu. In the "Corridor of Victory" a scene from the battle between Horus (Heru) and Seth (Typhon). Isis (Auset) kneels with her face defaced. Notice her exposed breast. This was a later Graeco-Roman innovation.

Possessing millennia of accumulated scientific knowledge developed in observation and charting movements in the heavens, as Bauval and Brophy argued, the inhabitants of **Nabta Playa** laid the foundation for pharaonic Egypt! The authors called these ancient Africans "precursors of the pharaohs!" Their arrival in Upper Egypt at about 3500 B.C. is very contemporary with Bruce Williams' discovery relative to the earliest monarchy at Qustol dated c. 3400 B.C. Evidently not the entire Nabta Playa community migrated for at least one Old Kingdom cartouche has been found in the vicinity, perhaps indicating pharaonic attempts to establish contacts with "ancestral beginnings." Who knows, perhaps it was "to see where we came from!"

3.   Many arguments were advanced to support the "Caucasian Egypt" theory particularly those explaining how the "Dynastic Race" arrived in Egypt, even though these visitors are credited with arriving during the Old Kingdom. That is, after a thriving southern kingdom had galvanized a powerful fighting force, employing the wherewithal of military logistics and ordinance ramifications, mastered the descent of the river, conquered a supposedly equally viable and functioning northern kingdom, began building temples and initiating state sponsored religious practices, established a monarchical form of government, possessed a numerical system numbering in the millions, and inaugurating a functional calendar, lends the view, the southern kingdom must have been well-organized administratively to have instituted the social, political and religious institutions Narmer put in place. These developments, within a few centuries led to the orientation and construction of the "Step," then "True Pyramid" and so much more. Dr. ben-Jochannan argued the "Silt Pyramid" of Nubia predated these two forms. Still, all were antedated by the wind-shaped phenomenon that created the natural pyramids over millennia in the hostile desert environment evident in Upper Egypt. Nevertheless, as the story goes, after all of these accomplishments, the Caucasian, "for some unknown reason" who left his native Southwest Asia environment and migrated to Egypt, arrived bringing his "superior mental attitude" after the native African had done all of the above. Naturally, that is to say, they came out and re-invented "Narmer's wheel." Significantly, there was no evidence of comparative accomplishments in the Caucasian home base, and he arrived with nothing but a "white skin and superior intellect," just as "for some unknown" reason he left. No one knows if he actually knew where his final destination would be! Since the route is generally desert-like, one could well imagine the hardships of the journey, a "struggle for existence," arriving thirsty, weary, desert whipped but with that "superior mental attitude," looking upon the accomplishments they encountered; again, they immediately set about reinventing Narmer's wheel!

4. The ancient Egyptians often painted themselves red and as the many theories of Egyptian origins collapsed, those leading the charge of a "Caucasian Egypt" offered the Egyptians were a Caucasian red race! Thus, there were "white Caucasian Egyptians," even Black Caucasian Egyptians, and now "red Caucasian Egyptians." Let us not lose sight, the Egyptians painted themselves red to be illuminated in the **pitch-black** darkness of the heavenly journey to the Hall of Judgment.

Nevertheless, filterings or survivals of Egyptians painted black in statuary, paintings and even papyrus, demanded examination of other possibilities. As it turned out, in his tremendously erudite *African Origins of Civilization*: *Myth or Reality* Dr. Cheikh Anta Diop stated the ancient Egyptians painted themselves red to be distinguished from other Africans! Dr. Yosef ben-Jochannan equally affirmed the ancient Egyptians painted themselves red because they were dead and also pointed out modern young Nubian brides were colored red with the Henna plant and sees this as a continuation of the ancient culture.

Into the Egyptian Mind. Erik Monderson strolling with Khafre's Pyramid at his rear.

Into the Egyptian Mind. Ghizeh Plateau. Massive granite pillars in vicinity of the Great Sphinx.

Into the Egyptian Mind. Ghizeh Plateau. View from within the Sphinx's sacred space, looking toward the Great Pyramid.

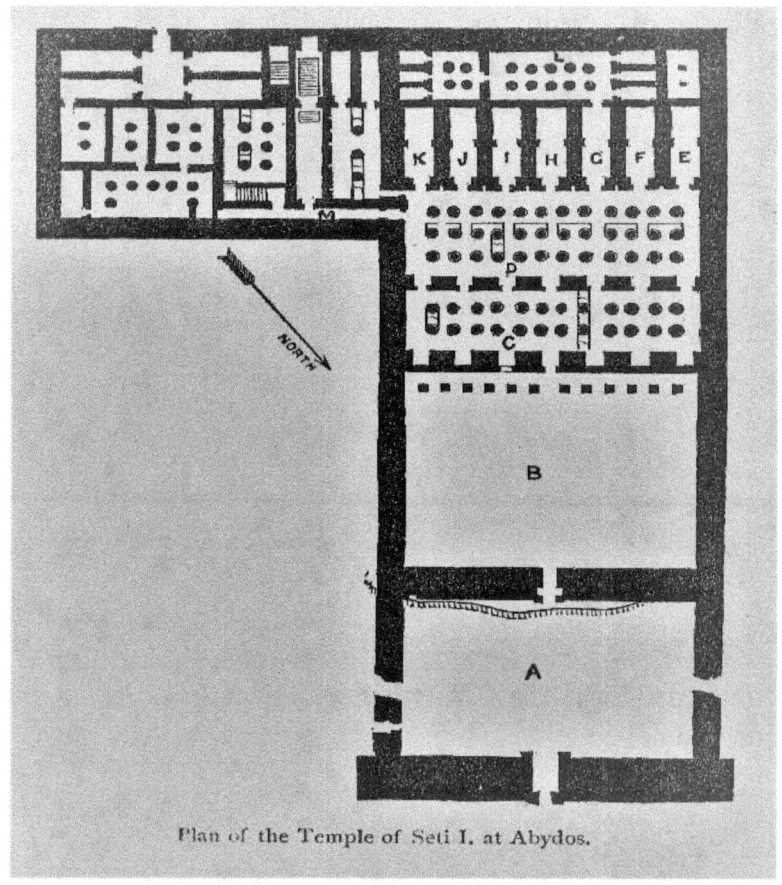

Plan of the Temple of Seti I. at Abydos.

SETI I'S TEMPLE AT ABYDOS TO OSIRIS

- A. First Court – Destroyed
- B. Second Court – Destroyed
- C. First Hypostyle Hall
- D. Second Hypostyle Hall
- E. Chapel – Sanctuary of Horus
- F. Chapel – Sanctuary of Isis
- G. Chapel – Sanctuary of Osiris
- H. Chapel – Sanctuary of Ra-Horakhty
- I. Chapel – Sanctuary of Amon-Ra
- J. Chapel – Sanctuary of Ptah
- K. Chapel – Sanctuary of Seti I
- L. Inner Sanctuary of Osiris

M. Gallery of the Abydos Tablet/List
N. Chapel of Nefertum
O. Chapel of Sokar
P. Hall of the Books
Q. hall of Sacrifice
R. Corridor of the Bull

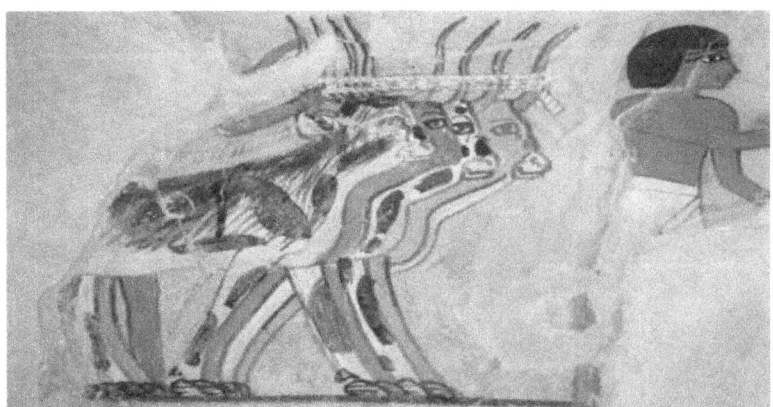

Into the Egyptian Mind. Egyptian Art. Taking the cows home.

Into the Egyptian Mind. Horus Temple at Edfu. Wearing the Double Crown with a falcon image before him, Horus (Heru) is borne in a throne Anubi (Anpu) on Heb in the "Corridor of Victory."

Into the Egyptian Mind. Egyptian Art. Papyrus.
The Judgment, weighing of the heart by Anubis (Anpu) (left) and Thoth (Tehuti) (right) before enthroned Ra-Horakhty.

Into the Egyptian Mind. Horus Temple at Edfu.
Pharaoh, in a colorful crown of horns, supporting white crown with feathers surmounted by disks and Uraei with disks, as he presents a sphinx presenting a vessel topped by uraeus with disk.

As a young student of ancient history this writer's professor, now seen as misguided, once stated the ancient Egyptians were painted red because they went into the sun and that their women who were painted a lighter color did not go in the sun but stayed at home. Yet, during the 20th Dynasty, Rameses III reported how safe he had made the country that women could come and go as they pleased and not be assaulted or molested in the street!

The Frenchman Henri L'Hote in his "Tassili Frescoes" in the Sahara and Mary Leakey in "Bushman Art" of East and Southern Africa who chronicled some 2000 Stone Age sites therein, mention the "predominant red" used by the artists. Recently, *The New York Times* in 2011 reported finding a "paint factory" with "red paint and brush" remains in Southern Africa dated at 107,000 years old. This factory "find" provided evidence of mixing paint from extracted iron ore. Similar sites dated to 150,000 years have also been assumed but then the clear evidence of "predominant red" had not been found. The southern African "paint factory" provided clear cut evidence of the process of extraction and paint mixing which not only indicated red was a form of cultural coloring but seems to push back the age of early man's thinking by several millennia before the time it's believed complex social thought processes actually began! With this "find" we could also associate a 1973 *New York Times* article chronicling discovery of an iron ore mine in South Africa carbon-dated at "43,000 Before Present." It is reasonable to assume iron ore extracts were available and could have been mixed and used by local artists though evidence of paint had not survived until the recent discovery.

Dr. Ivan Van Sertima argued in a lecture, a prevailing view entertained in Europe is that while scientists accept that man originated in Africa, the view is after migrating to people the world, the African stagnated. The Caucasian man, whom we know is linked to the African in his initial migration, and after he had conquered the harsh realities of the ice environment "returned to Africa to civilize the African." Now, we must not forget the units of culture, viz., Hieroglyphs, Petroglyphs, religion, architectural forms and river dynamics germane to the Nile Valley were absent in these migrants' places of origin. Even the Egyptians/Kamites have no record of these purported people and connections to their place of origin. Importantly, however, the paint factory discovery with evidence of paint extraction process that extended man's thinking practices beyond accepted time frames certainly makes obsolete the above claim.

Dr. Diop admonished the African who evades the issue of Egypt is either an educated fool or a neurotic. Prof. John H. Clarke pointed out "the people who preached racism colonized history" and "when Europe colonized the world, she colonized the world's knowledge." Thus, they both insist African history must be written by African historians! Maulana Karenga in his work **Ma'at** (2006: 16) reiterates Diop's contention, "that enduring attempts to deny the African character of ancient Egypt and recent claims that the racial or ethnic identity of the ancient Egyptians is irrelevant (Yurco 1989), although it is relevant for the rest of Africa and the world, are both products of an ideological 'scholarship' which grew out of an age of racism and imperialist expansion and the resultant 'need' for a justificatory ideology." This, he states, "led to a concerted effort to discredit dominated peoples through the manipulation of science and the falsification of human history, a falsification which in Africa's case involved depriving it of its most important classical civilization. The thrust seemed to have been one of taking Africans out of Egypt, Egypt of Africa, and then Africa out of human history. Such a project and view reaffirmed Hegel's and others' Eurocentric claims that Africa was a non-historical continent aided in justifying centuries of oppression and denial of African history and humanity. (Mudimbe 1988; Amin 1989)"

Further, Karenga reinforces the significance of the task ahead by revisiting Diop's "necessary condition" to achieve his "three basic goals" -

1) "to reconcile African civilization and history;"

2) "to build a (new) body of modern human sciences;" and

3) "to renew African culture."

In that case, he insists, in a new and systematic study of new paradigms posed by the body of knowledge, "Egypt will play in a reconceived and renewed African culture the same role that the Greco-Roman ancient past plays in western culture."

These admonitions mean we must vigorously challenge falsity and misconceptions and strongly aid African historiographic reconstruction so that the record is corrected to properly reflect the role of Africans in Egypt and in human progress.

Into the Egyptian Mind. Erik Monderson and young Egyptians at the Pyramids.

Into the Egyptian Mind. Horus Temple at Edfu.
Wearing Red and White Double Crown, Horus (Heru) in all his regal majesty.

Into the Egyptian Mind. Erik Monderson and more of the young Egyptians at the Pyramids.

Into the Egyptian Mind. Horus Temple at Edfu.
Wearing the Red Crown with horns, feathers and disk and sporting a short beard and necklace, elements have begun to deface the king's face. Again, we ask why?

Into the Egyptian Mind. Egyptian Art. Papyrus.
Picking grapes (left) and pressing wine (right).

Into the Egyptian Mind. Egyptian Art. Wearing the Leopard Skin, a Sem Priest pours a libation over a Nobleman and his wife who holds a meant and ankh.

2. LECTURE AT KARNAK TEMPLE, SATURDAY AUGUST 13, 2016 REFLECTIONS ON ANCIENT EGYPT
By
Dr. Fred Monderson

I. INTRODUCTION
II. WHO WERE THE ANCIENT EGYPTIANS

III. THE ROLE OF ARCHAEOLOOGY

IV. TEMPLES AND TOMBS
The Earliest tombs
Ten Temples at Abydos
The Middle Kingdom
New Kingdom
Graeco-Roman Temples

V. HISTORY OF EGYPT

VI. CONCLUSIONS

INTRODUCTION

Good Morning. It is a distinct honor and especial privilege to address men and women of deep thought, here at Karnak Temple, the "most select of places," home of God Amon, King of the Gods and maker of men, plants, animals, the earth and that dark and star-lit abode where the gods are born and dwell in harmony, purity and everlastingness. Ludwig Burkhardt reminded us, green and blue were just shades of black and we must remember Amon was described as so black, he was blue! Notwithstanding, we must stay vigilant, mindful and help to cease the disappearance of so much of this ancient culture. I'm reminded of seeing, in a back room at Medinet Habu the Gods enthroned with Amon at the head, represented as he is in

Luxor temple as God Min, and the same at Abu Simbel with **Black-face**. However, while this is an Egyptian preservative measure, last year Britain alone imported nearly 1500 pieces of artifacts. Now multiply this across the spectrum and you thus have a little idea of where I'm coming from. This phenomenon has been unending for more than two centuries, or should I actually say two millennia or more, if we go back to Persian, Assyrian, Greek and Roman plunder and expropriation.

I must first point out, I did not come here to educate you on Egyptology, I came here to learn from you and further seek to understand what this culture represents. This "Citadel" of theological, spiritual and cultural essence is the "Mecca of Egyptology," the place of the discipline's well-spring and I feel confident it is in good hands. I happened to be on my own adventurous pilgrimage at Karnak Temple and was encouraged to give a lecture essentially relaying some of what I know of the subject. Naturally, such an opportunity is not too often presented and so I accepted and has spent a few days in my hotel crafting a response that may seem a challenge but must be of a standard that respects and appreciates the opportunity to present to so distinguished an audience. Naturally I have questions of my own on which you can fill me in later. What was the actual cause of Queen Hatshepsut's death? How often have you seen a god with both hands empty? I saw one at Deir el Bahari temple, it may have been Sokar.

My name is Frederick Monderson, Dr. Fred Monderson. I am an African historian, retired educator and a journalist by trade. I have studied Egypt from the time I met Dr. Ben-Jochannan in 1972, that is more than 40 years ago. I am an Egyptologist with a profound interest in Egyptian temples, particularly its architecture. Photography is an avid passion of mine. I have photographed all the monuments from Abu Simbel to Sakkara. I have a book on Karnak Temple, one on Deir el Bahari as well as another on Medinet Habu with work in various stages on

Luxor, Ramesseum, Kom Ombo, Edfu and Philae. I have a work in progress on Abydos and Osiris and Hathor of Dendera. I'm fascinated by Egyptian archaeology. Not only have I studied Egyptian history as a student and taught it to the extent I was permitted, I have researched Egypt at the New York Public Library, Temple University and the Bodleian Library in Oxford, having spent two summers at Exeter College, Oxford in 1976 and 1981. I am a collector of ancient Egyptian Literature, history, religion, art and architecture and so have some familiarity with the subject.

I would like to begin by reading a poem dedicated to Amon, Amon-Ra.

POEM TO AMON-RA

O mighty Amon, the Greatest of the Black African deities, ithyphallic, you were from primeval times, Lord of Gods.
Your creativity radiated over an age, father of the gods, when worshippers praised your hidden nature.
Conquering peoples and places, they brought light and civility to the world, in your immortal name, multitudinous, more numerous, not known. The vanquished contributed wealth filling your treasury and your subjects, victorious in their imperial exploits, erected mansions in glory and praise of your being, Chief of the Great Ennead of the Gods, Self-Begotten, Lord of Heaven, Lord of Earth.
O Dweller in Anu, the Gods ascribe praise to you, maker of things celestial and things terrestrial, for you illuminate Egypt, President of the Apts.

Into the Egyptian Mind. Egyptian Art. Pouring a libation before a Nobleman and wife under a canopy as they sail on the Nile River.

Into the Egyptian Mind. Egyptian Art. Restoration of a defaced piece of portraiture.

Into the Egyptian Mind. Horus Temple at Edfu.
In the "Corridor of Victory," images of Horus (Heru) and Hathor (Athor) are defaced. Why?

Into the Egyptian Mind. Horus Temple at Edfu.
Horus (Heru) as Ra-Horakhty (left); Isis (Auset) as Hathor (Athor, center) and the king wearing horns, disk and feathers with uraei with disks. The thrones and feet are all aligned.

Beautiful child of Love, from relative obscurity you emerged in the Middle Kingdom and sat on your Sacred Mound of Creation.

That first time, seeking to complete the task of previous gods fallen short, you Created Brilliant Rays, Thunder in Heaven.
Black African rulers of that age imbibed in your inspiration, Lord of the Two Lands.
Mighty in Power, Lord of Awe-inspiring terror, they similarly manifested resolute courage, wisdom, intellect, and creative prowess.
They therefore gained success as Warrior Pharaohs, with mighty souls, all in your name, Fashioner of the Beauty of Kings, Priests and Artisans, O Lord of the Throne of Egypt.
All the Gods are three, Amen, Ra and Ptah and none like thee. Amen is his hidden name; Ra is his face, Ptah his body.

Power made by Ptah, Bull of Heliopolis, kings' architects shaped a society whose blueprint you encouraged in manifold attributes.
Lord of Scepter and Ankh, Frog, and Uraeus, Couchant Lion, your symbols include Beautiful Tiaras, Lofty Plumes, and Ureret, War, Nemes and Atef Crowns.
The prosperity you endowed your adherents generated artistic, scientific and linguistic creations, Lord of the Apts.
These first beneficiaries of your generosity toward mankind, erected temples as chapels simply to glorify your great name, Amon Lord of Thebes, Lord of the Two Lands, Lord of Might, Lord of Food, Bull of Offerings, Kamutef at the head of his Fields.
Lord of Victuals, Bull of Provisions, the gods beg their sustenance from you, Lord of Fields, banks and plots of ground.

Lord of Truth, Father of the Gods, Maker of Men, Creator of all animals, Black African kings, men of vision, fortitude and tenacity, benefited from an earlier age of African creativity. They synthesized, experimented and with vision and bellicosity bequeathed a creative era where craftsmen, philosophers, priests and kings, were motivated to extol your name to greater heights.

Lord of Radiant Light, you Exist into Eternity as Lord of Heaven, Lord of Earth, Lord of the Gods, Lord of the High Lands and Mountains, Lord of the Joy of Heart, Mighty One of Crowns.

Your Loveliness is in the Southern Sky and Your Graciousness is in the Northern Sky.

Your name is strong; your will is heavy.

Mountains of ore cannot withstand your might, for you set in order the kingdom of eternity unto eternity.

Lord of eternity, creator of everlastingness, you arise in the eastern horizon and set in the western horizon. Born early every day, you overthrew your enemies, steering oar, pilot who knows the water, Lord of the ship of the morning and ship of the evening, master of two stems. Beautiful form fashioned by Ptah, Ox with strong arm who loves strength; you are first in Upper Egypt, Lord of the Land of the Matoi and Prince of Punt.

Lord of Perception who speaks with authority, Lord of the Gods whose shrine is hidden, you are Lord of the Double Crown, Great Hawk who makes festive the body, fair body that makes festive the breast.

Beneficent God, you presided over a world as King of Kings. Lord of the Thrones of the Two Lands, Bull of your Mother, New Kingdom monarchs competed trying to out-do predecessors praising Amon, Greater than Great of the Primordial Deities, who continues to bless his champions.

Chief of Egypt, territorial conquests, ensuing wealth, architectural constructions, and religious and philosophical sonnets, extolled the name of Amon Presider of Karnak, who dwells in the Most Select of Places, in Power and Glory, Invisible and Creative.

As Chief of all the Gods, you fashion the deities, One in his actions as with the Gods.
Stablisher of all things, Lord of things that are, you Create all Life, Lord of the Sektet Boat and of the Antet Boat.

First Born Son of the Earth, Chief of Mankind, your Sanctuary at Karnak is a splendid piece of divinely inspired architecture. Master of the Double Crown, you receive the Ames Scepter.
Lord of the Makes Scepter and whip, your precinct, befits the Eternal Spirits of the Theban Triad, Amon, Mut, Khonsu, whose reigns encompassed millennia.
Priests manifested theological and sadly power from this sacred abode, constructed in stone while similar West-Bank 'Mansions of Millions of Years' profess Amon's august name, as Source of all Light in Heaven.
Lord of Karnak, King of the South and North, Lord of Things Which Exist, Stablisher of All Creation, You Last Forever, equips all lands, fashioner of all that exists, Just One, Lord of Thebes.

Beautiful boy whom the gods praise, maker of men and stars who illuminates the two lands, you are great of strength, Lord of Might, Chief who made the two lands, the Gods rejoice in your beauty, Amen-Ra, venerated in Karnak.
Lord of the Deeds Case who holds the flail, you are the Heliopolitan, first of his Ennead, who lives daily on truth.
The gods love to gaze at you when the Double Crown rests upon your brow, hawk in the midst of the horizon; you are beloved in the Southern Sky, and pleasant in the Northern Sky, possessor of praise, the Sun of Heaven.

Into the Egyptian Mind. Egyptian Art. Anubis (Anpu) has got Osiris' (Ausar) back while grapes hang overhead from the ceiling.

Into the Egyptian Mind. Egyptian Art. With mourners on display and a Sem Priest in leopard skin pours a libation and incenses the bier, as part of the "Open the Mouth Ceremony," the Deceased is poised to Sail.

Into the Egyptian Mind. Horus Temple at Edfu.
Pharaoh wears an interesting crown and presents a sphinx to defaced and enthroned Horus (Heru) and Hathor (Athor).

Into the Egyptian Mind. Horus Temple at Edfu.
In "Blue" or "War Crown" and wearing necklace, Pharaoh presents a platter of various victuals to Horus (Heru) in Double Crown.

Lord of Things that are, acting as Judge, Vizier of the Poor Who Takes No Bribes, your intellectual majesty enlightened the world in knowledge of arts and medicine.
Your inspiration pioneered astronomy, quarrying, navigation, stone-transportation, agriculture, mathematics, all gifts of the African mind. Generations of black men and women worship and praise you mighty Amon, King of the Gods, First Born, and Resting upon Ma'at. Amenemenes, Sesostris, then Ahmose, Amenhotep, Thutmose, Hatshepsut, Seti, Rameses, Merenptah and Piankhy, Shabaka, Shabataka, Taharka, were greatest adherents, physical father of these kings, Power of the Gods.
Amen-Ra the Justified, you give your hands to those you love and assign those you hate to fire.

The Gods love to behold you and they rejoice in your beautiful acts. These divinities acclaim you the Great House and Crown you with Crowns in the House of Fire.
Homage to you, Dweller in Peace for you are Successor to Ra. Fashioner of Kings and Queens, sole king among the gods, your collective wisdom schooled the Greeks and Romans, the newest converts.
They immersed in your wonderful cultural heritage, praising you with equal zeal and vigor.
Chief of all the Beings of the Underworld, Lord of the Nubians, Governor of Punt, King of Heaven, Amon the great African God, we beseech you, Lord of Eternity, today continue to make enlightening the Black culture of Kemet/Egypt, land of the ancestors.
Pour forth your salvation and ingenuity to inspire our people even more as they meet challenges in a new Millennium.

We African-American people view the ancient Nile Valley, Nubia and Egypt especially, as part of our cultural heritage. We appreciate Egypt. We have stood by Egypt. We have defended Egypt. We have learned from Egypt. We consider you Egyptians as the intellectual salt of the earth and would insist you must not lose your flavor. We look to you to be the embodiment of Ma'at, the practice of justice, truth, righteousness. In seeking truth; we see you as beacons. Though we might be half-way around the world, we expect your light must shine brightly, so from that a distance we can see and connect with our brothers and sisters here, grow and philosophically be strengthened to challenge the propagated falsity that now pervades the discipline in which you are all experts. What Dr. Ben Carruthers meant by his book *Intellectual Warfare* (1999) is actually a struggle for the minds and cultural heritage of African people and a battle in which we are engaged and we look to you, appreciate your role as constituting the depth of our strength as we confront falsity and *Isfit*. Most important, we firmly recognize "The existential data contradicts the symbolic representation" of this discipline, globally.

As the "Home Brigade" on the ground here we pray you must remain strong, vigilant and resolute in defense of this divine science manifesting in its theology, spirituality and art, sacred art, and architecture. In this cultivated attitude, you must establish and maintain order, not simply in your fieldwork, you must establish a code of conduct, behavior and dress for those visiting and entering these holy places. Some years ago, I was in a Mosque in Cairo and a young woman came in wearing a short dress. One of the people there came with a sheet and simply covered her up. I was in Medinet Habu two days ago and observed visitors wearing something a little removed from a bathing suit in a holy place. The guides must be your front-line agents in helping to nudge people to wear proper clothing leaving the hotel to these sacred sites. African-Americans will never come to Egypt, and enter a temple dressed like that because we respect and honor the intellectual, religious and philosophical achievements of the ancestors who tread this sacred land, as they occupied this sacred space in sacred time as they established Ma'at and schooled and helped launch the pageantry of human intellectual and cultural development mankind so wonderfully benefitted from.

Everyone has their preference. Dr. Ben Jochannan taught us not to go into the Sanctuary, "Holy of Holies," for in ancient times only the Pharaoh and High Priest entered therein. A great number of ancient people attended the daily ritual, viz., those of the book and liturgy, incense bearers, water carriers, those bearing food, vestments and oils, dancers, singers, guards, etc., but they never entered through the "doors of heaven," only the most revered were allowed in the God's sacred abode and presence. We recognize as Princes of the Realm, this does not apply to you because of the nature of your work, but it is something you must take note of.

You must also know and be gently reminded, we African-Americans, American-Nubians, love Egypt. We stand firmly on the frontline in defense of your glorious culture. You must feel confident in our work because we grow from it and are grounded in its most profound tenets. Like everyone else, we are not all good, though most of us are good. Together, as we work, teach, praise and resurrect and practice the old religion, ethical and spiritual tenets of the ancestors, Egypt must stay strong and like the first, may be the last, hope for mankind, humanity.

Now, right thinking Egyptians realize Europeans have tremendous influence in this country by virtue of their presence in numbers in Egypt and the money they spend as tourists among other factors, not least of which is foreign investments especially in the tourist industry. While there has been some slow-down of tourists recently, in times past there has been some 25 million visitors to Egypt annually contributing nearly a quarter of the national budget. More important, long in the study, Europeans have mastered the ancient hieroglyphic language and dominated the field of Egyptology even insisting for most of the first century of the discipline only Frenchmen head the Antiquities Department. To be clear, the Englishman Flinders Petrie defined the field of Egyptology to be knowledge of the writing, geography and history. Of course, one does not have to be master of all three at the same time.

It must first be pointed out, African-American scholars have long pointed to the multi-faceted nature of the problem, viz., antiquities collection and export; misrepresentation of the role of Black people whether in history, religion, art or even architecture as revealed through archaeology and its sister discipline anthropology; and most important defacement of the monuments and the art especially attacking the African features. First Chancellor Williams in *Destruction of Black Civilization* (1974) wrote about the glory and defeat then destruction of the ancient wonder. Dr. Carter G. Woodson in *The African Background Outlined* and *The Mis-Education of the Negro*, showed how forces of misdirection have mis-educated African people and forced them not simply to reject their history but to accept the world view as were created by non-Africans. Dr. Ben-Jochannan in his trilogy of works, *Africa: Mother of Western Civilization (*1970); *African Origins of the "Major" Western Religions* (1971); and *Black Man of the Nile and His Family* (1972) to which he added *From Abu Simbel to Ghizeh: A Guide Book and Manual* (1989) has been exceptional in defense of Egypt and what it represents to the African mind and body. In these works, many in pioneering style, he not only educated his people, pointed to many problems of misrepresentation, omission, plan of distortion and destruction of the monuments, as created around this subject. He also brought untold numbers of people to see the evidence and encouraged them to study and respect the Egyptian culture and people. He admonished, when visiting the holy sites be on the best behavior, never go into the sanctuary for only the pharaoh and high priest did so in ancient times. He also encouraged his students and those he influenced to write books, form study groups and never become complacent about Egypt. Equally and very early, another great defender of this wonderful Egyptian human and cultural experiment, J.A. Rogers in his books *Sex and Race* and *World's Great Men of Color* looked for the scattered evidence of the greatness of the African in the Nile Valley and elsewhere, particularly in Europe. W.E.B. DuBois, one of the great scholars-activists of the 20th Century wrote *Black Folks Then and Now* (1903), *The Negro* (1915) and *The World and Africa* (1946) dealing with ancient cultural achievements and showing how the problem of misrepresentation began and recommended what needed to be done. In the Post-World War era, George G.M. James wrote *Stolen Legacy* (1954) providing a very detailed and rather analytic exposure of how the "Greek Miracle" was actually an Egyptian remake. By mid-20th Century Leo Hansberry at Howard University in Washington, D.C., taught courses in Ancient Africa using Greek and Latin and modern European language sources as well as the new and mounting archaeological evidence; John Jackson in his *Introduction to African Civilization* (1970) and *Man, God and Civilization* (1974) instilled pride and appreciation in young African students as their cultural heritage in ancient Egypt was misrepresented.

Into the Egyptian Mind. Erik Monderson and young Egyptians on the Ghizeh Plateau beside Pyramid and Sphinx.

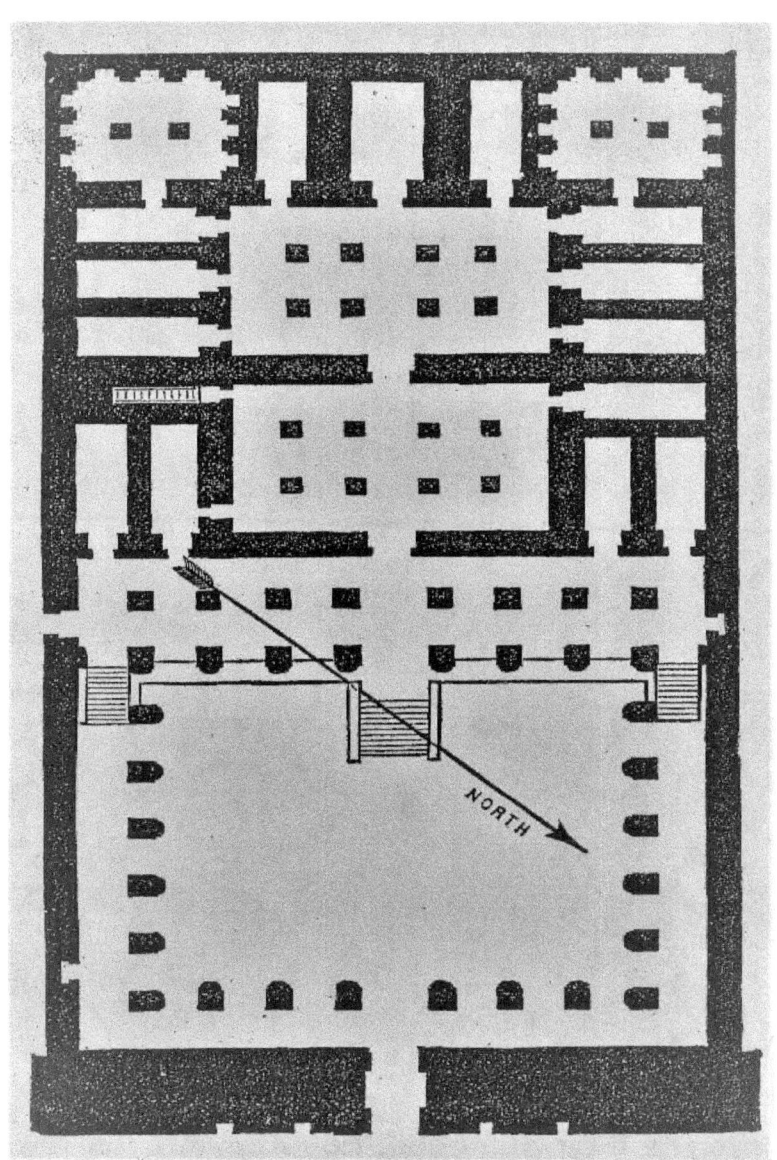

RAMESES II'S TEMPLE AT ABYDOS

    A.   Second Courtyard with Square Pillars and Osiride Figures
    B.   First Octostyle Hall
    C.   Second Octostyle Hall

D. Main Sanctuary
E. Isis Sanctuary
F. Horus Sanctuary
G. Chapel of the Ennead
H. Chapel of Rameses II
I. Chapel of Onuris
J. Chapel of Osiris
K. Chapel of Min
L. Chapel of Onuris
M. Chapel of Onuris
N. Chapel of Royal Ancestor
O. Chapel of Seti I
P. Room for Linen
Q. Room for Ornaments
R. Room for Offerings
S. Room for Offerings

Into the Egyptian Mind. Egyptian Art. With two "Eyes of Horus" overhead, as the male wearing necklace and heart vessel grasps the hand of the female, she presents a tray bearing two necklaces bearing chains with (1) a penis, Tet symbol and Hathor Girdle; and (2) a Beetle chain with Sun-Disk.

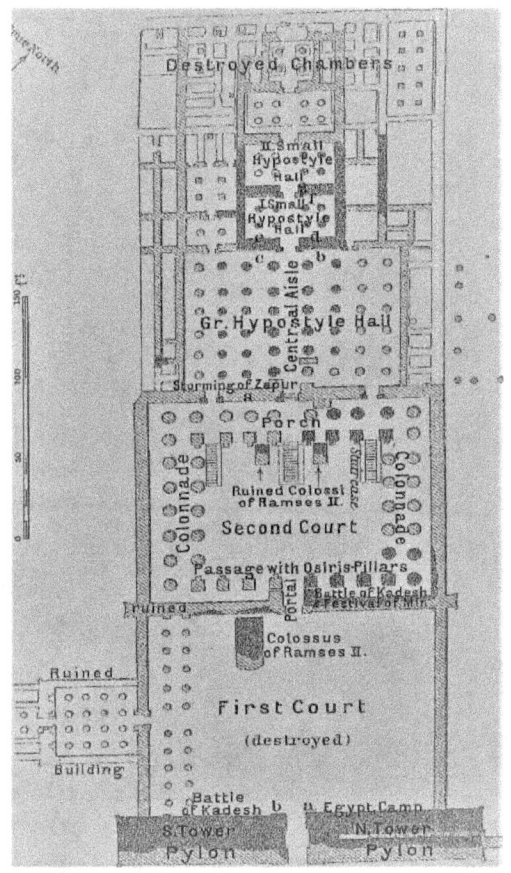

Ramesseum - Mortuary Temple of Rameses II.

a. Entrance Pylon (destroyed)
b. First Court (destroyed) but with remaining Osiride Figures and ruined colossal head stands here
c. Great Hypostyle Hall wit h Processional Colonnade split by a central line
d. First Small Hypostyle Hall
e. Second Hypostyle Hall
f. Transverse hall with 2 rows of 4 columns
g. Destroyed chambers.

Into the Egyptian Mind. Horus Temple at Edfu.
Pharaoh presents a platter with similar and varied condiments.

Into the Egyptian Mind. Dr. Fred Monderson on the Ghizeh Plateau with sphinx and Pyramid at his rear.

Into the Egyptian Mind. Horus Temple at Edfu. The King wears horns with dangling uraei with disks surmounted by White Crowns and feathers, as he prepares to drop pellets of incense.

We can't forget Duse Mohammed, an Egyptian living in England who encouraged and educated Marcus Garvey about the greatness of the African of Egypt and how his culture has been distorted and could be considered "A Culture in Captivity" abroad. This is so correct when we seek to assess the thousands of collections of antiquities in private hands, museums, and governments. There's a two volume *Egyptian Museum Collections Around the World*: *Studies for the Centennial of the Egyptian Museum, Cairo* (2002) with a Foreword by Zahi Hawass and Edited by Mamdouh Eldamaty and Mai Trad in which more than 120 scholars comment on one or a few other pieces in a particular collection but these institutions' Egyptian holding remain unimaginable. Of all these scholars, Dr. Ben early emphasized the great contribution the Nubian made to Egyptian culture.

We must understand, museums sometimes hide or not display important pieces for one reason or another. We know the "Low Dam" was built by the British in 1902 but as the nation expanded, by 1960 Gamal Nasser thought of the High Dam idea. In **UNESCO's** appeal to rescue Nubian temples to be submerged by Lake Nasser, the University of Chicago sent Keith Seele and a team who made a significant discovery at Qustol which was not revealed at the time but hidden in the Museum's basement. Ivan Van Sertima indicated he Seele, the great Egyptologist, wanted to take the secret to his grave. In his researches, Bruce Williams, a graduate student discovered and *The New York Times* published March 1, 1979, "The World Earliest Monarchy found in Nubia" dated at c. 3400 B.C. evidencing what became Egyptian Iconography, viz., enthroned pharaoh, the White Crown, incense burner, serekh, etc., 200 years later.

Now, as the historical evidence indicates, the French Revolution gave birth to the rise of Napoleon Bonaparte; who, suffering set-backs in Europe, relocated "to winter" by invading Egypt. He hoped, by holding Egypt, he would cut-off Britain's supply route to India's wealth. Napoleon was smart, along with his military apparatus he brought scholars called "savants" who in-between battles traversed the country studying the monument, drawing pictures of a culture, that for the most part had ceased to exist. Looking at the wonderful paintings of the Scottish artists David Roberts, among others, one gets an idea of how the desert had covered the monuments, the land and the ancient culture. So much so, people built their homes and lives on top of the settled dust. The mosque of Abu Haggag in Luxor is a good example of how the earth had covered the temple of Luxor and its entrance had to be readjusted when Maspero began clearing the temple. The Sphinx of Ghizeh is another example and this dated back to the 18th Dynasty. The "Stela of the Sphinx" recounts Thutmose IV's "dream" after falling asleep under the Sphinx. The God Harmachis admonished, 'if Thutmose cleared away the sand engulfing the Sphinx he would one day become king.' This he did and he became King of Upper and Lower Egypt.

So, as Napoleon was leaving France for Egypt, his wife Josephine asked, "If you go to Egypt, do bring me a little Obelisk!" This was an ominous sign relating to French antiquities collection and acquisition of Egyptian artifacts. Let us not discuss the Western Obelisk from Luxor Temple. Nevertheless, the savants studied the landscape and produced the book called *The Description of Egypt*. This important book opened Egypt to Europe but doubly and more important was its publication because all the artifacts the French collected, especially the Rosetta Stone, were demanded by the British who won the "Battle of the Nile." Nonetheless, for some reason, the book survived the demand and so outlived that encounter. It should be pointed out, the "Battle of the Nile" actually took place on the Mediterranean Sea. However, this naming phenomenon is important particularly as a strategy oftentimes an oppressor uses to gain control, consciously or unconsciously, of people's thought processes and by that fact, get them to do what is intended. History records, Islam came to Egypt in 640 A.D., A.H. 1! Ancient Egyptian *Waset*, the Scepter, became Thebes of the Greeks and Luxor, the "palaces," of the Arabs/Muslims. Similarly, in his lengthy career, Flinders Petrie, the "father of Egyptian Archaeology" employed the same strategy in continuing a tradition of change and exclusion, the Greek Priest Manetho had used when he wrote his *History of Egypt*.

Another important note can be seen in the American scholar, Dr. Ben Carruthers' comment, "Hegel, in saying Africa was outside the realm of history, took Egypt out of Africa and

Africans out of Egypt." Dr. Carruthers' book *Mdr Ntr - Divine Speech*, like so many others by African-American scholars minutely defended the theology, philosophy and mindset and form of governance of the Africans of Egypt. Because of their experiences in America the African-American alone stood against the false representation and mischaracterization of Egypt. They praised Egyptian/African culture, pointed out false claims and infinitesimally defended the ideas the ancients intended. Maulana Karenga wrote *Kemet and the African World View* (1986); *Selections from the Husia* (1989); and *Ma'at* (2004, 2006), all emphasizing philosophical and intellectual guideposts and providing forms of behavior that were of the highest ideals; Lester Brooks wrote *Great Civilizations of Ancient Africa* emphasizing greatness of culture; E. Jefferson Murphy also wrote *History of African Civilization* ((1972); then Tony Browder produced *Nile Valley Contributions to Civilization* (1992) detailing early types of achievements. There were many more but their defense of Egypt was a result of intense study, scholarship and challenge to correct the record in search for truth.

Following in the "Age of Metternich" "real politik" created the Middle East. But where is the Middle East, there is no such place, it is but a concept. And again, to emphasize how ideas influence people and who defended Egypt; Marcus Garvey, the great Black-American nationalist who claimed to speak for 400 million Africans worldwide in 1920, looked at the Pyramids. He did not say "How were they built?" He said, "How were they paid for?" He concluded they were paid for because the Egyptians had created a surplus economy that paid for its military defense and so provided peace and security for stable government to emerge and experiment in cultural units that established the wonderful Egyptian civilization manifested in their belief in God, hard work ethic, and practice of the Ma'at philosophy represented in justice, truth, righteousness. When the Egyptians had to fight they fought but when they didn't have to fight they were kind, generous and creative.

For eons, students were taught the "Fertile Crescent" began in Mesopotamia and curved towards Egypt. That agriculture, as we now know falsely, developed in South-West Asia at about 8000 B.C. arriving in Egypt around 4500 B.C. and then spreading to inner Africa thereafter, was the reinforced idea. Marcus Garvey, who was taught by an African-Egyptian named Duse Mohammed, said no! The "Fertile Crescent" began on the Nile and curved out and upwards towards Syria and Mesopotamia. Everyone knows, Egypt has always been the "bread basket" of this important crossroad of the ancient and modern world. Before and after Abraham's time, immigrants came to Egypt because of famine in their lands, but the Egyptians through a process of actively controlling the Nile's inundation by utilizing dams, dykes, canals and so on, produce that enormous surplus Garvey thought was necessary for the nation's wealth, peace and happiness. Naturally he was trying to encourage such industrial thrift among his own people in the New World.

Agriculture did not come to Egypt in 4500 B.C. It has been shown the Egyptians were practicing agriculture, planting barley, wheat and ember on the Nile as early as 16,500-14,500 B.P. That is 14,500-12,500 Before Christ. It is certainly before 8000 when agriculture developed in S.W.A. I will speak to this later but when it was revealed the discovery of an iron-ore mine in South Africa dated at 43,000 BP, that is 41,000 years ago. I asked Professor John Clarke what did this really mean? He said, for a people to be mining iron ore and that hematite was the basis for the red paint, remember red paint, it meant they had to have had a large population which also meant they had to be practicing agriculture to feed their people. Imagine agriculture at 40,000 years ago. We know, as the English archaeological journal *Man* has shown, in Upper Egypt, mealing holes for grinding corn speak to agricultural practices in catch basins areas where water had gathered after the inundation and sometimes seasonal rain. This dates to 11,000 B.C.

Into the Egyptian Mind. Egyptian Art. Tending the animals as part of farm chores.

Into the Egyptian Mind. Cairo Museum of Egyptian Antiquities. Erik Monderson stands before a seated scribe, representing pursuit of intellectual habits.

Into the Egyptian Mind. Egyptian Art. Couple with both hands empty and raised, even in adoration, is a rarity.

Into the Egyptian Mind. Egyptian Art. Guests at a banquet. Notice the unguent on her head that melts over time to bring the sweet-smelling odor.

Into the Egyptian Mind. Horus Temple at Edfu. A scene in the conflict between Horus and Seth. Holding a helmet crown with feathers, the king grasps a line.

Into the Egyptian Mind. Horus Temple at Edfu. A scene in the conflict between Horus and Seth. In the "Corridor of Victory" Horus (Heru) sits enthroned.

Nevertheless, and what Petrie did was to emphasize and use Greek/Roman names as did the Greek writers to identify Pharaonic people and places. Again, the vast area of the 4th Egyptian Nome, *Waset* became the Thebaid, Thebes. Still, even more, since the Greeks could not pronounce Egyptian names, Khufu, Khafre, and Menkaure became Cheops, Chephren, and Mycerinus and the general populace continue to use these and the names have stuck. Even further examples, the God Tehuti for Thoth; Tuthmosis for Thutmose; and Amenophis for Amenhotep. Interesting, it's hard to find scholars who will inform Amenhotep III, whose magnificent temple behind Memnon is being reconstructed, was actually black-skinned but so writes James Bonwick so in *Egyptian Ideas and Modern Thought* (1926: 288). In fact, Bonwick states: "As Amenoph III is represented as very dark in complexion, some say, as an Ethiopian, he introduced a southern type of religion. We read of his having a barge of 'the most gracious disk of the sun.'" That Thutmose I is similarly painted and shown being worshipped by an official in his tomb here in Luxor, yet this is a guarded secret. Many, especially guides and visitors will tell you of Hatshepsut's two obelisks at Karnak but not her four depicted at Deir el Bahari. Equally too, even the spelling of Sakkara, with Saqqara for Sakkara is a misnomer. Much more telling, at Luxor Temple, in the Court of Rameses II, the "Ramessean Front;" native Egyptian Guides rush to explain the Procession of the "Ascent of the Princes" to the sacred temple as depicted on the south-west wall, but never get to or seek to explain the "Nubian lady coming out of the cow's head;" nor even understand its significance. And so, omission and distortion, falsity reigned, as Europe came to dominate the field of Egyptology and to wield tremendous influence in Egypt by setting the standards that Afrocentric soldiers in the field must challenge in correcting the record.

Again, to emphasize the power of "naming" let us use the example of the cataracts. Today the First Cataract is situated at Aswan which should in fact be considered the Sixth Cataract. It is hard to imagine the Nile God setting out at the source of the Nile and on reaching the First Cataract he encounters he says, "I will name you the Sixth Cataract," then "I will name you the Fifth Cataract" and so on until he reaches Aswan and says "I will name you the First Cataract." After all, European scholars and writers in Egypt were engaged in explaining the culture to European writers and so colored their descriptions that became the standard practice and interpretation. Thus, we must recognize how a number of scenarios developed and became permanent fixtures as Europeans ascended the Nile. Another example will suffice. On entering the Great Pyramid on the Ghizeh Plateau, the large chamber was named the "Master Room." The same at Amarna, but this time the "Master Room" belonged to the "Mistress." The Egyptians have the same problem here at Karnak. This related to the First, Second, Third, Fourth, Fifth and Sixth Pylons on the principal east/west Axis. The Fourth Pylon of Thutmose I is actually the first, then he built the Fifth. Hatshepsut built the Eight, and Thutmose III the Sixth and the

Seventh. Amenhotep III built the Third, Rameses I and Horemhab built the Second and Horemhab again built the Ninth and Tenth Pylons, while the Ethiopians built the First. Thus, this naming may seem convenient for tourists, but within a historical context and for architectural purposes it is a problem.

II. WHO WERE THE ANCIENT EGYPTIANS?

Even modern-day Egyptians are to blame for the rich look down on the poor, the white look down on the black. I could find no "Black faces" on Egyptian TV. Even more important, many Egyptians who have comfortable lives acquiesce in the double standard and even those of Lower Egypt, rather than look up, they look down on those of Upper Egypt.

On my way to Cairo Airport I stopped at the Sadat Memorial. I could see two guards in the guardhouse dressed in red uniforms. One man, standing alone in the hot sun in the square said to me, "Let me see your passport." I asked "Why?" He said, "Unless I see your passport, you can't go in." I took it out, showed it to him, but won't hand it to him. He said, "You can't go in." Just then a bus with Asian tourists stopped. He didn't say a word to them and they went right in to the back of the Memorial. I had to turn back, get into my taxi and head to the airport on my way to Luxor where I feel more comfortable. I have been to Karnak more than a dozen times dating to 1989, 1990, 1991, 1993, 1995, 1997; 2003, 2005, 2008, 2010, 2012, 2014, 2015, and now in 2016. To this I may now add, 2017 and again 2018, and more recently 2019. I know the physical structure of Karnak! I have a photograph of practically every piece of stone found on the grounds.

Here at Karnak, I was asked "What do you like most about the temple?" I love Seti's decoration of the northern half of the Hypostyle Hall. I love Hatshepsut's "Red Chapel" in the

Open-Air Museum; I adore the "White Chapel" there; and I love the new signs that identify different parts of the temple. I also love the view from beside the Sacred Lake that shows the back of the First Pylon, the ruins of the Hypostyle Hall, and the two obelisks of Thutmose I and Hatshepsut. I don't like how the images are defaced, especially the females represented in the "African mold." The Sacred Lake's blue waters is magnificent especially when it reflects the Hypostyle Hall's ruins and the great Scarab. There is so much to love in a temple that took 2000 years to build. I also love the images of Rameses II's "Girdle Wall." Who could not love Thutmose III's *Akh Menu*. The "Taharka Column," the Ram-headed Sphinxes before the Northern and Southern Colonnades are also impressive. There is some dispute about how many columns were in the "Taharka Kiosk" that today retains 10 columns. Sir Bannister Fletcher in *A History of Architecture* gives 12 columns with the possibility for 14. Mariette identified 12. In discussions with Mr. Monsour a few years ago, he said there was no wall in ancient times around the Taharka Kiosk so there is a possibility there may have been more columns to the west. I love the decreasing size of the Pylons that regulate the light shining back into the temple after the sun has passed overhead, I recognize as one enters the temple, the floor rises and the ceiling lowers.

I also love the unending work ethic of the Egyptian man.

Henri Stirlin's edited *Architecture of the World: Egypt* (1963: 131) has indicated: "The Egyptian builders considered the problems of organization of work, economy and speedy construction to be of greater importance than questions of mechanics and technical progress, the use of tough materials or more effective tools, or a quest for a more lasting, lighter form of structure." However, while such problems were refined through the ages and with continued practice, no significant changes in construction techniques were made until the XXVth Ethiopian and XXVIth Saite Dynasties and the later Graeco-Roman Periods. These changes included "arch vaults, and improved methods of pre-planning foundations and stone-work." Equally, foundations varied according to size of building, wall or even obelisk and according to soil they were erected upon. Sterling (1963: 137) again comments: "The general principle was to dig a trench a little wider than the wall to be supported and to line the bottom of it with a thin covering of sand which was stopped from running away by little side walls made of brick. The real foundations were laid in these trenches: stones for the main walls, bricks for the less weighty features. The empty spaces were afterwards filled up with sand." To give an example, to construct walls at Medinet Habu 34 ½ feet wide and 60 feet high, they dug 10 feet deep in the clay's soil. Equally too, at Karnak some foundations as the 8th Pylon, built on clay, were 10 feet deep. On the other hand, at Deir el Bahari in the firmer soil beside the mountain, some walls had a foundation of 20 inches.

Into the Egyptian Mind. Erik Monderson stands behind the Ghizeh sphinx.

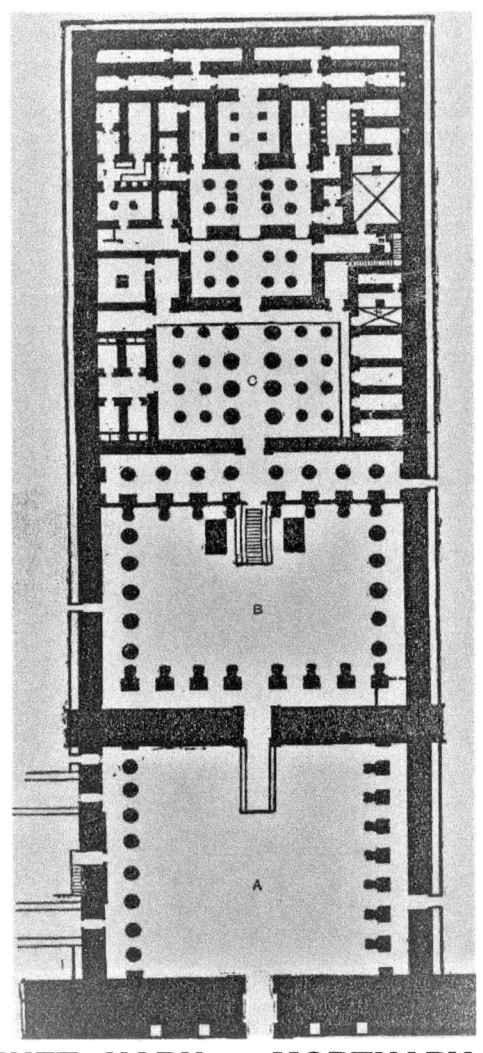

MEDINET HABU – MORTUARY TEMEL OF RAMESES III

- A. First Court
- B. Second Court
- C. First Hypostyle Hall
- D. Second Hypostyle Hall
- E. Third Hypostyle Hall
- F. Sanctuary

Into the Egyptian Mind. Egyptian Art. Young female mourners joined by an elder at a funeral. All wear white though the elderly lady has grey hair.

Into the Egyptian Mind. Horus Temple at Edfu. A scene in the conflict between Horus (Heru) and Seth (Typhon). The King in "Blue" or "War Crown" offers a platter with varied victuals to Horus (Heru) in Double Crown.

Into the Egyptian Mind. Horus Temple at Edfu.
A scene in the conflict between Horus and Seth. Wearing the Double Crown, Pharaoh pours a libation and prepares to incense Horus (Heru), himself in Double Crown.

Still, they never misused materials. Again, Sterling (1963:137) demonstrates: "The actual foundations were often composed of seemingly inadequate materials: small stones, sometimes set edgeways below a first course of large blocks placed lengthways or various elements taken from earlier ruined monuments. Huge squared blocks and drums or half drums of columns were set side by side, caving between them empty spaces unfilled by mortar. This motley collection of masonry frequently shifted ground causing fractures in the lower courses." Significantly, however: "From the twenty-fifth dynasty onwards, and especially during the Ptolemaic period, greater care was taken with regard to foundations: the great temples of later periods were built on proper platforms formed of several layers - up to nine or ten well-dressed slabs."

Lastly, I'm fascinated by the interplay of sacred space within sacred time, especially as Prof. Schafer has defined it.

WHO WERE THE ANCIENT EGYPTIANS?

So, who were the ancient Egyptians? Despite the many claims, they were not Caucasians who came from South-west Asia, "for some unknown reason" bringing "a superior mental attitude" to lord it over the natives. That is, the creation of a white upper class ruling over a black lower class who did all the work!

The well-known Zahi Hawass once said, "Tutankhamon is the only king we know exactly who he was because we found him in a sealed tomb." Despite all we know of the other pharaohs, we are not certain as we are with Tutankhamon. Therefore, everything is suspect but it is not only about the identities of the pharaohs but also the interpretation of the data and the unanswered questions that remain. Subsequently scholars were able to solve the mystery of Hatshepsut. That is, employing dental and other scientific sleuthing they were able to connect a missing tooth found in the Queen's toilet chest with a female mummy languishing in the by-ways of unidentified mummies. Apparently, when persons opened the chest, someone remembered there was a "Jane Doe" female mummy with a missing tooth. They were able to connect the tooth with the mummy and scientifically verify the identity of the Queen. In same manner, we must toss out all the old ideas about the Ancient Egyptians because under new and modern scientific investigations and analysis those theories quickly fall apart. Yet, we must recognize old ideas die hard therefore, those interested in the subject must be armed with a great many factual data to debunk falsity.

Dr. Yosef ben-Jochannan was my mentor and teacher. He told me essentially three things. "(1) At the time, there are 50 countries in Africa, choose one and become a specialist instead of a generalist. (2) When doing research on Ancient

Egypt, get the oldest materials you can find. I identified this as, essentially from 1870-1930. (3) Now that you have come to Egypt and seen what you have seen, what are you going to do with the knowledge?"

We know, according to W. Stephenson Smith *The Art and Architecture of Ancient Egypt* (1959) the earliest art in the Nile valley is to be found in Southern Upper Egypt proximate to Nubia and is dated to about 7000 B.C. In 1938, Henry Winkler visited the Eastern Desert of Upper Egypt and declared in his book, *Rock Drawings of Southern Upper Egypt* I (1937), the Pictographs he found there were made by "Mesopotamians" who settled the area some-time in the 3rd Millennium B.C. The Englishman Toby Wilkinson in *Genesis of the Pharaohs* (2003) dated these Petroglyphs of the Eastern Desert to "1000 years before Winkler's Mesopotamians." In his *Dawn of Conscience* (1933, 1934), the American James H. Breasted too denounced claims of Mesopotamian/Babylonian anteriority over Egypt as "not worth a credible response." In contesting misrepresentation in ancient Egyptian studies, the American Professor John H. Clarke argued, "Europe's claim to Egypt is not based on logic." Further, with significant effect, Dr. Clarke pointed out, "The people who preached racism colonized history" and "When Europe colonized the world, she colonized the world's knowledge."

In Western history, the Eighteenth Century of the Slave Trade is labeled "the century of trade" and the Nineteenth, "the century of production." As such, and upholding this contention and subsequent development, the Nineteenth and Twentieth Centuries are centuries of colonization, imperialism and racism. We should also label this period antiquities seizure and imprisonment! Therefore, as Egypt began to loom large in the Nineteenth Century, Europeans came to Egypt with a disdain for the people yet an appreciation for the culture and so they engaged in a form of "intellectual imperialism." You see, prior to the discovery of Egypt, the foundation of Western Civilization rested on the achievements of Greece and Rome.

In Edith Hamilton's *Mythology*, the world was created by the Greeks and thus, any explanation of historical events was aimed at European reading, consciousness and interpretation that put Europe and Europeans at global pinnacle from time immemorial! Today, all books on Western Civilization begin with a chapter on ancient Egypt, particularly its art. Using the question of logic just mentioned one has to ask, when did the Europeans come to Egypt, what did they bring, and what point of entry did they take.

We know, accordingly, "for some unknown reason" they left their homes in South-West Asia and migrated to Egypt. People doing well at home seldom seek their fortunes and to live abroad. Crossing the desert, they are challenged by its hostility and not equipped to overtake a people powerful enough to defend their land and project power abroad. In many respects this claim is really a mental exercise not supported by existential data. In some instances, they were said to be Armenians but this too cannot be substantiated. We know these Caucasians were said to have brought a "superior mental attitude" but this is all they were stated to bring. Now, these ideas were enunciated sometime around 1897 by M. Le Compte de Rouge who wrote, "Origin of the Egyptian Race," published in the *American Journal of Archaeology*. His arguments were based on the oldest evidence known belonging to the Old Kingdom. The evidence changed but the ideas remained the same. Flinders Petrie had not yet made his discoveries of First Dynasty evidence at Abydos which was done in 1900-1901. This is shown in his *Hierakonpolis* I (1900); *Royal Tombs of the Earliest Dynasties* (1901); *New Race* (1906) which was ultimately rejected because of its racist overtones; *Social Life in Ancient Egypt* (1923); and *Religious Life in Ancient Egypt* (1924). G. Elliot Smith, the anatomist working out of Manchester University, examined the mummies discovered in the Deir el Bahari "Cache" of 1881-1882 and those in 1898 in the Tomb of Amenhotep II. Smith was a bitter man! After he finished the examination of the mummies and washed his hands, the Egyptians rushed him from the room, paid him his fees and confiscated his notes. He was, however, able to publish his *Egyptian Mummies* through the Cairo Museum in 1905. He then wrote *The Ancient Egyptians and their Influence on the World's Cultures* in 1911, affirming the "diffusion" theory. In England, he chaired the "Committee" and initially produced "The Report on the Physical Remains" in 1912 and a more detailed "Report" along with others in 1914. He also wrote "Influence of Racial Admixture in Egypt" in *Eugenics Review* (1915). The interesting thing, there was no what we call "credible, critical pushback" on the reported findings, and this applies not only to his work but for much of the work produced by all the European writers who encountered and reported on Egypt. Of course, there were a few, Volney, Higgins, Massey, Hereen, Dart, Churchward, Greaves, etc., who were iconoclasts. Still more important, African scholarship in this field had not come into prominence at this time. There was credible European scholarship available challenging the misconceptions such as that of Count Denon's *Ruins of Empire* (1793); Godfrey Higgins *Anacalypsis* 2 Vols. (1836); Gerald Massey, Raymond Dart, Albert Churchward; Heeren, etc. What we do know is that at a certain time from approximately 1870-1930 a few people were dominating the intellectual and academic arena as well as giving speeches, oftentimes to raise money for excavation purposes but they were establishing and concretizing the ideas that came to dominate thinking relative to ancient Egypt.

However, and given that this credible anatomist who examined untold hundreds of mummies who did not specifically say they were European; still the assumption accepted was they had to be European. There is a rule that says, "possession is nine tenths of the law." Since Europe and America had hundreds of museums packed with Egyptian artifacts, European colonization was the practice worldwide, the "white man" was thought to be superior to everyone else and could claim, "Well, we have the Egyptian artifacts." So, the Ancient Egyptians had to be white! Today in the Cairo

Airport, in the most prominent places the Bazaar mannequin models are white; in the Bazaars in Cairo and Luxor, the Papyrus images of the ancient Egyptians are colored essentially white because no tourist will buy papyrus that looks African! The Italian Sergi coined the phrase "Mediterranean Race" to say the Egyptians were "brown, yet they were white. In the projected literature, there are "brown-skinned whites;" "black-skinned whites;" white-skinned whites" and "red-skinned whites." However, when we see black-skinned Egyptians they are either said to be black-skinned whites or they are "only painted black for the funeral ceremony!"

James Henry Breasted, an American Egyptologist of German heritage published *Ancient Records of Egypt* (5 Vols.) in 1905-06; *A History of Egypt* in 1907; *Development of Religion and Thought in Ancient Egypt* (1912); *Ancient Times* in 1916; *Conquest of Civilization* in 1926 and *Dawn of Conscience* in (1933) (1934). In the first issue of *Ancient Times* (1916) he described the Egyptians as "tall, thin. brown skin men" but when he reissued the book he changed to speak of "the great white race." Some have argued, because Rockefeller, the American billionaire, gave him money to start Chicago House, this was the quid pro quo payback. Seligman published his *Races of Africa* in 1930 and reinforced the false Caucasian claim in the "Hamitic Hypothesis" which held, "Any evidence of high culture found in Africa and Egypt was brought there by people of a white morphology." However, this idea was discredited as being racist and so has Petrie, Derry and Emery's "New Race" theory.

Into the Egyptian Mind. Egyptian Art. Size determines stature for as the nobleman in necklace and two heart-like vases around his neck, subordinates pour water over him as seen in the streams.

Into the Egyptian Mind. Horus Temple at Edfu. A scene in the conflict between Horus and Seth. In the "Corridor of Victory," Horus (Heru) in full battle mode prepares to spear Seth disguised as a hippopotamus (not shown).

Into the Egyptian Mind. Erik Monderson within the Ghizeh Pyramids perimeter.

Into the Egyptian Mind. Horus Temple at Edfu.
A scene in the conflict between Horus and Seth. Wearing a crown of feathers Amon as Min stands defaced in face and creative organ.

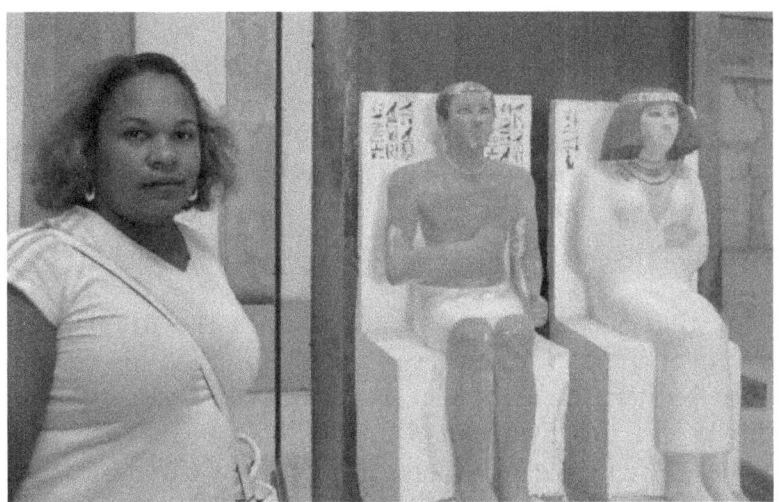

Into the Egyptian Mind. Cairo Museum of Egyptian Antiquities. Visitor Carmen stands beside a famous Old Kingdom couple Ra-Hotep and Princess Nofret.

Let's go back a bit. In 1820, two years before Champollion deciphered the hieroglyphs, an article in *The Gentleman's Magazine* (1820) described a mummy donated to the Hunterian Museum as "not like what we were taught" the Egyptians looked like. This mummy was of the Roman age, the skin color was described as "brown" and it turned black in four hours after being exposed to the elements. The Museum's artist, however, painted the mummy in its brown state before it turned black. In two years' time Champollion made his discovery and three years later in 1825 Auguste Granville, and English physician, did an autopsy on a mummy in London and declared the Egyptians were Caucasian, essentially same as Englishmen. Given the time from which the mummy came, the condition of the experiment, the state of the lab and autopsies this early in time forces thinking people to question whether his conclusions were based on logical evidence or a theory seeking support. Again, in regards the Hunterian "Roman Age" mummy, an important observation can be made. The "Roman Age" mummy was still brown-skinned after Persian, Assyrian, Greek and Roman invaders/conquerors who never brought their women but mixed with the native women. This was reported in *The History of British Egyptology 1549-1906* by John David Wortham, University of Oklahoma Press, Norman. Remember, in Roman times when Julius Caesar invaded England, he said, "The English were not fit to be slave."

Now, Dr. Cheikh Anta Diop, one of the greatest African minds that ever lived, a Senegalese Egyptologist, and his equally great assistant Dr. Theophile Obenga from the Congo attended the 1974 Cairo Symposium on the "Peopling of the Nile Valley." Being the "most prepared" at the Conference, they demolished the competing field of Western Egyptologists and wrote the final **UNESCO** Report underscoring the "fundamental blackness of Egyptian civilization."

A number of things need to be said about this brilliant African. He wrote in French and his book, *The African Origin of Civilization: Myth or Reality* was translated into English by Mercer Cook in 1974. Diop also wrote *The Cultural Unity of Black Africa* (1959, 1978) and *Civilization or Barbarism* (1991), *Precolonial Black Africa* (1987), *Black Africa: The Economic and Cultural Basis for a Federated State* (1974, 1987) as well as several other pieces. *African Origins*, however, destroyed all claims of a Caucasian Egypt, showing what the great German linguists, Erman, Eber and many others had said, the Egyptian language was Semitic was actually African in its structure and fundamentals showing parallels with many West African languages such as Wolof. For 100 years the Semitic origin held but even Wallis Budge when he issued his two volume *Egyptian Hieroglyphic Dictionary* in 1914, changed his position and admitted hieroglyphics was an African, not Semitic language. Wallis Budge, unlike most other Egyptologists did researches beyond Egypt's border in Nubia and elsewhere in Africa and was able to see much of Egyptian foundations in Nubia and beyond. He saw Isis, Osiris, Ptah, as coming from Central Africa.

Dr. Diop's book also showed Champollion recorded in the Valley of the Kings the Egyptian classification of man, where they listed Egyptian, African, Asiatic and European or Caucasian. As the good doctor reiterated, Champollion indicated and he affirmed, the European was on the lowest rung of the human ladder, a "veritable savage" untouched by civilization instead of being at the head of it. Equally and most important, Champollion's brother Francois around 1830 or so falsified his brother's letters about the ancient Egyptians and joined with others in the "age of Hegel" (1937) who "took Egypt out of Africa and Africans out of Egypt" as they helped create the notion of the Middle East and foreign invaders of Egypt. There is no such place as the Middle East. In fact, Europe itself is an extension of Asia. As usual, there being no "pushback," that Georges Foucart indicated, "The early Egyptologists made mistakes," and Dr. Leonard James affirmed, "Those mistakes were purposeful." Such falsity became the "accepted truths."

First, Diop discussed the "Falsification of History," pointing out how the "straw man" myth was created. Next, the good doctor examined all the arguments for a Caucasian origin and demolished each using comparative analogy referents as "Totemism," "Circumcision," "Kingship," "Cosmogony," "Social organization," "Matriarchy," "Kingship of the Meroitic Sudan and Egypt," "Cradles of civilization located in the heart of Negro lands," and "Language." Then he also used "melanin dosage," "blood groups," and physiological evidence of the pharaohs. Even more important, he included the primary source writings of nearly a dozen classical scholars who traveled among, lived with and observed the Egyptians of their time, even after the changes of time and circumstances.

He was particular in demonstrating African primacy in Old Kingdom foundation in all pharaonic customs, mores, iconography, religious beliefs, scientific beginnings, medicine, dentistry, astronomy, art and architecture, theology, study of the gods and much more.

Nonetheless and fast forward to Rameses II, his mummy was found in the "Deir el Bahari cache." When Gaston Maspero unrolled it is the 1880s, it was described as "brown with black splotches" which was published in *Biblical World* (1886) magazine. The "black splotches" was the stain from the same preservative material Elliot Smith mentioned in *Egyptian Mummies* (1905). Well, the mummy began to decay in the early 1970s and was rushed to a lab in Paris. Dr. Diop was qualified and the only Black man, Black African scholar, allowed in the chamber. Two things he observed and reported.

Last, the mummy of Rameses II was exposed to so much radiation it turned white. Now, if ever it is said the mummy of Rameses II is white, readers will know how it got that way. Second, or should I say first, the intestines of Rameses II contained residues of "New World tobacco." This was tremendously important at a time when the world was getting ready to celebrate 500 years of Columbus' voyage to discover the New World in 1992.

Dr. Diop got a lot of "pushback," remember that world, for scholars in the chamber admitted it was tobacco, but insisted it was an old-world strain of tobacco. Nevertheless, this pushback was not about the book *The African Origin of Civilization: Myth or Reality* (1974). However, he did affirm, "While the branches of this tree could use some pruning, its trunk and roots are fundamentally planted." The implications of tobacco in Rameses' stomach was tremendous. We know Herodotus, the "father of history" reported that Necho, a 26th Dynasty Pharaoh had sent ships to circumnavigate Africa. We know they got as far as the Cameroons in West Africa and reported its volcano was active. They called it the "Chariots of Fire." In 1992, evidence was presented at Temple University to show Abu Bakr, a king of the West African state of Mali sent many ships to the New World, more than 100 years before Columbus.

Into the Egyptian Mind. Egyptian Art. Have a bowl of "Popcorn" my Love, she could be saying.

Into the Egyptian Mind. Egyptian Art. Perfumed cones on the heads of this couple.

Into the Egyptian Mind. Horus Temple at Edfu. Pharaoh holds a bell-like object in one hand and the other remains free.

Into the Egyptian Mind. Erik Monderson, in the shade, admiring the Mammisi at Horus Temple at Edfu.

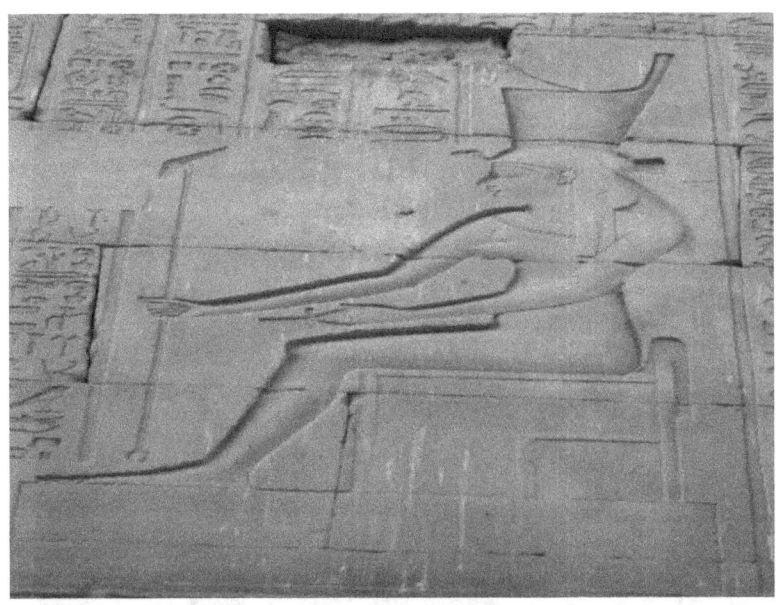

Into the Egyptian Mind. Horus Temple at Edfu.
Nephthys sits enthroned wearing the Red Crown.

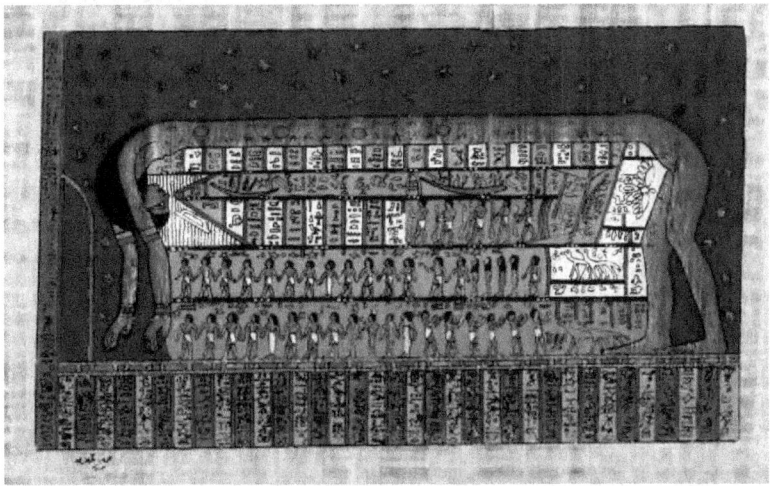

Into the Egyptian Mind. Egyptian Art. Papyrus.
Goddess Nuit and the Heavenly drama.

Into the Egyptian Mind. Cairo Museum of Egyptian Antiquities. Seated Old Kingdom statues depict the traditional seated pose.

Ivan Van Sertima, in his book, *They Came Before Columbus: The African Presence in Ancient America* (New York, Random House: 1976) has argued, the Mexican Olmec heads represented Africans who were in the New World before Columbus arrived. Even Albert Churchward in *Signs and Symbols of Primordial Man*, a student of Gerald Massey who wrote *Book of the Beginning*, (1882) *Natural Genesis* (1900) and *Ancient Egypt: Light of the World* (1912) Churchward showed, through migration, many ancient Egyptian ideas and concepts were adopted by New World Native Americans. This is not too different from Elliot Smith's "Diffusionist Theory" of Egyptian culture migrating and influencing other peoples and cultures. Additionally, an American scholar, Dr. Charsee

McIntire, has argued, "little Africans" were in the New World as early as 120,000 years ago. This important because the general consensus is that while Africa is the cradle of the human race, man migrated to people Europe and Asia, undergoing physical and morphological changes as he adapted to his new environment along the way. Some stayed in Europe and others continued on to Asia adapting to the climatic conditions along the way. Moving further along, the same man crossed the Bering Straits and arrived in the New World sometime around 12,000 - 10,000 B.C. and then he moved to people North and South America. However, *The New York Times* newspaper published an article a few years ago showing people of a region in Brazil, now a tourist attraction, painted red and this culture was dated nearly 24,000 years ago.

In 1971, the same *New York Times* had published another article on the discovery of an iron ore mine in South Africa dated at 43,000 Before Present that is about 41,000 Before Christ. Syncellus, a classical writer, mentions an Egyptian Tablet dating to 35,000 B.C. We know the Egyptian Precession lasted 26,000 years. It's been argued, to measure one Precession you have to measure it against two or possible three Precessions. Dr. Charles Finch in his book *The Star of Deep Beginnings* (1998) speaks of two Precessions. This means three or four. That is, 26,000; 52,000; 78,000, possibly even 104,000 years of Egyptian stargazing or astronomy.

Even further, in October of 2011 *The New York Times* again published the discovery of a "paint factory" in South Africa with "red paint and brush" in a pot. It's been carbon dated to 107,000 years ago. This idea of mining and mixing paint has "pushed complex thinking far back in time." Previously "complex thinking" in Europe especially, began about 40,000 years ago. There was belief of early paintings elsewhere in Africa nearly one hundred and fifty thousand years ago but this was the first-time actual paint and brush was discovered. In his book *African Origins*, Dr. Diop argued the ancient Egyptians painted themselves red to distinguish themselves from other Africans who were of different shades of black or brown in color.

The paleologist Mary Leakey, wife of Louis Leakey who found the fossil *Zinjanthropus Boisie* in Kenya, East Africa, and dated to 1.7 million years old as indicated in *The Progress and Evolution of Man in Africa* (1963) chronicled some 2000 prehistoric sites between South and East Africa, as Published in "Tanzania's Stone age Art" (1983) where early man painted on cave walls and in rest areas, using "the predominant red." Equally too, the Frenchman Henri L'hote discovered in the Sahara at Tassili and published in *National Geographic Magazine*, "The Tassili Frescoes" depicting African Black people painted red and whose existence was dated at 6500 B.C. and then "Oasis of Art in the Sahara." (1967)

The evidence is uncontroverted, yet falsity and misrepresentation persist. Nevertheless, as stated, the question was raised regarding how the Caucasians who arrived entered Egypt. First it was given they came by way of the Isthmus of Suez; next they were thought to come by way of the Horn of Africa and came through the Wadi Hammamat arriving at Koptos, home of God Min. Here Petrie discovered two massive wooden statues of Min, painted Black, that are now in the Ashmolean Museum, in Oxford. Min's earliest image, as Toby Wilkinson in **Genesis of the Pharaohs** (2003) revealed, was found among petroglyphs in the high rest areas of the Eastern Desert. This was the first image of a god known in history! Maspero argued, these arriving Caucasians crossed the Mediterranean, entering the Sahara they then entered the Nile Valley. Strange, he does not give these Tassili people the credit of being in the Sahara and entering the Nile Valley but gives much credit to migrants who crossed the Mediterranean. We must remember, Prof. Clarke reminded us, "Europe's claim to Egypt uses no logic."

We believe the ancient Egyptians painted themselves red because they were special. Gold and red are colors of the gods whose bodies were of these colors and they believed they were a god people, special. They built so many gods and temples. Imagine the Egyptians as a holy people, a great religious people. On a high holy day, a great nation at pray is an unbelievable experience!

Now, remember Elliot Smith and his Report; well Howard Carter, working for Lord Carnarvon, discovered Tutankhamon's tomb in the Valley of the Kings in 1922, 100 years to date after Champollion cracked the Code Hieroglyphic. The two statues guarding the burial chamber are painted black. In 1898, Mentuhotep II's statue was discovered in his Mortuary Temple at Deir el Bahari and excavated in 1903-04. Most of the great writers of that age literally ignored Mentuhotep until in 1959, W. Stephenson Smith in *The Art and Architecture of Ancient Egypt* wrote, "Mentuhotep had black flesh."

Now, I was in the Cairo Museum in 2005 and a young female Egyptian Guide told me Mentuhotep was "painted black for the funeral ceremony." I asked, "Who told you so?" and she replied, "My professors at the American University in Cairo!" Well, the American University in Cairo Press does good work but they must check what their professors are teaching. Elliot Smith in his *Egyptian Mummies* "let the cat out of the bag" by writing, the "black substance" on the mummy was a protective coating but the "brown color" of the mummies could still be observed beneath. *The Cambridge Ancient History* (Third Edition) Edited by I.E.S. Edwards, C.J. Gadd and N.G.L. Hammond, Vol. 1, Part 2 (1971) mentions the "preservative liquids;" "oils;" used in the embalming process. This must be the same substance. Nonetheless, the "painted black for the funerary ceremony" falsity is currently used for Tutankhamon's statues as told to visitors to the Cairo Museum. This falsity demands institutions as The American University in Cairo and its Press must insist these archaic ideas be discontinued. Significantly, there is need for more trained Nubian Guides in the Cairo Museum and those now operating, male and female, need to be retrained to be more sensitive to the realities of history. After all, there are more than 50 countries in Africa and Egypt needs to be sensitive to their concerns about falsification of the historical record. The American University in Cairo and its Press also need to sponsor a study and explain why 97 percent of statues and bas relief of pharaonic images, gods and queens especially, are defaced, disfigured. In the most obscure places and in public view, these figures are hacked. At Philae temple, on the first temple wall to the right in the Dromos there are many Ptolemaic images, especially females, in full view of the public and brightly displayed by the blazing sun, yet these European images are untouched. The same can be said for the "back wall at Kom Ombo Temple" opposite the "hearing ears" image and to the right of "physician's basin" and "Isis in the birth chair." These images with pointed noses are untouched. Also, many visitors to the Sanctuary area of Luxor temple marvel how "Greek" "Alexander the Great" looks, but his image is also untouched. However, the Amon-Min's "creative organs" are blackened from being "touched." It should also be added, while today there are nearly 54 countries on the African continent, only Egypt and Sudan have Egyptian artifacts. In shameless contradiction, little England has nearly 80 public museums and the United states 29 all housing "choice pieces" of Egyptian artifacts. This does not even consider "Private Collections. When Lord Carnarvon's heirs sold his "Collection" to the Metropolitan Museum of Art, it was considered exceptional because he always seemed to have had, "The pick of every crop!"

Into the Egyptian Mind. Egyptian Art. Portrait of a female beauty wearing a head bandana.

Into the Egyptian Mind. Egyptian Art. A female mourner kneels to weep before the encased mummy grasped by Anubis before internment in the funerary structure with a pyramid overhead encased in "Two Eyes of Horus," all before mountains to the right.

Into the Egyptian Mind. Double Temple of Elder Horus and Sobek. Upper portion of the left entranceway dedicated to the Elder Horus (Haroeris). Notice the varied capitals, the winged Sun-Disk overhead and uraei in rear.

Into the Egyptian Mind. Double Temple of Elder Horus and Sobek. Upper portion of the right entranceway dedicated to Sobek, the Crocodile God. Notice the two collections of Uraei atop panels. Varied capitals of the columns sit beneath the winged Sun-Disk on the Architrave.

Into the Egyptian Mind. Egyptian Art. Papyrus. Horus (Heru) introduces Nefertari to enthroned Ra-Horakhty and Hathor.

Into the Egyptian Mind. Double Temple of Elder Horus and Sobek. Erik Monderson in the Colonnaded Court showing columns with varied capitals, screened walls, and two faint winged-disks overhead the entrance façade.

Into the Egyptian Mind. Cairo Museum of Egyptian Antiquities. Two seated statues in the traditional pose.

A credible argument as to why the Tutankhamon statues were not destroyed when discovered by Howard Carter in 1922, is because of the publicity surrounding the tomb's opening. Of all statues, wooden ones are generally painted while others of stone reflect their natural color. With age, the black paint cracks and fall off the wooden statues or they can be easily removed from the statue. Do not be surprised, but sometimes skullduggery, exclusion, even "Doctoring occurs in Museum basement." In Pharaoh Haremhab's Valley of the Kings' tomb (he had another tomb at Sakkara); a wooden statue was discovered essentially intact though the details were not discussed. Elsewhere in the Valley of the Kings, many tombs contained pieces of broken wood bearing black paint. This is especially so for tombs opened since antiquity but some others discovered in the Nineteenth Century rushed to reveal, publish and reinforce ideas that supported the notion of European hegemony. These may very well be statues similar to King Tut's statues and these two statues may be the standard since no intact tomb remain where this particular feature could be observed.

Again, in 2005 this visitor overheard a male Egyptian Guide saying to a visitor, regarding Tutankhamon, "Not because the King looks black that his is Nubian." Well, nearby on a wall he is shown as bronze, trampling African enemies painted black. As such, if he is not Nubian, then he is Egyptian and most important, he is black! The female guide in the Museum also said, "I have never seen Osiris painted black!" Imagine a guide in the Museum who has never seen Osiris painted Black despite the many papyri on the walls and the numerous miniature wooden statues so painted. So, I searched him out and found many, many such statues. Elsewhere, in another room, two contingents of soldiers, one Nubian and one Egyptian stand side by side. The Nubians are painted black, the Egyptians painted red. I asked myself, "are the Nubians painted black for the funerary ceremony?" No. If they are, why are the other Egyptians not painted black for the funerary ceremony. Another important point, if Mentuhotep is painted black for the funeral ceremony, why is his Queen Kemsit painted black and considered a Negress. It can be pointed out, in the dining room at the Oberoi Hotel at Aswan, sphinxes, kings and gods are painted black as these, predominantly, Nubians remembers their "ancestors." Today, the Movenpick Hotel has taken over the Oberoi Hotel and these statues have disappeared. However, since this writer has photographs to this effect, this is not a mute issue. The same could be said for the enthroned divinities at Medinet Habu Mortuary Temple of Rameses III whose back room "has disappeared." There's a lot of work that needs to be done to correct such propagated falsity. The new Egyptian museum being built will present a number of problems and challenges because many pieces that attest the blackness of Egypt especially will be misplaced, omitted or sadly, destroyed. Nevertheless, their existence has been noted.

Alexander Moret in *The Nile and Egyptian Civilization* (1927) argued the Delta is the origin of Egyptian civilization. Dr. Diop took him to task in his book *African Origins*, demolishing his argument for primacy of the Delta. Pointing out, no significant evidence supports a Delta origin that is essentially based on theory not facts. Dr. Diop asked, "If the Delta was the origin of Egyptian Civilization, why are all the sacred sites and monuments in Upper Egypt?" That is, the great temples at Abydos, Karnak, Luxor, Abu Simbel, West Bank mortuary temples, Valley of the Kings, Queens, and Nobles, even the Graeco-Roman temples at Edfu, Dendera, Kom Ombo, Philae, etc., that attest to the primacy of Upper Egypt especially as evident in the pharaoh's *Suten Bat* title as King of Upper and Lower Egypt.

III. THE ROLE OF ARCHAEOLOGY

From as early as 1800-1880 there have been problems with how foreigners acquired antiquities and the manner in which they shipped them out of Egypt especially Prisse de Avennes who stole the Karnak Tablet, shipped the pieces downstream covered in boxes upon which Mariette sat unknowingly. First, we know Mohammed Ali seized power, decimated the Mamelukes and set about transforming his nation. He put Egyptians into the high ranks of the military; made land reforms benefitting the peasants; he sent Egyptians abroad to study at Western Universities; and he did internal improvements but did not borrow money from Western interests, so the nation was not indebted to foreigners. Sadly, during the 19th Century especially, the Egyptians did not understand the value of their antiquities nor did they pay attention to people coming and going and removing artifacts. We know of Giovani Belzoni, who discovered Seti I's tomb in the Valley of the Kings and began clearance of Abu Simbel Temple of Rameses II. He was an arch plunderer who destroyed mummies and other artifacts.

Elsewhere in Africa, Europeans were working to stamp out the Slave Trade, plant Christianity in Africa by encouraging agricultural pursuits; and generating trade for the expanding world market. "Spheres of influence" and "interests" began to be established. Adventurers began to penetrate the continent to discover its important geographical features, one of which was the source of the Nile. We have Burton and Speke competing and the naming of Lakes Victoria and Albert; the French dashing across the Sudan towards Fashoda and the British winning control of the Nile headwaters in Uganda. All this was taking place and brought more people to Africa. *The Description of Egypt* enlightened and encouraged visitors to this country and they were amazed by the marvelous architecture and art they encountered. Those who visited the newly opened Seti's tomb were dumb-founded by the art and religious meaning depicted therein. At Karnak, Champollion believed the Egyptians thought in terms of "men 100-feet tall."

Meanwhile, as low-level thievery began to export artifacts native Egyptians began searching and selling to whomever would buy, only much later would they begin to realize the artifacts were more valuable in Egypt rather than for the pittance they were paid for the various pieces. We know of the famous Rasul Brothers who discovered and robbed the Deir el Bahari "cache." The city of Luxor became notorious for the trade in illicit artifacts. The Winter Palace, famous as a place to stay, was an important hub for people to gather. In Aswan, it was the Old Cataract and in Cairo Mena House.

When, scholars as Rosellini, Lepsius, Birch, Chabas, De Rouge, Maspero and Erman struggled to place the language and culture on a firm footing publishing dictionaries and translating papyri. However, as this was taking place a number of developments began to transform Egypt and Africa by the early 1880s.

1.   The discovery of the "Deir el Bahari cache" of 18-20th Dynasty kings and queens.

2.   The rise of the Mahdi who killed General Gordon and in response the British sent General Kitchener who went about "executing his orders." After this Egypt came under the Egypt-Sudan administration headed by Lord Cromer.

3.   The Berlin Congress of 1884-85 "Partitioned Africa on Paper" setting the stage for the practical implementation and resultant colonialism throughout the continent with its "Direct and "Indirect" rule programs. In this, a number of studies were done to determine the zoological, botanical, mineralogical, and agricultural potential wealth and to generate export of resources to fuel the developing Industrial Revolution in Europe. Naturally they had to wipe out African resistance to take over of their land. The Germans in South-West Africa, the Boers in South Africa against the Zulus; and the French against Samori Toure building his empire in West Africa. Just as Queen Nzinga fought the Portuguese in Angola during the Slave Trade, Yaa Asantewaa in Ghana (the Gold Coast) fought the British in West Africa with their West African Frontier Forces. Native soldiers of the West African Frontier Forces knew the local languages, the terrain and the cultures and betrayed their people to the European overlord. This treachery facilitated defeat of national resistance and the onset of colonial rule. The Italians tried to colonize Ethiopia and were defeated by Menelik II at the Battle of Adowa in 1896. The colonial powers' armies were comprised of African conscripts commanded by European officers. In Egypt, the Egyptian

army was commanded by Egyptians since the days of Mohammed Ali.

Into the Egyptian Mind. Egyptian Art. In leopard skin, Priest performs a ceremony before a seated nobleman.

Into the Egyptian Mind. Egyptian Art. Let's get these cows to the market, fellas.

Into the Egyptian Mind. Double Temple of Elder Horus and Sobek. With outstretched winged sun-disk with uraei presiding, we witness the art of the Hieroglyphics.

Into the Egyptian Mind. Double Temple of Elder Horus and Sobek. Thoth (Tehuti, left) and Horus (Heru, right) pour ankh type libation to purify the King before he enters the temple.

Into the Egyptian Mind. Cairo Museum of Egyptian Antiquities. A colossal seated figure with two squatting females grasping his feet.

4. Then Flinders Petrie and Auguste Mariette arrived in the 1880s. Mariette was sent to collect artifacts for the

Museum in Berlin. Lepsius, who had been there earlier, collected some 15,000 pieces and shipped them back to Germany. After his 6-year stay in Egypt in which he excavated at several sites, Enos Brown "Excavations at Naga-Ed-Der, Where Prehistoric Man First Settled in Egypt" in *Scientific American* of March 30, 1907, says of Dr. J.C. Reisner, "the fruits of his labors and now being received. Hundreds of cases are being unpacked and their contents catalogued. They embrace an enormous number of objects, demonstrating the gradual progress of the arts from the earliest or Paleolithic age, the age of flint, through the period of its highest development in the Cheops dynasty, up to the time when Egypt sand to the position of a Roman dependency. The rise of civilization, from a period antedating the Christian era by 7,000 years, can be unerringly traced in the flints, pottery, carvings, statues, and inscriptions, found in ancient cemeteries or site of cities, ransacked to enrich the museum of an American university and to benefit, the scholars of the new world."

These two figures were each one man's total. Think of the thousands who worked in Egypt, excavating, collecting, even buying and shipping artifacts abroad. Petrie, in fifty years in archaeology and collecting, founded a museum in his name in London. Nevertheless, because of the deplorable condition of the subject in Egypt, Mariette convinced Ishmael Pasha to establish a National Museum in Cairo to house the artifacts he collected from excavation. That is, after he had shipped home his loot. From the time of Champollion's discovery an agreement held that a Frenchman must hold the top post in Egyptology in Egypt. Notwithstanding, Mariette had men digging simultaneously at 37 sites across Egypt. Exercising his stature, he restricted access to archaeologists and prohibited export of antiquities. Every time his name was mentioned people cursed.

Flinders Petrie had arrived to study and take measurement of the Giza pyramids as did Colonel Vyse who took measurements and studied the pyramids. General Pitt Rivers was active doing geological studies as was Colonel Lyons who surveyed the Nile and also the Temple of Isis and did a geologic survey of Egypt. The scholar Sir Garner Wilkinson, in Egypt since mid-century, living at Thebes did fantastic work in recording many images that have since disappeared. He published *The Ancient Egyptians* (1850) later to be edited by Samuel Birch. Petrie did establish high standards for his work that many followed as excavating practices and as such he earned the title, "the Father of Egyptian Archaeology." His Methods of Sequence Dating instituted at Naqada, using pottery from the Prehistoric period proved lasting. He showed the earliest form of pottery was of a superior quality.

The Frenchman Amelineau who found the "Tomb of Osiris" at Abydos reported the Anu of Upper Egypt were some of the earliest inhabitants of this land. They founded important cities at Esneh, Dendera and Heliopolis where God Ra was worshipped for the duration of dynastic rule. According to Heliopolitan cosmology, after God Ra had made the world, he created the Nubians, the Black people. Ra created Black people after he created the gods Shu and Nefnut, before he made other gods and the Egyptians or even Caucasians and Asiatics. How interesting!

These two men Petrie and Mariette not only established order in the antiquities field through systematic archaeological methods; but while Petrie's career in Egypt extended for some 50 years, he also accumulated a bibliography of nearly 1200 published pieces of work. Mariette, on the other hand, established the Museum in Cairo and today is surrounded by busts of men of similar Egyptological stature as his memorial stands on the grounds of the Cairo Museum of Egyptological Antiquities. However, as the work of excavation unfolded, the next thing was to determine how concessions were given to excavate the different fields of potential artifactual evidence of the ancients. With Lord Cromer as administrator, the British, chief of whom was Petrie and his school, were given lucrative concessions. Oxford and Cambridge Universities trained young scholars in Egyptology and encouraged them to do fieldwork at the various sites.

Amelia Edwards, an English artist went to France on holiday and it rained. So, she came to Egypt and wrote *Egypt and Its Monuments*: *Pharaohs, Fellas and Explorers* (1891). Impressed by what she saw, she founded the *Egypt Exploration Society* (*Fund*) in London. Those scholars trained at Oxford and Cambridge were sent to help excavate cemeteries and eventually lead their own expeditions across the country. Every year these field workers issued Reports and published books under the aegis of the Egypt Exploration Fund, the Egyptian Research Account and the Graeco Roman Branch whose institutions all assisted and helped publish studies on the ethnological, geographical and geological *Surveys of Egypt and Nubia* (1907-08) and much more. Together these institutions as houses of Egyptological knowledge amassed nearly 100 volumes of published works on temples, tombs, cemeteries across the Egyptian geographical landscape in what can today be called "Primary Sources of the Primary Sources."

Meanwhile, work was being done in translating papyri of pharaonic and Greek times. Complimenting Breasted's *Ancient Records of Egypt* (1905-06), *Records of the Past* (1876-1878), both Egyptian and Assyrian, were published with Samuel Birch as a principal editor. He also Edited Garner Wilkinson's *Ancient Egyptians*. Most of the Greek classics came to the West through Egyptian papyri.

Eventually, joining the British and French in Egypt, Germans, Italians, Swedes, Spaniards and many other nationals including Americans began seeking concessions to excavate in Egypt. Lord Cromer helped Maspero, who cooperated, and he was knighted by the British Crown. When Maspero was also away in France editing the *Pyramid Texts* he had discovered in 5th and 6th dynasty pyramids, he was replaced by Herr Brugsch and then De Morgan. De Morgan wantonly gave away untold numbers of artifacts across the world. He was succeeded again in the post by Maspero again through encouragement from Lord Cromer.

"Everybody was working!" Hundreds of and hundreds of excavators from all the nations involved collected artifacts and carried them home. Ludwig Burkhardt, Walter Emery, Arthur Evans, Frank Goodie, John Garstang, John-Philippe Lauer who reconstructed the Sakkara complex, Guy Brunton, Margaret Murray, Caulfield, Sommers Clarke, Batiscomb Gunn, Alan Gardiner, B.P. Grenfell, Edouard Naville who wrote "Origin of Egyptian Civilization," H.R. Hall, and more did excavations and as expected they all carried home souvenirs from Egypt. Add to this lot, those workers from German, France, Sweden, Italy, Turkey, America and an untold number of museums benefitted from Egyptian artifacts to which we can easily add the thousands of private collections. Thus, we are given some idea of the enormous number of artifacts were lost as Brian Fagan opened the door to understanding *The Rape of the Nile* (1975).

Into the Egyptian Mind. Egyptian Art. A figure kneels before the majestic Horus bird grasping a flail.

Into the Egyptian Mind. Egyptian Art. Horus (Heru) in Red and White Double Crown introduces a couple to enthroned Osiris (Ausar) in his Shrine while Horus' Four Sons stand between them.

Into the Egyptian Mind. Isis Temple at Philae. Close-up of a composite, varied, column with its abacus barely hidden supporting the overhead architrave.

Into the Egyptian Mind. Isis Temple at Philae.
View of another composite capital with its abacus partly hidden supporting the architrave below the decorated ceiling to the left.

Into the Egyptian Mind. Egyptian Art. Papyrus.
Flowers and bird in flight.

Into the Egyptian Mind. Cairo Museum of Egyptian Antiquities. A squatting scribe with the materials of his trade before him.

Erman in Berlin; Budge at the British Museum; Leclerc in Paris; Breasted in Chicago; Wilbur in Brooklyn, all had a significant impact not only in establishing firm foundations for study of the discipline but most important firmly implanting the interpretation of the subject matter in the minds of readership across the Western world. Newspapers, magazines, books, even publishing houses flourished; lectures were given, exhibitions were held every year displaying the newest finds from the field. Learned Societies such as the **British Society for the Advancement of Science** sponsored lectures by fieldworkers at the end of which, in question and answer periods, participants debated the issues but they never satisfactorily dealt with the substantive issue of who really the ancient Egyptians were. After all, this was an age of European imperialism. That is, military imperialism, geographical imperialism, and economic imperialism. With the mineralogical and other studies being conducted in the colonial areas of Africa and with the growing influence in Egypt under British Administration, colonialists and their adherents and agents created intellectual imperialism. As the 19th Century ended, the accepted gospel held, "The white man was superior to everyone" around the globe and this evolved as a strategy to control Europe's colonial holdings. Newspapers, magazines, reports became popular because they fueled an emergent "Penny Press" that informed of developments in the Egyptological field made by archaeology but even more important the belief that the Egyptians were Caucasians. Europeans essentially saw the Ancient Egyptians in themselves.

POEM TO RA - THE SUN GOD

O Ra, King of the Gods, you enjoyed a prominence matched by few divinities. You emerged at Heliopolis, and once absorbed, you extended your significance throughout dynastic times. Father of the Gods whose souls are exalted in the hidden place, your symbols are the Disk of the Sun, encircled by the serpent Khut, as well as Ankh, with scepter and tail from your waist. Self-begotten and Self-born creative vigor, Power of Powers with two uraei, you are a doubly hidden and secret god. Lord of Eternity, Sovereign of the Gods, you exist forever, Lord of Souls. You possess **14 Kas** or life force, as strength, might, prosperity, food, veneration, eternity, radiance, glory, fame, magic, authority, sight, and hearing and perception, Lord of Heliopolis, Supreme Power.

Sekhem, begetter of his gods, from Heliopolis, your priests influenced political developments in the Old Kingdom when

Pyramid builders incorporated your name into theirs, becoming Son of the Sun, hence the title Son of Ra. These kings erected sun temples with names as 'Favorite Place of Ra' and 'Satisfaction of Ra' all in Praise of you Lord of Rays. Self-Created, King of Heaven, Great Duration of Life, Lord who advances, you are the Soul that do good to the body. Governor of his Eye, Lord of Generation, invisible and secret, you are Governor of the Tuat, Double Obelisk God, Lord of the Eastern Bend, and Supporter of the Heavens who dwells in Darkness. Born as the all-surrounding universe, you send forth the plants in their season, Eternal Essence.

Maker of the Gods, Governor of your circle, Aged One of Forms, Memphis received endowments in the Middle Kingdom in Praise of thee, King of the World. The Priesthood of local gods linked their deity to the Sun God's name Ra, Mighty in Majesty, Vivifier of Bodies. The Theban triumph merged Amon with Ra assuming all of the ancient god's attributes as Maker of Heaven where you are firmly established. God One from the beginning of time, Mighty One of myriad forms and aspects, Creator of Laws Unchangeable and Unalterable, Lord of Truth your shrine is hidden. You are the Soul, which give names to his limbs, Body of Khepera, God of Souls who is in the Obelisk. You are Master of the Spheres who cause the Principles to arise.

Chief of the Earth, Lord of the Gods, Judge of Words, and the glory of Ra manifested in Amon at the Temple of Karnak. During the New Kingdom, Thebes gloried in the imperial age, and you were Opener of Roads in the Hidden Place, who confers his crown on Pharaoh. The Ruler of all the Gods, more strong of heart than all those who are in your following, you are maker of gods and men, Creator of Heaven, Earth and the Underworld. Divine Man-Child, Heir of Eternity, you are Chief of the Gods, Supreme in their Districts, being Crowned King of the Gods, Ram, Mightiest of Created Things. You Provide the Breath out of your Throat for the Nostrils of

Mankind, Fashioner of Himself, and Tonen who produces his members, Supremely Great One.

Provider of the Sovereign Chiefs, Governor of the Holy Circle, Ra as Amon brought victory and fame to those who followed his teachings and praised his name, as Crowner of Pharaoh. Proclaimed King of Earth, Prince of the Tuat, Governor of the Regions of Aukert, Souls in their Circles ascribe your Praises. Beautiful Being, Rays of Turquoise Light, you are Personification of Right, Truth and Goodness, O Mighty One of Journeys, Lord of the Gods, light of the lock of hair. Your Emblems secure entrance of the Dead Man into the Kingdom of Osiris. Chief of the Great Cycle of the Gods, your principles have become your manifestation. Chief of the Powers inhabiting the holy sphere, you raise your soul, hide your body, shine and see your mysteries.

Creator of Hidden Things, Lord of Heaven, Lord of Earth, for untold ages men praise the Exalted of Souls. The Maker of Eternity, Ra you sail a Boat of Millions of Years. In all your glory, you emerge in a Morning Boat Matet, becoming strong at Midday. The day's work done, and weak, you ride the Evening Boat Semktet. Confronting your mortal enemy Apep, fishes Abtu and Ant swim before the Boat of Ra with its defenders at the ready. United in Numbers, Destroyer of Darkness, Night, Wickedness and Evil, on the dawn of a new day, there are Acclamations of your Rising in the Horizon of Heaven, Only One. Soul that speaks, rests, creates the developed hidden intellects, you shine in your sphere and hide what it contains, moving luminary.

Ra, Lord of Truth, Lord of the Horizon, Horus of the East, Lord of Fetters of your enemy, protector of hidden spirits, you conquer the fiends of the underworld. Souls of the East follow and Souls of the West praise you, while you get Support of the Circle of Amenta. God of Life, King of Right and Truth, you are the World Soul that rested on his High Place. The Soul who moves onward, Opener of the roads in the Hidden Place,

One Alone with many hands, Ra, you are the Great God who lifted up his two eyes. You address your eye and speak to your head, the spirit that walks, that destroys its enemies, that sends pain to the rebels, you impart the breath of life to the souls that are in their place, Brilliant One who shines in the Waters of the Inundation.

Hidden Face, Glorious Creator of Eternity, you make beings come into existence in your creations in the Tuat. You rise like unto Gold, Great Light Shining in the Heavens illuminating darkness. Oldest One, Great One, you are Self-begotten, Self-created and Self-produced, the Soul Wo Departs at his Appointed Time. You existed forever and would exist for Eternity, Illuminer of Light into his Circle. Source of Life and Light, Glorious by reason of thy Splendors, you are Joy of Heart within your Splendor. Mighty One of Victories, Ra, how wonderful was your manifestation among early Africans, initiating laudable moral, spiritual and intellectual standards of creative genius, Mighty one whose body is so large it hides its shape, Double Luminary.

Into the Egyptian Mind. Egyptian Art. A figure with hand raised in adoration, kneels before two Anubi, tied with a single necklace.

Into the Egyptian Mind. Egyptian Art. With hands raised in adoration, this couple stands before male and female divinities enthroned. Notice the "Table of Offerings" before the Shrine.

Into the Egyptian Mind. Egyptian Art. Vultures with outstretched wings and grasping scepters, wears the White Crown (top) and the Red Crown (bottom).

Into the Egyptian Mind. Double Temple of Horus and Sobek. Colossal figure of Horus grasping scepter and ankh being offered a cone.

Into the Egyptian Mind. Cairo Museum of Egyptian Antiquities. Statues in different attitudes. Seated wearing necklace (left); striding with left foot forward and flap of the kilt to the right (center); and striding with flap of the kilt to the left (right). Objects in the hands are different.

Generator of Bodies, True Creative Power of Divine attributes, Sender of Light into his Circle, Ra you rise in the Horizon, and are Beautiful. So too, Rat, Mistress of the Gods, your female counterpart, Lady of Heaven, Mistress of Heliopolis. Hathor and Isis are also your companions. Mightier than the Gods, Glorious Being, Lord of Love, Double Sphinx god, you are Ruler of Everlastingness. God of Motion, God of Light, Lord of Might, you send destruction, fire into the place of destruction and destroy your enemies, Light that is in the Infernal Regions. Protector of hidden spirits, the Souls that Mourns, the God that Cries, you are the Soul One who avenges his children and who calls his gods to life when he arrives in the hidden sphere.

Aged one of the Pupil of the Utchait, Ra, Lord of the hidden circles, creative force who gathers together all seed, you are manifold in your holy house. Great One, who rules what is in him, you send forth the stars and make the night light, in the sphere of hidden essences. Master of the Light, Only One who names the earth by his intelligence, the vessel of heaven, Powerful, Ra in his disk with Brilliant Rays, Lord of Wisdom your precepts are wise. Lord of Mercy, at whose coming men live, you make strong your double with Divine Food. Creator of Hidden Things and Generator of Bodies, Enlightener of the Earth, Lord of the Gods who lights the bodies on the horizon, Africans need your continued illumination and Blessings now more than ever.

Into the Egyptian Mind. Cairo Museum of Egyptian Antiquities. Two Geniuses, Jean-Jacques Champollion who deciphered the Hieroglyphic script and Erik Monderson, Brooklyn genius.

THE ARCHAEOLOGY OF EGYPT
By
Dr. Fred Monderson

The Archaeology of Ancient Egypt is a fascinating subject that first stumbled then systematically reclaimed the rich Nile River cultural heritage from the misty past in which it lay buried in the debris of soil and time. As an emerging science, we can generally date Egyptian archaeology to the beginning of the 19th Century when Napoleon arrived, and his savants, after traversing the land in systematic study produced their *Description of Egypt* or *The Monuments of Egypt* based on linguistic and visual study of the language and monuments. By the end of the 19th Century archaeology had been placed on a more scientific footing and the mist was significantly cleared by then. The 20th Century saw the maturing of the discipline. Nevertheless, in all of this, as the Mighty Sparrow said in one of his songs: "Hurried birds make crooked nests," so the Story of Egypt was not correctly told because of the multitude of issues interplaying among global powers! During the age of colonization, from 1880 onwards as archaeologists began to reclaim ancient Egypt, with all the shenanigans going on, the work of the British archaeologists particularly emphasized rapid publication of discoveries to feed the rapidly expanding "penny press" and a public hungry for antiquarian knowledge to bolster "white supremacy" as Europe manifested its might globally.

As such, much was said but equally many errors and distortions as well as omissions entered the general body of knowledge and thus misinterpretations under-girded presentation of the historical record as to the people, origins and survivals of ancient Egypt. That is to say, the existential record or data contradicts the symbolic representation. From then to today, as scholars re-examine the "ancient records of the ancient records" generated between 1870 and 1930 particularly, much remains correct but many things have had to be correctly reinterpreted. Hence the need for reconstruction in African historiography because at the time of interpretation no critical African input was added to authenticate the corpus of new knowledge. Thus, archaeology and anthropology, its sister discipline, had as they say, "some pebbles in their shoes." There was never a broad interpretation of the information using as its cornerstone the full spectrum of the 8 major social sciences, viz., geography, archaeology, anthropology, history, sociology, economics, political science and psychology. Or, should I say "pushback" in critical historiographic analysis from credible scholars were never applied to question the findings and interpretations as put forward by European and American scholars, who were oftentimes biased in arguing from a Eurocentric view of the world. As such, again the symbolic representation contradicted the existential evidence.

Notwithstanding, Egyptian archaeology has helped define and establish parameters of Egyptology by its comprehensive excavation of viable sites and monuments throughout the land. On the one hand, the definition of Egyptology includes an understanding of the history, geography and language of ancient Egypt! On the other, the **Association for Study of Classical African Civilization** is much different because not only does it include examination and analysis of the entire Nile Valley's various forms of knowledge, it is not done from a European epicenter and not only studies this culture but vigorously reclaims its heritage. This African centered study of ancient Africa is not simply committed to comprehensive African historiographic reconstruction placing Africans as subjects not objects of this phenomenal historic dynamic by infusing the philosophic social exhilir of Ma'at, righteousness with its components or truth and justice to uplift the African mind from the European dead level to an inordinate level of consciousness enabling him to attain intellectual autonomy and seek to bring good into the world. However, in this cultural awakening, Dr. Ben-Jochannan not simply researched and wrote books, he taught his students, carried them to Egypt and exposed them to the wonders of the monuments, even explained their meanings to more fully assess the challenges and contradictions posed by modern archaeologists. However, while a great many African and African-American scholars viz., Edward Wilmot Blyden, Martin Delaney, W.E.B. DuBois, Marcus Garvey, Duse Mohammed, Drusilla Dunjee, Carter G. Woodson, John Higgins, John G. Jackson, J.A. Rogers, George G.M. James, Chancellor Williams, Ivan Van Sertima, Prof. Scobie, Asa Hilliard, Benjamin Carruthers, Maulana Karenga, George Simmonds, Molefi Asante, Cheikh Anta Diop, Theophile Obenga, Leonard Jeffries, Leonard James, even Walter Rodney among others, have incessantly extolled the blackness of ancient Egypt and the Nile Valley; the "warrior scholars" John Henrik Clarke and Yosef A. A. ben-Jochannan most adamantly had much to say about the people, culture and history of North-East Africa.

Dr. "Ben" as he was affectionately called, spent some sixty years challenging the distorted presentation of Egyptian history including significant omissions while setting the record straight as he brought the light and educated thousands, some say millions pointing out the intellectual crimes committed against Africa and its sons and daughters. Nevertheless, in this widespread examination, excavation or Archaeology, the now empowered and enquiring African minds have delved into not just temples and tombs, but cemeteries, and private dwellings and fortified buildings; even private and museum collections all along seeking truth. As such, and moving beyond Roman and Greek periods, structures where towns have remained intact as at Kuft, Kom Ombo, El Ayandiyeh, and even on the outskirts of Karnak at Thebes, these date to the Middle and New Kingdoms. Surviving towns and private dwellings date from the Twelfth Dynasty at Kahun and at Abydos where remains go back to the earliest times. The town of Tell el-Amarna, still standing, allowed archaeologists to reconstruct that important city of the religious revolution though this location suffered tremendously in the reaction having posed a challenge to Amon's supremacy.

At Tell el Maskhuta, the twin towns of Pithom and Rameses established connection with biblical times and events. The two fortresses at Abydos date to the beginnings of Egyptian history. Work of excavation was conducted on the ramparts of El Kab, Kom el Ahmar, el Hibeh, Kuban (opposite Dakkeh), of Heliopolis, and of Thebes where structures were still standing during the early development of the science of Archaeology.

Into the Egyptian Mind. Egyptian Art. An individual kneels in adoration before two lions guarding sun-disk traversing two mountains of the land, grasped by an ankh.

Into the Egyptian Mind. Egyptian Art. While an individual in a boat plucks fishes and birds from the river (above), others carry animals and vessels, perhaps in tribute.

Into the Egyptian Mind. Double Temple of Horus and Sobek. Pharaoh and alter ego offers to Horus (Heru) and Hathor (Athor).

Into the Egyptian Mind. Double Temple of Horus and Sobek. In White Crown, Pharaoh offers a golden apron to two ladies, Isis (Auset) and Nephthys.

Into the Egyptian Mind. Cairo Museum of Egyptian Antiquities. Striding individuals (top) carry scepter and staff of office. Clothing is different, head-dress is different and only one wears a beard.

Archaeology therefore revealed the earliest dwellings made of wattle and daub. Materials consisting of mud mixed with sand and chopped straw, were molded into oblong bricks then dried in the sun. Regarding mastery of the brick-making industry, Maspero (1914: 4) pointed out: "A good modern workman will easily turn out 1,000 bricks a day, and after a week's practice he will reach 1,200, 1,500 or even 1,800. The ancient workman whose tools were the same as those of the present day must have obtained equally good results."

An interesting consideration is the soil in which builders had to work. Equally we know the workers were of the poorest class. Today we call them fellahin, who built homes no different from their ancient counterparts. Many of the modern houses, built of concrete are quite different from those of the lower classes, and, are in several stories. For instance, today a father builds his house and a son builds above him and so on and you have the modern multistoried buildings, though not of a commercial type. This was not so in ancient times. Nevertheless, the private dwellings from the simplest huts to the biggest mansion all had certain features that archaeology has been able to reconstruct. Then we have fortresses built for military purposes and also civic structures designed for Government service and other civic activities. To this we add religious architecture as well as tombs, which the early archaeologists were more interested in. These eternal dwelling places for the gods were made of stone. However, the builders did not always use large stone or one type of stone to build temples.

In these temple constructions, Maspero in *Manual of Egyptian Archaeology* (1914: 53) described the type of materials they used: "The size varied greatly according to the purpose for which they were intended. Architraves, drums of columns, lintels, and doorjambs were sometimes of very considerable dimensions. The largest architraves known, those above the central aisle of the hypostyle hall at Karnak, average 30 feet in length. Each one represents a solid block of 40 cubic yards and weighs about 65 tons. Generally, however, the blocks are not larger than those in ordinary use among us. They vary from 3 to 4 feet in height, from 3 to 8 feet in length, and from 18 inches to 6 feet in breadth."

Seldom was a temple built of one single type of stone. In fact, variety was sometimes the rule. To this, Maspero (1914: 53) say further: "Some temples were built throughout in one kind of stone, but more frequently materials of various kinds and quality are associated, although in unequal proportions. Thus, the main buildings of the temple of Abydos are of very fine limestone, while in the temple of Seti I the columns, architraves, jambs, and lintels, all those parts where limestone might not be sufficiently strong, are in sandstone, granite, and alabaster. Similar combinations are to be seen in the temples of Karnak, Luxor, Tanis, Deir el Bahari, Ghizeh, and Memphis. At the Ramesseum, at Karnak, and in the Nubian temples, where all these materials are combined, the columns rest on a solid foundation of crude brick. The stones were dressed more or less carefully according to the position they were to occupy."

Into the Egyptian Mind. Cairo Museum of Egyptian Antiquities. Erik Monderson stands with Khafre and two goddesses in the background.

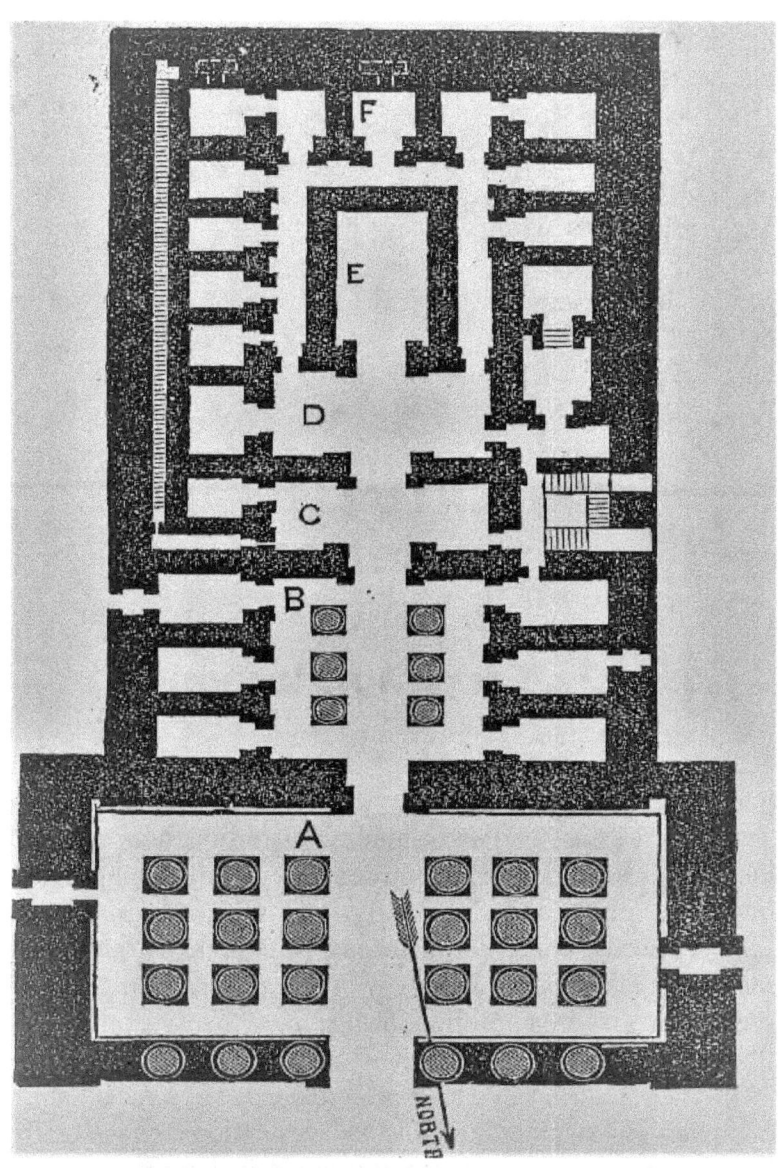

DENDERA TEMPLE OF HATHOR

A. Pronaos – First Hypostyle Hall
B. Second Hypostyle Hall – Hall of Appearances
C. First Vestibule – Hall of Offerings
D. Second Vestibule – hall of Ennead

E. Sanctuary
F. Per-Ur Chapel - Shrine of Egypt
G. Nile Room
H. Stairs to Roof
I. Laboratory
J. Harvest Rooms
K. Hathor's Wardrobe
L. Seat of Repose
M. Sacred Serpent
N. Treasury
O. Per-Neser Chapel – House of Flame
P. Per-Nu Chapel

3. EXISTENTIALISM AND SYMBOLISM
By
Dr. Fred Monderson

Despite the clear deluge of new revelations regarding interpretation of the data relative to ancient Egyptian religious and historical facts, art and ethnicity; distortion, omission and modern presentation, old representations still abound. It is interesting how upon close analysis its revealed this expert, scholar, even publisher, mistakenly interpreted a key data, idea, concept, which is generally due to the "rush to publish" scenario in that great information age more than a century ago. It's also generally agreed, the "Information Age of 1870-1930" was a period in which the most extensive reclamation of ancient Egyptian cultural history was undertaken generally through the work of archaeology aided in interpretation by anthropology, art-history, biometrics, anthropometry, in which these disciplines helped to define scholarly and adventurous men and movements of their age. Some time ago, to establish familiarity with the "Ancient Records of the Ancient Records," the master teacher Dr. Yosef A.A. ben-

Jochannan admonished this writer, in choosing Egypt as a field of anthropological research, "Get the oldest materials you can find and work from there." Thus, its manifest, the period is a lucrative treasure of relative data.

As such, the decision to study this era has revealed not simply the greatest body of ancient art and architecture, history, religion and even philosophical speculation exposing an enormous quantity of data relative to trade, economics, science, theosophy, theology, and cosmogony and cosmology, but more important, faulty extant existential reality that contradicts the symbolic representation in literature and artifacts designed to elevate Europe and denigrate Africa and things African.

Therefore, in those undertaking extending decades, a number of revelations spotlighted contradictions in interpretation of both the existential and symbolic record. That is to say, in aftermath of rampant disregard for the sanctity of ancient Nile Valley, Egyptian, cultural treasures in the form of mummies, statues, steles, tombs, temples, paintings, altars, papyri, scarabs, gold jewelry, religious writings, and a whole lot more; we see manifest a financial grab of cultural and historical riches, fulfilling requests of and greatly enriching museums and public and private collections. Still, in contradiction to this mindset and behavior, a number of good and decent men and women emerged to construct a systematic methodology that brought order to the chaotic method of Egyptian archaeological excavation and acquisitions acquisition by museums and public and private collections.

Even in this honest approach following that period, Brian Fagan labeled "The Rape of the Nile," the "White Man's Burden" mentality dictated excavators be recompensed for their efforts in being awarded meaningful artifactual, "choice" pieces that became prized possessions in worldwide collections. In addition, coming into possessions of significant portions of "finds" after the Egyptian authorities were rewarded their share of the "spoils," excavators and their respective societies networked worldwide in fund-raising efforts by doling out prized pieces to institutions and private individuals who could and did make significant contributions to "continue their work of excavation." In the ebullient and lucrative artifactual environment thus created, complimentary organs of publication in the form of journals, magazines, books, all in conjunction with an emerging and acutely active "penny press" and publishing houses, museums, academic institutions, spread the word, laid down the rule of interpretation of the newly discovered data reinforcing the above stated intent that emerged as the predominant view and order of representation today.

Into the Egyptian Mind. Double Temple of Horus and Sobek. Sobek and his consort.

Into the Egyptian Mind. Double Temple of Horus and Sobek. Pharaoh offers two "Eyes of Horus" to Horus while his consort pats his back.

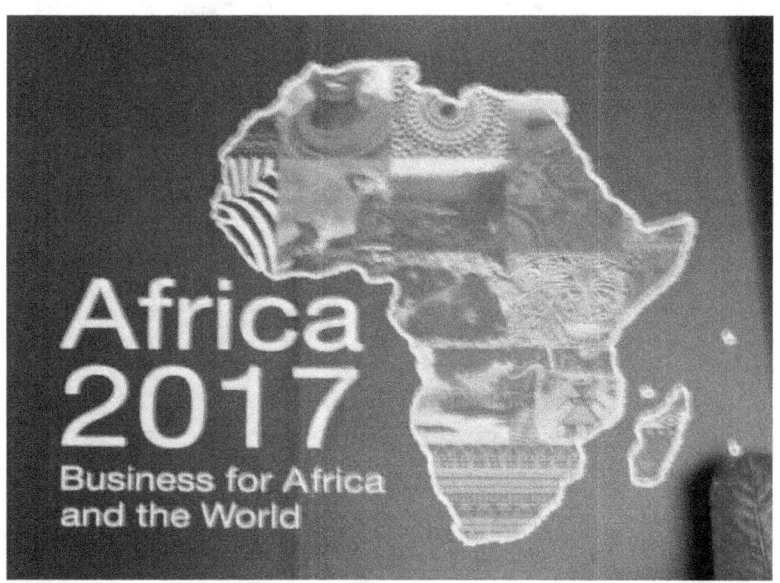

Into the Egyptian Mind. Cairo Museum of Egyptian Antiquities. "Africa 2017: Business for Africa and the World,"

Into the Egyptian Mind. Cairo Museum of Egyptian Antiquities. Three individuals who look essentially alike except for the hairstyle of the one in the middle.

As such, not only did men and artifacts loom large in the new scrutiny but contradictions began to be perceived in the existential and symbolic interpretation of the data, and projection; and, as in any close scrutiny, "rifts between the lutes" emerged thanks to the work of the diligent and meticulous contemporary iconoclastic researchers and analysts. There and then the true philosophic intent of "global white supremacy" stood unmasked from an age of European conquest and control of real property holdings in "colonial territories" in which the prevailing mindset as articulated by literary and academic schools of thought espoused that Europeans were created in a more superior mental and social mold than other peoples. After all, at the turn of the 20th Century, on the question of who were the ancient Egyptians, the prevailing argument and position held, "for some unknown reason" the ancient Egyptians left their "fatherland" and migrated west to find a "new fatherland" in Egypt. They brought and infused "a superior mental attitude" to the existing social setting and thus were responsible for the cultural and social bonanza known today as Egypt. That mindset categorizing the ancient existent reality created in modern symbolist interpretation an outgrowth of a flaunted and false belief system that held: "God is White!" He made man in his own image who is white and therefore psychologically and socially superior to all others particularly the Black, African, who is of an inferior status. Therefore, the white man who is thus superior in the natural and social order is destined to lord it over the Black equally created inferior in the natural and social order.

Let's not deal with the "curse of the black man" which got the white man a great deal of political and religious propaganda and economic and social advantage.

This is the rationale that guided the psychological and intellectual discourse resulting in social and religious degradation of the Black, whether emanating through the Biblical "Curse of Noah;" refusal to give equal status to

Balthazar the African among the "Three Wise Men;" the medieval degrading of blackness until convenient for New and wider World religious expansion following the Renaissance reawakening and this manufactured misconception feeding the rationale for slave trade and slavery manifesting in the most inhuman psycho-social degradation of the African spirit. This psycho-social development provided the wherewithal for plantation slavery transforming the New World in the dreaded chattel slavery system cloaked in "naked imperialism." As the abolitionist movement galvanized men and women of conscience, slave trade and slavery expansion, adventurism, establishment of "spheres of influence" for economic enterprise resulted in colonialism under the banner of "enlightened imperialism." We need remember Prof. John Clarke's absolutely correct observation that "The people who preached racism colonized history" and that "When Europe colonized the world she colonized the world's knowledge." As a result, in the "Scramble for Africa" resulting essentially in "Direct" and "Indirect rule" that characterized colonial administrations. This new mindset of "colonial holding" facilitated a number of agricultural, botanical, zoological and mineralogical investigations to determine the wealth of colonies so as to effectively administer them. In this guise, interest in antiquity enabled a focus in the cultural history that resulted in the creation and expansion of antiquarian societies, many with Journals which systematically and effectively spread the "Gospel of falsity" of white over black, resulting in intellectual imperialism and its machinations. In the case of Egypt, for the century of British conflict with Napoleon at the **Battle of the Nile** (1798) to General Kitchener at Khartoum (1882), British and other European adventurers and scientists began a period of Egyptian antiquities acquisition and data interpretation cloaked in archaeological and anthropological investigation that were meticulously, rigidly and falsely propagated within the "white supremacist mold."

This falsity of representation in what is being vigorously challenged; though the task is enormous. Since, "possession is nine tenths of the law" and European and American cultural and academic institutions became custodians of a great body of Egypt and Nile Valley knowledge and artifacts, this reality reinforces the false interpretation.

Into the Egyptian Mind. Egyptian Art. While fishes and birds frolic in the river above, individuals carry flowers, and animals in a procession.

Into the Egyptian Mind. Egyptian Art. Bound captives and animal parts all seem part of a sacrificial scene.

Into the Egyptian Mind. Egyptian Art. More of the above scene linking bound captives with offering accoutrements.

Into the Egyptian Mind. Egyptian Art. Offering ducks on two elongated vessels.

Into the Egyptian Mind. Cairo Museum of Egyptian Antiquities. Seated individuals who seem similar except for the hairstyles of two.

4. ANCIENT EGPYPT: THE STRUGGLE CONTINUES
By
DR. FRED MONDERSON

In this age of political and intellectual correction, one has to wonder, how lovers of Egyptology can remain intransigently misinformed about the origins and people who influenced and created the great Nile Valley civilization of ancient Egypt, in Northeast Africa. Prof. John H. Clarke long held, "The people who preached racism colonized history." This seems an uncontroverted fact, for clearly, the recovery, teaching, propagation and exhibition of the culture and history of ancient Egypt, has existed overtly and covertly in enmeshed racism, subtle and blatant.

All evidence to the contrary, the anti-Afrocentrists obdurately and with a vehemence inclandestine "slash and burn," any and all thoughts, writings, discussions, regarding the African nature of the Egyptians, the blackness of Egypt and the role of Africa, per se, in development and furtherance of Egyptian culture, affirmative evidence, notwithstanding.

What is significant, however, as African and African-American research scholarship becomes more sophisticated, profoundly analytic and more effectively ferret out the "little rifts between the lute," the falsity of the representation of Egypt is magnified and the *Paper Mache'* pillars supporting the false edifice has begun to crumble.

The "slash and burn movement" defending the "Caucasian origins of the ancient Egyptians," a la Derry, Emery, Petrie, Wortham, has attacked every credible black and some white scholars whose views oppose their own. It's as if to say, despite their own intellectual attainments, countless years of research, endless writing and publishing, teaching, lecturing, etc., Blacks cannot view Egyptian machinations objectively as if they have "an axe to grind." But, in fact, they do have an axe to grind; it is to set the record straight after centuries of falsity regarding ancient Egypt and Africa. For example, any attempt to so-call disparage Greek culture, is tantamount to a declaration of war and the defenders of Grecian "cultural and intellectual purity" who girdle themselves appropriately for academic combat.

Yet, reasonable minds can accept, in the history of cultural and technological development, mankind does not re-invent the wheel. *Ipso facto*, where there is physical contact between peoples, through trade or otherwise, there is cultural, technological or religious transfer of ideas.

The Greek miracle has often been highlighted in art, architecture, science, mathematics, philosophy, music, etc. However, the respectable Encyclopedist George Sarton, in responding to some commentary regarding the origins of Greek mathematics, simply stated: "The Greek miracle had been prepared by millennia of experimentation in Egypt. Rather than a discovery it's been a revival." This reminds of Prof. John H. Clarke's theory that: "Egyptian civilization was researched on the stage of the Upper Nile before making its debut in the Theater of Egypt." The "rehearsal" concept can be applied to Egypt and Greece. Now, this is applicable across the board within many of the Greek disciplines. Remember Goethe compared "Egyptian black basalt sculpture with Greek white marble." One of the classic Egyptian pieces, now in the Cairo Museum, is Khafre with Isis and the Nome Goddesses, and this is Old Kingdom, nearly two millennia before Greek prominence. The Egyptians had 28 soundings of music, similar to the Greeks and this was many millennia in the making. Egyptian philosophy is traceable through Imhotep, Ptahhotep, etc. Herodotus tells that the Greeks got their gods and religion from the Egyptians, and many of the pre-Socratic and Socrates influenced philosophers visited Egypt to learn philosophy.

The Egyptians invented the colonnade at 2600 B.C., and the highlight of the Parthenon, classic Greek architecture, is its columns influenced by the Egyptian colonnade. Regarding these, Champollion coined the name "Proto-Doric" to describe Middle Kingdom columns at Beni-Hassan and at Deir el Bahari during the New Kingdom, one and two millennia before the Greeks. Yet, when it comes to Egyptian influence on Greek culture, the "slash and burners" often remarked, 'What are you talking about!" And so, it is, denying Egyptian influence in Greek culture, yet proclaiming Caucasian influence in Egypt, and vehemently denying the blackness of Egypt and its connection to Africa.

To help this process and certainly as a challenge to Wortham and much of the arguments for migrating Europeans who entered Egypt, Africa, and developed the civilization, essentially lording it over menial blacks, the following important points are included.

1.   According to Heliopolitan belief, Ra created the gods then he created the people of Nubia. One has to wonder why Nubians were so high up in the creation process.

2.   The God Ptah was a pygmy not a European dwarf; as such a claim obfuscates the issue. The inherent idea of Ptah makes its historical appearance thousands of years before the appearance of Europe and its dwarfs.

3.   Henri L'Hote's "Oasis of Art in the Sahara" chronicles painting between 12,000 - 5000 B.C. Here he lists the "round heads" before 6000 B.C. and the "Pastoral peoples" who appear c. 5000 B.C. He says during this "Pastoral period," the "features of the archer painted during the Pastoral period,

suggests to me the presence of black people." For the art, their favored shades were yellow, red and brown. It is reasonable to suppose as the Sahara began to dry up, these people could have migrated to the Nile Valley. If we accept Maspero's "Theory" that European elements crossed over into North Africa then migrated to the Valley through the Sahara, are we to believe the Africans living there could not have done the same. Considering they did not have to cross over from Europe.

4. Mary Leakey's "Tanzania's Stone Age Art" in *National Geographic Magazine* (1983) refers to the choice of colors, where "The predominant red was made from ochre, which is derived from iron ore." Let's not forget *The New York Times* article of 1971 describing hematite mining in south Africa at c. 43,000 Before Present. These latter two articles connect the Egyptians and Ethiopians with the use of the red color. After all, Diop did write the Egyptians color themselves red simply to show some distinction with other Africans. But we know in the tomb of Tanutemon, the Ethiopian of the XXVth Dynasty, the wall was littered with red! This certainly questions the notion of "red Egyptians." While most pictures show Egyptian men painted red and the women a lighter color, some scholars have propagated the view, Egyptian women never ventured into the sun so they were shown as "light." However, Rameses III of the 20th Dynasty boasted, among the many things he accomplished, in addition to instituting peace and tranquility in his kingdom, he protected women, as the inscriptions indicates, that "they might go to and from where they would in security, no one daring to insult them on the way."

Into the Egyptian Mind. Egyptian Art. What goes through one's mind when standing in such a position.

Into the Egyptian Mind. Egyptian Art. As one group seems to be "frisked" (above), an individual is bastioned (beaten) (below), perhaps for taxes, as a high official looks on.

Into the Egyptian Mind. Double Temple of Horus and Sobek. A couchant Sphinx offers two ointment jars.

Into the Egyptian Mind. Double Temple of Horus and Sobek. A Nile Goddess offers the fruits of her Domain.

Into the Egyptian Mind. Cairo Museum of Egyptian Antiquities. Striding statues in different attitudes.

5. W. Stephenson Smith in *The Art and Architecture of Ancient Egypt* (1959) not only informed us Mentuhotep II had "black flesh," but that "the earliest forms of art appear in Upper Egypt and Nubia."

6. Hans A. Winkler in *Rock Drawings of Southern Upper Egypt II* (1938: 18) noted, in Southern Upper Egypt art first depicted the dynamics of their environment in the form of, "gazelle, stax, ibex, antelope, cattle, hare, lion, crocodile, fish, dog, horse. There are men with bow and arrow, with lasso, with staff, with flower, man smelling lotus-flower, man in adoring attitude, pharaoh on throne, pharaoh with mace; women; sailing vessels; Min, Mentu, Taurt, Anubis, Horus the flacon, uraeus." Most of these are included in the hieroglyphic depiction as the linguistics developed using their surroundings to create ideas for the language. This is somewhat consistent with Diop's and Arnett's view that hieroglyphics developed in Upper Egypt from the natural surroundings.

7.   The calendar was established by 4240 B.C., and by the First Dynasty, the two calendars (of 365 and 365 1/4 days) existed side by side.

8.   In the Prehistoric period weights were discovered in graves and this was evidence of its use in trade. Equally, gold was significant in development of weights for measurement of the precious metal.

9.   Mathematically speaking, numbers in the millions were established by Narmer's time, at unification, depicting captives counted in such high figures. It certainly took some time to develop use of these high numbers depicting captives.

10.   The lands to the south of Egypt were considered "god's land" and those individuals who knew how to dance "the dance of the gods" were honored persons. The Twa people, or Pygmies, as Old Kingdom evidence indicates, were good at dancing the "dance of the gods."

11.   Commentary has been made on the region of the eastern desert between the Red Sea coast, the Granite Mountains, and the Nile, and how difficult or "evil" was the passage without water. How convenient is the argument that one of the routes of the "originators of Egyptian civilization" is this same passage; and, one has to wonder how did these foreigners choose this location for passage, and how did they know what to expect at the other end of the journey?

12.   Bruce Williams discovered artifacts published in *The New York Times* of March 1, 1979 showing the earliest evidence of monarchy found in the region of Nubia at Qustol, with the depiction of enthroned pharaoh, sailing vessel, incense burner, white crown, serekh and palace facade, Horus figure, etc., centuries before Narmer.

13.   Bauval and Brophy in *Black Genesis*: *The Prehistoric Origins of Ancient Egypt* (2011) tell of the people of Nabta

Playa who are the earliest scientists who mapped the heavens. They were considered the "Precursors to the Pharaohs."

Therefore, the above are some factors that need to be considered in the equation of determining who in fact were the ancient Egyptians and where did they come from. We should never forget, the papyrus of the 19th Dynasty priest and nobleman, Hunefer, some have argued it's the "Famine Stele" which claimed regarding origins, "We came from the headwaters of the Nile, where the god Hapi dwells, at the foothills of the Mountains of the Moon." This is in the area of Mounts Kilimanjaro, Ruwenzori, etc., in Central Africa.

We must remember also, some of the theories regarding the origin of the Egyptians as Caucasian, are that they were "Boat people." Either they dragged boats across the desert they crossed or deny the invention of boats by a riverain people on the Nile whose Eastern Desert Petroglyphs were protohistoric prototypes of, among other features, "Boats of the Gods" in full-effect. Then we read they were a pastoral people. Well, L'Hote indicated that after the faceless "round heads" at 6000 B.C., the "Pastoral people" are dated at 5000 B.C., and they are "black people." Pastoralism was practiced at Nabta Playa. Therefore, pastoral way of life is certainly not alien to Africa.

Finally, since the Africans were in Africa, in the Sahara and on the Nile, one has to wonder when did the Caucasians, a la Wortham, arrive, and what did they bring. As far as it seems, all they brought was their "pretty white selves," and this smacks of the, now refuted, "Hamitic Hypothesis." To recall, the "Hamitic Hypothesis" argued, "any evidence of high culture found in Africa was brought there by people of a white morphology." Naturally, this theory has been discredited.

The seated scribe, out front, in the Louvre Museum in Paris, has blue eyes! The argument thus holds, "See the ancient Egyptians had blue eyes," all other evidence to the contrary.

We do know the Egyptians applied "inlaid eyes of glass" to their statues and that choice of blue eyes may have been an anomaly. Also, Wortham's one 1825 A.D. mummy dissection in London, "Correctly proves the Egyptians were Caucasian," is a faulty proposition. This "One swallow so its summer" theory forgets, "The Bones of Hen Nekht," of the First Dynasty, proves this king to be "Negro."

Regarding the tombs of Seti I and Rameses III, we are told, "The character of the four people in the first hall differs slightly from those of the former tomb."

"Four Blacks clad in African dresses, being substituted instead of the Egyptians, though the same name, Rot, is introduced before them."

What does all of this tell us? The Egyptians were Africans, black, and the modern records have been falsified to prove otherwise. Much of this is not "for some unknown reason" theory, but factually sound.

14.   Toby Wilkinson's *Genesis of the Pharaohs* (2003) discovered evidence of cultural features depicted in Petroglyphs that were "1000 years before Winkler's Mesopotamians."

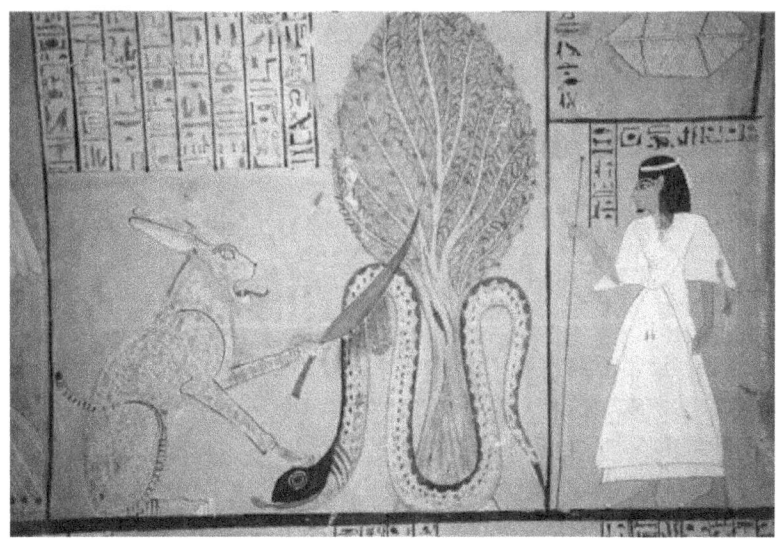

Into the Egyptian Mind. Egyptian Art. The "Great Cat" slashes the "Great Snake" hovering around the fruitful tree as the Nobleman looks on.

Into the Egyptian Mind. Cairo Museum of Egyptian Antiquities. A contingent of Nubian-Egyptian infantry on the march.

Into the Egyptian Mind. Double Temple of Horus and Sobek. A feathered king stands on a column with composite columns in the top rear.

Into the Egyptian Mind. Double Temple of Horus and Sobek. In White Crown with horns, feathers and uraei, pharaoh pour a libation and offers a plant. To the rear and above uraei and composite columns.

Into the Egyptian Mind. Cairo Museum of Egyptian Antiquities. Individual with hands crossed seeking solace looks peaceful.

5. GOD in Ancient Egypt!
By
Dr. Fred Monderson

The idea of "God" in ancient Egypt had been long in the making and depending on the scholar, who studied such, the conceptions varied and the age of such commencement restricted. The Pyramid Texts of the 5th and 6th Dynasties are considered the oldest surviving religious writings or for that matter, writing of any sort. Significantly, they remained unchanged until discovered in the 1880s. However, without question, the long march towards codification may have been two millennia in the making. Nonetheless, while Breasted dated these documents to the mid-4th millennium, c. 3500-3400 B.C., "refining" the dates of the chronology place these a thousand years after at c. 2500 B.C.

The contest of the "long" and "short" chronology is an argument not fully settled for the "Short Chronology" proponents seek to give Babylonia primacy over Egypt or certainly contemporaneity. Nevertheless, several scholars believe the Pyramid Texts in their codified form was millennium in the making. This meant, like all later forms of written literature were first spoken or experienced in oral form. Therefore, that would mean Egyptian and Nile Valley; religious beliefs may have been practiced for eons before finally having such experiences committed to writing. Albert Churchward believed such religious practices as spiritual expressions may be 300,000 years in the making.

Its general knowledge archaeology revealed much of ancient Egyptian cultural and religious practices and much of this was systematically done in the "Age of Reclamation" 1870-1930. The credit for such labors goes to European scholars, societies and institutions who not only excavated but others analyzed, codified and placed understanding in meaningful contexts to enable further study. However, much of this occurred in the

"Age of Imperialism, Exploration and Colonialism," and this in itself unfolded as Europeans ascended the Nile and penetrated Africa from different directions.

Nevertheless, as the record revealed, the archaeological excavation of Egypt, first Lower then Upper, was pursued and when this was exhausted, then Nubia became the next area of archaeological interest and exploration. Only within the last decades of the 20th Century were the desert regions explored to any great extent. As such, and important, while some desert exploration had been conducted in the first part of the 20th Century using camels for transport, these recent forays, using motorized vehicles have not simply covered more territory but equally made important discoveries that challenge the earlier revelations. In his *Genesis of the Pharaohs: Dramatic New Discoveries Rewrite the History of Ancient Egypt* (Thames and Hudson, 2003), Toby Wilkinson has explained in the Eastern Desert of Southern Upper Egypt, he found evidence of early Egyptian gods, the earliest of whom was "Min of Koptos" though his place of veneration was found much further south. He dates such "beginnings," "a thousand years before Winkler's Mesopotamians!" Similar cultural and religious "origins" beginnings were found in the Western Desert at Nabta Playa, somewhat west of Abu Simbel and revealed in *Black Genesis: Prehistoric Origins of the Pharaohs* (Bear and Company, 2011), written by Bauval and Brophy. This team, using a wide array of modern approaches to the study of history and historical sites, revealed evidence of science beginnings, viz., plotting the heavens, creating a calendar, pastoralism, etc., and worship of the "Cow Goddess!"

All this seems to say, while early scholars worked with honest intentions, they very probably got some things wrong and, the true purpose of research or the search for truth is to correct such when evidence to the contrary is found!

While there seems no definition for the term "God" in ancient Egypt, a number of ideograms as indicated by Alfred

Wiedemann in the article "God" (Egyptian) in Hasting's *Encyclopedia of Religion and Ethics* Vol. 6, 1913, have been used to depict the concept of divinity. Regarding this phenomenon, he wrote, "of the ideograms used for the term 'God,' the subsequent rather frequent figure of the star was derived from the occasional but never altogether systematic, identification of the gods with stars. The figures of the hawk or falcon for 'God,' and of the uraeus-serpent for 'Goddess' recall the incarnation of the sun gods (with which a large number of other gods were subsequently assimilated) as falcons, and of goddesses as serpents. The late usage of the three most sacred birds - hawk, ibis, and heron - instead of three hawks, as the symbol for 'God' is mere pictorial play. A much more frequent figure is the short axe, similar to that used by soldiers."

The star is understandable because of its distant mystique and so too the birds in their ability to soar into the heavens that seem to justify ancient man's quest to solve the mystery of divine personality and domain, "What's up there?" The axe, on the other hand, as a military weapon symbolizes strength and force thought to be a divine trait. Wiedemann describes this weapon's make-up: "The axe-head was let into a wooden helve and fixed with cords and was painted yellow or white to suggest the polished stone used for such tools in the earliest age and superseded later by copper or bronze. In the Nagada Period, instead of the single axe-head, we sometimes find two such - thin and almost nail-like - attached to the handle. This symbol always represents a weapon and in the inscriptions the standard, with which some have sought to identify it, is normally depicted in a different way." Among a number of war-like implements used in battle, the axe was synonymous with the term "Neter" meant "to strike," "knock down," or "throw" or even "to be vigorous" or even "powerful." In duplicate "Neter" came to mean "God" and further, "The god who by being removed creates everlasting life for himself." This designation meant the god was not indestructible because we know they were susceptible to injury or mal-intent, even death.

The question has always been whether the Egyptians practiced monotheism, polytheism or henotheism. However, while the latter two may have been practiced in the earliest times, many who have studied this issue explained monotheism was the actual practice from the beginning, Akhenaten's short-lived experiment, notwithstanding, suffices as the truest example! In fact, on this subject Wiedemann wrote: "The earlier Egyptologists believed that a species of monotheism must have existed in the Valley of the Nile.... Other scholars were of opinion that monotheism existed side by side with polytheism, but that it was known only to the learned, i.e., the priests and the learned."

While Alexander Moret may have coined the term "mysteries" to the Egyptian doctrines of immortality and of the ritual necessary for the attainment of the life beyond, "no evidence exist to support such nor that certain parts of the temple could only be entered by initiates. Thus, the only mysteries were 'magic words and ceremonies' known only to initiates." Nevertheless, the search to determine the true origin and nature of the religion, has engaged many minds, to which Wiedemann writes: "From the Egyptian texts scholar have laboriously collected such passages as would imply a higher conception of deity, or such as attribute to the deity the question appropriate to a god regarded as one. They have also found passages which speak of a god as the creator of all life and all existing things, as one who traverses eternity, the lord of infinite time, one who cannot be grasped by the hand, whose evolutions are a miracle, the outstretch of whose being knows no limits, and who is king in Thebes, and, simultaneously, prince in Heliopolis, and the "great of crowns" in Memphis. He cannot be seen, he listens to prayers, he turns his countenance to men according to their conduct; he is hidden, and his form is not known; he is alone and there is none beside him. These attributes, however, were not all ascribed to the same deity, but now one now another of them was regarded as the special property of Amon, of Ra, of Ptah, or of some other member of the pantheon. Even when the texts refer to the one deity, they speak also of other independent figures."

Into the Egyptian Mind. Egyptian Art. Oh, to be entertained musically while sitting together with the Missus.

Into the Egyptian Mind. Egyptian Art. Boating in the marshes while the procession carries flowers, fishes, birds and all good things.

Into the Egyptian Mind. Double Temple of Horus and Sobek. Offering a plant.

Into the Egyptian Mind. Double Temple of Horus and Sobek. Into the deep recesses of the temple where the Sanctuary stone altar rests.

Into the Egyptian Mind. Egyptian Art. Using cows to thresh the floor.

Into the Egyptian Mind. Cairo Museum of Egyptian Antiquities. Colossal seated black granite figure of, perhaps, Khafre.

Even further, Wiedemann states: "The one god is at most described, in a purely material sense, as the begetter, father, builder, conciliator, or king of the other higher powers. He is then, as such, the sovereign of the world of gods and men - one who corresponding for the time being to the earthly pharaoh, reveals his will to the subject by decrees. In all this, however, he is never more than Primer inter pares [first among equals]."

Still, syncretism was a practice frequently found in which such deities as Amon-Ra, Ptah, Hathor, Khnuphis, Isis and others are featured. However, with few exceptions, "the one god holds his dominating position only at a particular place, and even there the other gods are not absorbed in him but maintain their own function and individualities."

To explain this, Wiedemann writes further: "Each Nome found its supreme divine authority in its special deity. The god of the Nome from which the pharaoh had sprung was always regarded for the time as the most important of the Nome gods." This meant the pharaoh's god remained paramount only while his dynasty reigned and was relinquished when another pharaoh and god had ascended the throne. Nevertheless, both Ra and Osiris enjoyed a national following throughout most of dynastic rule. Nonetheless, political realities played into religious dynamics and in those eras of greatest stability and prosperity the recognized state god reigned supreme. As such, "on merely political grounds, the supreme position was held in the Old Empire by Ptah, under the Theban dynasty [Middle and New Kingdom] by Amon, and in the Saitic period Neith."

However, while certain gods were worshipped by the upper classes, conversely, the lower class worshipped gods more in keeping with their social realities. That is, whether as a farmer, a Nile dweller or household person, they recognized a god who could attend to their immediate needs. Explaining this,

Wiedemann (1913) puts into context: "The lower class in particular took but little cognizance of the Nome gods or of other gods worshipped by people of higher rank. They preferred to worship deities whose sphere of action was believed to be relatively narrow. Some of the popular deities could exercise their power at any time; others had special functions as, e.g., that of affording security against demons in general (Bes), at birth (Theuris), on entering the underworld (Amenthes, a form of Hathor), or that of protecting the corn (Nepera), etc."

Some scholars have argued for 'bi-forms" of the god such as Ptah-Imhotep, Hathor-Isis, Hathor-Amenthes, Amon-Min, etc., who "were invested with independent personalities and which sometimes, attained to an independent position in the pantheon. This took place, for example, in the case of Imhotep, 'he who comes in peach,' and Sechmet 'the mighty,' a secondary form of Sechet of Memphis. Probably Amon the 'hidden one' was likewise a special form of Min of Koptos, the god of fertility," then there were animal forms, and it was a crime (punishable by death) for the killing of its species, intentional or unintentional.

SYSTEMS OF DEITIES

Because the Egyptians invested their gods with human qualities in that they attained old age, became sick - even died; they also applied the family concept to their persons, forming groups. Wiedemann notes, "One such group after another was believed to have reigned as the king, or as the father and lord, or others as the enneads of Heliopolis. In other instances, we find certain smaller groups as the Ogdoad of Hermopolis, sometimes also in triads which might appear as families (father, mother, and son, in Thebes), usually very loosely connected, or in even less coherent unions (god and two goddesses in Elephantine) which never developed into trinities. Alongside of these we also find large families (the Osiris cycle), and various other arrangements.... The deities of a certain cycle in one locality might belong to an entirely different group in another. There was no single system embracing a majority of the pantheon, and, subsequently the functions of the individual deities were not everywhere denied in the same way." Some gods even had specific functions and responsibilities as Bes and Taurt mentioned above as well as Montu for war; creation to Ptah; sovereignty among the gods to Ra; and procreation to the goat deities.

ANTHROPOMORPHIC CHARACTER OF THE DEITIES

Anthropomorphically speaking according to Wiedemann, "The gods, while they might assume the external form of men, animals, plants, or even the products of human art, were always represented as having the feelings and needs of men. They required sustenance, food and drink were accorded to them in sacrifice. Even the obelisk, the embodiment of the sun-god, received oblations of loaves and beer. In the daily ritual worship, moreover, articles of clothing, ornaments, fumigations of incense as a protection against evil spirits, and the like, were consecrated to the deity in a fixed order of sequence. Attention was also paid to the housing of deities in temples and chapels and to making these acceptable to them by such accessories as groves, lakes, ships, attendants, slaves, etc."

All this, notwithstanding, a contract or covenant bound the worshippers and the worshipped in a seeming symbiotic arrangement where one depended on another. In this reciprocity relationship, "The worshipper attended to the needs of the god, and the god was expected to requite the worshipper with divine gifts – life, prosperity, health, happiness, victory." This is pictorially depicted in the temple reliefs [where] "we see the king and deity facing each other as parties to a contract and promising or actually bestowing their mutual gifts."

However, like all forms of contract, once one-party refuses to fulfill its obligations and then the agreement is broken. Wiedemann puts it this way: "Should a man, and especially a king, fail in his duty towards the gods, the latter do not further befriend him, and may bring calamity upon the whole country. While, if the deity does not perform his part, the man does not need to trouble any more about him, and, by way of punishing and injuring him, ceases first of all, by sending adversity to his enemies and prosperity to his votaries. He also revealed, his mind in the behavior of certain animals - whether they turned towards the man or away from him. Whether or not they took food from his hand, bellowed, entered certain chambers, and the like."

Al this notwithstanding, god in Egypt, the Nile Valley and elsewhere in Africa was generally generous, beneficent and loving to his adherents, worshippers, who reciprocated in the most obvious manner of ritual, praise and festivity.

Into the Egyptian Mind. Egyptian Art. A loving lion?

Into the Egyptian Mind. Egyptian Art. Making Presentations at family get-together.

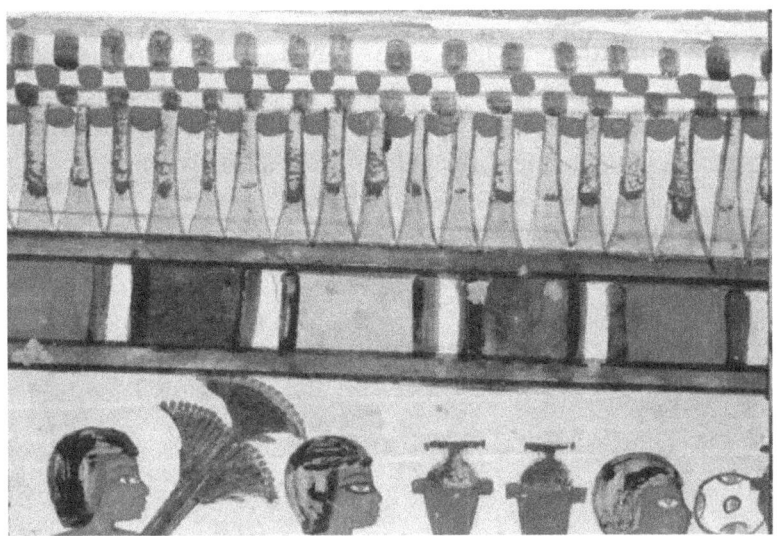

Into the Egyptian Mind. Egyptian Art. Miscellaneous.

Into the Egyptian Mind. Double Temple of Horus and Sobek. On a column, Pharaoh presents a Platter to Sobek, "Lord of Ombos."

Into the Egyptian Mind. Double Temple of Horus and Sobek. On a column, Pharaoh presents a Plant to Shu.

Into the Egyptian Mind. Cairo Museum of Egyptian Antiquities. Practically identical striding figures.

6. THE RELIGION OF ANCIENT EGYPT
BY
DR. FRED MONDERSON

I. Introduction

The Religion of Ancient Egypt is arguably the oldest on record, dating back several millennia even before Unification under Menes. This is probably before any other culture, perhaps only the Ethiopians southwards of Egypt, experienced such joys of sweet communion with deity. Albert Churchward believed this experience kept unfolding, being practiced for some 300,000 years.

Unquestionably it also influenced the manner in which other cultures would later enjoy this wonderful experience. Equally too, theirs' is certainly one of the oldest written forms of religious writings. For that matter, the Pyramid Texts bestow on us the oldest form of writing period, unaffected by editing and changes. Importantly, their equally oldest religious literature, discovered as it was in the pyramids remained, unchanged for millennia. This enabled scholars to understand not only Egyptian writing but also their literature as well, housed as it was in their architecture, adding also much about their skills as builders. Thus, and significantly, the writings discovered in the pyramids represented a process of religious development that probably extended for millennia back into the past.

However, and particularly for the problems of origins, Wallis Budge in *Egyptian Religion* (1900, 1991: 18) offers an interesting caveat, while affirming: "There is no evidence whatever to guide us in formulating the theory that it was brought into Egypt by immigrants from the East." Again, Budge (1991: 18-19) continued: "All that is known is that it existed there at a period so remote that it is useless to attempt to measure by years the interval of time which has elapsed since it grew up and established itself in the minds of men, and that it is exceedingly doubtful if we shall ever have any definite knowledge on this interesting point." Even more, Budge (1991) pointed out: "But though we know nothing about the period of the origin in Egypt of the belief in the existence of an almighty God who was One, the inscriptions show us that this Being was called by a name which was something like Neter, the picture sign for which was an axe-head, made probably of stone, let into a long wooden handle." That far back in time, some scholars have argued, the Egyptians were probably not very far removed from thinking like animals or savage peoples. Nevertheless, if we accept the view of science and the origins of man in Africa, this development of religious consciousness in this part of Africa may extend for thousands of years; first in oral then alter written form.

Notwithstanding, bridging this gap and positing a view of earlier Egyptian religiosity, even further, Budge (1991: 23) affirmed: "As a matter of fact, we know nothing of their ideas of God before they developed sufficiently to build the monuments which we know they built, and before they possessed the religion, and civilization, and complex social system which their writings have revealed to us ...." In this respect, "the primitive god was an essential feature of the family, and the fortunes of the god varied with the fortunes of the family; the god of the city in which a man lived was regarded as the ruler of the city, and the people of that city no more thought of neglecting to provide him with what they considered to be due to his rank and position than they thought of neglecting to supply their own wants. In fact, the god of the city became the center of the social fabric of that city, and every inhabitant thereof inherited automatically certain duties, the neglect of which brought stated pains and penalties upon him." However, what we do know of the early Egyptian religion with certainty is contained in their earliest writing called the Pyramid Texts.

Now, modern scholars on Egypt coined the name *Book of the Dead* that was really the *Book of Per-em-hru* or the *Book of Coming Forth by Day*. As such, the *Book of the Dead* evolved from the *Pyramid Texts* of the Old Kingdom and the *Coffin Texts* of the Middle Kingdom. In essence, these are a collection of spells that guided the soul in the afterlife and encompassed the judgment and what happened to an individual after death. Of this early religious literature, the *Book of the Dead*, Flinders Petrie (1906: 78) informs: "We can distinguish certain groups of chapters, an Osirian section on the kingdom of Osiris and the service of it, a theological section, a set of incantations, formulae for the restoration of the heart, for the protection of the soul from spirits and serpents in the hours of night, charms to escape from periods ordained by the gods, an account of the paradise of Osiris, a different version of the kingdom and judgment of Osiris, a Heliopolitan doctrine about the ba, and its powers of transformation entirely apart from all that is stated elsewhere, the account of the reunion of soul and body, magic formulae for entering the Osirian kingdom, another account of the judgment of Osiris, charms for the preservation of the mummy and for making efficacious amulets, together with various portions of popular beliefs." These ideas, therefore, cover the widest conception of the human intellect as it relates to the concept that death is not the final human experience. Equally, in anticipation of this drama, social and ethical tenets of righteousness, truth, justice as forms of Ma'at guided the individual's action in his daily life in preparation for the life after.

In *From Fetish to God in Ancient Egypt*, Wallis Budge (Oxford, 1934: 3-4) provided the explanation of the theological significance of the Egyptian belief system. He wrote, "The foundation of the popular opinion about the religious beliefs of the ancient EGYPTIANS was laid by the great pioneer of Egyptology E. DE ROUGE' about the middle of the last century. He stated that the EGYPTIANS believed in One self-existent, supreme, eternal, almighty god, who created the world and everything in it, and endowed man with an immortal soul, which was capable of receiving punishments and rewards. DE ROUGE's words were to all intents and purposes a paraphrase of the passage in NEWTON'S Principia in which the great scientist expressed his belief in the Unity of God who is supreme, infinite, omnipotent, omniscient, and absolutely perfect. Who is present always and everywhere! The various works of creation are the product of his ideas, and his existence is proclaimed by them."

Notwithstanding, and other than the *Book of the Dead*, there were, in addition, other literature as the *Book of Gates* and *Book of Am-Duat* that describe the drama that unfolds as the Sun God traverses the domain of the underworld. The *Book of Gates* describes the gates of the hours of the night. The *Book of Am-Duat* describes the successive hours of the night through which the boat of the sun god passes and the various monsters who tried to impede his journey so as not to arise on the horizon the next day.

Generally speaking, the *Book of Am-Duat* or *Book of What is in the Underworld* represents the beliefs of the Theban locality held by the Priests of Amen-Ra; while the *Book of Gates* are those held by the Priests of Osiris. These religious literatures are very old and extend to the earliest periods of Egyptian history, to a time before they were actually written. Nevertheless, we do know, by the time of the First Dynasty, a *Book of the Dead* was found in the temple of King Sempti. There was another found during the reign of King Menkaure (Menkaura) of the Fourth Dynasty. Even at these early times, these books were revisions of much earlier works. Additionally, over time the "Chapters" or *Book of the Dead* went through many versions or Recensions. These revisions were the "Heliopolitan Recension" done by the Priests of Ra at Heliopolis in the Old Kingdom. There were also revisions made as in the "Theban Recension" of the New Kingdom, and the "Saite Recension" of the Late Period of the XXVIth Dynasty. Over the years, through the editing, revision, duplications and expansions the "Chapters" were expanded to as many as 175 with certain chapters as number 125 becoming tremendously important.

Into the Egyptian Mind. Egyptian Art. With a little fuzz on the face, a raised empty hand implies adoration.

Into the Egyptian Mind. Egyptian Art. More of Miscellaneous.

Into the Egyptian Mind. Double Temple of Horus and Sobek. Close-up of a composite capital beneath architraves supporting the roof.

Into the Egyptian Mind. Double Temple of Horus and Sobek. Sunk-relief image of a deity with curved beard. Notice the side-locks of youth.

Into the Egyptian Mind. Egyptian Art. Papyrus.
From Queen to Goddess, two ointment jars.

Into the Egyptian Mind. Cairo Museum of Egyptian Antiquities. Various figures in varied attitudes. How nice these figures in the Museum do not have their noses broken but in American and European, museums most noses are broken!

Budge (1934: 25) adds more to our understanding of ancient Egyptian religious literature in the statement: "Among the earliest examples of religious drama may be mentioned the 'Book of Opening of the Mouth,' and the 'Book of the Liturgy of Funeral Offerings.' In the first work, the ritual acts and the spells are enumerated which were believed to have the effect of enabling the deceased to breathe, think, speak, walk, etc., in spite of the fact that his body was rough bound tightly with funerary swathing. In the second work, the object of which was to maintain the life of the deceased in the Other World, the KHERI HEB or chief priestly magician presents to a statue of the deceased a long series of offerings of meat, drink, unguents, wearing apparel, etc. As he presents each he repeats a spell, the effect of which could be used by the deceased in the Other World. Every act in every 'mystery' had originally a special signification or was symbolic of some well-known happening. Eventually the meanings of such actions were forgotten in many cases, but the repetition of the actions never ceased."

Nevertheless, these and so much more have shown that the religion of ancient Egypt is very unique. Even more so, that the three western religions of Judaism, Christianity and Islam which some scholars consider to be their foundation also have threads linking Egyptian Religion with eastern and even New World ritual and practice. Thus, the religion of ancient Egypt is very unique in that it is one of the earliest to emerge from the mist of antiquity at the crossroad of the ancient world. Principally it is a monotheistic religion emphasizing the unity of god that in later dynasties had elements of polytheism. It was solar or celestial and anthropomorphic and subterranean and boasted colorful representations of its principal gods, who in many respects, were manifestation of the same principle rather than the many gods the simple-minded encounters.

Explaining some aspects of the ancient Egyptian religious belief and godhead, G.K. Osei in *African Contributions to*

Civilization (African Publication Society, 1983) tells: "The creator is an active force. He commands; he guides; he inspires; and he ordains man's destiny." This "Oneness," is underscored by Budge (1934: 4-5) who offers the clarification: "There is no doubt that monotheism was a tenet of the Egyptian Faith, but it was entirely different from the monotheism of Christian peoples. When the **EGYPTIAN** called his god 'One,' or the 'One One,' or the 'Only one,' he meant exactly what he said and what the Muslim means today when he says, 'There is no god but God.' And that god was the sun in the sky from which he received light and heat and the food whereon he lived. The **EGYPTIAN** in his hymns called many gods 'One,' but these gods were all forms of the Sun god, and, as I understand it, he was a monotheist pure and simple as a sun-worshipper. It avails nothing to call his monotheism 'henotheism.' A time came when Osiris was associated with Khepri, the sun at dawn, and with RA at noon-day, and with Temu as the setting sun, and the Pyramid Texts make it clear that under the VIth dynasty Osiris usurped all the attributes and powers of the 'Sun, the One lord of heaven.' There was, of course, a time when men thought that the Sun-god had no counterpart, no offspring, and no associate or equal." Thus, there was clearly a combining of gods in this early period. However, let us also seek to understand; while the sun was a manifestation of God, it was actually the magical, mystical essence behind the sun which was actually god. This was a sort of "power behind the throne" belief syndrome

The religion of ancient Egypt is also unique because the principle of divine right was enshrined in the belief of god working in the king as guardian of the state. In this respect, Frankfort (1961: 30) tells: "The Egyptian state was not a man-made alternative to other forms of political organization. It was god-given, established when the world was created; and it continued to form part of the universal order. In the person of Pharaoh, a superhuman being had taken charge of the affairs of man. And this great blessing, which ensured the well-being of the nation, was not due to a fortunate accident but had been foreseen in the divine plan. The monarchy then was as old as the world, for the creator himself had assumed kingly office on the day of creation." Even further, Frankfort (1961: 30-31), in referring to the creator, great god, continued: "Pharaoh was his descendant and his successor. The word 'state' was absent from the language because all the significant aspects of the state were concentrated in the king. He was the fountainhead of all authority, all power, and all wealth. The famous saying of Louis XIV, L'etat c'est moi, was levity and presumption when it was uttered, but could have been offered by Pharaoh as a statement of fact in which his subjects concurred. It would have summed up adequately their political philosophy."

The religion of ancient Egypt very early established the notions of heaven and hell and the philosophical tenets and principles that applied, thereto, viz., Ma'at, righteousness, truth, justice, balance, reverence, deference, order, etc., that guided the individual's ethical behavior and standards of conduct as such related to the expectations of this other worldly drama and reality. The religion of ancient Egypt is again unique in that it presented the earliest comprehensive religious writings that have survived, unchanged and unedited, until discovered in the 19th Century. In this early manifestation of the creative Egyptian, African, mind, the religion established parameters and paradigms of religious experience people would forever more aspire to. In this Ma'at was a powerful social utility that was also a tremendous dynamo creating ethical standards to guide and shape the society. As a result, later civilizations benefited tremendously owing a great debt to this ancient Egyptian, African, experience.

The religion of ancient Egypt with its many and essentially African characteristics boasted several principal deities worshipped at different centers throughout the nation. An established Priesthood serviced each deity, and in order to avoid conflict, they tried to synchronize their dogma. The king, as the gods' representative on earth, built temples throughout the land and though favoring one god in one particular time, was also beneficent to the others, though to a lesser extent. In the evolved building and associated practices, their architecture developed decorative features in stone as a lasting testament to their god. In their building practice, different types of temples were constructed to the god, the king and nation. The effort enabled the decorative arts to flourish and a number of industries that fed the ubiquitous religious demands were generated.

The religion of ancient Egypt is unique because very early it preached the dynamics of the afterlife and so became a true engine of molding social and ethical behavior. The science of the funeral, building and decoration of tombs, practice of mummification, the final judgment, the Negative Confessions, the philosophic maxim of Ma'at, and reward for the good life, were all themes and practices that not only molded their culture but later civilizations came to emulate much they had initiated. For worshipping and ritualizing the gods, a priesthood developed that managed the god's estate and catered to the religious aspirations of the people and they also encouraged furtherance of the arts, study of the heavens, practice of medicine, teaching of bureaucratic administrative principles, serving mundane needs of ordinary citizens, etc. Thus, in the relationship that developed with the gods, Egypt became an imperialist nation sanctioned by a divine spirit. As such, imperial pharaohs wielded the sword and conquered, then of the accumulated booty heaped untold wealth on their favorite divinities resulting in the building of enormous structures for religious worship that furthered agricultural practices, the craft of boat building, navigation of the Nile and much more. In the totality of this interaction, religion helped to advance science that in turn advanced civilization and thus Africa, through Egypt and the Nile Valley, can be considered not simply the mother of invention but also the dynamo fueling human progress.

The unmistakable fact of all this is that the *Pyramid Texts*, *Coffin Texts* and *Book of the Dead* are the oldest existing religious literature and monotheism is the basis of Egyptian religion. In this Egyptian, African, religious experience and drama, while the fortunes of their other gods rose and fell, the worship of Osiris remained consistent throughout dynastic times. In the practice and experience of worship and ritualizing the gods, temples became larger, more durable and decorative, all this while the social and ethical rewards of Egyptian religion helped shape human behavior ultimately benefitting the cause of humanity. The bureaucracy that aided religious worship, managed the god's estate, catered to the afterlife requirements of the individual souls and in this interaction, religion advanced the development of knowledge and civilization. All this the African bequeathed to the world, while not getting the proper credit for this legacy in the much distorted and falsified modern conception of humanity's long march along the evolutionary path of human development.

In the enormous compendium of the *Book of the Dead*, there are more than 172 "Chapters" and some versions of "Chapters" are duplicates, making correctly 153 "Chapters." Still some "Chapters" seem more important than others and "Chapter" 125 is probably the most important. It is comprised of 4 parts, an Introduction, the Negative Confessions, Conclusion, and Psychostasia or Weighing of the Heart. The latter part, takes place in presence of 12 great gods of Egypt, who are Ra-Harmachis, Temu, Shu, Tefnut, Seb, Nut, Isis, Nephthys, Horus, Hathor, Hu and Sa. Thoth and Anubis are also involved in weighing the heart. However, the Papyrus of Hunefer mentions 14 gods and the Turin Papyrus lists the 42 gods to whom the **Negative Confession** was recited.

Why there are 42 confessions is not certain. Some scholars such as Dr. ben-Jochannan believe they are part of a larger body of 147 confessions. However, we do know for sure, the "eater of the dead," Am-mitt, was a woman, whose "Forepart is that of a crocodile, her hind part is that of a hippopotamus, and her middle is that of a lion." Why a woman, we do not know! Perhaps it is because she gave birth similarly when Goddess Nuit gave birth to the sun-god in the morning and swallowed it at evening time. She then gave birth again, this time to the stars that twinkle. Nevertheless, Am-Mit stood at the judgment hoping the deceased would fail that process, not having lived by the tents of Ma'at or righteousness, and then would become her "lunch."

Into the Egyptian Mind. Egyptian Art. Two ladies holding Sistrums.

Into the Egyptian Mind. Egyptian Art. Figures in different attitudes surrounding a broken, seated statue in a Naos.

Into the Egyptian Mind. Double Temple of Horus and Sobek. Sobek, "Lord of Ombos."

Into the Egyptian Mind. Double Temple of Horus and Sobek. Presenting a baboon representing Thoth.

Into the Egyptian Mind. Cairo Museum of Egyptian Antiquities. Various figures in different attitudes. Again, the noses are intact.

No one knows when the Judgment actually happens, whether immediately upon death or whether there is a waiting period or whether it's after the burial or mummification. One thing is certain, each soul is judged individually and the deceased hoped, when the heart was being weighed against a feather in the Hall of African Judgment, his (or her) heart would not speak negatively against him and this was determined by the life he lived on earth. Now, after a successful Judgment and declared "True of Voice" or "Justified," he attained to the heavenly "Elysian Fields" with its components of "Fields of Reeds," "Field of Peace," etc., that place of righteousness and spiritual purity. In the earthy preparation for this process, Reid (1925: 117) believed essentially: "The Egyptian ideal was to avoid those things that are denied and to do those things that are affirmed."

Symbolism, whether of logic or magic, was very much part of the Egyptian conception of cosmological, theological, metaphysical practices even equality in social matters. While there appeared four principal gods, Ra, Ptah, Amon and Osiris; their realms, solar or celestial and subterranean were oftentimes not contradictory but complimentary, even fused. Throughout, the belief was held that the gods gave everything to Egypt and Egypt should give everything to the gods. This view therefore pervaded every aspect of their earthly and otherworldly existence. In all of this, magic played an important part in the society, and magical provision for the dead in the future life became an accepted fact from the earliest times. This idea of magic ultimately led to the lavish decoration of the tomb, placement of stelae, in and outside tombs, where passersby would recite the inscription for magical transformation of their intent or through the deceased spirit willing the goodies within reach to magically enrich or entertain him.

THE NEGATIVE CONFESSIONS

1. I have not done Iniquity
2. I have not robbed with violence
3. I have not done violence to any man
4. I have not committed theft
5. I have not slain man or woman
6. I have not made light the bushel
7. I have not acted deceitfully
8. I have not purloined the things which belong to God
9. I have not uttered falsehood
10. I have not carried away food
11. I have not uttered evil words
12. I have not attacked any man
13. I have not killed the beasts that are the property of God
14. I have not acted deceitfully
15. I have not laid waste the land which has been ploughed
16. I have never pried into matters to make mischief
17. I have not set my mouth in motion against any man
18. I have not given away to wrath concerning myself without a cause
19. I have not defiled the wife of a man
20. I have not committed any sin against purity

21. I have not struck fear into any man
22. I have not encroached upon sacred times and seasons
23. I have not been a man of anger
24. I have not made myself deaf to the words of right and truth
25. I have not stirred up strife
26. I have made no man to weep
27. I have not committed acts of impurity, neither have I laid with men
28. I have not eaten my heart
29. I have abused no man
30. I have not acted with violence
31. I have not judged hastily
32. I have not taken vengeance upon the god
33. I have not multiplied my speech over much
34. I have not acted with deceit, and I have not worked wickedness
35. I have not uttered curses on the king
36. I have not fouled water
37. I have not made haughty my voice
38. I have not cursed the god
39. I have not behaved with insolence
40. I have not sought for distinctions
41. I have not increased my wealth, except with such things as are justly mine own possessions
42. I have not thought scorn of the god who is in my city

These "Confessions" helped mold the social, moral and ethical conduct of the life of the ancient Africans, Kamites, called Egyptians of the Upper and Lower Kingdoms, also known as Tawi/Kemet the Greeks named Egypt.

II. The Antiquity of Egyptian Religion

It is difficult to establish the antiquity of ancient Egyptian religion but suffice to say that by the time of the Badarian,

Amratian and Gerzean pre-dynastic culture sequence, religious expressions were already evident in the graves of these early people. The objects included in the "goods of the grave," attest to belief in an afterlife and in a god figure. For example, warriors were buried with their weaponry, farmers their implements and craftsmen their tools so as to continue their "professions" in the next life. In time, those who could afford it had interred in their final resting place the **Book of the Dead** to help as guide in the afterlife drama. Stepping out of the mist of prehistory, by the time of Unification at the First Dynasty, Narmer established the worship of Ptah at Memphis. On his slate palette the Goddess Hathor, whose origin Budge determines is Nubian, is evident and this lets us believe their creation stories were perhaps, at least, centuries old by this time. Given that, Ra's worship at Heliopolis may have been contemporary or preceded by the religious worship of the upper kingdom. Many of the creator gods were already in existence. So, having established the prehistoric origins of Ra, Ptah, Thoth, and since Narmer was a Theban, it's easy to accept Amon and his family as being in existence even though they did not come into prominence until much later. Given these gods, certainly the "followers of Horus" precede Narmer; thus, we can assume Osiris his father, whom the ancients believed went north from Nubia or Ethiopia must have been around, though he too does not become prominent at Abydos until around the second and third dynasties. Petrie found large wooden statues of Min at Koptos that were painted black dating to this earliest period. These are now housed in the Ashmolean Museum in Oxford, England. Many scholars associate this god with the Africans of Upper Egypt and further South. Importantly, this puts Min among the earliest company of gods. In fact, Toby Wilkinson in *Genesis of the Pharaohs* (2003) identified Min as the earliest imaged god in history and found in the Eastern Desert of Upper Egypt among other depictions, early Petroglyphs, he determined were "1000 years before Winkler's Mesopotamians."

That aside, we can easily say, "Essentially, two main religious systems emerged in Egypt. First, the state cults were organized, with the temples and priesthood, to ensure the survival of the Gods, Egypt and the King." Then there is the term we apply today called "household gods" that fits the second category of deities. Margaret Murray in *The Temples of Egypt* (1931) says of these "household Gods": "They were worshipped at small, domestic shrines, and had neither temple, divine cults or priesthood, but were approached by people at all levels of society for help and guidance in everyday matters."

As religious expression expanded, rituals played an important part in the mortuary, or god or cult, temples. Murray adds further: "In the cult temple, there were two main types of ritual. The most important ritual (known as the Daily Temple Ritual) was carried out three times per day for the resident god in every temple and dramatized the common-place events of everyday existence, providing food, clothing, washing and regular attendance for the god's cult-statue in his sanctuary. The second type of ritual, the festivals, varied in content from one temple to another, each being based on the mythology of the particular resident deity. These were celebrated at regular, often yearly intervals and marked special events in the god's life, such as marriage, death and resurrection. A main feature of most festivals was the procession of the god's statue outside the temple giving the crowds their only opportunity to see the deity and participate in the worship."

There was also a royal ancestor or mortuary cult festival where the daily offerings from the divine temple worship was presented to the king's dead ancestors so that they could one day welcome him into their company.

Rawlinson's *Ancient Egypt* (1893: 38) explained the dual, common and divine, nature of Egyptian Religion in the following statement: "Beside the common popular religion, the belief of the masses, there was another which prevailed among the priests and among the educated. The primary doctrine of this esoteric religion was the real essential unity of the Divine Nature. The sacred texts, known only to the priests and to the initiated, taught that there was a single Being, 'the sole producer of all things both in heaven and earth, himself not produced of any,' 'the only true living God, self-originated,' 'who exists from the beginning,' 'who has made all things, but was not himself been made.' This Being seems never to have been represented by any material, even symbolical, form. It is thought that he had no name, or, if he had, that it must have been unlawful to pronounce or write it. He was a pure spirit, perfect in every respect - all wise, almighty, and supremely good. It is of him that the Egyptian poets use such expressions as the following: 'He is not graven in marble; he is not beheld; his abode is not known; no shrine is found with painted figures of him; there is no building that can contain him;' and, again: 'Unknown is his name in heaven; he doth not manifest his forms; vain are all representations;' and yet again: 'His commencement is from the beginning; he is the God who has existed from old time; there is no God without him; no mother bore him; no father hath begotten him; he is a god-goddess, created from himself; all gods came into existence when he began.'"

Into the Egyptian Mind. Egyptian Art. While baboons welcome the Boat of Ra (above), various attitudes of the deceased in the Afterlife.

Into the Egyptian Mind. Egyptian Art. "Well, I'll just take my boat and mosey on down the river."

Into the Egyptian Mind. Karnak Temple of God Amon. Handaka, Chief of security explains an aspect of the Wars of Seti I to Erik Monderson in 2018.

Into the Egyptian Mind. Double Temple of Horus and Sobek. Truly, Sobek, "Lord of Ombos."

Into the Egyptian Mind. Double Temple of Horus and Sobek. Preparing incense pellets as offering.

Into the Egyptian Mind. Cairo Museum of Egyptian Antiquities. With one seated scribe above, three striding figures and one at a standstill.

Even further, Rawlinson (1893: 38-39) continued: "The other gods, the gods of the popular mythology were understood in the esoteric religion to be either personified attributes of the Deity, or parts of the nature which he had created, considered as informed and inspired by him. Num or Kneph represented the creative mind, Phthah the creative hand, or act of creating; Maut represented matter, Ra the sun, Khons the moon, Seb the earth, Khem the generative power in nature, Nut the upper hemispheres of the heavens, Athor the lower world or under hemisphere; Thoth personified the Divine Wisdom, Ammon perhaps the Divine mysteriousness or incomprehensibility, Osiris the Divine Goodness. It is difficult in many cases to fix on the exact quality, act, or part of nature intended; but the principle admits of no doubt. No educated Egyptian conceived of the popular gods as really separate and distinct gods. All knew that there was but One God, and understood that, when worship was offered to Khem, or Kheph, or Maut, or Thoth, or Ammon, the One God was worshipped under some one of his forms or in some one of his aspects. He was every god, and thus all the gods' names were interchangeable, and in one and the same hymn we may find a god, say Ammon, addressed also as Ra and Khem and Tum and Horus and Khepra; or Hapi; or Osiris as Ra and Thoth; or, in fact, any god invoked as almost any other. If there be a limit, it is in respect of the evil deities, whose names are not given to the good ones."

III. The Egyptian Holy Books have exerted a tremendous influence on the religion and social behavior and practice of man in the Nile Valley.

a. The *Pyramid Texts* were found in pyramids of the 5th and 6th Dynasties of Kings Unas (5th), Teta (Teti), Pepi I, Merenra and Pepi II (6th) at Sakkara. R. Engelbach in *Introduction to Egyptian Archaeology with special reference to the Egyptian Museum*, Cairo (1961: 225) is of the view: "They are written in a far more ancient language, however, probably of the IIIrd Dynasty or even earlier, and as such are of extreme importance in the study of the ancient language. The texts are exclusively connected with the welfare of the dead king; they consist of incantations whereby his place in the sky and the other prerogatives of a dead king are assured to him, and they also incorporate the ritual which was recited in connection with the daily offerings made in the pyramid-temples. The discovery, quite recently, of an almost complete version of the Pyramid Texts on the walls of a tomb of a noble of the XIIth Dynasty at El-Lisht, shows that these texts were known some 500 years after the VIth Dynasty, and were, at any rate in this case, applied to a non-royal personage. During the IXth to XIth Dynasties, many excerpts from the Pyramid Texts are found written, usually in ink, inside the large coffins of that period. These are now known as the Coffin Texts."

He concluded: "A curious feature in the Pyramid Texts is that figures of fishes are never found; the religious or other reason for this is unknown." Even more important, there are no illustrations in the Pyramid Texts. Budge in Egyptian *Heaven and Hell* (1905: 3) addresses this in his explanation: "That the Egyptians possessed artistic skill sufficient to illustrate the religious and general works which their theologians wrote or revised, under their earliest dynasties of kings of all Egypt, is evident from the plain and colored bas-reliefs which adorn the walls of their mastabas, or bench-shaped tombs, and we can only point out and wonder at the fact that the royal pyramids contain neither painted nor sculptured vignettes, especially as pictures are much needed to break the monotony of the hundreds of lines of large hieroglyphics, painted in a bluish-green color, which must have dazzled the eyes even of an Egyptian."

b.   The *Coffin Texts* of the Middle Kingdom were a continuation of the *Pyramid Texts* of the Old Kingdom that were now written on the insides and outsides of coffins as opposed to being written on the walls of pyramids. We are told: "The Coffin Texts contain an important collection of spells composed on behalf of non-royal personages and comprise incantations against hunger, thirst and manifold dangers of the Underworld, and incantations for enabling the deceased to assume whatever form he pleased, and incantations by virtue of which he could remain in the enjoyment of his former pastimes and partake of the society of his relatives and friends. Part of the interest of the Coffin Texts lies in the fact that they form a link between the Pyramid Text and the later 'Book of the Dead;' spells from both compilations occurring in them. The *Coffin Texts* appear to have been anciently called 'The Book of Justifying a Man in the Underworld;' when read by priests, the spells were called 'transfigurations' or 'spiritualizations.' No complete copy of the Coffin Texts has been found on papyrus, but spells from it occur on New Kingdom papyri. Mutilations of figures of animals, birds and serpents also occasionally occur on some versions of the Coffin Texts."

The *Book of the Dead's* magical spells, were to be recited by the dead man, to protect himself from injury, demons and the 'second death.' They were also to enable him to emerge from his tomb, to accompany the gods, to secure acquittal at the Judgment, and be able to enjoy the fruits of heaven or the Elysian Fields.

c. The *Book of the Dead* continued the religious traditions of the Old and Middle Kingdoms, only now the religious ideas were written on papyrus called books, consisting of "Chapters" of the rituals. Naturally they incorporated much of the earlier religious beliefs.

In part, for example, C.W. Goodwin (1873: 104) discusses: "The 115th Chapter of the Turin Book of the Dead" containing "a very remarkable legend relating to the city of **An or Heliopolis**. This chapter belongs to a group of ten extending from the 107th to the 116th all of which have reference to the recognition by the deceased person of the Ba-u or Spirits of certain localities where he meets them. Several of these chapters contain very antique legends explanatory of the ceremonies observed in certain towns. Thus, Chap 112 professes to explain the origin of the worship of Horus in the town of Pa. Chap 113 had a legend explanatory of the commemoration of the finding of the bands of Horus in the word of Chem. The 115th Chapter .... Contains ... an account of the destruction and reproduction of the race of man in the city of Heliopolis." Continuing: "The title of the chapter is 'The Chapter of going forth to heaven, of penetrating the shrine, of knowing the spirits of Heliopolis.' The word ammahu translated 'shrine' appears to be specially applied to that part of an Egyptian temple where the sacred relics of the gods or heroes were deposited. King Piankhi is said to have visited the holy place called Zersa near Heliopolis and there to have offered oblations to Tum and his circle of gods in the house of the circle of gods, in which is the shrine (ammahu) of the gods."

Accordingly, the story continued: "'I was a great one in time past among the great ones.' 'I was a creature among the creatures.' 'Gods and men are all described as being created with the exception of Ra the self-produced. The meaning of this passage is that the deceased claims to have appeared as a created being in some primeval period of time, and to have played a part in a previous state of existence upon the earth.' He says: 'I appeared before One-eye.' One eye in this case may be an epithet for the Sun, the eye and light of creation. 'When the circumference of darkness was opened, I was one among you.' 'I know the spirits of An.'"

Into the Egyptian Mind. Egyptian Art. Oh, those perfume cones used at parties and festive gatherings.

Into the Egyptian Mind. Karnak Temple of God Amon. Handaka, an Associate and Erik Monderson north of the Great Hypostyle Hall.

Into the Egyptian Mind. Double Temple of Horus and Sobek. Majestic portrait of Isis (Auset) as Hathor in the Queen Mother Vulture Crown, mounted on a mortar sporting horns, disk and feathers. Notice her face is not defaced because she looks so European, though one breasts is exposed.

Into the Egyptian Mind. Double Temple of Horus and Sobek. Image of a King in White Crown.

Into the Egyptian Mind. Cairo Museum of Egyptian Antiquities. Two statues, one seated, one striding (legs with left foot forward). Look at them noses!

Into the Egyptian Mind. Egyptian Art. Floral challenge to the desert environment.

As the explanation goes: "The passage is one of great difficulty, although all the words of which it is composed are known. The reading Atum, of the Hays papyrus, does not help us and appears to be a mistake. 'The most glorious Atum proceeds from it, even to the limits of the things which are visible.' 'I know how the woman was made from An.' literally, the curly haired, is the name of a curled wig worn by the priest in certain ceremonies. It is a title of Hathor and is applied to the votaresses of Hathor. 'This took the form of a curly haired woman.' 'Then he took the form of a curly haired woman.' 'It is the curly headed of An.'"

Again, C.W. Goodwin discussed: "On the 112th Chapter of the Ritual" (Nov-Dec 1871: 144-147) and "Another Chapter of the Knowledge of the Spirits of Pa." The deceased addresses the Great Body dwelling in Zxati (16th Nome of Lower Egypt, the Mendesian) in the city of Anpu or Anu, also the bird-catcher who reigned in Pa. These personages are styled 'the elders who are without end.' 'Do you not know wherefore the town of Pa was given to Horus?'

"'Horus says to Ra, Grant that I may see the creatures of thy eyes, see as it (thy eye) sees them.' Ra says to Horus, 'Look I pray thee, at this black hog.' Said Horus to Ra, 'Behold my eye is as though Anepu had made an incision in my eye. Then we were grieved at heart.'" Let us also note, beneath the hairy black hog or pig, the skin is white!

He continued: "Anpu said to the gods: 'Put him upon his bed; he will get well. It was Seth who came and took the form of a black hog. Then he fomented the wound of the eye of Horus. These words explain the cause of the accident. When Ra invited Horus to look at a black pig as one of his own creations, the evil Set came and presented himself in the form of that animal, and Horus looked upon not only a creation of Set but Set himself. Hence the injury to his eye.' Said Horus to the gods - Who are about him - 'When Horus was in his childhood the cattle of the gods were his oxen, his goats, his pigs - They are Amesta, Hapi, Tau-ma-f, and Kabh-senu-f, whose father is Horus, whose mother is Isis.' Horus says to Ra. - 'Grant me my brother in Pa and my brother in Xen, to be within me (in my power) and to be with me, for an eternal portion.'"

IV. The Centers of Worship

There are several other features of the religion of ancient Egypt that sets it apart from so many ancient religious beliefs. Its monotheistic nature is affirmed by Budge (1934: 44) who holds that: "There is no doubt that the EGYPTIANS included monotheism among their dogmas, but it is impossible to say when their theologians evolved it. Two forms of it existed, a higher and a lower. The higher is the monotheism of Ptah of Memphis, the spirit God, the Eternal Mind, who existed before everything else, and created matter by thought, and the lower is the monotheism of Ra of Heliopolis. But the African monotheism of 3800 B.C. or earlier, though not to be compared with that of modern Christian people, is a remarkable spiritual achievement."

a.   Ra was worshipped at Heliopolis and was considered one of the oldest Egyptian gods. "Temu or Ra, the great god of Heliopolis, was a material being, and the source whence he came was NUNU, the great primeval abyss of water. Water existed before Ra and was regarded as the oldest thing in the world, and therefore the 'father of the gods.' The cult of Ra, i.e., worship of the Sun-god, was well established at Heliopolis long before the union of the North and the South by MENES .... The Pyramid Texts show that he had recourse to masturbation in order to produce the twins Shu and Tefnut and the peoples of the Sudan. His cult was gross and material, and the benefits which the Egyptians hoped to receive from him, were material, virility, fecundity, robust health, and abundant offspring both human and animal .... As men expected Ra to give them great material prosperity on earth, so after death, in heaven they rely upon him to provide them with divine meat and drink and apparel, and unstinted gratification of their carnal appetites. In no prayer to Ra can be found a petition by the suppliant for spiritual gifts, or any expression indicating his need of divine help for his soul. During the great festivals when a statue of the god was carried by the priests around the town or through the country the people in crowds appeared before him, for by this act they discharged a religious obligation and, so to say, acquired merit, and they expected the god to give them in return health, strength, virility, and prosperity."

Interesting enough, when the argument is made for an Egyptian origin outside of Africa, one has to wonder why their great god Ra made the "people of Nubia" so early in his work of creation! Are we to believe the Europeans who migrated to Egypt very early created the people of Nubia? Or, should we also believe the Nubians were Europeans? Nevertheless, the Nubians were created before the Egyptians. How interesting!

b.   Ptah was worshipped at Memphis after Unification when Narmer or Menes established the beginning of the first dynasty and initiated the Dynastic period. He was a god of creation as well as a patron of the arts and artisans. He was, together with Thoth, a constructioneers who created the heavens. While considered 'Father of the gods' Ptah Nunu and 'god of the great abyss of water,' he wears the solar disk and plumes. As Ptah-Tanen 'the oldest earth-god in Egypt,' he holds the crown of Seker (horns, disk and plumes) and also holds the triple scepter. However, in his most popular form as Ptah of Memphis he is shown as a mummy god, with arms emerging, from his closely-fitted garment, at his chest and holding his scepter, wearing a beard and menat hanging from the back of his neck.

He was also a pygmy god. The pygmies originated in Central Africa, source of earliest gold and it's no wonder some of the earliest goldsmiths are pygmies. Equally, they knew how to dance the "dance of the gods" coming, as they did from "the land of the gods!"

Continuing, Budge (1934: 13-14) added: "From the text which was rescued from oblivion by **SHABAKA** we learn that PTAH, the Great and Mighty, had eight principal forms among which were PTAH-NUN, and PTAH-TANEN. He therefore preceded NUN and TANEN in existence and he was their creator, and he created them by an effort of his heart or mind. Thus, PTAH was the oldest being the priests could imagine, and he was the Eternal Heart or Mind and was self-created. The male part of PTAH begot TEM or TEMU or RA, and his female portion was the mother of the Sun-god of Heliopolis. And, like Ra, Ptah was the father and mother of men, and he conceived and fashioned and made the gods. Tem was a form or figure of Ra …. Tem produced the gods Shu and Tefnut by masturbation and self-impregnation, whereas

Ptah produced the gods by the motions of thoughts of his mind. Horus, the oldest Sun-god in Egypt, acted as the heart or mind of Ptah, and Thoth, the god of wisdom, as his tongue. What the heart of Ptah thought passed on to Thoth who translated it into words, which were uttered by the one great almighty mouth, from which everything which is hath come, and everything which is to be shall come. Though Thoth was the Word-god, his actual creative power was derived from the magical pronouncement by Ptah, who alone knew how to utter the words with the correct intonation."

Into the Egyptian Mind. Egyptian Art. Even in the afterlife, work has to be done, so recruit the "Missus."

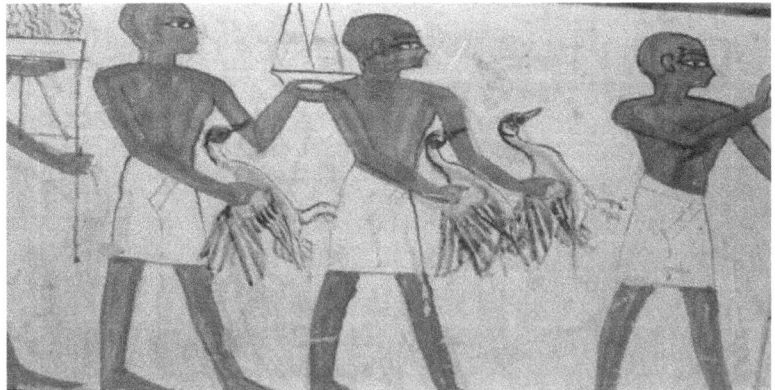

Into the Egyptian Mind. Egyptian Art. Let's give up these birds and these pyramid cones.

Into the Egyptian Mind. Double Temple of Horus and Sobek. With her European nose in public view, Isis as Hathor stands undefaced. This European nose gets no treatment in a place of high-visibility!

Into the Egyptian Mind. Cairo Museum of Egyptian Antiquities. A wonderful head with characteristic hair and broken nose.

c. Amon or Amen, later Amon-Ra or Amen-Ra rose to prominence in the Middle and New Kingdom after the successes of his Theban adherents. He dominated the country and the ancient world for more than a good millennium until Egypt became too weak to defend itself and continue its imperialist policies. He was on the same level as Ptah, even possessing some of his powers. Budge (1934: 17-18), quoting Sir Alan Gardener explained the nature and attributes of Amen, Amun or Amon in the following:

I. Amen's origin. He was self-created and as he fashioned himself none knoweth his forms. He existed first as the Eight Gods of Khenemu (Hermopolis), [The head of this Ogdoad was Thoth.] then he completed them and became one. He became in primeval times, no other being existed, there was no god before him; there was no other god with him to declare his form; all the gods came into being after him. He had no mother by whom his name was made; he had no other who begot him, saying, 'It is even myself.' He shaped his own egg; he mingled his seed with his body to make his egg to come into being within himself. He took the form of Tanen in order to give birth to the Pautti (Companies of the?) gods.

II. The hiddenness of Amen. His body is hidden in the Chiefs. He is hidden as Amen at the head of the gods. Amen is one; he hides himself from the gods and conceals himself from them.

III. His oneness. His Unity is absolute.

IV. He was a Trinity, i.e., he had three persons, or characters.

V. His name. His name is more helpful to a man than hundreds of thousands of helpers. The gods cannot pray to him because his name is unknown to them. The man who utters the secret name of Amen falls down and dies a violent death. His name is victory.

VI. Amen as lord of time. He makes the years, rules the months; ordains nights and days. The night is as the day to him. He the One Watcher neither slumbers nor sleeps.

VII. The beneficence of Amen. He breaks evil spells, expels sicknesses from the bodies of men. He, the Physician, heals the Eye, he destroys the Evil Eye (?), he releases men from hell, he abrogates the Destinies (or Fates) of men at his good pleasure, he hears all petitions and is present immediately he is invoked, he prolongs or shortens the lives of men at will, to the man he loves he adds to what Fate has decreed for him, and to the man who sets him in his heart he is more than millions. He was a Bull for his town, a Lion for his people, a Hawk that destroyed his attackers, and at the sound of his roaring the earth quaked."

"From what has been said above it is quite clear that there was a monotheistic element in the Egyptian Religion. The Spirit-god Ptah was One, the material god Ra was One, and Amen who was claimed by his priests to be both Spirit and Matter was One." And even Ptah, Ra and Amen were considered one in unity.

d.   Osiris was worshiped in several places throughout the land of ancient Egypt/Kemet/Tawi but his head was buried at Abydos and his heart was buried at Philae. As a result, these two locations became the principal centers for his worship. However, while Philae was given status it did not accord with Abydos where his principal mysteries were conducted. From the earliest times kings chose to be buried at Abydos. They built temples there as Petrie has confirmed finding 10 successive layers of temples; nobles erected stela if they could not be buried at Abydos; the dead, as indicated in illustrations, made the pilgrimage to Abydos to be near the god symbolically; and today this site boasts a surviving temple, of the New Kingdom. The temple of Seti I at Abydos is a significant survival from the Ramesside Period and it boasts the finest surviving religious art of the entire land. His son Rameses II has a temple at Abydos, also richly illustrated. However, it has not survived the ravages of time and man, but a walk through will provide a glimpse of what it may have looked like in its heyday. Seti's father Rameses I also built a temple in the vicinity of Abydos.

e.   In addition to the above state centers of worship, Hermopolis boasted the cosmology of the Ogdoad, worship of the 8 gods with Thoth at its head. This notwithstanding, Thoth belonged to the Ra cycle of gods. Denise M. Doxey in *The Oxford Encyclopedia of Ancient Egypt* Vol. 3 (2001: 398-400), in explaining that Thoth was associated with science, medicine, cosmology, writing, nature and the afterlife as well as music, states: "As a moon god, Thoth regulated the season and lunar phases and counted the stars. Hence, he was associated with astronomy, mathematics and accounting. As the god of scribes and writing, Thoth, 'the lord of the sacred word,' personified divine speech. Seshat, the goddess of writing and literature, was said to be either his wife or daughter. By the Middle Kingdom, Thoth as a god of wisdom and justice was connected with Maat, the personification of rightness and world order. The Greeks viewed him as the source of all wisdom and the creator of languages."

"At Hermopolis, Thoth was worshipped as a cosmogenic deity, believed to have risen on a mound from the primeval chaos to create the Ogdoad consisting of Nun and Naunet, Heh, Heket, Kek, Keket, Amun and Amaunet, coordinated male and female couples representing various forces of nature. In solar religion, Thoth and Ma'at navigated the bark of Re." Even further, Doxey continued: "The principal cult center of Thoth was Hermopolis, ancient Egyptian Khenemu, near the modern town of el-Ashmunen. This was the site of a major new Kingdom temple, at which Amenhotep III claims to have dedicated a pair of thirty-ton quartzite baboons."

Into the Egyptian Mind. Egyptian Art. Oh yes, since work has to be done in the afterlife, let's get the "Missus" out to help sow some seeds. How is it Tutankhamon and Mentuhotep II are "painted Black for the funerary ceremony" and this couple, in the afterlife retain the same brown or red color as in paintings.

Into the Egyptian Mind. Karnak Temple of God Amon. Erik Monderson and some of the Karnak Men!

Into the Egyptian Mind. Double Temple of Horus and Sobek. Close-up of Presenting a golden girdle. Again, this "European nose" gets "no treatment!"

Into the Egyptian Mind. Double Temple of Horus and Sobek. Yet another image of Isis (Auset) as Hathor that is not defaced. What a beautiful nose!

Into the Egyptian Mind. Cairo Museum of Egyptian Antiquities. An alabaster Sarcophagus with lid.

Into the Egyptian Mind. Egyptian Art. A colossal figure sits and overseers workers, a "Table of Offerings" and workers making a report.

As an explanation of Thoth's creative powers, Maspero (1891: 2) tells: "The voice without speech was reputed to have the same effect as the two combined, and had been, according to certain Egyptian schools, the agent of Creation." That is: "The Supreme God who is reputed to be the God of Creation, opens his mouth, and the gods come out of it, either the gods generally, or some particular god. Once come forth, the gods each set to work on that which they were predestined to accomplish. These texts have hitherto been translated under the influence of the preconceived idea that what was here meant was a formula, and not an emission of the voice: but this is only an instinctive interpretation, and the Egyptian phrases simply state the fact of a Divine mouth opening and gods issuing from it."

He goes on to quote from a magical book in Greek that says, inter al, the magician addresses himself to Thoth. "'I invoke thee,' he says, 'Oh Hermes, thou who containest everything in every speech and dialect, as thou was first celebrated by the subordinate, the Sun, to whom the care of everything is entrusted.' The solar forms then salute Thoth, who answers them thus: 'And speaking, the god clapped his hands, and burst seven times bursts of laughter. Kha, Kha, Kha, Kha, Kha, Kha, Kha, and when he had done laughing, seven gods were born,' one for each burst of laughter, as we see. When Hermes first laughed, light appeared, to light everything; and the Creation began to take place. He laughed six times in succession, and each burst of laughter gave birth to a fresh being and a fresh phenomenon; the earth, feeling the sound, in its turn gave utterance to a cry and bowed itself, and the waters were divided into three bodies (masses). Then were born Destiny, Justice, Opportunity, the Soul. The last, at its birth, first laughed, then wept, whereupon the god gave forth a breath, bent him towards the earth and produced the serpent Python, which is possessed of universal prescience. At the sight of the dragon the god was struck with stupor, and clacked his lips, whereupon an armed being appeared. The god, seeing this was again struck with stupor, as at sight of a more powerful one than himself, and, lowering his eyes towards the earth, exclaimed, Iao! The god who is master of everything was born of the reach of that sound."

V. The Temple as Sanctuary for the Gods and Place of Worship and Ritual

a. The nature of the temple architecture was dictated by the geography, period, royal family or dynasty in power, and the wealth they possessed in order to endow their god. Since the house of the god was a thing of eternity, the building was constructed in stone and had to be quarried from some distance where good stone was located. This endeavor thus gave birth to a number of enterprises and disciplines, not simply quarrying, flat bottom boat building for transport but more important actual mastery of the Nile to move the large stone, even obelisks "to place of erection." Once the stone was removed to the place of erection, the structure was further finished and beautified with elaborate artistic renderings that depicted the ritual and other facets of the pharaoh's existence, as it related to worship of his god.

b. Pylon and Court were parts of the temple entrance that the visitor encountered as well as the pharaoh when he came to pay homage to his god. The pylon was generally decorated on the outer face and there were openings for flagstaves that flew flags of the god, Nome and nation. The Court was generally a hub for invited guests of the temple but also decorated with kiosks, shrines, altars, statues, sphinxes, even small temples.

c. Halls and Colonnades were decorated features that carried the various themes and rituals of the temple and showcased the wealth of the particular god worshipped there. The walls depict the ritual of the temple showing the king in adoration of his god, sometimes assisted by other gods. In some respects, in total, this architectural feature became "the glory of Egypt."

d.   The Sanctuary was the place where the divinity rested in absolute darkness that only the pharaoh or high priest dared to enter. Naturally, because the ritual was very complex, both king and high priest were assisted by subordinates. Interestingly enough, as one ventured deep into the temple, the floor rose and the ceiling sank so that the Sanctuary became the highest point in the structure. In the Sanctuary, there was an altar upon which the lustrations of the god were performed. However, incense, as part of the ritual of fumigating the god against evil forces, was never burnt on the altar, but in an incenser in some corner of this inner recess.

e.   Adjoining chambers were designed to accommodate the vestments and liquid and solid offerings of the ritual, as well as the elements of the god's toilet. Oftentimes these adjoining chambers contained a library as well as served as a bark station for the god's ark or boat. Sometimes these adjoining chambers were decorated. Additional chambers were shrines for associated gods connected with the principal divinity and the temple.

VI.   The Afterlife Dynamic

a.   The tomb was an important part of the individual existence and great effort was made to prepare and furnish it correctly since he hoped to dwell there for an eternity. The nature of the tomb varied with the time period referenced in the religion and the particular individual interred there. In the Old Kingdom, the pharaoh was buried in pyramids and before that in the earliest tombs, as at Abydos and Memphis. Here at Abydos, there were real tombs and cenotaphs or dummy tombs were at Sakkara, burial site of the Memphis capital. These eternal resting places were decorated with 'goods of the grave;' or as the Cairo Museum calls them, 'funerary furniture.' The 'dummy tombs' or cenotaphs at Sakkara were duplicates with the exception of the body of the deceased. However, they contained much the deceased would require in the other world. The only thing missing was the body. Notwithstanding, Seti I's temple at Abydos is important for a number of reasons. First, as a 19th Dynasty monarch, the king had access to Old, Middle and New Kingdom compounded knowledge. The Abydos Tablet, in Situ, still in place, contains the names of 76 kings from Menes or Narmer to Seti I, deified as a god. Dedicated to Osiris, the "God of the Dead," the temple was actually a memorial to the archaic kings buried in the desert. The center line is oriented towards those tombs. Given these factors, the temple honors such kings! *Ipso facto*, the Abydos ones are the real tombs and Memphis is actually the cenotaph. The purpose of two tombs was to emphasize the dual nature of the pharaoh as king of upper and Lower Egypt. Some scholars have argued, it was a worship and a mortuary temple. This dual nature was also thought to apply to the Hypostyle Hall at Karnak, in which Seti played a principal part in its construction and decoration.

Into the Egyptian Mind. Egyptian Art. Date palm trees beside the River.

Into the Egyptian Mind. Double Temple of Horus and Sobek. Isis as Hathor wearing the Queen Mother Vulture Headdress with a mortar supporting horns and disk and feathers. Notice her breast.

Into the Egyptian Mind. Double Temple of Horus and Sobek. No, its not the same image of Isis as Hathor with her breast exposed, though she wears horns and disk.

Into the Egyptian Mind. Cairo Museum of Egyptian Antiquities. Colossal seated figure with miniature figure beside his feet.

By the time of the Old Kingdom, officials preferred to be buried near the king's pyramid, so much so that since he was assured the immortality of heaven, being in his shadow enabled them to share in his good fortune! As such, cemeteries for such Nobles became systematic, well-organized and thought or laid-out funerary arrangements. By the time of the Middle and New Kingdom, there developed what was called "democratization of the afterlife," in that by that time not simply the king, but practically everyone could get to heaven, as did the king, providing one lived the good life as dictated by the tenets of Ma'at embodied in righteousness.

Tombs of the kings, queens, nobles and artisans of the New Kingdom were dug into the mountains at Thebes and were equally and tremendously decorated with scenes of this world and the next. For security reasons this was begun by Thutmose I. While some tombs depicted social themes, others emphasized the afterlife and were replete with literary themes, al illustrated, outlining the drama of the underworld. Most Middle Kingdom tombs have not been found and when this happens, it would provide a bonanza of religious, artistic and social factual data that would further refine our understanding of Egyptian belief and practices.

b. Mummification began very early in the Old Kingdom and reached a high state of perfection by the time of the New Kingdom. In fact, some scholars see mummification as beginning in Nubia before dynastic rule began. Nevertheless, great effort was made to mummify the deceased in preparation for the dynamics of the afterlife. Herodotus tells us there were three types of mummification based on the economic status of the deceased with the wealthy being more elaborate in their choice of preparation and decoration. This mummification process aided the development of science, and as a result, medicine and treatment of the sick as well as dead. It also helped in creating a written record of anatomy and physiology as well as a medicinal pharmacopeia based on plant and animal mineral and other constituent elements.

c. The Judgment was an important part of the Egyptian's other-worldly experience and seems he prepared for it from the earliest times of his existence in social and economic readiness. In order to get to the Judgment, once dead, the individual had to navigate a set of pylons and portals with dangerous obstacles seeking to impede his entry in the Underworld as he headed to the Hall of Judgment. By having the right knowledge and words of power he was able to overcome such obstacles and arrive at the Hall of African Judgment where his heart was weighed against a feather of truth, Ma'at. This was called the **Psychostasia** where sometimes as few as a dozen and as many as forty-two judges sat and observed the process. Thoth and Anubis as well as Am-mit 'searched' the deceased before finding him guilty or not, that is 'true of voice,' or 'justified.' Upon the latter, it was announced by Thoth and the assessors or jurors affirmed his findings, then the deceased was introduced to Osiris, the Egyptian god of the dead.

d. Before the actual weighing of the heart against the feather of Ma'at, the deceased had to make the 42 "Negative Confessions" affirming that he did not commit those unacceptable behaviors. The "Negative Confessions" were said to the 42 assessors, variously thought to represent each of 42 nomes, but some scholars, such as Dr. ben-Jochannan, believed they were part of a greater body of more than 147 such confessions. Equally there was a body of 'positive confessions' the deceased made as well indicating he had done these good or positive things in aid of his fellow citizens.

e. The notion of standing before your god at the end of your existence was a horrifying feeling and inherently it steered individuals to live a positive and constructive lifestyle based on the practice of righteousness. This does not, however, lead us to believe all Egyptians lived right and truthfully.

f. The reward for the good life lived on earth is peace of mind in this world and eternal bliss in the next. Some people believe goodness is an outstanding moral virtue that allows the individual to live in harmony with his surroundings, people, places and even things and animals. "It makes you sleep sound at nights." However, the whole notion of goodness is an essential prerequisite of being able to survive the judgment and live among the immortal "Lords of Righteousness" in the next life and enjoy the eternal bliss of heaven.

VII. Worship and Ritualizing the Gods

a. The Priesthood very early developed into a professional organization with a many-faceted functionality. This gained them the power of not only being protectors of the god because of their close relationship, but also having a significant impact on the society in general because of their technical, intellectual and scientific know-how. As full-time intermediaries between the gods and king and people, their power grew immensely, owing to a number of beneficial incentives as endowments, tribute, benefits from temple owned rented and worked lands and manufactured artifacts for trade. Very early they acquired a tax-free status and came into control of much wealth because of perennial endowments they were responsible for administering as guardians, in order to propagate the memories of deceased persons. Soon kings and nobles were not only lavishing great wealth on the gods and by extension on the priesthood, but the weak ones also became very wary and afraid of the power of this multi-faceted body that could interpret the wishes of divinity.

Into the Egyptian Mind. Egyptian Art. Looks like these gentlemen and these ladies are going to a festival for they are carrying birds, flowers, and more.

Into the Egyptian Mind. Egyptian Art. Workers in different attitudes while performing their functions.

Into the Egyptian Mind. Musician playing on a 7-string Harp.

Into the Egyptian Mind. Double Temple of Horus and Sobek. Close-up image of Bastet, the Lion Goddess, sporting a sun-disk with uraeus.

Into the Egyptian Mind. Double Temple of Horus and Sobek. Offering "Two Eyes of Horus."

Into the Egyptian Mind. Cairo Museum of Egyptian Antiquities. Carmen and Mentuhotep II, 11th Dynasty Pharaoh who built his mortuary temple at Deir el Bahari.

The article "Religion" in Ian Shaw and Paul Nicholson *The British Museum Dictionary of Ancient Egypt*, (1995, 2003: 244-245) explains: "Ancient Egyptian state religion was concerned with the maintenance of the divine order; this entailed ensuring that life was conducted in accordance with Ma'at and preventing the encroachment of chaos. In such a system, it was necessary for religion to permeate every aspect of life, so that it was embedded in society and politics, rather than being a separate category. The Egyptian view of the universe was capable of incorporating a whole series of apparently contradictory creation myths. This holistic view also led to the treatment of prayer, magic and science as realistic and comparative alternatives, as a result it made good sense to combine what might now be described as medical treatment with a certain amount of ritual and recitation of prayers, each component of the overall treatment giving the same aim; to suppress evil and maintain the harmony of the universe."

The temples and their attendant priests therefore served as a perpetual means of stabilizing the universe. Each day they attended to the needs of the god (who was thought to be manifested in the cult image), made offerings to him, and thus kept the forces of chaos at bay. A distinction is sometimes made between, on the one hand, the important state gods (Horus or Isis) and local deities (Banebdjedet at Mendes), and, on the other hand, the "popular' or 'household' deities such as Bes and Taweret."

b. An important function of the priesthood, beside worshipping and ritualizing the gods, was the responsibility of managing the estate of the divinity. This economic responsibility allowed the priesthood to venture into and play an essential role in the society. They collected taxes, owned their own land and farms, maintained ships on the Nile River that carried their merchandise of food, arts and crafts they manufactured for purposes of trade. There were towns given as endowments and they had to manage these so their prosperity could be multiplied. The priesthood owned untold cattle, chickens, hectares of land, ships, slaves, gardens, orchards, vessels of wine, beer, oil, and the technical sophistication to engage in all forms of trade and craft, from building, quarrying, and transportation to artistry. They built, educated others, extended the realms of science, pursued mathematics, medicine; engineering, farming, and essentially "managed the society," while serving their god. Their power became so immense the pharaohs, weak ones, that is, kept a close eye on this religious power that also combined economic, scientific and moral power while also having political implications and the rule of law. This latter became so acute that the priesthood was able to seize power in the 21st Dynasty, after the collapse of the New Kingdom.

c.   Circumstances in relationship within the society and challenges from neighbors created an imperialist outlook and pharaohs took the sword to nations abroad while they quelled resistance at home. Warrior pharaohs pursued an imperialist policy of conquest and incorporation into their very extensive empires with concomitant demands of tribute on the nations they conquered and allied with. Much of the ensuing wealth they accumulated from their exploits abroad was lavished on the gods and priesthood, enabling them to build fabulous temples with the wealthiest decorations and providing enormous gifts of gold. In their relationship with the gods they were given his blessing which translated into victories with attendant wealth that in turn became temple endowments. This state of affairs continued for centuries and as the nation grew wealthier, the priesthood benefited and their god became still wealthier, they managed his wealth, and so this continued. When there were no young, vigorous and strong pharaohs to defend Egypt, their numerous enemies were attracted by the wealth of the state temples and priests whose fortunes were untold. The temples then were, for moral and economic reasons, among the first targets of invading forces that looted the holy places, desecrated the sanctuaries of the gods, and carried off much of their wealth and people.

d.   Religion advanced science because of its essential role in the society since the principal proponents were also the intellectual elite and this beat back the mist of ignorance. Astronomy, medicine, mathematics, government, law, education, building, quarrying, farming, arts and crafts, trade, theology, Theogony, metaphysics, mummification, perhaps even warfare, sanctioned, those essential ingredients that propel society and civilization, and can be traced to the practice of religion and praise of the gods. Thus, the Nile River whose effluence flowed from Central Africa manifested in a tremendous gift of spirituality, religious expression and social creativity that enlightened Egypt and the world.

Into the Egyptian Mind. Egyptian Art. Oh yes, have the Missus out there doing her share of the chores in the Afterlife.

Into the Egyptian Mind. Egyptian Art. Workers in different attitudes performing their functions.

Into the Egyptian Mind. Double Temple of Horus and Sobek. Intricate and details of the wonderful hieroglyphs.

Into the Egyptian Mind. Double Temple of Horus and Sobek. More of the intricacies and beauty of the Hieroglyphs.

Into the Egyptian Mind. Cairo Museum of Egyptian Antiquities. Three similar statues found as part of a larger cache.

References

Budge, E.A. Wallis. *The Egyptian Heaven and Hell*. New York: Dover Publications, (1905) 1996.
_____. *Egyptian Religion*. New York: Carol Publishing Group: A Citadel Press Book, (1900) 1991.
_____. *From Fetish to God in Ancient Egypt*. London: Oxford University Press, 1934.
Doxey, Denise M. "Religion." *The Oxford Encyclopedia of Ancient Egypt*. Vol. 3. London: Oxford University Press, (2001: 398-400).
Frankfort, Henri. *Ancient Egyptian Religion*. New York: Harper and Row, Publishers, (1946) 1961.
Goodwin, C.W. "On the 112th Chapter of the Ritual." *International Congress of Orientalists* (November-December, 1871: 144-147*).*
_____. "The 115th Chapter of the Turin Book of the Dead." *International Congress of Orientalists* (1873: 104).

Maspero, Gaston. "Creation by Voice and the Ennead of Heliopolis." 9th *International Congress of Orientalists*, (1-10 September, 1891: 1-10).

Murray, Margaret. *Egyptian Temples*. London: Sampson Low, Marston and Co., Ltd., 1931.

Osei, G. K. *African Contributions to Civilization*. London: African Publication Society, 1983.

Rawlinson. *The Story of the Nations*: *Ancient Egypt*. London: T. Fisher Unwin and New York: G.P. Putnam's Sons, 1893.

Shaw, Ian and Paul Nicholson. "Religion." *The British Museum Dictionary of Ancient Egypt*. London: The British Museum, (1995) (2003: 244-245).

Shorter, Alan W. *The Egyptian Gods*: *A Handbook*. London: Routledge and Kegan Paul, (1937) 1981.

Into the Egyptian Mind. Egyptian Art. At a Banquet, a Sem Priest pours a Libation.

Into the Egyptian Mind. Egyptian Art. More of workers in different attitudes.

Into the Egyptian Mind. Double Temple of Horus and Sobek. Nile Gods bring the fruits of their Domain.

Into the Egyptian Mind. Double Temple of Horus and Sobek. More Nile Gods bring the fruits of their Domain.

Into the Egyptian Mind. Egyptian Art. As their female counterparts look on, two gentlemen greet.

Into the Egyptian Mind. Cairo Museum of Egyptian Antiquities. Bust of a figure in Nemes Headdress and short beard. One eye is inlaid.

Into the Egyptian Mind. Egyptian Art. Guests at a banquet wearing perfumed cones on their heads. The little ones are under the chairs.

Into the Egyptian Mind. Cairo Museum of Egyptian Antiquities. A double seated statue with fishes and other features.

7. RIGHTEOUSNESS
By
Dr. Fred Monderson

Proverbs 14: 34-35 admonished "Righteousness Exalteth a nation; but sin is a reproach to all people!" Thus, it is my unquestioned insistence, if you must lead me, then you must lead me in the "paths of righteousness."

Into the Egyptian Mind. Egyptian Art. While two large figures carry a basket, smaller figures wrestle and sit in contemplation.

Into the Egyptian Mind. Double Temple of Horus and Sobek. Nile Gods bring the harvest fruits of their Domain.

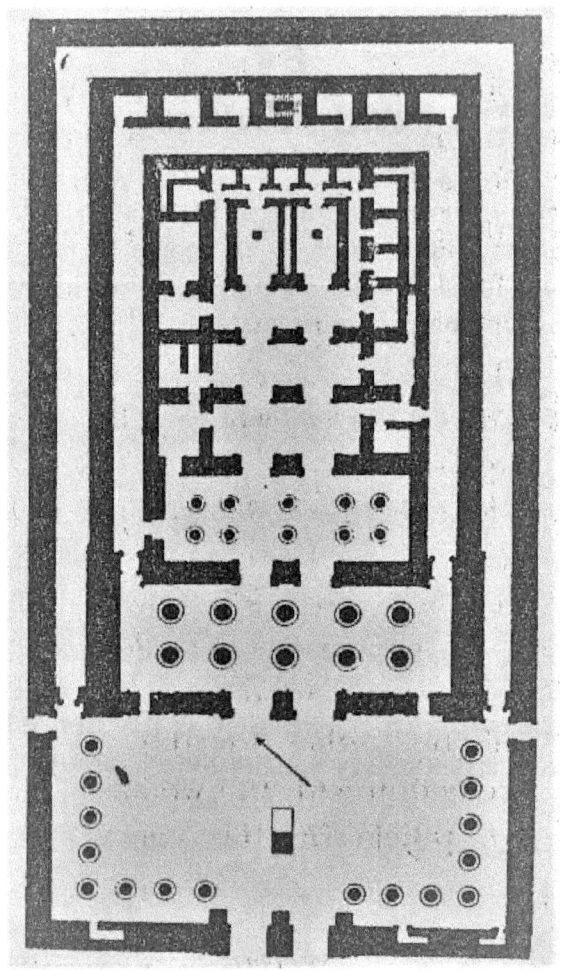

KOM OMBO TEMPLE OF SOBEK AND HAROERIS (Elder Horus)

1. Dual Entrance Gate
2. Forecourt
3. Altar
4. First Hypostyle Hall
5. Second Hypostyle Hall
6. Outer Vestibule
7. Middle Vestibule

8. Inner Vestibule
9. Outer Passage
10. Inner Passage
11. Sanctuary of Sobek
12. Secret Chamber or Priest Hole
13. Sanctuary of Haroeris (Horus the Elder)
14. Stairs
15. The Rear Passage and Back Wall
16. Chapel of Hathor
17. Mammisi of Ptolemy VII
18. Nilometer

Into the Egyptian Mind. Cairo Museum of Egyptian Antiquities. Sphinx figure of a king with a short beard.

Into the Egyptian Mind. Cairo Museum of Egyptian Antiquities. A colorful stele depicting beneath "Two Eyes of Horus" a seated noble smelling flowers, with his wife and having libation done to them while others share the space of their expression.

I wish to thank Prof. Loncke for inviting me to make this presentation. As the leader of the **Guyana Branch of the Pan-African Movement**, now in its 27th year, I believe to found, lead, nurture and sustain such a movement is like raising a child to manhood. Much more important, however, navigating the crosswinds in that growth process is in itself a dangerous task because in righteousness you seek the salvation of an entire people. As you all know, Prof. Loncke is not a leader who seeks glory in the spotlight of flashing cameras and newspaper pandering, but is comfortable in organizing and setting in motion events that significantly further the interests, cultural and otherwise, we African people seek after. That role, therefore, signals her steadfast and continuing commitment to the true ideals of the fathers and mothers who laid the foundation for the mental, moral, intellectual, even economic and political liberation of African people, at home and abroad.

The task before me, "Righteousness as a hallmark of ancient African ethical behavior" is a challenging one, more especially relevant in these times and one I gladly accept.

In Ancient Egypt along the banks of the Nile River, it was expected the Gods, King, nobles, administrative officials, and general masses would act in a righteous manner, with an eye and heart to the future.
In this way, the society would maintain its equilibrium and enjoy the fruits of blessedness with an eye and heart to the future existence. Never were a people more oriented towards a future life. They believed this life was a temporary sojourn but the afterlife was for eternity and this had a bearing of their practice of righteousness. After all, the Afterlife experience is where the gods dwelt and people wanted to be gods and to dwell among the gods, in a place of spiritual and cosmological purity.

In their ethical and spiritual consciousness, there were two realms of righteousness or heavenly bliss. There was the celestial heaven ruled by Ra, the Sun-god, and the earthly or heavenly kingdom ruled by Osiris. Ra was first, Osiris came later. Ra, the Sun-god was a visible manifestation people saw everyday who brought light to see and helped grow their crops. Osiris was a good king murdered by his jealous brother Seth and who rose from and became Judge of the dead. Both their abodes were places of righteousness and anyone who wished to dwell therein must practice righteousness and be "justified" or "purified" at Judgment. However, while the Pyramid Texts tells the king would soar like a hawk to the heavenly kingdom, they faced the reality the body was buried in the earthly realm of Osiris.

One of the first acts of wickedness was the killing of Osiris (Ausar) by his brother Seth (Typhon). His sister Isis (Ausar) and her sister Nephthys (Nepthi) searched and found the body; reconstituted it and applying Isis' magic enabled her impregnation of a son named Horus (Heru). Osiris had to be justified at Heliopolis and he was defended by Thoth the legal eagle of the gods. Ra sent Anubis to protect Osiris from Seth's wrath. After his birth, Isis raised the young Horus who as an adult sought vengeance. Seth found the body of Osiris after he impregnated Isis and decapitated it into 13 pieces. Isis searched along with Nephthys and finding each piece, buried it. The head was buried at Abydos and the heart at Philae.

Because Osiris was considered a king of Egypt who had been a good king, his son Horus sought to succeed him and he was again defended by Thoth and declared, "Justified" then enabled to succeed his father as rightful King of Egypt. The father could not rule so he became king of the underworld and judge of the Dead assisted by Thoth, Horus, the four sons of Horus, Isis and Nephthys, and 42 judges. There was also Ammit, eater of the dead who, if your heart was heavier than a feather, then you became her lunch. Why a woman became the eater of the dead no one knows for sure!

The earliest form of literature preserved for us is the Pyramid Texts. The Pyramid Texts of the Old Kingdom were religious and ethical ideas inscribed in the Pyramid tombs of the last king of the Fifth and four kings of the Sixth Dynasty. James Henry Breasted dates them to 3500 B.C. but they were thought to be at least a thousand years earlier as a collection of oral sayings. By the Middle Kingdom, in opening the portals "of the afterlife," the Pyramid Texts were inscribed on the inside and outsides of coffins and thus became the "Coffin Texts" In the further "democratization of the Afterlife" during the New Kingdom, these religious writings were now made into book form or papyrus and illustrated with black and white, later colored, vignettes and by this time had become portable. Their purpose was essentially to map or depict the journey of the soul after death as it traveled to the judgment in the "Hall of Double Maati" or "Two Truths." Along the way there were gates or pylons guarded by spirits or monsters and the deceased had to know each guard's name to be allowed to pass. Thus, the Book of the Dead had the magical knowledge to empower and enable his passage. As such, the power of the word, whether in the head or the hand, became an indispensable weapon. There were essentially two forms of religious practices by these ancient Africans, the religion of the masses and the religion of the intelligentsia. While all persons sought righteous practice in daily life, elements of the intelligentsia trained to free the shackles of daily existence to be prepared for the Afterlife existence. That is, prepared, they want to arrive prepared!

Into the Egyptian Mind. Egyptian Art. Couple kneeling with empty hands raised in adoration.

Into the Egyptian Mind. Egyptian Art. Classic image of a cat ascending the lotus to secure eggs or even a bird, with a mouse below.

Into the Egyptian Mind. Egyptian Art. Still more Nile Gods bringing the fruits of their Domain.

Into the Egyptian Mind. Double Temple of Horus and Sobek. More Nile Gods bringing the fruits of their Domain.

Into the Egyptian Mind. Cairo Museum of Egyptian Antiquities. Face of Akhenaten with the beard and floral decorations in rear.

The Grand Vizier Ptahhotep in the 27th Century Before Christ affirmed: "Established is the man whose standard is righteousness, who walketh according to its way." Demonstrating such, a contemporary noble told of his good deeds, "I speak no lie, for I was one beloved of his father, praised of his mother, excellent in character to his brother and amenable to his sister," that is, according to James Breasted's *Dawn of Conscience* (New York: Charles Scribner's Sons, 1934: 117). Again, another noble boasted, "The king praised me. My father made a will in my favor. I was excellent, one [beloved] of his father, praised of his mother whom all his brothers loved." It was said and required of the Vizier, who is second to the king, the state's chief administrator, that he "must do justice because the great god of the state abhors injustice, and not solely because the king enjoins it." That great god is Ra, the first king of Egypt. However, the righteous human king seeking the greatest good, reminded his subordinates, "It is an abomination of the god to show partiality." This required that individuals, especially government officials, "speak the truth, do truth (or "righteousness"); for it is great, it is mighty, it is enduring." Righteousness is believed the embodiment of the goddess Maat. Thus, we see the God, king, nobles, administrators and the masses all regarded the practice of righteousness as of prime importance in this world and the next.

In that early age of emerging enlightenment and intellectual consciousness nourished by righteousness, a son states in his tomb inscriptions, "Now, I caused that I should be buried in the same tomb with this Zau (his father) in order that I might be with him in the same place; not however, because I was not in a position to make a second tomb; but I did this in order that I might see Zau every day, in order that I might be with him in the same place." This is not simply for love of one's father but a true manifestation of righteousness.

In same way, this much-prized level of attained consciousness earned through love and respect for others is lucidly stated by

The Eloquent Peasant to the high Steward Rensi in the 23rd Century Before Christ: "Righteousness is for eternity. It descendeth with him that doeth it into the grave, his name is not effaced on earth, but he is remembered because of right." Equally, because of the chaotic state of society about 2000 B.C., the Egyptian prophet Neferrohu, predicted a coming savior who will rescue Egypt from the decadence of the First Intermediate Period. He remarked: "The people of his time shall rejoice, the son of man shall make his name forever and ever, Righteousness shall return to its place, unrighteousness shall be cast out." It was as **Isaiah** 59: 14 has said, "and judgment is turned away backward and judgment standeth afar off; for truth is fallen in the street and equity cannot enter." Again, we see written on a tombstone of about the 22nd Century Before Christ a, "A man's virtue is his monument, but forgotten is the man of ill repute."

Therefore, we see, this idea of "righteousness" embodied in "truth," "justice," balance, order evolve as the Egyptian state emerged from the mist of history, first as a family unit, manifesting influence at home and then abroad, community, petty state and as a national state institution. Equally, as religion came to play a significant role in the people's lives, their principal divinity, the Sun-god was not simply recognized as the first king of Egypt but also the embodiment of righteousness. That is to say. The ruler must be righteous otherwise his subordinates will act in rampant unrighteous fashion.

We recognize, in that evolution and while the Archaic Period comprising the First and Second Dynasties grappled with the challenges of unification, by the Old Kingdom three important developments had taken place. First, the construction of the pyramids as an eternal resting place for the Pharaoh as son of the Sun-god. Second, we recognize the compilation and preservation of the Pyramid Texts, perhaps a millennium in the making, and their preservation in the Fifth and Sixth Dynasty structures; that is in the pyramids of the last king of the Fifth and four kings of the Sixth dynasties; and third, emergence of social thinkers and philosophers whose thoughts and writings extol the virtue of righteousness and their being critical of non-practitioners.

In this, their efforts came to outlast the pharaonic system. A good example of some of these cherished wisdom thoughts as they relate to righteousness are embodied in the follow writings: "The Song of the Harp-Player," "Tales of the Eloquent Peasant," "The Misanthrope," "Neferhotep," "Just Abhorrence of his Name," "The Corruption of Men," "Death a Glad Release," "The High Privilege of the Sojourner Yonder," "Admonitions of Ipuwer," "Prophesies of Neferrohu," and "Ameni of Beni Hasan," just to name a few.

Characterizing the mentality of the African and his aspirations for what is good, "The Egyptian," Breasted wrote, "always thought in concrete terms and in graphic form. He thought not of theft but of a thief, not of love but of a lover, not of poverty but of a poor man: he saw not social corruption but a corrupt society. Hence Ptahhotep, a man meeting the obligations of office with wholesome faith in righteous conduct and just administration to engender happiness, and passing on this experience to his son; hence the Misanthrope, a man in whom social injustice found expression in the picture of a despairing soul who tells of his despair and its causes; hence Ipuwer, a man in whom dwell the vision to discern both the deadly corruption of society and the golden dream of an ideal king restoring all; hence the Eloquent Peasant, a man suffering official oppression and crying out against it; hence even the Instruction of Amenemhet, a king suffering shameful treachery, losing faith in men, and communicating his experience to his son. The result was that the doctrines of these social thinkers were placed in a dramatic setting, and the doctrines themselves found expression in growing out of experiences and incidents represented as actual." (217-218)

Given, such early and qualitative thinking places the development of the Egyptian, African, mind much earlier than other ancient peoples, whom modern misinformed and even racist scholarship have sought to withhold credit, by denying the role of Blacks in Nile Valley civilization. Again, the following quote from the American Egyptologist James Henry Breasted (1934: 145-147) pushed back seriously against the thought of an Asiatic origin of the Egyptians, who almost a century since are still "stuck in park!" Breasted writes to demolish this falsity in a somewhat lengthy quotation stating: "As we thus look forward and our eyes are inevitably drawn Asiaward it becomes clear at once why Western Asiatic civilization lagged behind in such development. In the Egyptian conception of a great administrative and moral order, designated Ma'at, we must recognize the highest manifestation of ancient oriental civilization. Here is a conception which, as we have seen, was obviously the product of a millennium of social and governmental evolution in a great unified, continuous, orderly, and ever more highly organized national life. This conception of an administrative and moral order, although vaguely adumbrated in beautiful pictures of a righteous king two thousand years later by the Hebrew prophets, did not clearly emerge in Western Asia until the advent of Zoroaster and his great moral system after the rise of the Persian Empire under Cyrus and his successors. The history of Western Asia shows quite clearly why it was earlier impossible. In Egypt, developing through the Second Union and the Old Kingdom, we have civilization as the product of more than a thousand years of social experiment within the guiding forms of a stable, stimulating, and vigorous national organization, possessed of the vitality to endure for over a millennium; whereas Babylonia, the earliest outstanding Western Asiatic state, continued throughout that thousand years to suffer constant disorganization in the petty wars between the insignificant city-states of which it was made up during the greater part of that millennium. Even before its beginning Egypt had already left the struggles of the local city-kingdoms far behind. Material civilization is doubtless as old in Western Asia, as it is in Egypt, but civilization in its broadest aspects is the product of a long social evolution. Hence the arguments of the archaeologists, who, on the basis of such things as copper axes and the craft of the goldsmith, would place Babylonian civilization, which had had no earlier date than that of Egypt, are too superficial to be worthy of refutation.

Into the Egyptian Mind. Egyptian Art. Nobleman Sennutem and wife in adoration before the Gods.

Into the Egyptian Mind. Egyptian Art. As one worker bows on the ground, two individuals of official type look outward.

Into the Egyptian Mind. Double Temple of Horus and Sobek. Still more Nile Gods bringing fruits of their Domain.

Into the Egyptian Mind. Double Temple of Horus and Sobek. In the temple's rear corridor, Colossal figures do their thing.

Into the Egyptian Mind. Egyptian Art. While offering a plant to enthroned Amon-Ra, Pharaoh also pours a libation into two vases.

Without question the political, social, and, in general, the civilized development of mankind along the Nile was many centuries older than in Western Asia. Indeed, in religious, social, and political experience Babylonia was at least a thousand years later than Egypt."

Naturally, J.H. Breasted had his own contradictions to wrestle with. After the brilliant successes of his *History of Egypt* (1905) and *Ancient Records of Egypt* (1906-07), he published *Ancient Times* in 1916. Here he described the Egyptians as "tall, thin, brown men" but this changed in a later re-issuance of that work, where he began extolling "the great white race!" Some scholars argue, because John D. Rockefeller, Jr., provided means to support the University of Chicago's work in its Egyptian epigraphic survey, this tainted his outlook. Nevertheless, his scholarship was impeccable, but he did deny Asiatic place of origin influencing Egypt. Now we have evidence of an even earlier dates from the Eastern and Western Deserts of Southern Upper Egypt. Thus, this further confronts and compounds the false claim of a "Caucasian Egypt."

As such, and again, we must accept that the ancient Africans who inhabited the Nile River Valley can be considered the originators and trendsetters of wisdom and ancient moral and ethical belief and practices. Extolling Egypt, considered a part of that creative workshop, in that work, James Breasted (1933: 116-117) further acknowledges, "The family as the primary influence in the rise and development of moral ideas." Again, he states, "Moral discernment has its roots in the life of the family." Even more, "moral impulses in the life of man have grown up out of the influences that operate in family relationships."

He then quotes W. McDougal in *An Introduction to Social Psychology* (Boston, 1926: 74) who had written: "From this emotion [parental tenderness] and its impulse to cherish and protect, spring generosity, gratitude, love, pity, true benevolence and altruistic conduct of every kind; in it they have their main and absolutely essential root, without which they would not be." Even further, "This intimate alliance between tender emotion and anger is of great importance for the social life of man, and the right understanding of it is fundamental for a true theory of the moral sentiments; for the anger evoked in this way is the germ of all moral indignation, and on moral indignation justice and the part of public law are on the main founded. Thus, paradoxically as it may seem, beneficence and punishment alike have their finest and most essential root in the parental instinct."

Again, emerging human consciousness expanded outside the family to the community and ultimately the nation state comprising a ruler, administrators and the public they served. Therefore, these Africans ultimately helped define the parameters of practiced ethical and moral behavior establishing connections between the principal gods, their son the King and the people, both high and low, which he was expected to "shepherd." It was, therefore, his responsibility to lead his people in a just manner and instruct his administrators, judges, nobles, of their obligation to administer justice equally to all. As an example, in the case of religious practice, as the son of the dominant god, the king was responsible to perform the daily liturgy of the ritual of praise in the temple as the Chief Priest. Since he could not be in every temple in his kingdom, every day, to perform the daily ritual, he created or in fact supported his religious second, a High Priest, who administered a religious bureaucracy responsible for worshipping and ritualizing the gods. In similar fashion, since the king had to manage the societal dynamics of his kingdom he created a civic bureaucracy headed by a Vizier or Prime Minister to administer the social and political institutions of the state. Combined, their actions pertained to the living and the dead with repercussions for their experiences in the Afterlife dynamics. In this emerged the standard principle that these individuals be the epitome of righteousness and that they administer justice and be truthful in all their dealings. They must never allow, as Isaiah 64: 6 says, "All our righteousness have become filthy rags." Thus, for an administrator to accept a bribe was considered an abomination to the god; that is, the king and his father, the Sun-god.

In seeking to comprehend this powerful social admonition, the Sun-God was adjudged the "creator of righteousness" who "lived on righteousness" and "fed on righteousness" and as his son and earthly representative, the king was expected to manifest, demonstrate, uphold and practice righteousness. Further, he expected this attribute and its twin pillars of "truth" and "justice" to be paramount in all dealings, among high and low, but particularly from those servants of the state with whom he entrusted this task. But of course, this has not always been the case! Criminal behavior in its many guises, whether in robbery, theft, bribery, corruption, can be considered "as old as the hills." Knowing this, the king as son of the Sun-god strove to be the model of righteousness not simply because he was head of state but particularly because he himself was to be judged in the Afterlife.

Thus, put within a legal context, James Breasted (1934: 128) wrote: "The moral worthiness of the deceased must of course, in accordance with the Egyptian's keen legal discernment, be determined in legal form and by legal process. We have seen that the nobles refer to judgment in their tombs, and that even the king was subject to such judgment, because he was expected to wear his crown of righteousness, righteously. Indeed, not even the gods escaped it; for it is stated that every god who assists the Pharaoh to the sky 'shall be justified before Geb (the Earth-god).'" To explain this further he states: "The translated Pharaoh, who is thus declared just, continues to exhibit the same qualities in the exercise of the celestial sovereignty which he receives. 'He judges justice before Re on that day of the feast, (called) 'First of the Year.' The sky is in satisfaction, the earth is in joy, having heard that King Neferkere (Pepi II) has placed justice [in the place of justice]. They are satisfied who sit with King Neferkere in his court of justice with the just utterance which came forth from his mouth.' It is significant that the king exercises this just judgment in the presence of Re the Sun-god. Similarly, in the Solar Utterance we find it affirmed that 'King Unas has set justice therein (in the isle where he is) in the place of injustice." For this reason, the king devised a number of measures to combat such improper behaviors, and these ranged from punishment to reward, and this could take many forms. Principal among these were appointment of men of great integrity such as the Vizier whom the king further instructed as to the proper behavior in executing his proper responsibilities.

As the society matured in Ancient Empire stages, theologians defined what came to be called the "Negative Confessions" designed for an Afterlife Judgment where the deceased denied practicing some 42 behaviors that were either criminal in nature or unrighteous or unethical in their practices. Again, the king was also subject to this same yardstick as part of his own Judgment to determine whether he had been righteous; whether he had practiced righteousness on earth; and whether he demanded it and even prosecuted it as behavior practice of his subordinates; all to be admitted to dwell with his brother gods in that wonderful Afterlife abode.

Into the Egyptian Mind. Egyptian Art. Sennutem seems to be opening a window to the Afterlife.

Into the Egyptian Mind. Double Temple of Horus and Sobek. More Nile Gods do their thing.

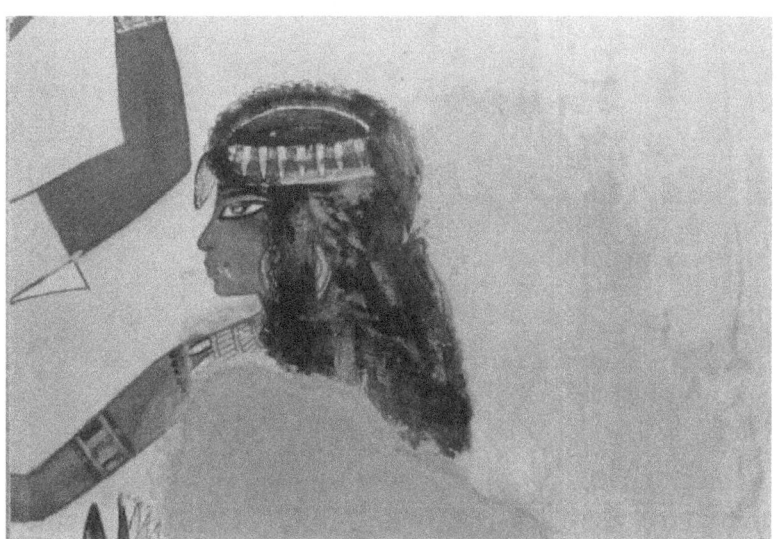

Into the Egyptian Mind. Egyptian Art. Perhaps the raised hands are in adoration of this extraordinary beauty with hair!

Into the Egyptian Mind. The Vulture and the ubiquitous face.

Into the Egyptian Mind. Beauty of the Hieroglyphics. Cartouche.

Into the Egyptian Mind. Cairo Museum of Egyptian Antiquities. Carmen Monderson stands before a kneeling statue of Hatshepsut of the 18th Dynasty.

In as much as science today acknowledges the first humans were Africans, objective scholarship must recognize the seekers after knowledge and concomitant righteous behavior were original and these were hallmark African behaviors. After all, these African Egyptians believed their god Thoth invented knowledge, Ptah constructed the heavens with his help, and Ra created righteousness that also became an attribute of Osiris, the god who reigned in the Afterlife and judged the dead. As such, then, these moral and ethical gems of society may very well have diffused to other ancient societies themselves coming into vogue and molding the personalities of their cultural experiences through practices of righteousness as a sheet anchor in their moral and ethical understanding morphing into religious behavior in a conception of a higher sense or Afterlife phenomenon beyond this mundane world of human existence.

For example, if we examine the quest for "righteousness" among ancient nations, in as much as they emerged after the Egyptian Africans, the Babylonians, Buddhists, Jews, Greeks and Romans, and especially Christians, all reveal an unending moral and spiritual quest not simply to better the physical, psychological and moral nature of man but also to inculcate a philosophical consciousness and longing for near perfection in human experience, particularly for example, righteousness to fulfill the criteria to qualify for entrance into whatever their version of the heavenly kingdom. Notwithstanding, and regarding this Afterlife experience, the Africans of the Nile Valley in North-East Africa believed, according to their theological construct of this Afterlife, the heavenly experience was both a celestial and terrestrial phenomenon. Nonetheless, except nihilists, people of all societies were content to work for the "greater glory" that inherently improved their human qualities and conditions on earth, in the belief, sometimes, of a better world to come.

As will be shown later, we must therefore agree, Righteousness is a state of being practically every ancient

African aspired to in this life and hoped to boast of practicing as an ideal when he asserted such standing before his God. Naturally in that elevated practice and spiritual consciousness, he had to be equated with Osiris who possessed the necessary attributes of righteousness in order to be considered "Justified." This state of righteous consciousness, called by many names as "Ma'at" or "balance," "order," "truth" and "justice," was reflected in many types of behaviors, themselves designed to mold the individual into a being who practiced qualities that not only benefitted himself, but also reflected the actions of the society and of the gods. Thus, righteousness in its ideal and practice must be considered an attribute of the living, the dead and the divine.

Given these factors, the record is replete with individuals who either cried out for justice, instructed the young and official class, prophesied the coming of redeemer kings or boasted in admonitions, autobiographies, on tombstone stele and in tomb inscriptions, issued the call for or explained how they practiced righteousness in many walks of their social and religious experiences. A good example of this is recounted in an article entitled "Egyptian Righteousness" by A.M. Blackman in *Encyclopedia of Religion and Ethics* Vol. 10 [Edinburgh: T. and T. Clarke, 1918] which quotes from *Hieroglyphic Texts from Egyptian Stelae*, Etc., in the British Museum, (London: 1911-14, 1, Pl. 47, line 11f) where a noble affirms: "I came forth from my city, I came down into my Nome and I spake the truth therein, I did righteousness therein.' 'I am one who loves good and hates evil....' 'There is no iniquity that has issued from my mouth. There is no evil that my hands have wrought.' 'I was a righteous man upon earth.' 'Never did I do any evil thing unto any people.' 'I am a noble pleased with righteousness, conforming to the laws of the Hall of the Two Rights.'" Thus, these Nile River state individuals never tired of boasting of practicing "righteousness" and its twin virtues of "truth" and "justice."

A further example of praise of the twin pillars supporting righteousness states: "Truthfulness seems to have been highly esteemed, and was particularly looked for in the great and powerful. 'Speak not falsehood, thou art great,' says the Eloquent Peasant to the high Steward Rensi; indeed, such a one must 'destroy lies and create truth [or 'right']'" Again, "an Old Kingdom noble asserts that he was straightforward in the royal presence and free from falsehood. Says another: 'I spake the truth which the god loves every day.'" Papyrus Prisse recounts among the Admonitions of Ptah-Hotep insistence that "one act in accordance with right, free from falsehood." Apparently, the Sun-God instructed, 'Speak the (Ma'at) truth, do right (Ma'at), for it is great, it is mighty, it is enduing.' In the Psychostasia or Judgment, one of the Negative Confessions the deceased asserts: 'I have not spoken lies,' or 'I have not spoken lies knowingly.'

The Egyptian courts of law are replete with individuals seeking justice for some transgression against them. The pharaoh constantly demanded judges dispense justice impartially, never favoring the rich over the poor. The Chief Justice must make particularly sure his rulings are never questioned! "The viziers, Nomarchs, and high officials who governed and administered the laws were expected to exhibit a high standard of justice." As such, 'men expect the exercise of justice in the procedure of the vizier.' He 'must not be a respecter of persons or show partiality for that is what the god abhors.' "He must not, however, go to the other extreme and act like the vizier Akhthoi, who discriminated against some of his own kin in favor of strangers, in fear lest it should be wrongly said of him that he favored his kin dishonestly; 'that' we are informed, 'is more than justice.' The ideal judge must be 'a father of the lowly (*nmh*), a husband of the widow, a brother of the forsaken, the garment of the motherless … one who comes forth at the voice of him who calls. If such a one veils his face against the violent, who shall repress crime? A judge must be as unerring and impartial as the balance!"

The story of the Eloquent Peasant is an excellent example of good speech but also a call to justice and reminds officials of their responsibilities to act justly. The peasant says: "Is it not wrong, I suppose, a balance that is awry, a tongue of a balance that is faulty, a righteous man that has swerved (from the right path)?" As such, one official describes himself as: "A man of truth (or righteousness) before the Two Lands, equitable and righteous like Thoth ... more accurate than the plummet, the likeness of the balance."

Another Old Kingdom official boasted, "Never did I judge two brothers in such a way that a man was deprived of his father's property." Again, a Middle Kingdom official stated: "I did not pursue after mischief for which men are hated. I was one who loved good and hated evil, a character who is loved in the house of his lord.... Now as for any commission which he (the king) bade me attend to, viz. giving a petitioner his right, attending to the claim of one who has been wronged, I always did it in reality .... I was passionate against violent persons. I did not take a thing (i.e. a bribe) wrongfully in order to conduct a transaction." Intef of the New Kingdom, boasted of, "Tuning his face towards him who speaks truth; disregarding him who speaks lies; not discriminating between him whom he knew and him whom he did not; going about after righteousness; indulgent in hearing petitions; judging men so that they are satisfied; ... free from partiality; acquitting the righteous; driving away the plunderer from him whom he plunders; the servant of the oppressed." Thus, in a legal dispute seeking justice, both parties must come out feeling justified with the verdict!

THE RIGHTEOUS MAN

He must demonstrate generosity and benevolence; practice avoidance of slander; be honest and practice fair dealing; demonstrate faithfulness, obedience and deference to superiors must be his strong suit; he must show hospitality;

demonstrate piety towards the dead; demonstrate sexual morality; have regard for old age; practice regard for parents, wife and near relatives; have a good temper; carefully avoid rancor; show gratitude and avoidance of pride; be humble in his dealings; practice discretion and avoidance of loquacity; avoid crimes of violence.

Into the Egyptian Mind. Egyptian Art. Oh, how enchanting this lotus smells.

Into the Egyptian Mind. Egyptian Art. It appears individuals await instructions from seated noble with chariot at their back.

Into the Egyptian Mind. Egyptian Art. Cartouche (*Hennu*) with raised-relief characters (Cleopatra).

Into the Egyptian Mind. Characters in "Sunk-relief."

Into the Egyptian Mind. Cairo Museum of Egyptian Antiquities. Floral tile decoration from Amarna.

SUN-GOD AND RIGHTEOUSNESS

The Sun-god is the creator and champion of righteousness. The Sun-god lives on righteousness. The Sun-god loves righteousness. The Sun-god maintains the balance. The place in which judgment is had must always practice justice. The

Sun-god is the ideally righteous king. The people must always feel confident of justice in the place of justice.

OSIRIS AND RIGHTEOUSNESS

Osiris was originally the proto-type of all dead and god kings. The influence of the Osiris myth on Egyptian ethics has been significant. Upon being vindicated and found "True of Voice" in Heliopolis, Osiris was acknowledged king and judge of the dead. Osiris was recognized as the god of righteousness.

OTHER GODS AND SOLAR RIGHTEOUTSNESS

The Judicial Council in Heliopolis is where the kings were judged and also crowned. Thoth was scribe of the gods who invented knowledge, music, and writing, assisted Ptah in mapping and construction of the heavens, and then he defended Osiris in the Council. The "Four Apes" in the "Boat of Ra" were "Lords of Righteousness" and so too "Turn Face" the Celestial Ferryman who ferried the souls across the lake to the "Place of Judgment." The "Assessors of Osiris" in the "Broad Hall of Two Truths" are also entitled "Lords of Righteousness." The "Crocodile Gods" are considered as "Lords of Righteousness" and "Righteous Ones." All inhabitants of the Osirian
Kingdom as well as local gods who acquire ethical quality are righteous.

INCENTIVES TO RIGHTEOUSNESS

Incentives to righteousness are many including the Posthumous Judgment before the Judge of the Dead. Those who "Done what their god praise" fit the criteria. Future accountability is a powerful incentive that regulates conduct. The **Tale of Khamuast** is a good example for good behavior. The "Book of the Dead" characterizes the journey after death, mapping the path and explaining what happens in the "Hall of Two Truths" or "Double Maati." Then it describes the passage into eternal life. Fear of God is a good incentive as well as the contemplation of Rewards or punishments during this life. There are other rewards. The righteous man will be accorded a "good death" and a "good burial" to begin a "new, blissful life." As such, this righteous man's heirs will succeed to his possessions. Equally, the desire to stand well with the pharaoh is another, and the desire to stand well with the community is also a powerful incentive. Lastly, man's conscience is a great motivator for right conduct. That is, the conscience is a barometer of right and wrong!

JUSTIFICATION OF THE DEAD

Osiris is king and also the ideal prototype of the justified dead. Some methods of obtaining justification deemed righteous, by the deceased for inclusion to the Kingdom of Osiris, included an association with the god himself declared "Justified" or "True of Voice." The pilgrimage to Abydos was to symbolically visit the Home of Osiris as well as to participate in the Mysteries sacred to Osiris which are all powerful incentives. He must undergo "Purification" to be admitted.

(1)   He could bathe in special pools while alive;

(2) He could have this purification done by individuals dressed as the gods;

(3) Before he enters the "Hall of Two Truths" he is cleansed by two goddesses and receives the name of "Stone of Righteousness!"

The powerful Chapter 125 of the Book of the Dead named the "Negative Confessions" is part of this justification process. That is, while his heart is being weighed against a feather he states 42 times, "I did not do so and so …

There is also a "Positive Confession" where he states "I did this…" and possessing magical formulas are also helpful.

Now, in turning to some examples of other ancient nations seeking righteousness and attendant virtues; we must acknowledge all peoples essentially seek the same outcomes in their cultural, religious and spiritual aspirations. The first of these representative societies is described by T.G Pinches as "Babylonian Righteousness" in Hastings' *Encyclopedia of Religion and Ethics* (1918) where he speaks of an inscription called "warnings to kings against injustice" which shows what "righteousness on the part of the ruler was expected to be. He was to favor justice and to be well-disposed towards his people, his provinces and the intelligent ones of his land. He was not to favor roguery, when the king was favorable to the work of Ea (the god of Wisdom); the great god would set him in the knowledge and understanding of righteousness." Thus, the king and all others in authority came to have a reputation for righteousness, justice and similar virtues. The king, therefore, became sacred in the eyes of the people because of his "uprightness and integrity, love for his subjects, and fair and benign conduct with regard to them." The great ruler Sargon was called "King of Righteousness" (Justice). He was a "speaker of righteousness (good);" and Senacherib's grandson Ashurbanipal calls himself "King of righteousness," even "the lover of righteousness."

The Buddhist recognizes righteousness as a term of human relations and conduct. Thus, he believes the order of the universe is such that "wrong-doing leads to punishment and right-doing to reward." However, his ideal of righteousness - the state of the Saint - is to become independent of the universe and free from any desire for it."

In the Old Testament, righteousness is similar to truth, sincerity, firmness and denotes generally what is true, right, fitting, or conducive to the end in view. A.R. Gordon states in his article on "Righteousness" that the term is "primarily interpreted in terms of social usage. The righteous man is he who adheres loyally to the moral and religious customs of his people, while the 'wicked' sets them at naught." "Thus, Abraham's righteousness consists in a scrupulous regard for Yahweh and His commandments (Gen 12 - 1), combined with signal manifestations of that lavish generosity towards one's kindred (13 - 5) and hospitality to passing strangers (18 -1) which have always been reckoned among the most sacred obligations of the dutiful tribesman. David also identifies 'righteousness' with the magnanimity which he has shown towards Saul, in refusing to stretch forth his hands against the Lord's anointed,' even when the Lord has 'delivered him into his hand (1 S 26 - 33).'"

In the prophetic ideal of righteousness, we see, in wake of Jewish military successes and forgetful of the Covenant, "rich men used their wealth to 'trample the face' of the poor, refusing him an honest wage, ousting him from field and home, in high places there was neither security and for the debt even of a pair of shoes selling him into slavery (Is 3 - 14; 5 - 8; Am 2 - 6, Mic 2 - 2, 3 - 1, 3 - 11), such oppression there was neither security nor redress. The judges at the gates openly accepted bribes and perverted justice (Is 1 - 22, Am 6 - 12, Mic 3 - 11) while religion itself was made a cloak to cover wrong-doing (I 1 - 11, Am 2 - 7)." But Amos rebelled, insisting "Let justice roll down as waters and righteousness as an everlasting stream." Here Amos equally laid it down as a principle, "righteousness is no mere body of customs, still less a legal status conferred on fallible authority; it is the living essence of social ethics, embracing alike honesty in business - fair weights and balances, standard wages and prices - and impartial justice in the law-courts."

Among Christians, Christ is said, according to **Matthew** 3-15, to have come "to fulfill all righteousness." Things had so deteriorated in his time; many were "persecuted for righteousness sake." It was said John "the Baptist" came "in the way of righteousness" as a "representative and preacher of righteousness." His job was simply to identify Christ, baptize him, prepare and set him on the way! Christ for his part said, "For I say to you, that except your righteousness surpasses that of the scribes and Pharisees, you shall not enter the kingdom of the heavens."

Into the Egyptian Mind. Egyptian Art. Individual with unusual hairdo, holds lotus flower and duckling.

Into the Egyptian Mind. Egyptian Art. A stunning beauty raises her arms in adoration.

Into the Egyptian Mind. Double Temple of Horus and Sobek. Sunk relief depicting a headless four-legged animal and a Red Crown.

Into the Egyptian Mind. Double Temple of Horus and Sobek. An eye watches lapwing in flight.

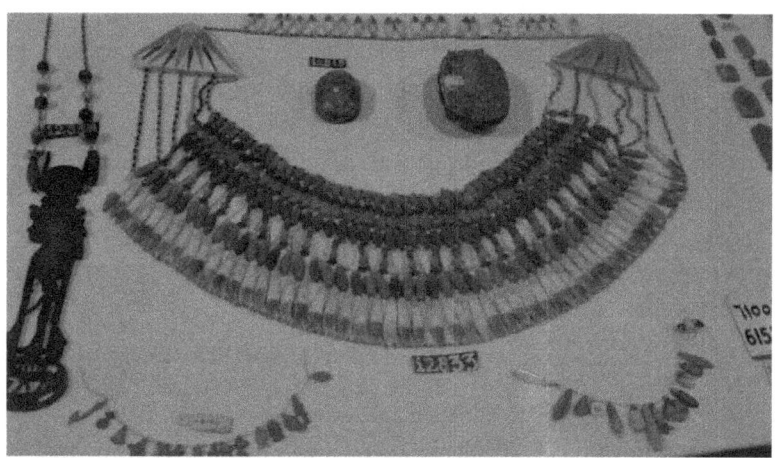

Into the Egyptian Mind. Cairo Museum of Egyptian Antiquities. Wonderful necklace of precious stones and assorted jewelry.

There was some contention that his teachings contravened the long-standing "Old-laws." However, Christ said of the "right conduct of his disciples, just because it is based on a more spiritual Law, will be far wider in range than the scribal righteousness." But he did not in formal language apply the terms 'righteousness' to the results of obedience to the Law in its more spiritual interpretation.

Almsgiving, fasting and prayer were assumed to be righteousness because they were commanded by the law, but the "Sermon on the Mount" goes further. Jesus the Christ said, "Seek ye first the Kingdom of Heaven and its righteousness" without which you cannot enter. What he seemed to imply is that people give alms, fast and pray every day, yet many are not righteous! In contrast with the Pharisaic righteousness based on the Old Law, true righteousness is a right condition of the heart, caused by a right understanding of the spiritual tenor of the Law, which issues in right conduct. But this is never called 'righteousness.' Thus, throughout the Sermon Christ seems to be employing the term as a known conception, using it therefore, as it were, in inverted commas.

In St. Paul's message (**Romans** 14-7) he writes: "The Kingdom of God is not meat and drink, but righteousness and peace and joy in the Holy Spirit." It is most natural to suppose that he uses the word in the large and somewhat infinite sense which everyone understands. What it signifies is that there is a standard of conduct - a standard determined not simply by the nature of the person who is to exhibit the character or quality of righteousness, but by his relation to other persons or things - and that the requirements of this standard have been met."

Just as we recognize "Justice or righteousness of god in the Bible is sometimes loving kindness to the just and unjust," among the Greeks and Romans we look for a definition of the terms first among two prominent philosophers Plato and Aristotle, where (1) Plato defines justice as "Be this" rather than "Do this" which means for him justice is social. "But he emphasizes equality of service in the voluntary acceptance of natural inequalities not the equalization of rights and rewards."

In the germ of the myth of Plato's Protagoras, "Zeus established a civilization by sending alows and olkn to mankind. Hesiod also anticipates the complaint of Job, Theognis, the Sophist Trasymachus, Sophocles, the speaker in Plato's Republic, and Euripides, that the righteous man is not visibly rewarded. It is commonly said that the personification of olkn begins with the description of her banishment by wicked men."

In a fable of Archilochus there is an appeal to Zeus who regards both the Hybris and the Dike of beasts. This may be little more than the literary tone of Kipling's 'law of the pack' and Aristophanes' 'law of the birds.' Pindar echoes Hesiod with the compound beasts 'unwitting-of-justice.' Mimnermus says the truth is the most just of all things."

We are further informed, among the Greeks, "The idea of justice is especially prominent in Solon, the earliest of Attic poets. He speaks in almost Aeschylean metaphor of those who regard not the august foundation of Dike. He associates the doctrine of the late punishment of the wicked with the omniscience of silent Dike, who sees and knows all things, and surely overtakes the evil-doer at last. He prays for wealth - but not unjustly gained. He boasts that he has harmonized might and right, and amuses Plutarch by the archaic naiveté of his sayings that the sea is the most 'just' of things when the winds do not vex it."

Anaximander says, "All things that are born must die" and "paying the penalty to one another for the injustice (of individual existence?)." Heraclitus says "All things are just in the sight of god, but men conceive some things to be unjust and some just." "Wise men tell us," Socrates says, "that it is love and order and sobriety and justice that hold together gods and men and the whole world, which is therefore a cosmos - an order, not a licentious disorder."

Phocylides believes, "In justice is comprehended all virtue" which Theognis embellished with "Every man is good who is just" and that "The most beautiful thing is justice, the best is health, the most delightful, to win what one loves."

Aristotle expresses, "Neither the evening star nor the morning star is so admirable" as justice or righteousness.

Pindar expresses the "idea of justice in his praise of commercial cities - Corinth, and his beloved Aegina, that deals fairly with strangers."

In Aeschylus Dike, the daughter of Zeus, the embodiment and the accomplishment of the law, is frequently personified with bold metaphor. Whereas, in that case we find, the Prometheus "raises the theological problem of the justice of Zeus who keeps justice in his own hands."

"The Agamemnon trilogy emphasizes the awfulness of sin, the certainty of retribution, the irremediability of spilt blood, the law that the doer must suffer. The Furies, the ministers of the older law, claim to be strictly and straightly just. But already in the Agamemnon we hear of another law, that wisdom comes through suffering; and in the final symbolism of the Eumenides the Furies become the gracious goddesses, and the letter of the old law of an eye for an eye is superseded by a law of grace and atonement."

Now, reflecting back on Plato, one author explained, "The artistic design of the Republic required him to regard justice in its subjective aspect an entire righteousness, the harmony, unity, and right functioning in division of labor of all the 'parts' or 'faculties' of the soul."

Next, in seeking righteousness among the Hindu, we look toward the Rig-Veda and finds its expression in the term RTA, "the equivalent of the Avestan asa, which denotes primarily the cosmic order, and then the order of the moral law, and the performance of the   sacrifice, on the other."

"Righteousness is thus accordance with general and with this agrees its constant association with truth (satya) considered with reality. This opinion demands the virtues of a simple society - consideration in domestic relations, political loyalty, truth in friendship, abstention from crimes such as theft and murder, and from women faithfulness in wedded life; not unnaturally in hymns closely associated the sacrifice much more stress is laid on the merits of liberality than on such manly virtues as courage in war."

Nevertheless, we must give the Egyptian, Nile Valley African credit for creating and preserving evidence of the earliest form of social consciousness we label as "righteousness."

Into the Egyptian Mind. Egyptian Art. Individual shown previously in other profile holds flower in one hand but does not smell lotus in other.

Into the Egyptian Mind. Egyptian Art. Workers meet to converse.

Into the Egyptian Mind. Double Temple of Horus and Sobek. Before entering a temple, Pharaoh is baptized by Horus (Heru, left) and Thoth (Tehuti, right).

Into the Egyptian Mind. Double Temple of Horus and Sobek. Horus (Heru) hands instrument to king in White Crown with two goddesses at his rear.

Into the Egyptian Mind. Egyptian Art. Papyrus. Pharaoh in a fighting mood, shoots an arrow from his charging chariot.

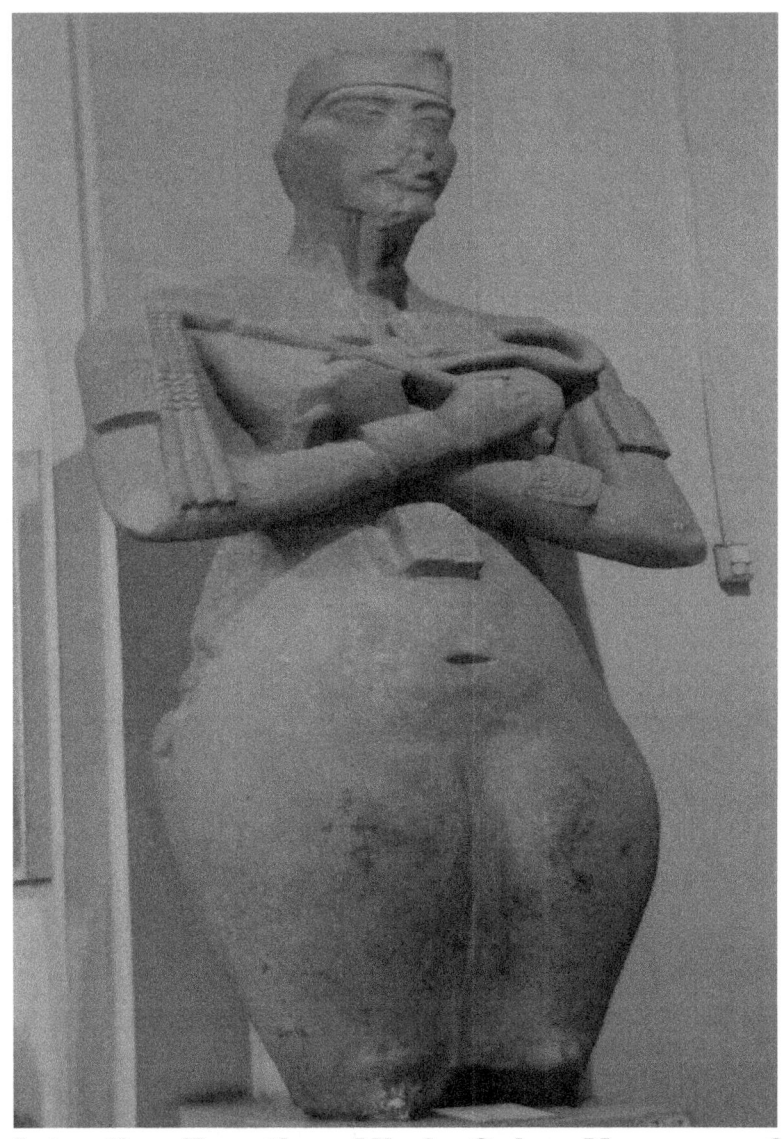

Into the Egyptian Mind. Cairo Museum of Egyptian Antiquities. Statue of Akhenaten (Amenhotep IV) grasping scepter and flail.

"Man's moral ideas are the product of social conditions and forms part of a social process." But, remember, no individual can make a conscience for himself; he always needs a society to make it for him." Thus, across the social landscape we see individuals asserting their righteous behavior. For example, on a statue was engraved, "I had these statues made by the sculptor and he was satisfied with the pay which I gave him." A steward left a tomb inscription affirming, "As for everyman who had done this for me (that is, has worked on his tomb), he was never dissatisfied. Whether craftsman or quarryman, I satisfied him." A Nome ruler said, "I gave bread to all the hungry of the Cerastes Mountain (his domain). I clothed him who was naked therein. I filled its shores with large cattle. I satisfied the wolves of the mountain and the fowl of the sky with [flesh] of small cattle. I never oppressed one in possession of his property so that he complained of me because of it to the god of my city; but I spake and told that which was good. Never was there fearing because of one stronger than he, so that he complained of it to the god. I was a benefactor to it (his domain) in the folds of the cattle, in the settlement of the fowlers.... I spake no lie, for I was one beloved of his father, praised of his mother, excellent in character to his brother, and amicable to [his sister].

King Sahure's chief physician says, "Never did I do anything evil towards any person," while a contemporary priest also boasted, "Never have I done aught of violence towards any person."

Of King Pepi it is said, "There is no evil which King Pepi has done. Weighty is this word in thy sight, O Re!" Again, "This King Pepi is justified, this King Pepi is praised."

King Userkaf is called "A doer of righteousness (Ma'at)." King Unas comes forth to righteousness (Ma'at) that he may take it (Ma'at) with him. Again, "King Unas goes forth that he may bring righteousness (Ma'at) with him."

Finally, the Vizier Ptahhotep uttered these words, "I have attained one hundred and ten years of life, while the king gave to me rewards above those of the ancestors because I did righteousness for the king even unto the grave." Accordingly, Breasted assessed, in such conduct, "we are contemplating the emergence of a sense of moral responsibility as it was gradually assuming an increasingly mandatory power over human conduct, a development which was moving towards the assertion of conscience as an influential social force." Again, he argues, "While the individual's claim to worthy character might be based on his spirit and conduct in his relations with his own family, father, mother, brothers and sisters," it was the community and state that began to mold his consciousness about a greater cultural, ethical and moral responsibility."

Lastly, Ptahhotep admonishes, "Be not proud of thy learning. Take counsel with the unlearned as with the learned, for the limits of a craft is not fixed and there is no craftsman whose worth is perfect. Worthy speech is more hidden than greenstone, being found even among slave-women at the mill-stone." Or, it can be found among fisher-women in the marketplace.

"The friendless peasant pleading with the grand steward says to him, 'Beware! Eternity approaches.' Ameni, the great lord of Beni Hasan, sets forth upon his tomb door, as we have seen, the record of social justice in his treatment of all as the best passport he can devise for the long journey. Over and over again the men of the Feudal Age reiterate in their tombs their claims to righteousness of character. 'Sesenebnef has done righteousness, his abomination was evil, he saw it not,' says an official of the time on his sarcophagus. The mortuary texts which fill the cedar coffins of this age show clearly that the consciousness of moral responsibility in the hereafter was greatly deepened since the Pyramid Age. The balances of justices to which the peasant appealed so often and so dramatically are now really finding place in the drama of justification hereafter. 'The doors of the sky are opened to thy beauty,' says one to the deceased; 'thou ascendest, thou seest

Hathor. Thy evil is expelled; thy iniquity is wiped away, by those who weigh with the balances on the day of reckoning.' Just as the peasant so often called the grand steward the balances of justice, so the deceased may be possessed of character as true and unswerving as the scales themselves. Hence, we find the Coffin Texts saying, "Lo, this X (name of the deceased) is the balances of Re, wherewith he weighs truth' (or righteousness). It is evident also those are the balances of truth and who the judge who presides over them. It is as before the Sun-god, before whom Osiris had been tried. A similar connection of the judgment with Re places righteousness in the cabin of the Solar Barque.

The moral requirement of the great judge has become a matter of course. The dead says: "I have led the way before him and behind him. He loves righteousness and hates evil, upon his favorite ways of righteousness whereon the gods lead. When the dead man entered those righteous paths of the gods, it was with a sense of moral unworthiness left behind. 'My sin is expelled,' he says, my iniquity is removed. I have cleansed myself in those two great pools which are in Heracleopolis.' Those ceremonial washings which were so common in the Pyramid Texts have now become distinctly moral in their significance. "I go upon the way where I wash my head in the Lake of Righteousness,' says the dead man. Again, and very often the 'deceased claims that his life has been blameless:' 'I am one who loved righteousness, my abomination was evil.' 'I sit down justified, I rise up justified.' 'I have established righteousness; I have expelled evil.' 'I am a lord of offering; my abomination is evil.'"

In summation, in the Chapter of Justification before Thoth, Hereditary Prince of the Gods, the deceased speaks in reference to his justification, along "the beautiful path of justification. When Thoth defended Osiris' justification, it became clear that Osiris Ethical Justification, as put in the mouth of the deceased who says: "'I perish not, I enter as truth, I support truth, I am lord of truth, I go forth as truth, I enter in as truth.'…Even more significant, the god says, 'I am Osiris, the god who does righteousness, I live in it!" I therefore close with the admonition of 1Timothy 6: 11, which admonishes, "O man of God, flee these things: and follow after righteousness, godliness, faith, love, patience, meekness!"

Into the Egyptian Mind. Egyptian Art. Workers in different attitudes.

Into the Egyptian Mind. Friends greeting at Luxor.

Into the Egyptian Mind. Egyptian Art. Young girl in the nude.

Into the Egyptian Mind. Double Temple of Horus and Sobek. Beauty of the Hieroglyphs.

Into the Egyptian Mind. Double Temple of Horus and Sobek. While a defaced Horus (Heru) sits enthroned, Pharaoh offers two small vases of flowers.

Into the Egyptian Mind. Cairo Museum of Egyptian Antiquities. Floral patterns of Akhenaten's time at Amarna.

8. THE SANCTUARY
By
Dr. Fred Monderson

The especial designation ancient Egyptian Sanctuary, has been applied both to the temple itself and also to the particular spot or location within where the image of the god resides. That is, viewed from a distance, the temple is the Sanctuary of the god. Viewed from within the temple, the Sanctuary is the "Holy of Holies" where the image of the god rests in the quiet solitude of his darkened abode. In the latter instance specifically, it is unique but also the most important part of the temple.

Generally different from most other religious sanctuaries where the ceremonies are performed; the Egyptian Sanctuary has its own special peculiarities. For example, in a Christian church, the congregation gathers in the Sanctuary to hear and participate in the ceremony. However, it is not so in an ancient Egyptian Sanctuary. First, the general public never ascends into the inner reaches of the temple; only members of the high priesthood do. Located beyond or adjacent to the Hypostyle Hall, the "Holy of Holies," is never visited by anyone except the king and a designated high priest. Naturally, these individuals are assisted by deputies who sing the songs and play music, read the verses, burn the incense, carry the solid and liquid offerings, water, etc. Nevertheless, and except as active participants, even while the god's covered statue in the sacred bark may be observed in the procession outside the "Holy of Holies" and within and outside the temple as seen by the general public, these people are not privileged to enter or view the divinity in his sacred realm. Still, on the holiest festivals the god's image is sometimes bare to the Faithfull's gaze for an instant peek! Importantly, however, it should also be pointed out, the iconic Dr. ben-Jochannan always instructed his students to never enter the Sanctuary because, he reiterated, in ancient times only the high priest or pharaoh could access the spot and behold the god, enjoy the ambience of the chamber and even participate in the ritual dynamics of his resting place. However, having said such, a number of factors can be pointed out regarding the Sanctuary in ancient Egypt.

One of the most important purposes and intent of the Sanctuary has been as a place of shelter for the god's image manifestation on earth. In addition, because the Egyptians invested their god with human attributes, lustration and sustenance became necessities on a daily basis and this became incorporated into the official liturgy of worship.
In fact, this daily lustration in the Sanctuary was actually a carbon copy of that undergone by the sun-god in heaven.

Significantly, however, "The whole object of official worship, as represented in the temple reliefs, was to obtain the favor of the divinities for the Pharaoh. In return for the offering which he presents to them they provide him victory, gladness, life, stability, health, good fortune, abundance, millions of years, the duration of Re, an eternity of jubilees, etc. The very temples of the gods were erected by the king that he might receive in return the 'duration of heaven,' 'hundreds of thousands of years,' and that he might 'be granted eternity as king.' Thus, the designation of every ritual act, 'giving [var. doing] this or that to [for] his father [var. mother] NN.' Is followed by the words 'in order that he may make an 'Endowed-with-life' like Ra forever,' the 'Endowed-with-life' being the king himself."

In the beginning when the god arose from the murky depths of the primeval ocean, he stood up on a sacred mound and as the waters receded, shelter was required. It has been postulated that the first architects were priests. In contact with divinity, they were instructed on how to construct the shelter or Sanctuary. At first this was simply a basic lean-to covering with a rag on a flag pole to indicate a sacred place, with also a fence to keep out animals and people. As the society matured, the god's home became more sophisticated being built with more lasting materials, first brick then stone.

Though there were several versions of creation, that of the Sun-God at Heliopolis predominated in the earliest times and the king was regarded as the Son of the Sun-God and also his High Priest. The temple ritual also depicts him as sole officiant. However, because he could not be in every temple, for every god across the country, he created subordinates to officiate for every god and temple throughout the land to conduct the daily ritual. This is also the time when much of the religious ritual became standard practice across the land and for the duration of dynastic rule. Significant, and given such, when the pharaoh visited the temple's Sanctuary accompanied by his second, the high priest, he would break the seal over the closed door and enter, offering some greeting. As this was, however, infrequent, the high priest did so several times on a daily occurrence; thus, his actions were dictated by a prescribed liturgy.

Recently, I visited Egypt and traveled to a small temple in the desert at El Kab, accompanied by my Guide Showgi Abd Rady. After the doors were opened, he said, "Let me go in first!" Once inside he then offered a greeting, "Hotep!" to the kneeling figure facing the door. Not as similarly brief, yet, this is not unlike the greeting the pharaoh or high priest would offer in salutation as they entered the God's space. Adolf Erman, of whom it's been said, "He was the only modern man who knew exactly what the ancient Egyptians meant," best puts this dynamic which occurred in approach to the god's darkened space, to begin the three divisions of the daily ritual, i.e., incense, toilet and feeding, then a parting greeting. He states, for example, at Abydos, the priest began communication with the God offering incense from within the adjacent Hypostyle Hall, according to Erman in *Life in Ancient Egypt* (London: MACMILLAN AND CO., 1894: 273-74) as he recited: "I come into thy presence O great one, after I have purified myself. As I passed by the goddess Tefnut, she purified me … I am a prophet, and the son of a prophet of this temple. I am a prophet, and I come to do what ought to be done, but I do not come to do what ought not to be done."

Therefore, for the most part, as an example, at Karnak the Sanctuary sits alone outdoors detached just to the rear of the Hypostyle Hall separated by one or more courts, obelisks, chambers, beyond the Wadjit! However, at Abydos the shrine is just atop the incline beyond the Second Hypostyle Hall within the covered temple. As such, "He then stepped in front of the shrine of the god and opened the seal of clay with these words. 'The clay is broken and the seal loosed that this door may be opened, and all that is evil in me I throw (thus) on the ground.' When the Door was opened, he first incensed the sacred uraeus snake, the guardian of the god, greeting it by all its names; he then entered the Holy of Holies, saying: 'Let thy seat be adorned and thy robes exalted; the princes of the goddess of heaven come to thee, they descend from heaven and from the horizon that they may hear praise before thee…. He then approached the 'great seat,' i.e., that part of the shrine where the statue of the god stood, and said: 'Peace to the god, peace to the god, the living soul, conquering his enemies. Thy soul is with me, thine image is near me; the king brought to thee thy statue, which lives upon the presentation of the royal offerings. I am pure.'"

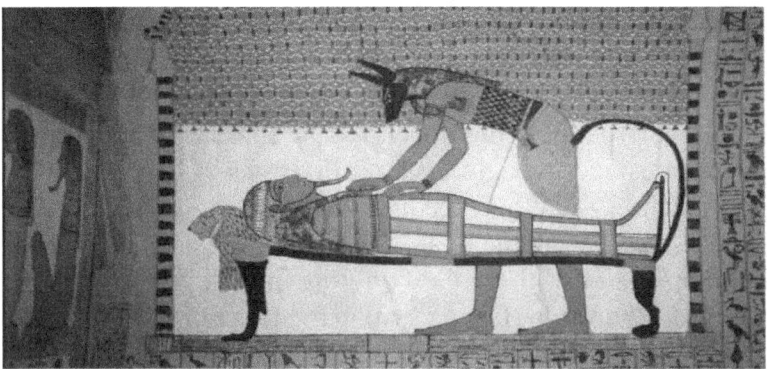

Into the Egyptian Mind. Egyptian Art. Anubis administers to the mummy in the tomb of Sennutem.

Into the Egyptian Mind. Egyptian Art. Workers climbing stairs and moving stuff.

Into the Egyptian Mind. Double Temple of Horus and Sobek. Goddesses in Red and White Crowns usher Pharaoh to meet Sobek, "Lord of Ombos."

Into the Egyptian Mind. Vulture Goddess with outstretched wings serves as protector of the temple.

Into the Egyptian Mind. Cairo Museum of Egyptian Antiquities. Lotus flowers from Akhenaten's Amarna.

However, as already stated, since the pharaoh only occasionally participates in the daily ritual which dictates the god is awoken, incensed, lustrated or having his morning toilet then fed three times daily, the priest conducts the chores. Important also, because there is much to be done, procession, hymns, chanting, bringing clothing, food, etc., the Pharaoh and High Priest are also assisted by senior priests in the temple. Adolf Erman in *Life in Ancient Egypt*, translated by H.M. Tirard (London: MacMillan and Co and New York, 1894: 273) describes some aspects of the ritual. He states: "The daily acts of worship performed by the priest du jour are known from several contemporary sources to have been essentially the same in the case of the various gods. Whether it was Amon or Isis, Ptah or the deceased to whom divine honors were to be paid, we always find that fresh rouge and fresh robes were placed upon the divine statue, and that the sacred chapel in which it was kept was cleansed and filled with perfume. The god was regarded as a human being, whose dwelling had to be cleansed, and who was assisted at his toilet by his servants. These ceremonies doubtless differed both in detail and extent at the various sanctuaries; e.g., the priest at Thebes had about sixty ceremonies to perform, whilst at Abydos thirty-six were found to be sufficient. The form and object of the worship however were always the same, though the details might vary. As a general rule also, the priest had to recite an appointed formula at each separate ceremony."

Now, having opened the door and in the God's presence, Erman further states, the priest had to "kiss the ground, throw himself on his face, throw himself entirely on his face, kiss the ground with his face downwards." Then he began to incense the chamber. Important, also, while the king is often shown with a hand incenser, incensing the god, in the Sanctuary a stand-alone incenser is also used. However, incense is never burned on the altar but in an incenser set in a corner on the floor.

In the *Encyclopedia of Religion and Ethics* article "Worship (Egyptian)" (Edinburgh: T and T. Clark, Vol. 12, 1921, 778), A. M. Blackman describes what he terms "The Pre-Toilet Episode." Regarding that part of the daily ritual he writes: "Having undergone purifications in the water of the sacred pool or tank, the priest entered the temple, reciting a formula as he did so his first act after entering the temple was to kindle a fire, a blow-drill being used for that purpose, or perhaps only a spindle and 'hearth.' The priest then picked up the principal part of the censer, which was of metal, usually bronze, and in the form of an outstretched arm with the hand open palm upwards. Taking hold of the rest of the censer, the little brazier in which the incense was burned, he fixed it in its place, namely in the open hand at the end of the arm. Having filled the brazier with burning charcoal from the fire he had previously kindled, he set incense thereon, and, holding the smoking censer in one hand, proceeded to the sanctuary, the double doors of which were bolted and the bolts secured with a clay seal. The bolts seem often to have been tied with a strip of papyrus to which the clay seal was affixed. The priest broke the seal, drew back the bolts, and opened the doors of the sanctuary, whereupon the sacred boat was disclosed with the cultus-image enshrined therein."

"After the unfastening of the seal, and presumably the opening of the doors, the priest sometimes burned incense in honor of the uraeus goddess. On beh1olding the image, the priest made a profound obeisance, 'kissing the ground prone,' as it was said, or 'placing himself upon the belly stretched out flat.' Then, standing or kneeling, he chanted first a hymn in honor of the divinity - lifting up both his hands as he did so in the attitude of worship, or else burning incense - and after that a second hymn in honor of R'yt, the female counterpart of the sun-god and identified with Hathor. The priest next offered the image scented honey, or a figure of the goddess Ma'at, and then burned more incense. Having swept the floor of the sanctuary with a cloth, he was now ready to 'lay his hands upon the god,' i.e., take the image out of the boat or naos in order to perform its toilet.'

After the greeting and incensing, then next the God's toilet is done and he is dressed. Erman (1894: 274) described the dressing, giving an example on how the toilet of the god was performed. "He laid his hands on him. He took off the old rouge and his former clothes, all of course with the necessary formulae. He then dressed the god in the robe called the Nems, saying: 'Come white dress! Come white dress! Come white eye of Horus, which proceeds from the town of Nechebt. The gods dress themselves with thee in thy name Dress, and the gods adorn themselves with thee in thy name Adornment.' The priest then dressed the god in the great dress, rouged him, and presented him with his insignia: the scepter, the staff of ruler, and the whip, the bracelets and anklets, as well as the two feathers which he wore on his head, because 'he has triumphed over his enemies, and is more splendid than gods or spirits.' The god required further a collarette and an amulet, two red, two green and two white bands; when all these had been presented to him the priest might then leave the chapel. Whilst he closed the door, he said four times these words: 'Come Thoth, thou who has freed the eye of Horus from his enemies - let no evil man or woman enter this temple. Ptah closes the door and Thoth makes it fast, closed and fastened with the bolt." These sequence of events, though at Abydos were no different at Karnak. Here, at Karnak, Erman states: "according to the Theban rite, for instance, as soon as he saw the image of the god he had to 'kiss the ground, throw himself on his face, throw himself entirely on his face, kiss the ground with his face turned downwards, offer incense,' and then greet the god with a short psalm."

Again, in a different spin, Blackman (1922: 778b) describes "the toilet." He writes: "The priest's first act after 'laying hands upon the god was apparently to divest the images of the clothing and ornaments in which it had been arrayed the previous day and to remove the pat of scented grease that had been placed on its forehead. Then, placing the image on a little heap of sand, which he had previously poured out for that purpose, and having fumigated it with incense, he proceeded to sprinkle it with water, first from four *nmst* and then from four *dsrt*-vessels, or else with water from one so-called vessel. He then censed the image again, cleansed its mouth with different kinds of natron, and yet again censed it. Having thus purified the image, he began to dress it, putting on the white head-cloth and arraying it in white, green, red, and dark red cloths in succession. After decking it with ornaments, he anointed it with unguents and then painted its eyelids with green and black cosmetic. Either immediately before or immediately after this application of unguent and cosmetics the priest invested the image with royal insignia - a diadem, *uas*-scepter, crook, and whip. The toilet episode was probably brought to a close with a final burning of incense."

Naturally, after his bath and dressing then came the feeding. Again, Erman (1894: 275) offers: "Not only had the priest to dress and serve his god, but he had also to feed him; food and dress had to be placed daily on the "Table of Offerings," and on festival days extra gifts were due." He continued (1894: 277) further: "If we leave on one side the less important items, such as honey, flowers, incense, etc., and consider simply the various meats, drinks, and loaves of bread placed on the tables of offerings, we shall find as follows: every day of the year the temple received about 3220 loaves of bread, 24 cakes, 144 jugs of beer, 32 geese, and several jars of wine. In addition to this revenue, which was doubtless chiefly used for the maintenance of the priests and the temple servants, special endowments were established for special days. There were extra offerings for the eight festivals which recurred every month. On the second, fourth, tenth, fifteenth, twenty-ninth, and thirtieth days of each month, 83 loaves, 15 jugs of beer, 6 birds, and 1 jar of wine were brought into the temple; while on the new moon and on the sixth day of the month the offerings amounted to 3656 loaves, 14 cakes, 34 jugs of beer, 1 ox, 16 birds, 23 jars of wine. Still more important were the offerings on great festival days, of which there was no lack in the ecclesiastical year of ancient Egypt. Thus, for instance, a feast of ten days was solemnized in the last decade of the month Choiakh to the Memphite god Ptah-Sokaris-Osiris; the temple of Medinet Habu took part in this festival."

Into the Egyptian Mind. Egyptian Art. Out there alone doing the boating thing.

Into the Egyptian Mind. Egyptian Art. Workers in different attitudes under supervision.

Into the Egyptian Mind. Double Temple of Horus and Sobek. Horus (Heru) makes a Presentation.

Into the Egyptian Mind. Double Temple of Horus and Sobek. Pharaoh approaches Horus (Heru) with Hathor at his rear.

Into the Egyptian Mind. Cairo Museum of Egyptian Antiquities. Miniature figures of kings with arms crossed holding scepter and flail.

Blackman (1921: 778-79), in a more explicit focusing on "The Presentation of food-and-drink offerings," writes. "The procedure observed at the presentation of food - and drink-offerings in the temple liturgy seems to have been practically identical with that observed at the corresponding part of the funerary liturgy. This is indicated among other things by the fact that in the temple reliefs depicting a divinity being fed there is sometimes inserted above the altar or offering-table, and between the divinity and the chief officiant, a so-called list of offerings identical to all intents and purposes with the lists occurring in the tomb reliefs and paintings. This is only to be expected, since every divinity was regarded for cult-purposes as an Osiris.

Before the offerings could be laid upon it, the table or altar had to be purified. The act of placing offerings on the altar or table, or else on mats spread upon the ground, was variously termed 'setting out the repast upon the altar,' 'setting down the divine offering,' 'setting down the repast.' When thus engaged the officiant either stood or knelt.

The god's meal having been laid before him, two closely connected ceremonies, the one being apparently in immediate succession, the one being variously designated 'presenting the repast,' 'presenting the divine offering,' 'performing the presentation of [or 'causing to be produced'] the divine offering,' and 'performing the presentation to, causing to be produced a great oblation for, NN,' and the other being termed 'bringing the god to his repast.'

At the former ceremony, the officiant extended his right arm and bent the hand upwards in the prescribed manner and pronounced the formula beginning with the words 'an offering which the king gives.' When the king is depicted performing this ceremony, he is often shown holding a mace and staff in his left hand. The recitation of the formula 'An offering which the king gives, etc.,' was closely associated with, and, on the analogy of the funerary liturgy, was doubtless preceded by, the burning of incense and the pouring out of a libation of water. At the ceremony of bringing the god to his repast the officiant recited a formula calling (*dwt*) upon the god to come to his bread, beer, roast flesh, etc."

The act of consecration, by which each item of food and drink was finally made over to the god, was termed 'stretching out the arm four times.' According to the temple reliefs, it was performed in the following manner. "The king, standing before what was to be offered stretched out over or towards it four time the so-called *hrp*-baton, which he grasped in his right hand; in his left hand, he held staff and mace, or else this hand hung at his side holding the symbols of life."

In the series of temple reliefs depicting the god being fed is one representing the king in the act of 'elevating' a 'tray of offerings' 'before the face' of the divinity. Does this scene represent one special episode in this part of the liturgy; i.e., after the pronouncement of 'An offering which the king gives, etc., was a specimen of the offering elevated in the presence of the cultus-image? More probably the scene is a summation of a series of elevations; for doubtless, as in the funerary liturgy; each particular item of food mentioned in the list of food - and drink-offerings was elevated at its presentation to the accompaniment of a special formula. In the funerary liturgy, according to Utterances 108-171 of the Pyramid Texts, each item was elevated four times."

In addition to the meal laid out before the image of the principal divinity in the sanctuary and before the images of the co-Templar divinities in the adjacent chambers, offerings were also laid, of course, upon the great altar in the forecourt. "If the procedure in the temple of the Aton at El-Amarna prevailed also in other Egyptian temples, it was upon this altar that the Pharaoh mostly laid his oblation."

Thus, with the incensing, dress and feeding done, the priest removed his footprints from the floor and closed the door. However, even though the god had returned to his sacred abode, the festivities continued since the great offerings had to be consumed. Notwithstanding, Blackman (1921: 779b) explained further: "The removal of the footprints" thus: "The final act of the chief officiant before leaving the sanctuary, shutting the doors, and affixing the clay seal to the bolts, was to obliterate all traces of his own and his assistant's footprints. This he did by sweeping the floor with a cloth or with a besom made of twigs of the *hidn*-plant. In the sanctuary of the temple of Derr, on either side of the door, is a representation of Rameses II holding a cloth for sweeping the floor in one hand and a vase (for sprinkling it?) in the other."

With the liturgy done we now turn to the structural dynamics of the temple. In the construction of the temple, as the holiest spot in the building, the Sanctuary is located well into the rear of the enclosure. It sits on the highest point, so much so, in the approach inwards, the floor rises and the roof declines giving it that elevated look. A Sacred Lake is situated in close proximity so that the priests could wash frequently to abide by that old adage, "Cleanliness is next to Godliness!" On special festivals, the barges of the temple gods are allowed to float on the lake.

The axis or center line, another important feature of the temple, represents the orientation of the temple. Sir Norman Locklear in *Dawn of Astronomy* (1894) argued, in the earliest times, temples were oriented towards some celestial body such as stars. This meant the temple and its axis may be north/south, east/west, or any variation therein according to a heavenly body's movement.

Karnak Temple is oriented east to west signifying the path of the Sun God, Ra or Amon-Ra, as he traveled across the sky, over his home. In Hathor's Temple at Dendera, the Chapel of Nuit contains an image depicting the sky goddess shining her rays on the temple. This then shows how important the god's home is and its contact with or relationship with the heavens. Mentuhotep II's temple across the Nile River at Deir el Bahari was also oriented east/west to face Karnak, home of Amon, or Amon-Ra, a manifestation of the Sun God. So too was Hatshepsut's temple built alongside some five hundred years later. Amenhotep III's Luxor Temple was also built facing Karnak. When Rameses II extended the temple by adding the "Ramessean Front," a Peristyle Court of columns, statues and altars, he re-directed the addition along a slightly different line to also face Karnak.

The axis line was thus very important for a number of reasons. Importantly it guided the construction of the structure in orientation to the dedicated divinity. Luxor temple is unique for it boasts three axes. Two axes are contained within the Amenhotep II part. However, of these two, one is an "invisible axis" beneath the floor and one rests above. Rameses II's "Ramessean Front" added a third axis in his Peristyle Court. Nevertheless, as in the case of Karnak temple, some kings or even individuals of distinction were permitted to place their statue there. While no such fixture would be placed in the Sanctuary, statues were placed in front of or in the Hypostyle Hall, a short distance away. In front of the Sanctuary at Karnak, statues of Amon and Mut, placed there by Tutankhamon and bearing his and his wife's images, represent the god and goddess and both face the center line or path of the Sun God. This is also the case of two surviving statues in the Hypostyle Hall. There are also two colossal statues of Rameses II in the Great Court just before the Second Pylon at Karnak. They too face the center line generally identified as the Processional Way. Even the seated colossal statues of Rameses II before the pylon and in the Court at Luxor also look out towards Karnak. All these statues face the east/west center line at Karnak. Thus, from a distance Karnak is the God's Sanctuary, but once there, it is the "Holy of Holies," that is the Sanctuary! Nonetheless, as the Karnak temple expanded a second axis on a north/south path, was opened linking the temple of Mut and Luxor, even farther south. Significantly, along this north/south axis, even distant in the "Ramessean Front" the statues do not face that extant center line but towards the principal east/west of the greater Karnak temple where the Sun God travels. Interesting, at Karnak beyond the Pylon in the Great Court, the Kiosk of Seti II, the Temple of Rameses III, the Sphinxes and all statues face the center line.

Into the Egyptian Mind. Karnak Temple of God Amon. Erik Monderson with "Karnak Me" beside the sacred Lake.

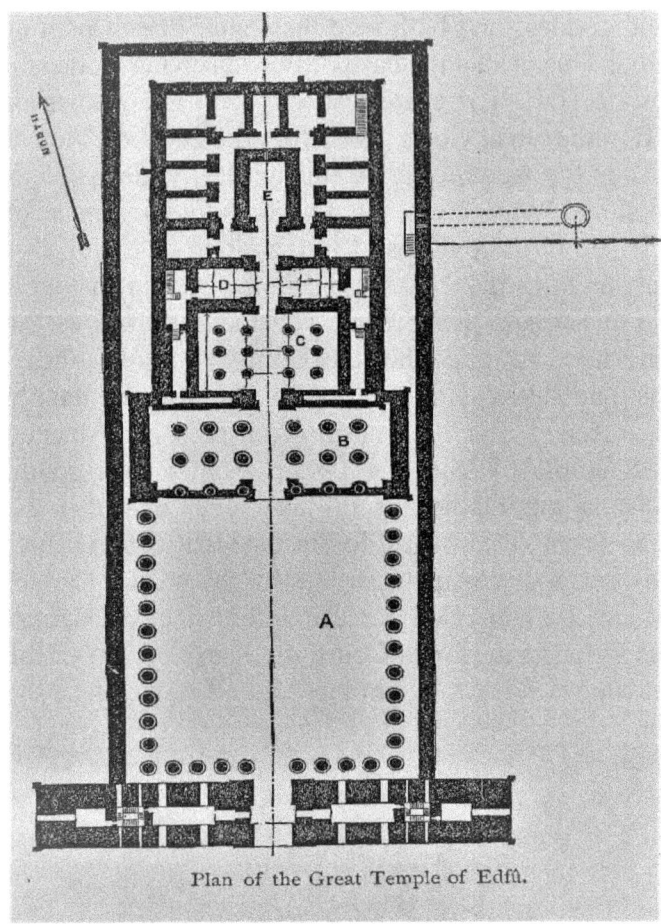
Plan of the Great Temple of Edfû.

Plan of the HORUS TEMPLE AT EDFU

A. First Court – Peristyle
B. First Hypostyle Hall
C. Second Hypostyle Hall – Festival Hall
D. First Vestibule – Hall of Offering
E. Sanctuary of Horus
F. Chapel of Min
G. Chamber of Linen
H. Chamber of the Throne of the God
I. Chamber of Osiris
J. Chamber of the West
K. Tomb of Osiris

L. Chamber of Horus (The Victory)
M. Chapel of Khonsu
N. Chapel of Hathor
O. Chapel of the Throne of Ra
P. Chapel of the Spread Wings
Q. Sun Court
R. Stairs to Roof
S. Library
T. Chamber of Unguents
U. Passage of Victory – Ambulatory

Into the Egyptian Mind. Egyptian Art. Notice how she caresses her man.

Into the Egyptian Mind. Egyptian Art. Individual hoisting a carrying device on his back.

Into the Egyptian Mind. Double Temple of Horus and Sobek. Goddesses lay hands on Pharaoh before Sobek and his consort.

Into the Egyptian Mind. Karnak Temple of God Amon. Erik and a friend beside the sacred Lake with the 9th Pylon in rear.

Into the Egyptian Mind. Cairo Museum of Egyptian Antiquities. On a stela, a goddess places the ankh to the nostrils of an individual holding a bow and arrow as a scorpion stands between them. Below a kneeling figure raises both empty hands in adoration before a "Table of Offerings."

However, this temple of Rameses III of the 20th Dynasty is unique for a number of reasons.

(1) This is a complete temple, built by a single king and located in the Great Court, perpendicular to the principal east/west axis. In essence, it is built to face the axis.

(2)   While parallel to the principal north/south axis on the extending of Karnak southward, Rameses' temple is on its own and a separate axis.

(3)   Rameses' temple boasts two standing statues before the entrance. It consists of an enclosure wall, a Peristyle Court with a dozen standing Osiride Figures, six on each side, before its Hypostyle Hall that entrances its Sanctuary.

(4)   Interesting still, the Osiride statues of this Court face this mini-temple's north/south axis line and not the east/west center line of the greater temple.

The pylon at Karnak was an important entranceway feature attached to the Enclosure Wall. This Enclosure Wall, sometimes more than twenty feet high and ten feet or more wide was designed to safeguard events within the temple from prying eyes and ears outside. It also served as a defense mechanism. Karnak itself has ten pylons. These are six on the east/west axis and four on the north/south axis.

Sanctuaries are either open or closed. Karnak is an open Sanctuary with two chambers. Facing east towards the Sanctuary, the left part is open and the right part is closed. Of course, it is in the reverse as the god looks out to admire and bless his creations! To the right the god resides in utter darkness. To the left, the chamber is open with an altar upon which the God is placed to receive the energizing first rays of the sun in the morning. Sometimes he is removed from his right-side utter darkness and placed on the left side altar to bathe in the early morning rays of his celestial manifestation. Then, having traveled across the sky the last rays of the sun are thrown back on the Sanctuary. The first six pylons are arranged so that decreasing amounts of sunlight shines back towards the Sanctuary. Today's First Pylon's aperture is larger than that of the succeeding five pylons towards the Sixth Pylon where the opening is very small and so the last light is regulated.

Thus, the importance of the Sanctuary is underscored for, in the ancient world, when conquerors invaded, the first thing they did was attack the temple and home of the god who was viewed as the nucleus of the society and temple. Equally, riches of gold, statues, utensils, were here and constituted a prize of seizure.

All this notwithstanding, while Karnak boasted an open Sanctuary, temples at Deir el Bahari, Luxor, Mut, Abu Simbel, and even the late temples of Edfu, Esneh, Kom Ombo, all have closed Sanctuaries. Interesting, all New Kingdom monarchs built a Mortuary Temple across the Nile River on the West Bank. There they were worshipped in life and when they became gods after death. These "Mansions of Millions of Years" all have closed Sanctuaries and generally face the path of their father the Sun god; in a way oriented towards Karnak across the river.

Into the Egyptian Mind. Egyptian Art. With perfumed cones on their heads sporting bandanas, this couple raises their hands in adoration.

Into the Egyptian Mind. Egyptian Art. Farmers doing their tasks of hoeing the soil and dropping seeds.

Into the Egyptian Mind. Double Temple of Horus and Sobek. Miniature version of Sobek wearing Sun-Disk and Uraeus on a platform with Heb to its rear.

Into the Egyptian Mind. Cairo Museum of Egyptian Antiquities. Under the Aten Disk (Sun) with hands as its extended rays, Akhenaten and his wife Nefertiti sit with their children in a family portrait.

9. THE QUINTESSENTIAL FACE
BY
Dr. Fred Monderson

Ask anyone, "What is the Quintessential Face of Ancient Egypt?" and any number of answers will be supplied. For example, the classic image of Egypt is the "Great Pyramid" among the Ghizeh Pyramid Group; but there are in excess of one hundred pyramids along the Nile in Egypt and Nubia. In some instances, it is the "Sphinx of Ghizeh" that is considered the image of Egypt because of its age and the thought it has seen so much down through the ages. However, while these colossal images have survived the destructive nature of time and man, there is much that has not survived such ravages of the ages. As such then, we can still search, among what has survived, to arrive at the best example of what can be considered the quintessential image of ancient Egypt! Yet, that image, that face is hiding in plain view and despite the destruction it is there for all to see!

The first two above examples represent excellence in Egyptian art and architecture, not simply because they withstood the challenges of time but attest to the best in art and architectural creativity and building practices. Still, despite all this, perhaps the best and most quintessential image is that of a face not given true recognition and this is important. Of course, the issue goes to the heart of the ethnicity question of 'Who were the ancient Egyptians?'

We could begin with Dr. Jacob Carruthers pointing out, in the fabrication of a "Caucasian Egypt," "Wilhelm Hegel took Africans out of Egypt and Egypt out of Africa!" In *The African Origin of Civilization: Myth or Reality* (1974), Cheikh Anta Diop eloquently presented Jean Jacques Champollion's explanation of his understanding of the ancient Egyptian conception of the status of the four races of man being Egyptian, African (Black, Negro, Nubian), Asian and Caucasian (white). He perceived this order as being from the highest to the lowest! Diop was in full agreement and laid particular emphasis on the great man's honesty. Diop further pointed out how Champollion's brother distorted the genius' intent in fostering a false view of the role of Caucasians in Egypt while seeking to deny that of the African, Nubian, Negro, Black, in this Nile River culture of North-east Africa.

And so, as European expansion in the Eighteenth Century and production in the Nineteenth Century manifested concurrent with the escalated Slave Trade that gave way to radical adventurism, creation of "spheres of interest" and ultimately the Berlin Congress' Partition of Africa, the image of Europeans was projected as larger than life as they conquered, trampled upon and dominated large segments of the globe. As such, despite Champollion's 1822 decipherment of the *Code of Hieroglyphs* and reports on the role of Africans in Egypt, the created Caucasian "straw man" reinforced the unfolding imperialism and resulting colonialist mentality reshaping human perception of reality. This enabled emerging scholarship on Egypt to begin falsely "flying the flag" in articulating "the party line" which is increasingly being proven today to be more a myth than anything.

The interesting observation is, despite the great Egyptologists' contributions to understanding the language and culture of ancient Egyptian history, we must recognize either their acquiescence in perpetuating the falsity or silence in avoiding or challenging this reality reshaping understanding of the true nature of Ancient Egypt. Nevertheless, in the contemporary ossified climate in which teachers, students and the general public have all been gorged on the falsity of a "Caucasian Egypt," arguments to support such have been advanced for a "Red Caucasian Egyptian;" "White Caucasian Egyptian;" even a "Black Caucasian Egyptian." Notwithstanding, at the 1974 **UNESCO** Symposium on "The Peopling of the Nile Valley" Dr. Cheikh Anta Diop and his associate Dr. Theophile Obenga towered over their Lilliputian competitors because they came enormously prepared with facts to support their arguments regarding the People of the Nile Valley and Ancient Egypt. In their scholarly presentations buttressed by classical and more constructive or objective assessments of the issue, they proved the notion of a "Caucasian ancient Egypt" is a false, a fake and sinking ship!

This position was arrived at in an eloquently articulated presentation by Dr. Diop as has also been argued in his *The African Origin of Civilization: Myth or Reality*. Thus,

(1)   Egypt was a Negro, African Civilization.

(2) Classical scholars from Herodotus onwards, all affirmed in many settings, the Egyptians were Black Africans.

3. Jean Jacques Champollion gives evidence of the African nature of Egyptian, not Caucasian, civilization.

4. Counts Volney and Denon as well as Godfrey Higgins of *Anacalypsis* fame, argued for an African, Negro Egypt.

5. Many French scholars as Amelineau, Mussellard, etc., affirmed such evidence.

6. Even English-speaking writers as Winwood Reade, Gerald Massey, Raymond Dart and Alfred Churchward came to the same conclusion.

7. Though Wortham in *The Genesis of British Egyptology* (1971) argued the Egyptians were Caucasians, based on Augustus Granville (1825) dissection of an Egyptian mummy, the modern scholar David O'Connor in contradiction affirmed "the Egyptians were not White!"

It is interesting, in an article in the *Gentleman's Magazine* of 1820, five years before Granville autopsy, the writer commented on a mummy donated to the Hunterian Museum and noted though from the Roman period; that "it [the mummy] did not look like we were accustomed to believe" Egyptian mummies looked like: and that the cadaver had all the attributes of Negro features. However, this reference is not in David Wortham's bibliography.

8. Even William Arnett in his *The Predynastic Origin of Egyptian Hieroglyphs*: *Evidence for the Development of Egyptian Hieroglyphics in Upper Egypt* (Washington, DC: University Press of America, 1982) argued, while Cheikh Anta Diop in *The African Origins of Civilization*: *Myth or Reality* **proved** the "Egyptians were not Caucasians" he,

however, did not prove they were Negroes because bones from the archeological evidence cannot prove such!

Into the Egyptian Mind. Egyptian Art. Sennutem and wife face the Gods in his tomb while, to the right, Anubis administers to the mummy, and above two Anubises stand guard beneath "Two Eyes of Horus."

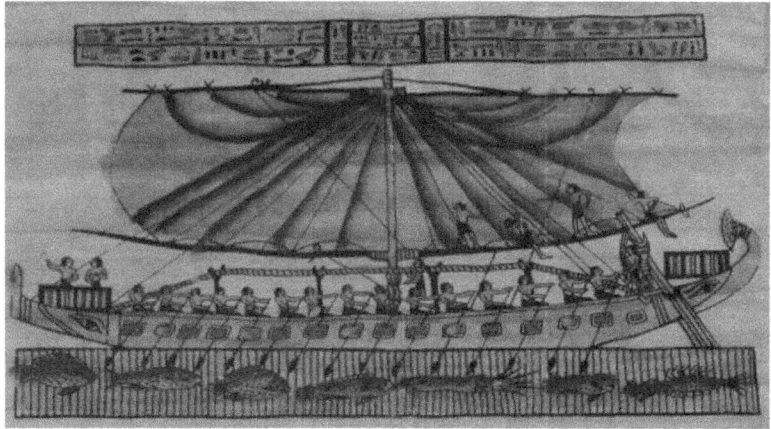

Into the Egyptian Mind. Egyptian Art. Ship in full sail with oarsmen and evidence of fish and other life.

Into the Egyptian Mind. Egyptian Art. Farm work of ploughing the soil using a cow to pull the wooden hoe.

Into the Egyptian Mind. Double Temple of Horus and Sobek. Upper entrance of the temple showing twin sun-disks with uraei, architrave and varied capitals, while at the bottom (left and right) lines of uraei stand over panels in the screened walls.

Into the Egyptian Mind. Cairo Museum of Egyptian Antiquities. Akhenaten and Nefertari and two children offer flowers in adoration of the Aten disk.

Into the Egyptian Mind. Karnak Temple of God Amon. Erik Monderson just east of the Akh Menu besides twin statues.

Into the Egyptian Mind. Double Temple of Horus and Sobek. A winged sun-disk with uraei above the cornice as a protective device.

Like Aristotle's confusing statement that "Ethiopians and Egyptians are cowards because they are black" Arnett's contention that Diop proving the Egyptians were not Caucasians and that they were not Negro "is another of those conundrums." However, to the contrary, Diop did provide a litany of evidence for his contention that the Egyptians were truly African. Nevertheless, what is unmistaken, he did prove any contention they were Caucasian is false and misleading.

This lengthy preamble brings me to the purpose for this article. Sometime ago it dawned upon me amidst some of the most sensitive locations on decorative temple inscriptions, a face, and African Face, is displayed prominently. So, I searched him out.

First, Ludwig Burckhardt indicated this fellow is a "Prince of his city!"

Given that much has been destroyed and defaced, particularly on statues and relief inscriptions on walls, "the face" is probably first survived and noticed on the "White Chapel" built by the 12th Dynasty king Usertsen (Senusert) I, now on display in Karnak temple's "Open Air Museum."

From then on, because it is "hidden in public" in inscriptions for all to see, the face appears everywhere begging the question "Why is it an African and not a European face we see here?" Or, more importantly, "Why is an African face, image, in the most sensitive positions in the ritual, in the litany of Egyptian religious and philosophic thought?" There can only be one answer. The African, Negro, Black image is essential to the culture of Ancient Egypt for which it gave birth!

Into the Egyptian Mind. Egyptian Art. A kneeling beauty.

Into the Egyptian Mind. Egyptian Art. The drudgery of work, or as they call it, "Pulling Bull."

Into the Egyptian Mind. Double Temple of Horus and Sobek. In the Court, remains of the columns of the Southern Colonnade with other columns further on. Notice the Photographer's tripod to the right.

Into the Egyptian Mind. Double Temple of Horus and Sobek. Another and better view and arrangement of the colonnade in the "Peristyle Court."

Into the Egyptian Mind. Cairo Museum of Egyptian Antiquities. Heads of various shapes and attitudes.

Into the Egyptian Mind. Cairo Museum of Egyptian Antiquities. A black basalt bust of a truly beautiful woman in all of its intricacies.

10. THE PYLON
By
Dr. Fred Monderson

The Pylon is an essential feature of an ancient Egyptian temple. It is a gateway providing access beyond the enclosure wall. Within the temple it is a dividing line. At the entrance connecting the Enclosure Wall, it is a protective device for the temple's occupants and happenings. It slopes upwards, generally high and broad with openings at the top to host flag-staves to fly various flags, that is, whether for the actual temple, the god, Nome or nation. Its massive nature along with the Enclosure wall is to keep out prying eyes and keep within sounds of activities conducted in the temple. The Enclosure Wall as an extension of the pylon is also a mechanism to ensure the God's and occupants' safety in times of unrest or invasion. It is generally believed; the two halves of the propylon represent the two goddesses, Isis and Nephthys, and serve as windows to the sun-god's access.

The 20th Dynasty Temple of Rameses III at Medinet Habu has an outer enclosure wall some have described as an Asiatic Migdol. At one time of unrest, the entire surrounding community sought refuge behind its walls and its massive nature withstood penetration from the threatening hostile forces. Thus, the Pylon and Enclosure Wall provided a fundamental purpose, safety for all within its walls. The importance of the God dictated the size of the temple with its Enclosure Wall and Pylon. However, though the Pylon is an entranceway into the temple, not every entrance into the temple is a Pylon. For instance, Karnak Temple is residence of Amon or Amon-Ra, principal God of the Theban Triad and most important deity of the New Kingdom. Very unique, this "architectural museum," Karnak, boasts 10 pylons and 6 entrances, but only 2, the First and Tenth Pylons are linked to entrances. Of the 10 Pylons, 6 are on the principal east/west Axis line that represents the path of the Sun god whose temple it really is. The other 4 Pylons are on a north/south axis linking this temple to 2 temples further south. These are dedicated to the God's wife Mut and his Southern Harem Luxor Temple. To the extreme east of the temple, the Gate of Nectanebo is not considered a Pylon. However, a similar gateway to the South is considered a Pylon, the Tenth.

The east gate was dedicated by Nectanebo of the 26th Dynasty and the northern gate led to the temple of Montu, the Theban war god. This Montu temple to the north and the temple of Mut to the south were self-contained structures related to the Theban god Amon-Ra resident at Karnak. Essentially then, the north temple belonged to the "Northern Group;" the Temple of Karnak comprised the "Central Group;" the Temple of Mut, the "Southern Group. Each had its own enclosure wall with pylons, smaller temples within but was contained within an even greater Binding Wall. Therefore, the Karnak Complex is nothing but a complex of pylons and walls replete with decoration.

Karnak Temple of Amon Ra is a quintessential temple; for one thing, there are temples within this temple. It has been described as "vegetative construction" because, in its present state, it took nearly 2000 years to build. Over that duration various monarchs vied with each other to please their father, the Son god, and so constructed a temple, added a pylon, portico, a kiosk or chapel, column, statues, altar with much wall space.

One of the contradictions in recording Egyptian history and even applied to this temple is the numbering of the first 6 pylons at Karnak. The New Kingdom monarch Thutmose I built the first 2 Pylons, today numbered four and five. His daughter Hatshepsut built the Seventh and his son Thutmose III built the Sixth and Eighth. Amenhotep III also of the 18th Dynasty built the Third Pylon. The Second Pylon is associated with Horemheb and Rameses I of the 19th Dynasty, while the Ethiopians, some say Saites, built the First or last Pylon which remains unfinished.

While Hatshepsut built the Seventh Pylon on the North/South Axis, Thutmose III followed her and built the Eighth Pylon on this axis. Horemhab not only assisted Rameses I to build the Second Pylon where he hid many bricks from the broken-up temple of Amenhotep IV, the Amarna Revolutionary, but he also built the Ninth and Tenth Pylons, enclosing the Temple to the South. Thus, in the ascent to the temple as the king would proceed along the Processional Way, by modern counting, the visitor encounters one through six on the east/west axis and seven through ten on the north/south axis.

Into the Egyptian Mind. Egyptian Art. Guests at a banquet while individual in leopard skin prepares to pour a libation before seated official. Notice children under the chairs.

Into the Egyptian Mind. Egyptian Art. Boating, fishing and catching birds in the marshes.

Into the Egyptian Mind. Double Temple of Horus and Sobek. View of Horus (Heru) aisle deep into the temple with lines of uraei left and center.

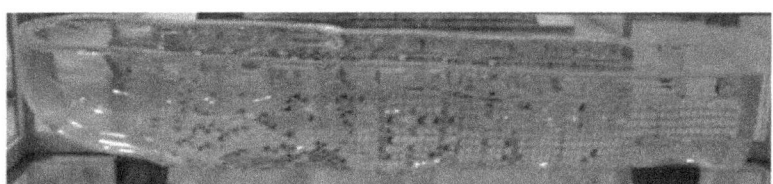

Into the Egyptian Mind. Cairo Museum of Egyptian Antiquities. A mummy case cover made of a clear material decorated with inlaid precious stones.

Into the Egyptian Mind. Double Temple of Horus and Sobek. Along the left side aisle of Horus (Heru's), into the deep recesses of the temple, past the colonnades, towards the Sanctuary.

Into the Egyptian Mind. Cairo Museum of Egyptian Antiquities. Seated statues of a couple as both wears the White Crown. He also wears the Nemes Headdress, a New Kingdom innovation.

The First Pylon remained unfinished and therefore undecorated. The others were decorated but have, for the most part, been destroyed.

Each Pylon had its specific name and peculiar characteristics, whether illustrations or inscriptions. It is generally preceded by or enclosed by a Court. Karnak in all its majesty, notwithstanding, the most celebrated is the Great Pylon at Luxor Temple. This is because, on its outer face, Rameses II engraved the characteristics of the famous Battle of Kadesh. Many scholars have studied its contents including, Breasted, Dumichen, and Gayet. The original part of the Luxor Temple built by Amenhotep III boasted 2 Pylons. Then Rameses II added his Peristyle Court or "Ramessean Front" and enclosed this with the Great Pylon. Then he placed 4 statues before it; two seated and six standing as well as two obelisks. One of the Obelisks remain in place while the other stands erected in the Place de La Concorde in Paris, France. There are two seated and several standing or striding statues, between the columns of the Peristyle Court. While Amenhotep III built this temple, on an earlier sacred foundation and Rameses II built his addition and even though several pharaohs as Rameses I, Seti I, Tutankhamon and Horemheb did repairs to it, it is still considered a single temple in all its majesty. Karnak, on the other hand, a compilation of temples added to and alongside the principal structure along the main axis, was by different pharaohs over an extended, 2000-year, period.

THUTMOSE I

"I come to thee, lord of gods; I do obeisance [before] thee, in return for this that [thou has put] the Black and the Red Land under (the dominion of) my daughter, the King of Upper and Lower Egypt, Makere (Hatshepsut), who lives forever, just as thou didst put (it) under (the dominion of) my majesty ...."

"Thou has given to me the kingdom of every land in the presence of the Two Lands, exalting my beauty while I was a youth ... [the Black Land] and the Red Land are under my dominion. I am satisfied with victories, thou hast placed every rebellious land under my sandals which thy serpent-diadem has bound, bearing their gifts; thou hast strengthened the fear [of me] .... Their limbs tremble, I have seized them in victory according to thy command; they are made my subjects; [they come to me] doing obeisance, and all countries with bowed head. Tribute ... the heart of my majesty is glad because of her ... [the petition] concerning my daughter Wosretkew, King of Upper and Lower Egypt, of whom thou hast desired, that she be associated with [thee] ... [that] thou mightiest assign this land to her grasp. Make her prosperous as King ... mayest thou [grant] for me the prayer of the first time, my petitions concerning [my] beloved (fem.) under her majesty (fem.)"

PYLON

PYLON III ERECTED BY Amenhotep III

Western Pylon - (Breasted, **Ancient Records of Egypt**, Vol II, 885)

"The bow-rope of the Southland [in it] and the stern-rope of the Northland, even his majesty revealed himself like Ptah, was skillful-minded like Him-South-of-His-Wall (Ptah), searching out excellent things for his father, Amon-Re, King of the Gods, making for him a very great pylon over against Amon. Its beautiful name which his majesty made was: 'Amon-Has-Received-His-Divine-Barque,' a place of rest for the lord of the gods at his 'Feast of the Valley' on the western voyage of Amon to behold the western gods, in order that he may endow his majesty with satisfying life."

PYLON III Breasted Vol. II No. 889

"King of Upper and Lower Egypt: Nibmare, Son of Re: Amenhotep (III), Ruler of Thebes, who is vigilant to seek that which is useful, the king, who has erected another monument for Amon, making for him a very great portal against Amon-Re, Lord of Thebes, wrought with gold throughout. The Divine Shadow, as a ram, is inlaid with real lazuli wrought with gold and many costly stones; there is no instance of doing the like. Its floor is adorned with silver; towers (*sbh.t*) are over against it. Stelae of lazuli are set up, one on each side. Its pylons reach heaven like four pillars of heaven; its flag staves shine more than the heavens, wrought with electrum. His majesty brought gold for it in the land of Karoy (*K'-r'-y*) on the first victorious campaign, slaying the wretched Kush."

No. 903

... Flourishing and established, which his son, Khammat (Amenhotep III) made for him. The number of these things is ... flourishing in every garden, sweet in fragrance of all flowers, ... a great [pylon] over against the temple, [its door] made high and wide, of cedar of ... it illuminates this whole land, its beauty seems like the horizon of heaven....

Into the Egyptian Mind. Double Temple of Horus and Sobek. Thoth (Tehuti, left) and Horus (Heru, right) wash or baptize Pharaoh before he can enter to officiate in the temple.

Into the Egyptian Mind. Karnak Temple of God Amon. Erik Monderson stands between the statues of Amon and his wife Mut, placed just before the sanctuary by Tutankhamon after the Restoration following the Amarna Revolution.

Into the Egyptian Mind. Egyptian Art. Beauty on display.

Into the Egyptian Mind. Egyptian Art. Walking the cows!

Into the Egyptian Mind. An old photograph showing the gods on display.

Into the Egyptian Mind. Karnak Temple of God Amon. Erik Monderson stands before Thutmose I's Obelisk.

Into the Egyptian Mind. Double Temple of Horus and Sobek. Adoration to Horus on a column.

Into the Egyptian Mind. Double Temple of Horus and Sobek. Offering a pyramid to the god. Notice both king and god are standing on the same plane.

Into the Egyptian Mind. Cairo Museum of Egyptian Antiquities. In "Blue" or "War Crown" pharaoh enters an incense pellet.

PYLON IV Breasted IV 889

"As a memorial of his rule in Thebes, Shabaka left the following record of a restoration by him on the fourth pylon of the Karnak temple" '[King Shabaka he made (it) as his monument for his father], Amon-Re, lord of Thebes, preside over Karnak, restoring the great and august gate (*sb*) : 'Amon-Re-is-mighty-in-Strength,' making for it a great overlay of fine gold, which the majesty of King Shabaka, living forever, brought from the victories, which his father, Amon, decreed to him; the great hall (hy.t) being overlaid with fine gold, the south column and the north column being wrought with gold, the two lower lips being of pure silver made ..."

Into the Egyptian Mind. Egyptian Art. Sennutem and wife in gesture of adoration before the Gods.

11. ARCHITECTURE OF ANCIENT EGYPT
By
Dr. Fred Monderson

The architecture of ancient Egypt was its great glory. Beginning with the simplest materials in the pre-dynastic age, the craft of building grew from use of windbreaks, and mud and daub to erecting shelters, to unfired or sun-dried then fired bricks and finally into the more durable material, stone, transported on the Nile from quarries sometimes from great distances. Papyrus stalks lined homes and roofs. Now, while the buildings of kings or commoners were constructed of wood and other perishable material, the temples of the gods were made of stone befitting a deity who represented everlastingness. The temple was said to be 'made of fine stone to stand for eternity.' Yet, this notwithstanding, while the dwellings of kings and commoners ascribed to social conventions, the temple of a god was shrouded in magical symbolism and mysteriousness. This reality not only symbolized the eternal nature of the deity, it also represented the notion of the coming into being of that divinity and the subsequent dynamic admonitions regarding the temple's security and the ritual and liturgy upon which his existence was daily practiced.

This metaphysical construct can be conceptualized if, in going back to earlier times one understands, as Yoyote explained: "A pyramid may perhaps be compared with the primordial rock where the sun was born, and the tunnels in the Valley of the Kings with the passages in the netherworld where the sun regenerated itself." The temple, on the other hand, was a primordial hill from which the god emerged from the waters of chaos at creation. The hypostyle hall with its massive columns was a "forest as at creation."

Notwithstanding, G. Baldwin Brown in "Origin of Monumental Architecture in Egypt" (1903: 219) compares these two forms of architecture and arrives at an interesting conclusion. This is explained as he, Brown argued, "For a building to merit the term 'monumental' something more is wanted than mere size. Loosely designed edifices of multitudinous parts may, like some of the early Renaissance palaces... cover a vast extent of ground, but their want of consistency and style offends that aesthetic sense." Nevertheless, "The principle that size is not the criterion of the monumental applies in ancient Egypt. The tourist is there chiefly impressed by two buildings, the Great Pyramid and the Temple of Karnak, and he generally accords to each the same tribute of awe and admiration. But, aesthetically speaking, the two buildings are very different, and it is by no means necessary to place Karnak, or any New Empire structure, on the same artistic level as the older work. The latter, as we shall see perfectly fulfils the conditions of the monumental. It possesses prodigious mass treated by the constructor with the most austere self-abnegation in the refusal of ornament and details, and is the very embodiment of style. The former, the Temple of the New Empire, possesses mass only in the mechanical sense of a vast number of cubic yards of stonework, but there is no such treatment of the mass as to convey the impression of the monumental. It has abundant detail and a superfluity of ornament, but the various parts have not passed through the crucible of the imagination to issue thence worked into a harmonious unity."

He goes on to comment, in the same critical method, "In the famous hypostyle halls of the Egyptian temples the supports are far too crowded, so that the effect of an interior is quite lost. They are immeasurably too numerous and too bulky for the work they have to do in supporting the roof, while the form of them suggests soft and yielding rather than rigid material. We may compare them with the Doric columns of the Greeks. In both cases the original support was of plant origin, in Greece the tree-trunk, in Egypt the tall and swaying stem of the papyrus, or even at times the pulpy and succulent stalk of the water-lily; but when the Greeks transferred the plant form to stone they petrified it, so that it bears a thoroughly lithic character. The Egyptians contended themselves with preserving the shape and character of the plant stem and only copying it on an immense scale of enlargement in stone. Hence the form and the material are out of accord, and the effect of the corpulent Egyptian column is that of a gigantic and overgrown baby. The most effective part of the Egyptian temple is after all the pylon, for this, though crude enough, is in its frontal aspect a sort of crystallization of the vertical cliffs bounding the Nile valley, that form the background of every Egyptian landscape. Similarly, the obelisk is the crystallization of the upright unwrought stone or menhir. As such the pylon and obelisk come more or less into line with the pyramid and mastaba of the Old Empire, which are crystallizations of the mound or tumulus, the most natural and most primitive funeral monument."

Equally too, since the temple was a fortress for the god-force dwelling within, it had to be equipped with all manner of protective, nurturing, decorative, ritualistic and service paraphernalia, first to invite the divine visit and to make the god feel comfortable at home, nurtured, satisfied, worshipped to provide resulting beneficence. As such then, temple architecture came to represent all that was good within the society and hence it was endowed with elaborate ritual, the buildings exhibiting lavish wealth fueled by the successes of imperial warrior pharaohs whose New Kingdom exploits bequeathed enormous riches to the society and temples.

In explaining this phenomenon of how religious beliefs influenced architectural developed intermixed with mortuary practice, James Henry Breasted in *The Dawn of Conscience* (New York: Charles Scribner's Sons, 1934: 57) offered in this respect, wherein the "Pyramid tomb was a solar symbol of the highest sacredness rising above the mortal remains of the king to greet the sun who's offspring the pharaoh was." These accomplishments rested upon Old Kingdom foundations, philosophical and practical, evolved from architectural experiment and representation dating back to the earliest times of philosophic and theological emergence as man's artistic and architectural consciousness formed and became crystallized.

Therefore, while the culture created and could boast of domestic, civil, religious and mortuary, even military structures, architecture thus came to embody not simply the quarried stone for the building endowed by pharaoh to house the deity, but much more. It possessed a magical, mystical, esoteric metaphysical significance that was brilliant in its conception and execution. In its multi-faceted dynamic religious and philosophic belief, temple architecture came to embody one or more Avenue of Sphinxes, gates, pylons, propylon, with flagstaves and flags, an axis or two, enclosure walls, forecourts and inner courts, doorways, portals, stelae, walls, doors, colonnades, columns, stone drums, capitals, architraves, pavements, floors, shrines, statues, kiosks, a sacred lake, obelisks, decorations, gardens, trees, halls, chambers, the Holy of Holies or Sanctuary, altars, Nilometers, sphinxes, standards, libation vases, incense-burners, as well as animals, viz., - cattle, geese, chickens, pigs, horses, donkeys, lions and the implements used by the priests, stewards, priestesses, their kitchens, vine cellars, crypts, bakers, confectioners, store houses, gold and other precious stones, treasury, a library, craftsmanship, gardens and even more as reflected in the wealth of the priesthood. To this we may add industrial crafts for temple decoration and trade that encouraged flourishing and competing schools of arts and crafts that produced jewelry and other statuary masterpieces.

No less significant, the architecture of Egypt was not simply symbolic but a living entity, for it fed upon and fed multitudes; or should we say, it fueled social systems engaged in the protection, nurturing, worshipping, and ritualizing of the deity on a daily and repetitious basis all to benefit the society. Ritual, magic and decoration went hand in hand. The

"Overseer of the Works," the ritualist and master mason and decorator, all cooperated to give life to their building projects. Maspero has pointed out, at Deir el Bahari, a ceremony was performed with white sand laid out, sacrificial animals killed and the blood let to run, tools bearing the name of the founder, perhaps in a cartouche, was placed there, offerings made, breaking of statues at the site of erection that were all part of blessing and providing protection for the temple embodied in the foundation that marked the beginning of construction that represented the guiding light seed-germ that came to bless the structure's contemplation and proved the spark of philosophic protection. Thus, the builder consecrated the living home of the deity. Equally, as in the decoration of tombs, magic was utilized and enabled to give life to what was represented in its spiritual, mystical and art and architectural wholesomeness.

7

Into the Egyptian Mind. Egyptian Art. Members of an orchestra at work.

Into the Egyptian Mind. Egyptian Art. Papyrus.
Outstretched wings of Horus (Heru) figure wearing Sun disk and grasping ankhs.

Into the Egyptian Mind. Karnak Temple of Amon. Hatshepsut's standing Obelisk, looking south towards the Ninth Pylon.

Into the Egyptian Mind. Double Temple of Horus and Sobek. In White Crown, Pharaoh offers a cow with horns and disk to Hathor.

Into the Egyptian Mind. Double Temple of Horus and Sobek. In White and Red Double Crown, pharaoh offers a plant.

Into the Egyptian Mind. Cairo Museum of Egyptian Antiquities. Unusual image of four, Hathor, Osiris (Ausar), Pharaoh and his consort.

Now, to understand the path through the social and politico-religious system just sketched we must trace the architecture of Egypt from the prehistoric beginnings through the early kingly burials at Abydos as well as the fortresses there at the beginning of the dynastic period; the Memphis "white wall;" seek to understand the emergence and significance of the dynamic Step-Pyramid of Zoser; follow the evolution of Snefru's "bent" and "red" pyramids, and the next stage in the "true pyramid" at Ghizeh, necessitating the expanded "pyramid complex" concept concurrent with the sun temples of the fifth dynasty; linked by the Middle Kingdom temple at Deir el Bahari transmitting to arrive at New Kingdom struggles and in imitating the early art forms and finally Graeco-Roman architecture trailblazing. Some scholars have argued the pyramid originated in Nubia in the form of silt and more anciently "natural wind shaped pyramids." Several of these latter can be seen in Abu Simbel area and along the road to and therefrom.

By the New Kingdom, principally three types of temples were in use, the god or worship temple such as at Karnak and Luxor; the mortuary temple or "Mansion of Millions of Years," as Hatshepsut's at Deir el Bahari, Rameses II's Ramesseum and Rameses III's Medinet Habu. The west bank, "land of the dead," was decorated with mortuary temples of all the New Kingdom pharaohs, with all facing the Nile but more particularly Karnak on the other side of the river. Unfortunately, the principal surviving examples today's tourists visit, Deir el Bahari, Ramesseum, Medinet Habu, Seti I's temple at Gurneh, and even the temple of Merenptah, that is now closed, are interesting ones that have withstood the ravages of time and the destructive hand of man. In addition, there was the processional temple, such as the Middle Kingdom "White Chapel" of Sesostris I, reassembled and now in the Karnak "Open Air Museum;" there also is Hatshepsut's "Red Chapel," both were profusely decorated representing masterpieces of art and architecture constructed by individual pharaohs. There were others such as kiosks, chapels, Speos, grottos, etc. This processional temple was designed as a resting place to house the god, manifest in his statue, when he left his main sanctuary generally in procession as part of a festival celebration. Surviving Kiosks to the Theban Triad as in the Great Court at Karnak and in the "Ramessean Front" at Luxor Temple are other forms of processional temples for worship of the deity outdoors and away from the sanctuary. However, the Kiosk at Abydos, dedicated to Isis, Horus and Seti I are within the temple and near the Sanctuary in the Osirian complex at Abydos as opposed to others in the "open air." Interesting however, while the Processional Temple is generally open at both ends, the Kiosk is closed at the back end.

Recognizing the timelessness of this great science, architecture in ancient Egypt has thus been of several forms.

However, while the society created domestic, civic, military, and religious and mortuary, this paper will focus primarily on religious, mortuary and tomb architecture. In "The Sources and Growth of Architecture in Egypt," *Journal of the Institute of British Architects* (Vol. III, Third Series, 1901: 340) W.M. Flinders Petrie, in his article proposed to show the transformative use of "new material to shape the evolution of building." He states: "The use of wrought materials, and the form which result from such; then the use of wrought wood; of stone, rough and lastly, the development of the pillars." In this, he further elaborates: "The unwrought materials, which were everywhere at hand in Egypt, were palm-ribs, papyrus, reeds, maize stalks, and mud, together with palm-fiber roughly twisted. At the present day a native sets up a row of maize stalks for a fence, binding them by weaving some stalks in and out in opposite directions along the upper part. Needing a closer lien for shelter, he places the stalks touching, and lashes on some cross stalks by means of palm string. This stage is seen in an enclosure in a scene on the great mace head of Narmer (4800 B.C.) To keep out the wind this wall of stalks is plastered with mud, and so a hut is formed." Even more: "A striking sight of the beginnings may be seen any day in a nomad settlement on the desert edge. Side by side stand (1) a black goat-hair Arab tent, long and low, open always on the leeward side; (2) a tent fenced along part of the open side with a row of maize stalks; (3) a tent fenced all round with maize; (4) a tent in a maize fence mud-plastered; (5) a dwarf wall of brick round the fence; (6) a high brick enclosure with a tent inside to roof it, the tent ropes stretching out through the wall; lastly, a roof is put on the wall, and the tent has disappeared."

From the earliest period, architects began using the simplest materials such as leaves and branches for windbreaks; they added Nile mud, using leaves to create a strengthened mud and daub to build the earliest structures. Then they graduated to brick, un-burnt and burnt types. Later, as quarrying and river transportation methods advanced, they began using stone transported from great distances to place of erection. The first stone use has been dated to the tomb of King Den of the First Dynasty and King Khasekhemwy of the Second Dynasty. This material, nevertheless, came into very general use by the Third and Fourth Dynasties.

Now for the types of structures they erected, like all builders, the Egyptian was concerned with the location of his building and how it blended with the environment. In every age, as the nature of building construction changed in its evolution, different challenges faced the architect. The massive pyramid required a different foundation, special orientation than a New Kingdom temple or tomb. Nonetheless, whatever the type of building, the design was harmonized with the landscape. For the pyramids, the area was cleared to the bare rock and the dimensions set out before building commenced. Despite what may have been said in absence of surviving places of construction, the geometrical and mathematical precision produced and the architect's mathematical and spiritual professionalism argued against any such claims. After all, especially in Egypt, any argument from the absence of artifactual evidence is not a credible one. That is, however, to the exclusion of the false notions that the North influenced the South and that Asiatics or Caucasians ruled Egypt. That is before the Greeks, Romans, Persians and Assyrians, as well as the Hyksos.

This notwithstanding, there were other issues regarding these constructions. Henri Stirlin's edited *Architecture of the World: Egypt* (1963: 131) has indicated: "The Egyptian builders considered the problems of organization of work, economy and speedy construction to be of greater importance than questions of mechanics and technical progress, the use of tough materials or more effective tools, or a quest for a more lasting, lighter form of structure." However, while such problems were refined through the ages and with continued practice, no significant changes in construction techniques were made until the XXVth Ethiopian and XXVIth Saite Dynasties and the later Graeco-Roman Periods. These changes included "arch vaults, and improved methods of pre-planning foundations and stone-work." Equally, foundations varied according to size of building, wall or even obelisk and according to soil in which they were erected. Sterling (1963:137) again comments: "The general principle was to dig a trench a little wider than the wall to be supported and to line the bottom of it with a thin covering of sand which was stopped from running away by little side walls made of brick. The real foundations were laid in these trenches: stones for the main walls, bricks for the less weighty features. The empty spaces were afterwards filled up with sand." To give an example, to construct walls at Medinet Habu 34 ½ feet wide and 60 feet high, they dug 10 feet deep in the clay's soil. Equally too, at Karnak some foundations as the 8th Pylon, built on clay, were 10 feet deep. On the other hand, at Deir el Bahari in the firmer soil beside the mountain, some walls had a foundation of 20 inches.

Into the Egyptian Mind. Egyptian Art. In his shrine, Osiris (Ausar) holding Crook and Flagellum being watched over by "Two Eyes of Horus."

Into the Egyptian Mind. Karnak Temple of God Amon. Erik Monderson stands in the Great Court before Rameses and Binta Anta's statue on the East/West Axis line the sun God travels daily.

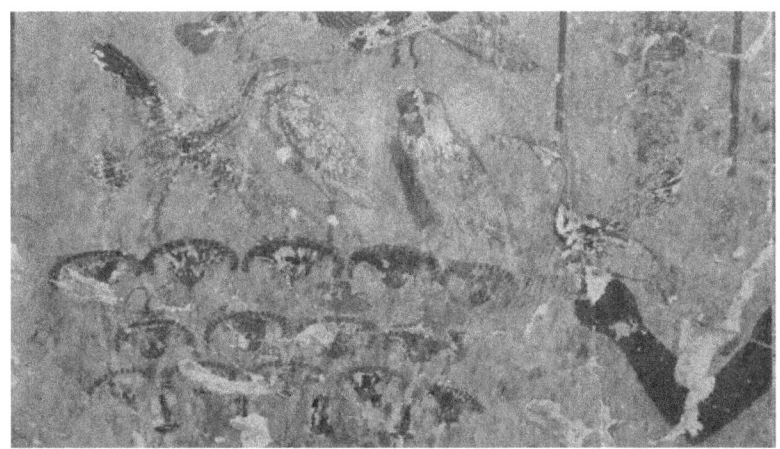

Into the Egyptian Mind. Egyptian Art. Hunting birds among the flowery marshes.

Into the Egyptian Mind. Double Temple of Horus and Sobek. View of the Court with some of its columns before the Temple's entrance.

Into the Egyptian Mind. Cairo Museum of Egyptian Antiquities. Colossal size pharaoh grasps Egypt's enemies by the hair and about to deliver the "death blow."

Still, they never misused materials. Again, and further, Sterling (1963:137) demonstrates: "The actual foundations were often composed of seemingly inadequate materials: small stones, sometimes set edgeways below a first course of large blocks placed lengthways or various elements taken from earlier ruined monuments. Huge squared blocks and drums or half drums of columns were set side by side, caving between them empty spaces unfilled by mortar. This motley collection of masonry frequently shifted ground causing fractures in the lower courses." Significantly, however: "From the twenty-fifth dynasty onwards, and especially during the Ptolemaic period, greater care was taken with regard to foundations: the great temples of later periods were built on proper platforms formed of several layers - up to nine or ten- of well-dressed slabs."

In addition, transportation of stone from distant quarries took place primarily during the Inundation period when the river was high and thus, water made the stone more manageable and these sites became more easily accessible. Flat bottom boats were generally used to transport stone, especially obelisks. Deir el Bahari temple has a surviving illustration showing two obelisks being transported on these boats drawn by smaller tugs. Lighting also played an important part in their buildings and the clerestory window became an important feature in the New Kingdom temples at Karnak, the Ramesseum and Medinet Habu. The *Akh Menu*, Festival Temple of Thutmose III at Karnak seems to have the earliest form of the clerestory. The Processional Colonnade with the nave higher than the flanking areas allowed light into the temple's space. Equally too, roofing and ceilings varied according to temple. Some temples had windows, others did not. Of course, mathematics was an essential part of their construction methods and techniques. Egyptian geometry as applied to architecture was key. They used primarily the simplest materials, which perished early; the palaces of kings were made of simple materials, primarily clay and mud-brick. However, the temples of the gods and burial places of the kings were reinforced with stone. Civil projects, to the extent that they were in pivotal places such as gateways, wharves for landing craft, public buildings, etc., all utilized stone.

Military fortifications were built to garrison forces particularly in foreign lands. Nevertheless, some of the oldest such ruins are found at Abydos and date to the beginning of dynastic times. Here too, in this city, some of the earliest and evolving tombs were built for pharaohs of the First and Second

Dynasties. These earliest and budding architecture experiments certainly reflected high quality craftsmanship whose efforts withstood time and the elements and left evidence of their existence and techniques of building.

Religious architecture included pyramids, mastabas, temples and later rock-cut tombs. There were god or worship temples, mortuary temples, kiosks or processional temples as well as chapels. Alexander M. Badawy in the article "Egypt" in the *Dictionary of Art* (Edited by Bernard S. Myers, London, 1969: 329) discusses the cult temple and states, the god or cult temple and the king or mortuary temple were the most important religious structures. Of the two, the god or worship temple was still more important. He writes: "The temple is the 'castle of the god' who was embodied in the small cult statue of gilded wood set within a naos (shrine). The representative temple as exemplified by those built by Rameses II and Rameses III at Karnak is laid out symmetrically along a longitudinal axis. Its tripartite plan (the three transverse parts) consist of (1) a pylon (monumental two-towered gateway); (2) a courtyard, usually having columned porticoes on one or more sides; (3) a hypostyle columned hall with a central nave, bordered by tall columns and flanked by two lower aisles; and (4) at the rear a Sanctuary with a naos and several subsidiary chambers. The levels of the floors of the various parts are higher towards the rear while their ceilings become correspondingly lower. This gradual reduction in the height of the apartments, combined with a reduction in the lighting, tends to impress the worshipper with the hallowed mystery of the Sanctuary." Even further, Badawy (1969: 329) continued: "All the walls and columns are usually of stone, carved and painted with scenes and hieroglyphs related to the ritual performed in the various rooms. The layout conforms to the system of harmonic design that controls the growth of the structure by accretion whereby the later courtyards and pylons added in front are larger than the earlier ones according to set proportions."

More mortuary than religious, were tombs to house the bodies of kings, queens, nobles and artisans. It gained the name "eternal house" because, according to belief, the deceased hoped to spend eternity in this structure. As early as predynastic times, poor people were generally buried in sand pits where the dry soil accomplished natural mummification quickly and easily and this phenomenon helped reinforce the concept of immortality and led to the development of the practice of mummification as a practical aspiration of the dead. However, on the other hand, during the Old Kingdom the pyramid combined mortuary and religious structures. The Mastaba was more mortuary and social as their decoration depicted the owner's status and sometimes daily activities. Some of these were very elaborate with large rooms with lots of decorative scenes proving great usefulness to scholars. As an important architectural construction, Mentuhotep II's temple and pyramid at Deir el Bahari is the best example of surviving Middle Kingdom temple architecture that provided transitional building techniques and decorations from the Old to the New Kingdom. This structure comprised a pyramid on a raised platform reached by ramps and a Peristyle Court and Hypostyle Hall with many pillars and columns as well as burial spaces dug into the mountain-side.

In "The Beginning of the Egyptian Style of Architecture" Professor Sir Martin Conway in *Journal of the Royal Institute of British Architects* (Vol. X, Third Series, London: 1908: 373) explained essentially, the Egyptian style of architecture "appears to have arisen about the time of the Fourth Dynasty, and to have rapidly developed during the Fifth. The elements of which it was composed, or from which it was derived, existed earlier, but not till the Fourth Dynasty were they definitely compounded into an architectural style applicable, and thenceforth continually applied, to buildings in stone."

There is "evidence that the palaces and doubtless most other buildings of the early dynastic period were built of crude brick, and that the architecture of that time was an architecture of mud and reeds, not of stone, still less of wood. The characteristic feature of exteriors was the rectangular niche - niches within niches. The supports were bundles of reeds, or clustered bundles, plastered over with mud and modeled above, for capital, into the likeness of buds or flowers. It would be easy to construct imaginary restorations of such buildings, but they would not carry us further that our bare statements carry us."

Even further, Sir Conway continued: "Thus far we have obtained no information whatever as to the origin of Egyptian stone-architecture. Of the beginnings of stone building Professor Petrie has already told us the important facts. He has actually revealed a granite pavement in a chamber of the tomb of the First Dynasty king, Den, but so far was that from being an architectural feature that it was actually covered over by a layer of mud-bricks. He has further brought to light the first known chamber built of stone, which is that of King Khasekhemui, of the Second Dynasty…. All this, however, is mere building, not architecture. The same statement is true of the Step-Pyramid of Sakkara, which dates from the Third Dynasty. That is built of stone, but if it ever possessed any architectural features no trace of them has survived. It contained indeed a chamber covered with glazed tiles, a decoration no doubt adopted from contemporary crude-brick buildings, which, like similar buildings in Chaldea, would naturally be so decorated by people who knew the art of glazing; but such flat wall decoration, without division of areas of any special adaptation to the chamber, is no more an architectural feature than so much wall-paper would be. The decoration can, of course, be made an architectural feature - as it was in Persia - but the tile decoration of the third pyramid chamber is not in any sense architectural. The lesson of the Meydum pyramid and its adjacent chapel is the same. The masonry is better; the pyramid approaches without actually reaching the developed type, but it is in no sense a work of architecture."

Into the Egyptian Mind. Egyptian Art. With Thoth (Tehuti) on point, Ra-Horakhty and team sails the heavenly ocean in Sennutem's tomb.

Into the Egyptian Mind. Egyptian Art. A Procession carrying all manner of objects and articles.

Into the Egyptian Mind. Double Temple of Horus and Sobek. Classic view of the Court's Colonnade before Kom Ombo's entrance and its towering architectural beauty.

Into the Egyptian Mind. Double Temple of Horus and Sobek. Another view of columns from the court with the temple's monumental and majestic architecture in background.

Into the Egyptian Mind. Cairo Museum of Egyptian Antiquities. Another foursome of Hathor as Isis (Auset), Osiris Ausar), the King and Ra-Horakhty.

In the evolution of mortuary architecture, internment changed from the Old Kingdom pyramids and mastabas for kings and queens to tombs for high officials and nobles so that by the New Kingdom, for security reasons, Thutmose I chose to move from the burial on the plains to begin hidden burials in the Valley of the Kings at Thebes. By the middle of the 20th Century of our era, a total of some 65 tombs had been found hidden in this select burial place. Today that number has increased and the number of Noble tombs have also increased. "The dig continues." On the principle of the kings' internment, there was a separate burial place for other important individuals as named the Valley of the Queens, Valley of the Nobles, even Valley of the Artisans. A great deal of the nation's cultural history is preserved in the painting of these tombs, though much has been desecrated and destroyed. The last is most important, for, though the artisans built for kings, queens and nobles, they used the same techniques and decoration practices to embellish their final resting places. More important, however; imperial military adventure and the allure of captured wealth not only attracted many to the call but the reward was great and much of the riches went into temple construction and decoration.

Every part, feature, utility or location of a type of architecture had its own peculiarity, whether the foundation, floor, ceiling, walls, decoration, quarrying, transportation, each had its own character. However, some have argued, as the society progressed from the Old through the Middle and New Kingdom, as the society in general and the rich in particular got wealthier, temple size increased. Thus, as temple size increased, so Pylon size also increased outward from the "Holy of Holies" while in the reversed configuration, pylon apertures decreased allowing less light to shine backwards as the sun passed overhead at day's end. Flower gardens and vines for grapes as well as other plant forms were cultivated in some temples or just beyond their walls enhancing the beauty of the architectural layout while these gardens produced flowers to supply the daily temple ritual. There were other gardens that provided the victuals of consumption for the priestly class and workers assigned to the temple.

Now let us briefly sketch the history or evolution of building practice from the earliest times. Let us begin with Memphis.

1. Memphis - The White Wall - At unification, Narmer or Menes diverted the Nile River near Memphis, creating a plain of dry land where he founded his administrative and capital city. He built around it an enclosure wall, painted it and hence the title "white wall." This was the first significant civic construction in ancient Egypt. However, it is interesting, Professor Sir Martin Conway in "The Beginning of Egyptian Style of Architecture" in *Journal of the Royal Institute of British Architects*, (November 1902-October 1903) Vol X, Third Series, does not consider this an architectural construction. In fact, he says regarding the topic, "That style appears to have arisen about the time of the Fourth Dynasty, and to have rapidly developed during the Fifth. The elements from which it was composed or from which it was derived, existed earlier but not till the Fourth Dynasty were they definitely compounded into the architectural style applicable, and thenceforth continually applied, to building in stone." Nevertheless, in this new capital, he built a temple and established the worship of the God Ptah. While this "white wall" structure has generally disappeared, it noticeably remains in literature and mythology.

In these architectural beginnings, on the other hand, Badawy (1969: 329) notes: "The embryo of the cult temple can be recognized in the tripartite plan of the archaic shrine of Khentiamentiu at Abydos. The strictly symmetrical plan of the cult temple is projected at right angles to the river bank. Its walls and columns are covered with religious scenes in low relief, stuccoed and painted to offer visual instruction to the illiterate masses. Cult temples grew by accretion, attained extensive proportions at Thebes. Most of the structures were built on top of earlier remains or on hallowed ground."

2. Step-Pyramid of Zoser - By constructing the Step-Pyramid for the Third Dynasty King Zoser at Sakkara, Imhotep stands large at the beginning of Egyptian building/architectural history, and for that matter in world architectural construction history. This structure was the first significant building utilizing stone as well as containing a number of new features including the colonnade, standing and engaged columns, the enclosure wall, false entrances, cobra friezes, glazed tiles, multi-story construction, great court, "dummy buildings," a temple for worship, a court for running the Heb Sed race; etc. Much of this, still stands 4,600 years later which says something about this earliest form of construction/building techniques as well as its builder. Of course, Imhotep was more than an architect, he is considered the world's first multi-genius. He was an astronomer, mathematician, priest, medical doctor, administrator as Grand Vizier and poet. He has been credited with the saying of the ages: "Eat, drink and be merry, for tomorrow you die." His tomb, thought to be in the Sakkara area, has never been found. For his medical prowess, he was later deified as a god of medicine and praised by the Greeks in their Hippocratic Oath, as the personage Aesculapius. This Step-Pyramid of which there were several represented the earliest multi-tiered structure in history and while other large buildings have disappeared these buildings remain; some revealed others are still buried.

3. Snefru's Bent-Pyramid - Snefru, the last king of the Third Dynasty or first king of the Fourth Dynasty built two pyramids and experimented with the true pyramid. The two pyramids are the "Red Pyramid" and the "Bent Pyramid." The "Bent Pyramid" "collapsed," or so it is thought, but it set the stage for his son Khufu in the Fourth Dynasty to accomplish the "true pyramid at Ghizeh." Rather than ending the Third Dynasty, Snefru also gets credit for beginning the Fourth Dynasty, though in fact the Third and Fourth Dynasties should be fused. It needs be pointed out; it's believed the idea of the pyramids finds its prototype in the natural pyramids carved in the sand-blown highlands of which some are seen at Abu Simbel temple in the south of Egypt. There are also pyramids in Nubia that are as numerous as those in Egypt.

4. The True Pyramid at Ghizeh - The "True Pyramid" is the highlight of the "Pyramid Age" of the Old Kingdom. Built to harness the unemployed population at inundation time, as a final resting place for the pharaoh and to awe his contemporaries, it is a masterpiece of architectural accomplishment, building techniques of great exactness and administrative organization and manpower utilization. Having withstood time, it continues to awe, inspire and amaze attesting to the ingenuity of ancient African architectural creativity. Some have argued it still radiates philosophic, mystical, spiritual, theosophical, epistemological and metaphysical power. It is truly an amazing work of architectural construction. The author of *A Search in Secret Egypt*, Dr. Paul Brunton, a mystic, spent the night in the Great Pyramid and reported on the spirit and manifestations of "ancient Egyptians still resident in the monument" who admonished him to live life as if to "bring good into the world" as Maulana Karenga, creator of Kwanza, has himself admonished!

5. The Pyramid Complex - When we see the Pyramids, say of Ghizeh, in pictures or from a distance, the only things visible are three triangles against the horizon and the inner workings and juxtapositioning of the architectural layout is seldom considered. The Pyramid was housed in a complex, a sort of mortuary village. The Pyramid Complex consists of an Enclosure Wall surrounding the entire complex; a Causeway or walkway into the structure; and a Valley Temple at the river's edge, where the deceased is first introduced into the surroundings of his final resting place. Moving further along this path evident is a Sacrificial Altar and Sun Temple with the king's massive Pyramid in the center of the complex. Off to the right there would be Magazines for storage, a Great Court and equally a Heb-Sed Festival Pavilion and an open area Court for the king to run the Heb-Sed race of rejuvenation, at first celebrated after 30 years of rule. There would be "Dummy Buildings" symbolizing the north and south kingdoms of his unified nation. Before the pyramid there would be Solar Boat Pits with buried boats to ferry him across the sky. There were five pits found near Khufu's Great Pyramid. Off to one side would be smaller pyramids for his female relatives and on the other, Mastaba Tombs for officials and nobles, who wished to be buried in the shadow of their god-kings in his pyramid. These courtiers' Mastaba tombs were laid out with block and street-like precision in sectional cemeteries. Oftentimes there was a God temple within the complex. Beyond the wall were found workmen's dwellings from where they lived, were injured, treated medically, even died and were buried as they labored on those national or civic projects.

6.   The Sun Temples of the Fifth Dynasty - The Sun Temples of the Fifth Dynasty sought to emphasize and incorporate a temple to the god as well as one to the king. They generally had an outdoor altar where ceremonies and worship of the Sun God took place. Many innovative and associated features characterized this form of building.

7.   Middle Kingdom - Mentuhotep II's Middle Kingdom temple at Deir el Bahari, the most complete and oldest surviving temple at Thebes, represented a transitional form from Old Kingdom to New Kingdom building practice. It encompassed all the elements of a pyramid on a raised platform with ramp, colonnades, a Peristyle Court of pillars and Hypostyle Hall with columns, and shrines or Sanctuary up against the face of the mountain. There were also burials of princesses discovered here though no one knows what happened to the king's body. A valley temple lay at the river's edge and this led to the temple. Along this pathway lay a tree-lined Avenue of Sphinxes. In the temple, a statue of the king was found wearing the Heb Sed Festival gear, the Red Crown of the north and his skin painted black; or as W. Stephenson Smith in *The Art and Architecture of Ancient Egypt* has indicated, Mentuhotep had "black flesh!"

Into the Egyptian Mind. Egyptian Art. A priest pours a libation and incenses the monarch Amenhotep I and his mother Aahmes-Nefertari (painted black) before the image of "Hathor coming out of the Mountains."

Into the Egyptian Mind. Karnak Temple of God Amon. Erik Monderson stands in the Plaza before the temple's Great Pylon.

Into the Egyptian Mind. Double Temple of Horus and Sobek. On a column, offering Double Uraei wearing Red and White Crown.

Into the Egyptian Mind. Double Temple of Horus and Sobek. Pouring libations from two vessels before Osiris (Ausar) in White Crown.

Into the Egyptian Mind. Cairo Museum of Egyptian Antiquities. Image of youngster with hand to his mouth before the great bird.

The assumption is that there was also a similar statue of him wearing the white crown and in the same attitude as the other. Some have written there were actually six statues. It would certainly be something if the other statues were found with Mentuhotep wearing the White Crown and painted red! This would certainly put to rest the notion of the "Red Egyptian." This falsity was, however, unlikely since he was **Black!**

8.   New Kingdom - The New Kingdom broke with the past and made a separate temple to worship the god and one for the dead king, called his "Mansion of Millions of Years." They also separated the location of their siting. The burial place was also separated from the mortuary temple. While not absolutely so, worship temples were located on the east bank, "land of the living" and mortuary temples on the west bank, "land of the dead." One scholar believed Seti I conceived of the Hypostyle Hall at Karnak as a Mortuary Temple in a Worship Temple. Then there was a later period worship temple to Hathor on the west bank near Deir el Medina. Of course, there was a third temple called processional, in which the god rested when traveling away from his main sanctuary. Karnak and Luxor, the Temple of Mut and that of the War god Montu, were typical worship temples of the New Kingdom and situated on the east bank of the Nile, "land of the living," at Thebes. Practically every New Kingdom monarch built a mortuary temple to his deified self. The west bank at Thebes was host to many. Not many have survived the ravages of time and man. The principal ones visited today are at Deir el Bahari, Ramesseum and Medinet Habu. The temple of Seti I at Gurneh has survived, been repaired and is now open to visitors.

The Mortuary Temple of Seti I at Abydos dedicated to Osiris, the god of the dead, is only one of many built here at the home of the judge of the underworld. While the ritual drama of the African Judgment took place in the Hall of the Double Maati at Heliopolis, here at Abydos the ritual of the death and resurrection of the god took place, where the head of Osiris was buried. Here, the God stood at the Stairway to heaven. The main structure of this temple has survived well and has colonnades in the lower and upper Hypostyle Halls and very good colored illustrations. Some scholars have argued that Seti's temple is not simply to the God Osiris but to Seti's predecessor kings whose burial sites are not far off in the desert.

Petrie found 10 successive levels of temples at Abydos dating back to the beginning of dynastic rule, where evidence of some important kings was discovered, including that of Khufu, builder of the Great Pyramid, who worshipped here. Perhaps there were others of perishable materials of the Prehistoric Period but none remain, only those beginning at the start of the dynastic period. Nonetheless, this temple of Seti has the best surviving illustrations in all of Egypt to this date. Though dedicated to Osiris as his principal temple with requisite inner chapels, as indicated, his head was buried at Abydos. The temple was actually a monument to the archaic kings, Dynasty One and Two, who were buried in the desert to which the central axis of the Holy Site points.

9. Late Period - Architectural constructions continued into the Late Period particularly during the XXVth Ethiopian and the XXVIth Saite Dynasties. All the principal worship sites received new construction, reconstructions, repairs, endowments, embellishments, additions, etc., during this period, attesting to Ethiopian and Saite concern and respect for the gods and culture. Building practices received new impetus especially in the XXVth Dynasty under the Ethiopians where foundations were more firmly laid out to support walls particularly. The XXVIth Dynasty also experienced some of the construction techniques upgrade.

10. Greek and Roman Periods - Building of Egyptian temples never finished during the Greek and Roman periods. In fact, these foreign conquerors added a significant feature of inundating the temples with inscriptions that helped retain much of the ancient ritual representing examples of art and liturgy of even earlier times. New features also entered the illustrations in terms of how individuals were represented. At Kom Ombo we see Cleopatra's breast exposed. The Mammisi or "birth house," where the god was born was added as a new feature during Roman times. The temple of Horus at Edfu has supplied a tremendous amount of detail regarding the early ritual practice and decoration. Each temple had one and some had two Nilometers to measure the significant volume of the river at Inundation time.

Esna, Edfu, Kom Ombo, Dendera, Philae and Kalabsha are all surviving temples of the Greek and Roman Period built by Egyptian architects along ancient specifications under foreign over-lordship. Kalabsha, however, was first built during the New Kingdom. Much of surviving temples are built on even earlier sacred foundations taking them back to the earliest times. Certainly, Edfu and Dendera are among these. Clearly there were changes in these Graeco-Roman temples from the much older ones. However, even with changes they did continue the tradition of building and ritual and worship with basically the same elements and practices.

Now let me wind down and sketch the architectural layout of the temple.

First and foremost, after conceiving and laying out the dimensions of the temple, a foundation ceremony had to be conducted to mark the conception and commencement of building of every temple. Sir Gaston Maspero discovered evidence of such a foundation ceremony at Deir el Bahari and another at Luxor Temple. Thus, this ceremony is a given for all major temples whether worship or mortuary. Second, every temple was given a name in its original conception. That is, not the modern name given through location or in association with the builder but given by the founder as to why he or she built it. This also applies to major projects, as for example, the reason Hatshepsut gave for erecting her obelisks at Karnak.

Thus, Karnak, Deir el Bahari, Luxor, Ramesseum, Medinet Habu, all had names and statements regarding the reason for building these temples.

In this respect, Alexander Badawy in *A History of Egyptian Architecture: The Empire* (1968: 154-55) wrote: "The temple is usually the 'castle of god (Egyptian *hwt-netjer*), but the desert temples and the rock-cut temples are often called 'strongholds.' The mortuary temples on the western bank of Thebes or the cult temples at Soleb (Nubia) or at Redesiya provide examples. This conception is emphasized in the text itself (Soleb) '… making for him an excellent fortress, surrounded with a great wall, whose battlements shine more than the heavens, like the great obelisks ….' The enclosure of the mortuary temple of Thutmose IV at Thebes is the 'Fortress-of-Menkheperura' and it is actually filled with captives from Kharu and Nubia. Rock temples are explicitly said to be hewn out of the cliff: Rameses II, the great specialist in rock temples, says about his small temple for his wife at Abu Simbel: '… he made (it) as his monument for the Great King's-Wife, Nefertari, beloved of Mut …, a house hewn in the mountain of Nubia, of fine, white and enduring sandstone, as an eternal work.' His father Seti I had described the work on the rock temple at Redesiya: "… that there should be made by digging in this mountain, this temple, where is Amon…."

This naming of things as in the personality of the individual was very important to the ancient Egyptian. Among the nine parts of the soul, the name was considered very important for without it the individual did not exist. In similar fashion, as Badawy states: "The temple is usually 'like heaven, beautiful, pure, glorious and excellent.' Its pylons 'reach heaven and the flagstaffs the stars of heaven.' They are 'of real cedar, wrought with Asiatic copper, their tips of electrum, approaching heaven.' 'Two mighty obelisks of red granite, with pyramidions of electrum, rise at the double façade of the temple.' The columns 'wrought with electrum,' usually in stone, but originally in wood. The shrines 'of sandstone, ebony or enduring granite, lined inside with electrum, or gold of the best of the hills, are placed upon a base of alabaster from Hat nub.' Doors are 'of new cedar, of the best Terraces (Lebanon), mounted in real black copper and wrought with inlaid figures in electrum or gold, representing the great name or the shadow (of the god),' 'like the luminous mountain-horizon of heaven.' The 'shadow' of the god is the representation of the deity on the copper lining of the door as if coming out of his temple. Pavements are covered with silver or gold, and offering tables are of silver, gold, bronze, or Asiatic copper. One boasts of using the 'beautiful stone of Ayan, fine white sandstone, every splendid costly stone,' or finally 'that never was done the like since the beginning.' In the description of restoration work the building is said to have been in ruin. The walls were rebuilt in stone and brick, ruined doors replaced by new ones, and wooden columns by stone ones."

Into the Egyptian Mind. Egyptian Art. Clasping hands, Anubis (Anpu) escorts the deceased.

Into the Egyptian Mind. Egyptian Art. A sailing boat with numerous oarsmen plying the Nile.

Into the Egyptian Mind. Egyptian Art. Horus (Heru) in flight with his eye watching, from the **Tomb of Pashedu**.

Into the Egyptian Mind. Karnak Temple of God Amon. Erik Monderson before the twin-statue of Rameses II and Amon-Ra at the entrance to the Hypostyle Hall.

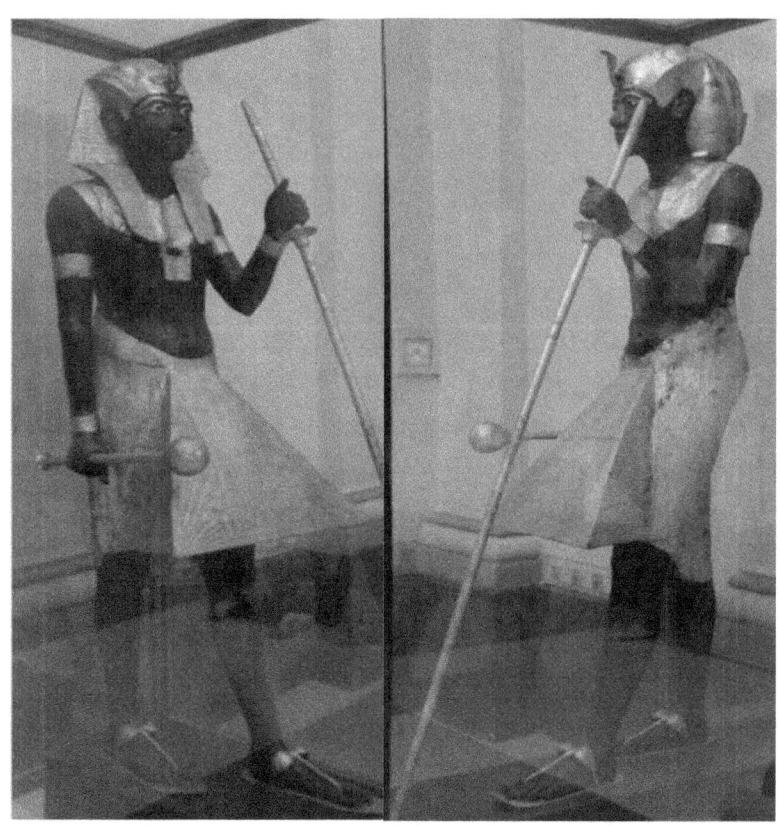

Into the Egyptian Mind. Cairo Museum of Egyptian Antiquities. The now famous two statues of Tutankhamon, depicting the king's actual color, Black.

Even further, Badawy (1968: 155-156) states: "The names of the temples can express a quality of the building or of its lord: 'Shining-in-Truth (Temple of Amenhotep III at Soleb), 'Most-Splendid' (Temple of Thutmose III at Deir el Bahari, 'Splendor-of-the-West' (small temple at Medinet Habu). 'Splendid-is-the-Seat-of-Amun' (small temple at Medinet Habu), 'Heat-which-is-in-Aten' (Sanctuary of Harakhte at Karnak built by Akhenaten). Sometimes the name clearly expresses ownership: 'House-of-Nib-mare' (temple of Amenhotep III at Memphis), 'Temple-of-the-Son-of-Seti-Meryamon-in-the-House-of-Amon (northern part of the

Hypostyle Hall at Karnak, by Seti I), 'House-of-Usermare-Meriamon-in-the-House-of-Re' (temple of Rameses II at Derr), 'Temple-of-Ramses-Meriamon-in-the-House-of-Amon' (temple of Ramses II at Luxor.) Or the name may designate the deity to whom it is dedicated: 'House-of-Amon-on-the-West-of-Thebes (mortuary temple of Amenhotep III), 'Temple-of-the-Spirit-of-Seti-Merneptah-in-the-House-of-Ptah,' 'Temple-of-the-Spirit-of-Seti-Merneptah-in-the-House-of-Amon-on-the-West-of-Thebes' (mortuary temple of Seti I). Parts of the temple such as shrines and doors are also named: 'Amon-has-received-his-divine-barque' (pylon in the mortuary temple of Amenhotep III), Amon-Mighty-in-Wealth" (door of Thutmose at Karnak), 'Mernmare-is-rich-in-food' (door of Rameses II in the temple of Seti at Abydos), 'Usermare'-is-splendid-in-strength' (door in the temple of Rameses II at Serre), 'His-Great-Seat-is-like-the-Horizon-of-Heaven' (Holy of Holies of Thutmose III)."

Equally significant, when the pharaoh visited the temple there was much fanfare on the part of officials, priests, musicians, etc. The typical scene is a visit to Karnak temple, where the king's barge docked. From the Quay at the riverside the pharaoh disembarked upon arrival. In some cases, a canal connected the river to the temple's entrance. In others, an Avenue of Sphinxes led to the First Pylon. At Karnak, for example, there were two small obelisks erected before the temple's entrance pylon, while at Luxor there were two seated statues, two regular sized obelisks and four standing statues in front of the pylon. Of the four, statues at Luxor, one standing statue remains while parts of at least two lie reassembled nearby. While Luxor's Eastern Obelisk is still in place on its pedestal, only the pedestal of the Western Obelisk remains as the shaft was given to King Louis Philippe of France in 1836. Given the temple is built out from the sanctuary, nevertheless, as one enters both the Luxor and Karnak temples the earliest parts are to the rear and the later parts are first encountered.

At Karnak, the visitor encounters an Avenue of Cori-sphinxes; sphinxes with rams' heads fronted by a miniature figure of the king between the paws; all stand on an elevated pedestal, leading to the temple's Pylon entrance. The Pylon is a massive gateway with a tower that was attached to the enclosure wall and designed to block out the temple's doings from the prying eyes and ears of outsiders. This enclosure wall also created the fortress that protected the god and his retinue within. On the Pylon were flagstaves flying flags of the temple's divinity, the national god, the Nome and nation. Some pylons are decorated while others are not, depending on whether it was finished or not. Even though it took nearly 2000 years to construct, Karnak temple remained unfinished. Some have held, called away to fight wars of national significance, the pylon was unfinished and not decorated. However, resting on the inner face of the Southern half of the pylon, a mud ramp remains indicating how the heights were scaled. The two westernmost columns of the Southern Colonnade behind the Southern row of sphinxes, and beside the mud ramp remain unfinished, indicate how such columns were erected as segmented square drums and then pounded into the rounded columns as compromising the other columns in this colonnade. At the eastern end of the same southern colonnade abutting the western wall of Rameses III's perpendicular situated temple, the last column is also unfinished.

Beyond the Pylon is a Great Court where most noble visitors came and this was as far as they got. In such a Court, there were shrines, kiosks, an altar or two, sphinxes, statues, colonnades, and much more. At Karnak, a smaller temple of Rameses III was built in the south-west corner of the Great Court on a north-south Axis. At the north-west end of the Court there is a Kiosk to the Theban Triad, Amon, Mut and Khonsu, built by Seti II of the Nineteenth Dynasty. The remaining intact columns of Taharka, of which various numbers of ten, twelve and fourteen are given, represents this king's Kiosk in this Court. A portico led to the Second Pylon which served as the western face of the Hypostyle Hall. Also, at Karnak, a temple that took 2000 years to build, a Processional Colonnade centered the great Hypostyle Hall. Beyond this, another, the Third Pylon led to another Open Court. Beyond this a Fourth Pylon, actually the first such structure built at Karnak. Between the Fourth and Fifth Pylons were obelisks erected by Thutmose I. Between the Fifth and Sixth Pylons, Hatshepsut erected two other obelisks. Before the smaller Sixth Pylon Thutmose III erected two pillars highlighting the emblematic papyrus and lotus symbols of the Upper and Lower Kingdoms under unification.

Thutmose III and his father Thutmose I built the Sixth Pylon before the Sanctuary. With warrior pharaohs, Thutmose I and III, each placed a separate line of Osiride statues and papyrus bundle columns along this path towards the Sanctuary in an area called the Wadjit.

Unlike any other New Kingdom sanctuaries, the one at Karnak was open at the east and west ends so the sun could shine through on rising and setting. There was a Sacred Lake nearby so priests could wash themselves before officiating and the god's barge could sail here on festive occasions.

In the south-west portion of this second axis bearing a number of courts and pylons, seventh through tenth, the Temple of Khonsu, the third member of the Theban Triad stood. Its entrance Pylon was fronted by a number of recumbent lion sphinxes. An Avenue of Sphinxes led out from there. From the tenth pylon, an Avenue of Sphinxes led three miles linking Karnak and Luxor temples.

Perpendicular to the original east-west axis, four other pylons were added on a second axis linking the original temple with the god's wife Mut's temple to the south. The gods were generally shown as a family of husband, wife and son. Interestingly, on the east-west axis, the statues face the center of the axis on the Processional Way, while on the north-south axis they face north along the path of this second axis. In this national temple, called "the palaces" there were a total of some 22 temples of differing sizes to various gods and goddesses who were also worshipped at Karnak, besides the Theban Triad of Amon; Mut, his wife; and Khonsu, their son. Given that the Theban Ennead at Karnak comprised only 15 members, not every divinity had a temple there and some may have more than one or a monarch may build more than one. That is the case with Rameses III who built this miniature temple in the Great Court, the temple of Khonsu further and another in the temple of Mut. Beside Khonsu's temple, Rameses III built a temple to Osiris.

East of the main Sanctuary is a Court of the Middle Kingdom with an altar and remains of pillars. Beyond this Thutmose III built his Festival Temple, the *Akh Menu*. Rameses II came by later and finished the hypostyle hall begun by his grandfather Rameses I and his father Seti I. Then he erected a "Girdle Wall" to enclose the original temple on the east-west axis running along the Sanctuary, the Middle Kingdom Court, and the *Akh Menu*. Beyond the *Akh Menu* chapel to worship Thutmose III was decorated with the "Botanical Garden" and in the vicinity is where priests were trained in temple ritual. Beyond this Rameses II built the "Temple of the Open Ear. Further on, Taharka erected a second Kiosk before the Eastern Gate. Just to the north lay the treasury and further on the Temple of Ptah with the Goddess Sekhmet still in situ.

There are six gates or entrances to Karnak, though today as in ancient times, the most important one was on the west nearest the river.

Columns play an important role in the religious architecture of ancient Egypt. In the colonnade represented in the Hypostyle Hall (a roofed enclosure with columns) and an open court, a Peristyle, with columns on one or more sides generally with a roofed walkway between the columns and the wall, generally called a roofed ambulatory. The columns can be decorated or plain. Beside the Sacred Lake, just nor of where Hatshepsut's broken obelisk lies, Taharka erected another of his building at Karnak. Flinders Petrie in "The Source and Growth of Architecture in Egypt" in *Journal of the Royal Institute of British Architects*, London, Vol. VIII, Third Series (1901: 349) summarizes the evolution of the Column in the following: "Columns of maize stalks bound together are commonly used in huts at present; and stalks bound and plastered with mud are the usual supports of the heavy swinging shaduf used for raising water. Hence, we can understand one early form of column which shows the splaying base needful to prevent crushing, and the spread top, bound round for some way down."

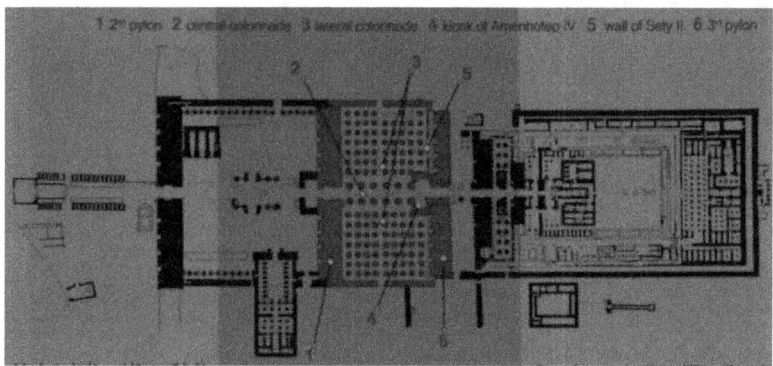

Into the Egyptian Mind. Karnak Temple of God Amon. Plan of the Temple with the area of the Hypostyle Hall emphasized.

Into the Egyptian Mind. Egyptian Art. Kneeling before a sumptuous "Table of Offerings."

Into the Egyptian Mind. Egyptian Art. Wailing women stand before colorful wooden coffins at a place of burial.

Into the Egyptian Mind. Double Temple of Horus and Sobek. View of the upper reaches of the temple's columns and capitals.

Into the Egyptian Mind. A very friendly Chef at the Sonesta Hotel, Luxor, Egypt.

Into the Egyptian Mind. Egyptian Art. Out there sailing with the Missus and child is an exhilarating experience, beyond imagination.

Into the Egyptian Mind. Cairo Museum of Egyptian Antiquities. One of King Tutankhamon's more famous personal bedroom pieces.

"The wooden column appears as an octagon in the models found in the First Dynasty, and in the actual pieces which I have found in the Twelfth Dynasty, and the copies of such in stone at Beni Hasan."

"The fluted column is found copied in ivory in the First Dynasty tombs, and is well figured as a hieroglyph in the Fourth Dynasty."

"The most peculiar form of column is that derived from the tent-pole, as figured in the hieroglyphs. This was the origin of the strange form known as the inverted bell capital in the Eighteenth Dynasty at Karnak."

"The lotus column has been discussed by M. Foucart, whose work I had the pleasure of bringing to your notice recently

(*Journal of Royal Institute of British Architects*, Vol. IV, 3rd Series, p. 361) The earliest example known is of the Fifth Dynasty (about 3600 B.C.), and shows the stems of papyrus bound together, and then decorated with lotus flowers and buds. The later examples of the Twelfth Dynasty, of the Eighteenth Dynasty, and of the Nineteenth and Twentieth Dynasties, show a series of lamentable decadence. Each age in Egypt had its special excellence. In the Eighteenth Dynasty, a delicate and freely flowing ornamental treatment; in the Fifth Dynasty, the finest figure sculpture; in the Fourth Dynasty, the grandest constructions; and in the First Dynasty the most lavish use of hard stones for hand objects and table furniture. Diorite, porphyry, and such materials were cut in thin and beautiful forms with a familiarity which was never known in later times. But every branch of art, when once it had fully grown, decayed rapidly, and the later work in every respect cannot bear comparison with the older triumphs."

Into the Egyptian Mind. Egyptian Art. Papyrus.
Youth in leopard skin attire incenses Osiris (Ausar) while Isis (Auset) as Hathor holds a Sistrum and meant.

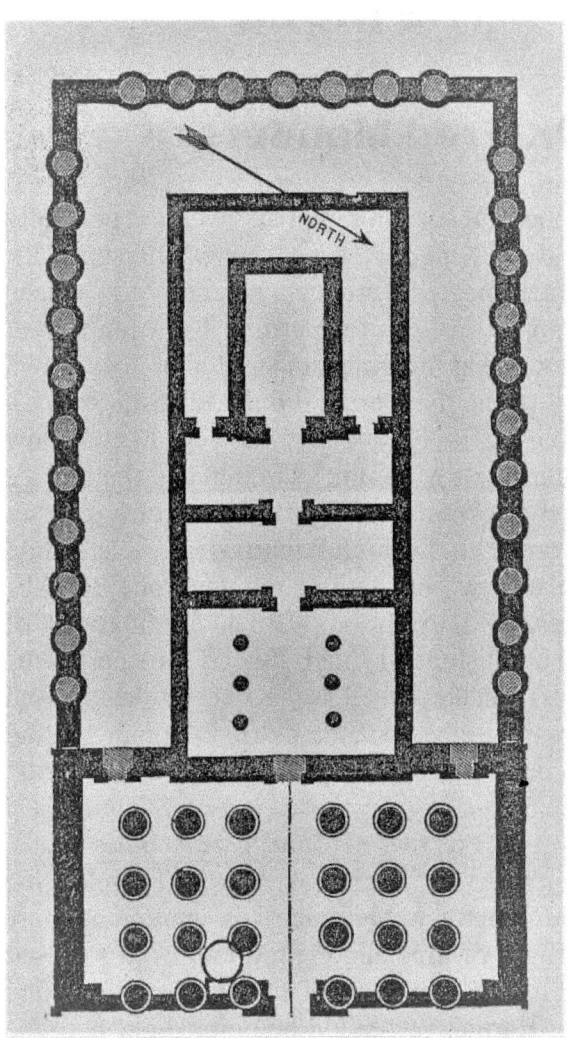

Esneh Temple of Khnum. 24-columns in the pronaos, while others in the plan are buried in the surrounding earth covered area.

12. THE KIOSK
By
Dr. Fred Monderson

The Kiosk is a wonderful ancient Egyptian invention generally confined to the New Kingdom based on extant survivals. Despite the oftentimes negativity attached to Queen Hatshepsut's persona, she was responsible for a number of cultural innovations that became standard practices down through dynastic times. Not only did Hatshepsut build a Sanctuary at Karnak, subsequently destroyed and now restored in the "Open Air Museum;" she initiated the voyage of the God to visit the West Bank mortuary temples of other monarchs; her temple at Deir el Bahari is an outstanding architectural and artistic innovation; the four obelisks she erected at Thebes, two extant at Karnak are marvels of engineering accomplishments; and the art in apartments beside the extant Sanctuary as well as that decorating the "Red Chapel" attest to the highest standards of Egyptian art and architectural excellence very early in the Eighteenth Dynasty.

Consistent with her creative *Avante garde* innovations, Hatshepsut constructed a Kiosk at Luxor Temple that encouraged the building of that temple. This creation not only withstood the ravages of time and expropriations of man but served as model for the Kiosk at Seti I's temple at Abydos and that of Seti II's at Karnak. It should be pointed out both the Luxor and Karnak Kiosks are outdoor structures while that at Abydos is indoors!

Nonetheless, these Kiosks are all dedicated to the Theban Triad of Amon, Mut and their son Khonsu. Thus, in approach to the Kiosk, Amon's shrine sits in the center, that of Mut to his right, the viewer's left, and that of Khonsu to his left, the viewer's right.

There is an interesting development relating to the three surviving Theban Triad Kiosks. The Kiosk is essentially a closed processional temple designed as a way-station chapel for the God en-route to and from the temple's principal sanctuary. The images of the two outdoor structures at Karnak and Luxor are badly damaged though that of Abydos remains remarkable well-preserved, because it is indoors.

Ancient Egyptian architects favored sites previously considered sacred when choosing to erect a temple. Evidence indicates the Luxor site was in use during the Middle Kingdom, perhaps earlier. A small temple was built there by Aahmes at the establishment of the New Kingdom. Following Amenhotep I and Thutmose I, Hatshepsut's architect Senmut constructed the Kiosk in what would have been a courtyard of the existing temple and dedicated it to the Theban Triad of Amon, Mut and Khonsu.

Again, this construction has a unique history, not because it was built by Hatshepsut but also because of its existence and location. First, in aftermath of Hatshepsut's reign following her demise, Thutmose III's adherents attacked evidence of the Queen's reign by smashing her Deir el Bahari temple with its numerous statues of the Queen. Next the king enclosed her two principal obelisks at Karnak to prohibit their viewing by members of the priesthood and members of the public privileged to enter this far into the temple. In addition, wherever the Queen's name appeared in Cartouche, efforts were made to erase or substitute if for another. Fortunately, several of the Queen's cartouches escaped the hands of destruction. Further, Thutmose III exchanged the Queen's name for his, confusing later admirers as to who actually built the Kiosk. This was also done at her Deir el Bahari temple. Thutmose also expropriate the Queen's Eighth Pylon on the North-South Axis at Karnak Temple.

At Luxor, the Kiosk was in place when Amenhotep III tore down the ancient temple and built his classic structures on the outskirts of Hatshepsut's construction. It is interesting that these two temples, large and small, are not only enclosed sanctuaries but face each other. That is, while the resident God at Amenhotep's temple, Amon, looks out to face his principal Sanctuary at Karnak; in Hatshepsut's Kiosk, the Theban Triad may have been predisposed to look toward the earlier structure whose principal location was long sacralized.

Given the Kiosk was dedicated to Amon and his family, during the Amarna Revolution, when Akhenaten advised his adherents to erase the God's name, the Kiosk suffered at their hands. In the next or 19th Century, Rameses II expanded Amenhotep III's original temple by adding the "Ramessean Front" with statues and altars and erected the Great Pylon enclosing the Kiosk in its Peristyle Court. Rameses also added his name to the Kiosk as he has done in so many of his other expropriations. While discusses here in general, the Kiosk of Trajan at Philae needs to be included in any discussion on this form of Egyptian Architecture. Granted, it is late in its construction but it naturally falls within the same category in Egyptian Architecture.

Into the Egyptian Mind. Luxor Temple of Amenhotep III and Rameses II. The Nile Gods Uniting the Land" at the base of Rameses II's seated statue before the Great Pylon.

Into the Egyptian Mind. Egyptian Art. Affixing the perfumed cone on the head at a banquet.

Into the Egyptian Mind. Luxor Temple of Amenhotep III and Rameses II. Statues coming out from between the columns in the Court of Rameses II, called the "Ramessean Front."

Into the Egyptian Mind. Luxor Temple of Amenhotep III and Rameses II. Again, statues coming out from between the columns in the Court of Rameses II, the "Ramessean Front."

Into the Egyptian Mind. Cairo Museum of Egyptian Antiquities. A decorated stone coffin with lid.

Rameses' father Seti I, built the Abydos Temple dedicated to Osiris. In fact, seven divinities were worshipped in this temple. These are the Triad of the Osiris Cycle comprising Osiris, Isis and Horus; the three great gods of the Empire, Ra-Horakhty, Amon-Ra and Ptah; and lastly the deified Seti I was included in this temple of several gods! Each divinity had his own entrance into the temple but Rameses closed six and retained the central entrance.

The Kiosk of Seti's temple is the best preserved of the three surviving kiosks. It contains some of the most beautiful artistic renderings of any place in the Nile Valley. Juxtaposed to the inner sanctuary of Osiris worship, the Kiosk is not only well-preserved in its beautiful entirety but it certainly played a crucial role in the ritual of Osiris worship.

Thus, this form of religious architecture proved to be multi-functional in its intent. First, dedicated to a triad, it contained separate compartments for each. The illustrations and images addressed the specific divinity. In the case of Luxor and Karnak, these were Amon-Ra, the sun god; his wife, Mut the Earth Goddess; and their son, Khonsu, the Moon God. At Abydos it was Osiris, God of Resurrection and the Dead; his wife, Isis; and their son, Horus the Younger. However, with the Kiosks, at Karnak and Luxor it was Amon, Mut and Khonsu. At Abydos, it was Osiris, Isis and Seti I.

The Luxor and Karnak Kiosks built in the outer or Great Court, "Ramessean Front," enabled the general public to be part of the celebrations conducted there. While some of Egyptian society's upper crust could enter the Great Court and beyond the Great Pylon, many common folks did not even enjoy this privilege. However, this is probably as far as these could go into the temple with few exceptions. At Abydos, neither noble nor commoner could enter the temple's inner Osiris Sanctum to be part of the ritual celebration.

It is interesting, being situated in the outer court at Luxor and Karnak affording public access also proved a detriment to the Kiosk. When enemies invaded and sacked the city and temple, this Great Court structures including the Kiosk was the first casualty resulting from hatred directed toward the nation and its god. Conversely, the Abydos Kiosk, located deep within the temple did not suffer the same fate.

It can therefore be said; the Kiosk was part to the regular temple ritual though dedicated to respective divinities. It did differ in some respects housing a separate bark for each divinity. Even more, Hatshepsut's Kiosk's outer face differs from that of Seti II's. It is fronted by four papyrus bundle columns and a decorated architrave showing the king dancing before the enthroned God. Seti's temple face is undecorated and plain. The Abydos shrine is decorated at the entrance and within.

Into the Egyptian Mind. Egyptian Art. Ptah (left), Khepre (center) and another god, defaced.

Into the Egyptian Mind. Egyptian Art. Hathor (left), Thoth (Tehuti, center) and Osiris (Ausar, right).

13. SALVATION
By
Dr. Fred Monderson

For the ancient Egyptian the concept of salvation dynamics which, for the most part, occurred in the Afterlife was dependent on a life lived and guided by preparation and the precepts of Ma'at, viz., right, justice, righteousness, enabling the deceased to stand confidently at the Judgment and to be rewarded with positive reception in the realm of the blessed. This promise of heavenly bliss was considered a desired honor. There, in that glorious hereafter, Salvation meant being able to work, play, relax, enjoy being among the gods and doing all the things that brought happiness on earth, in the actual participation in festivals and feasts, even after he was gone, still being conducted on earth. Now, this existence among the blessed dead for whom Salvation was an earned and just reward, meant the deceased had acquired near god-like status, could do the things the gods did and would probably enjoy such status for all eternity similar to that of "the imperishable stars."

This conception is explained further by Aylward Blackman in an article entitled "Salvation" in Hasting's *Encyclopedia of Religion and Ethics* Vol. 11 (1920) where, accordingly: "The blessed dead we are told dwell in heaven as the intimate companion of the sun-god. It is said of him, 'who has reached (the existence yonder) without wrongdoing' that 'he shall continue yonder like a god, stepping forward boldly like the Lords of Eternity." The Bai of such a one 'shall abide beside the Lord of All, his name shall be good in the mouth of the living.' 'A righteous dead person, we are also informed, has his place in the Hall before the great god (Osiris), or he is clothed in fine linen and is near Osiris.' Again, he may dwell in the Field of Earu or Field of Offerings, the great city, the possessor of winds, where he is a mighty one (*sekhem*) and a blessed one (*ikh*) and where he ploughs, reaps, eats, drinks, copulates, and does all that is done on earth.'"

Notwithstanding, Mr. Blackman yet describes these examples of posthumous happiness as "confused and conflicting." This may be to the modern mind, buttressed by the vicissitudes of historical explanation, the progress of knowledge and the bone of skepticism, but to the ancient Egyptian this was not strange at all! That is to say, first and foremost, these ancient Africans were pioneers in the workshop of consciousness creating first edition thought processes that would shape human thinking certainly down to our time. Second, as time and circumstances dictated, competing schools of religious, social, ethical, and scientific thought evolved and theologians struggled to be receptive of new ideas, and yet succeeded in harmonizing and seemingly not be in conflict of conception and practice of their respective ritual. Therefore, for the most part, two predominant schools of religious thought still predominated depicting the glorious hereafter or future existence beyond the grave.

On the other hand, recognizing the primacy of the Egyptian notion of salvation and that that state of mental preparation began long before death, George G.M. James in *Stolen Legacy*

(New York: Philosophical Library, 1954: 27) even referencing C.H. Vail in *Ancient Mysteries*, p. 25, affirmed: "The earliest theory of salvation is the Egyptian theory. The Egyptian Mystery System had as its most important object, the deification of man, and taught that the soul of man if liberated from its bodily fetters could enable him to become godlike and see the Gods in this life and attain the beatific vision and hold communication with the immortals."

To uphold such a contention, he goes on to state, "Plotinus defines this experience as the liberation of the mind from its finite consciousness, when it becomes one and is identified with the Infinite. This liberation was not only freedom of the soul from bodily impediments, but also from the wheel of reincarnation or rebirth. It involved a process of disciplines or purification both for the body and the soul. Since the Mystery System offered the salvation of the soul it also placed great emphasis upon its immortality. The Egyptian Mystery System, like the modern University, was the center of organized culture, and candidates entered it as the leading source of ancient culture. According to Pietschmann, the Egyptian Mysteries had three grades of students (1) the Mortals i.e., probationary students who were being instructed, but who had not yet experienced the inner vision. (2) The Intelligences, i.e., those who had attained the inner vision, and had received mind or nous and (3) The Creators or Sons of Light, who had become identified with or united with the Light (i.e., true spiritual consciousness). W. Marsham Adams, in the 'Book of the Master,' has described those grades as the equivalent of **Initiation, Illumination and Perfection**. For years they underwent disciplinary intellectual exercises, and bodily asceticism with intervals of tests and ordeals to determine their fitness to proceed to the more serious, solemn and awful process of actual Initiation."

Into the Egyptian Mind. Erik Monderson stands on the Ghizeh Plateau before the Great Sphinx in 2018.

Into the Egyptian Mind. Egyptian Art. The deceased stands before the seated gods in Sennutem's tomb.

Into the Egyptian Mind. Egyptian Art. Papyrus. King Tutankhamon and wife relax under the Aten's protection.

Into the Egyptian Mind. Egyptian Art. Carrying the Mummy's coffin to its place of deposit.

Into the Egyptian Mind. Luxor Temple of Amenhotep III and Rameses II. In the "Ramessean Front," "fat cows" as part of the Procession of the Sons of Rameses II going to Luxor Temple. Notice the "Nubian Lady" coming out of the head of the cow.

Into the Egyptian Mind. Luxor Temple of Amenhotep III and Rameses II. Another fat cow in the Procession of the sons of Rameses going to the temple.

Into the Egyptian Mind. Egyptian Art. Papyrus. Out with the family fowling and fishing in the Marshes.

Into the Egyptian Mind. Cairo Museum of Egyptian Antiquities. Another personal chest of Tutankhamon, decorated, showing the king in battle.

Even further, Mr. James continued, "Their education consisted not only in the cultivation of the ten virtues, which were made a condition to eternal happiness, but also of the seven Liberal Arts which were intended to liberate the soul. There was also admission to the Greater Mysteries, where an esoteric philosophy was taught to those who had demonstrated proficiency. (*Ancient Mysteries* C.H. Vail p. 24-25) Grammar, Rhetoric, and Logic were disciplines of moral nature by means of which the irrational tendencies of a human being were purged away, and he was trained to become a living witness of the Divine Logos. Geometry and Arithmetic were sciences of transcendental space and numeration, the comprehension of which provided the key not only to the problems of one's being; but also to those physical ones, which are so baffling today, owing to our use of the inductive methods. Astronomy dealt with the knowledge and distribution of latent forces in man, and the destiny of individuals, races and music. Music (or Harmony) meant the living practice of philosophy i.e., the adjustment of human life into harmony with God, until the personal soul became identified with God, when it would hear and participate in the music of the spheres. It was therapeutic and used by the Egyptian Priests in the cure of diseases. Such was the Egyptian theory of salvation, through which the individual was trained to become godlike on earth, and at the same time qualified for everlasting happiness. This was accomplished through the efforts of the individual, through the cultivation of the Arts and Sciences on the one hand, and a life of virtue on the other. There was no mediator between man and his salvation, as we find in the Christian theory."

The Abode of Ra, the Sun-god, was a heavenly or celestial existence while that of Osiris was an earthly or underground manifestation. The architects of both schools recognized and reconciled their differences and so encouraged a harmonious relationship. That is, in the realm of the dead, the practicalities of these two abodes never conflicted but complemented; for, when Ra proceeded to make his night-time circuit underground, after traveling across the sky during the day, he recognized and temporarily aided Osiris and his denizens. In some respects, this "higher religion" of Ra worship was enjoyed by the upper class, viz., king and nobles, intellectuals, existing from the earliest times. Osiris worship, on the other hand, though it only came into official recognition in the later Old Kingdom, while some believe it may extend millennia prior, became the religion of all people but more especially the poor who experienced the hardships of this life but were rewarded with the promise of pleasantries in the next if they lived by the precepts that were noble and not self-serving. That is, providing righteousness and truth had been paramount in their dealings on earth casting similar aspirations in the Afterlife.

The reward of eternal life was an earned prize though the requirements changed overtime whether in the Old, Middle, or New Empires or even Late Period. Justification through righteousness molded the behaviors of the king, his nobles and the masses in general. James Henry Breasted in *Dawn of Conscience* (New York: Charles Scribner's Sons, 1934) emphasized that material possessions in this world had no value in the next. He quotes the social prophets and theologians who, as an example, after the great particular architectural accomplishments of the Pyramid Age, critiqued the lavish outlay of wealth that had fallen into decay. Surviving literature of the age attest to the quality of intellectual prodigiousness but that the only garment the deceased could rely on was his righteous behavior while on earth. In the Judgment, whether in Ra's celestial abode or Osiris' earthly kingdom, the deceased's life was an open book, meticulously examined to determine qualification for the other-worldly existence into eternity.

The king was the first subject of Judgment as early as the Old Kingdom. Whether determined by tradition or intellectuals and advisers at his court, the king not simply strove to be a pillar of righteous consciousness but sternly insisted his administrators be upright in their dealings and that every man gets his just due in his appeal for justice.

Breasted, in *Dawn of Conscience* (1934: 73) further explained the significance of the stellar and solar faiths and how the king's future in the Afterlife was molded by requirements of this heavenly dynamic. He states: "Two ancient doctrines of this celestial Hereafter have been co-mingled in the Pyramid Texts. One represents the dead as a star and the other depicts him associated with the Sun-god, even becoming the Sun-god himself." However, "while the stellar and the solar elements are found side by side, the solar beliefs predominate so strongly that the Pyramid Texts as a whole and in the form in which they have reached us may be said to be of solar origin. The solar destiny was perhaps suggested by the unfailing daily reappearance of the Sun. Death was on earth; life was to be had only in the sky, where the king is lifted high above the universal domain of mortal men:

'Men fall,
Their name is not
Seize thou King Teti by the arm,
Take thou King Teti to the sky,
That he die not on earth,
Among men.'"

Even more, he continued, "This idea that life was in the sky is the dominant notion, far older than the Osirian faith in the Pyramid Texts. So powerful was it that Osiris himself is necessarily a celestial and solar hereafter in the secondary stage, in which his myth has entered the Pyramid Texts." (74)

Therefore, the posthumous happiness mentioned above was contingent on the deceased receiving a favorable verdict at the judgment and such a verdict as determined by the life, a virtuous one, he lived on earth. As an example, according to Blackman, "Osiris himself did not attain to his position of king and judge of the dead until he had undergone trial before the Judicial Council of gods at Heliopolis and had by them been proclaimed 'justified' or 'righteous (true) of voice.'"

Thus, the deceased sought to identify with Osiris as his passport to this happiness, for "Originally only the dead pharaoh was identified with Osiris, who appears in the Pyramid Texts as the prototype of all dead pharaohs, the dead pharaoh par excellence. This identification ensured to the deceased pharaoh the same renewed and glorified existence as that of the god. As Osiris lives, he also will live. As Osiris dies not, he will not die. As Osiris was not destroyed, he will not be destroyed." Even further, "the gods do for the deceased pharaoh what in the first instance they did for Osiris. Nut, the mother of Osiris gives the dead Pepi his head, united for him his bones, puts together his limbs for him and places his heart in his body! Isis and Nephthys may also perform this service for him and [he is then] embalmed by Anubis and revivified by Horus. As a representative or successor of Osiris, the departed is said to be a blessed one or spirit (*ikh*) and to be mighty as a god. His soul (*bai*) is within him and his power (*sachem*) behind him. Finally, the dead pharaoh must appear before the Judicial Council of the gods, by whom, like Osiris, he is pronounced 'Justified,' 'righteous of voice,' thanks to the pleading of Thoth, who also made Osiris to triumph over his enemies. He can now enter upon a glorious existence according to one conception, in heaven, or, according to another in the west."

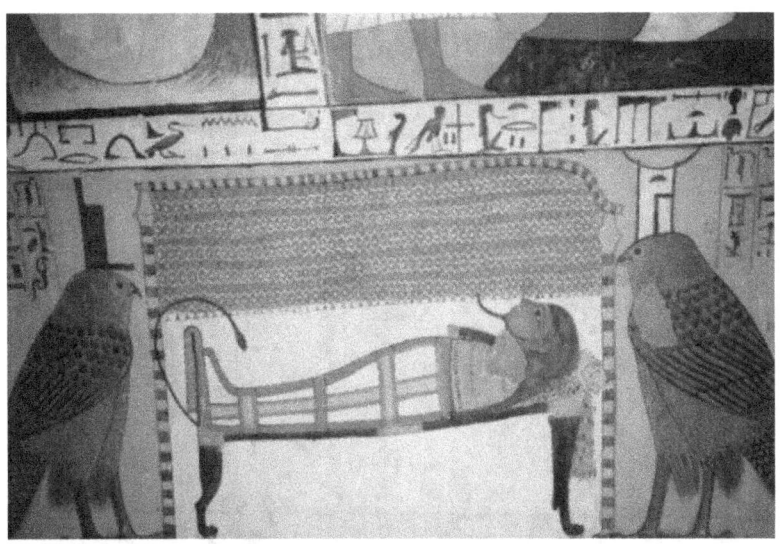

Into the Egyptian Mind. Egyptian Art. As the deceased lies in his bier, Isis (Auset, left) and Nephthys (right) as hawks, stand guard.

Into the Egyptian Mind. Egyptian Art. The King leads a procession before the Sem Priest in Leopard Skin followed by the Queen and fan bearers.

Into the Egyptian Mind. A dignified female, Nefertari, wife of Rameses II, wearing the "Queen Mother Crown."

Into the Egyptian Mind. Nephthys sits to the rear wearing the Red Crown.

Into the Egyptian Mind. Cairo Museum of Egyptian Antiquities. One of Tutankhamon's Gold Chests.

As for the god and the king; so it was for other members of the society; first the nobles and later the masses. As such, "After the VIth Dynasty, every dead person was identified with Osiris, and the custom then arose of appending to the deceased's name the Osiris epithet 'Justified' the tendency therefore was to regard the deceased as 'righteous' or 'Justified,' not on his own merits, but, owing to his identification with Osiris, his personality and acts becoming merged in those of his righteous and justified prototype."

Throughout the Egyptian state's ebb and flow, the literature is replete with theologians and social critics either decrying the conditions of the time or praising one King or another for some accomplishment. In their poor burials, the great masses have bequeathed modern man little by way of the written word. However, the noble class and officials have left plenty, whether in papyrus form or stele or tomb inscriptions and illustrations extolling their behaviors in service and rewards given by the king in quest of the righteousness that was so godlike. Breasted calls attention to a noble in the 27th Century Before Christ favored by the king who tells in his "Autobiography" of his good fortune. According to Blackman, "'He [the dead Unas identified with Osiris] is justified by what he hath done. ... The Two Rights have held the legal hearing. Shu was witness. The Two Rights have ordained that the thrones of Geb belong to him, that he should raise himself up for that which he desired, that his limits which were in concealment should be joined together, that he should unite with those who are in Nun, and that he should put an end to the words in Heliopolis."

Accordingly, the verdict essentially reads: "'Atum, father of the gods, is satisfied, Shu and Tefnut are satisfied, Geb and Nut are satisfied, Osiris and Isis are satisfied, Seth and Nephthys are satisfied ... with that great and mighty utterance that came out of the mouth of Thoth in favor of Osiris, treasurer of life, soul-bearer of the gods. Anubis who reckons the hearths, he reckons the Osiris Pepi from among the gods who belong to the earth unto the gods who are in heaven.

Even further, the prayer is offered: 'O Thoth, who justified Osiris against his enemies, justify NN. Against his enemies even as thou didst justify Osiris against his enemies before the judicial council ... in Heliopolis.'"

All this, notwithstanding, an important distinction need be identified as existing between the deceased and Osiris. That is, while the Pyramid Texts of the Old Kingdom pertained to the king's salvation, the Middle and New Kingdom Coffin Texts and Book of the Dead respectively, enabled all deceased persons to be accorded the right to that heavenly bliss. In that arrangement, the deceased, possessing all the requisite righteousness attributes was thus identified with Osiris, Judge of the Dead. However, making a distinction between, the deceased and the God, Blackman writes: "It should here be noted that a deceased person was identified with Osiris only in his earlier role as a dead god-king who had been killed and revivified, and who finally had triumphed over his accusing enemies at the trial before the Judicial Council in Heliopolis. The deceased is clearly differentiated from Osiris in his later role of Judge of the Dead."

Into the Egyptian Mind. Egyptian Art. Pashedu before Ra-Horakhty and another divinity.

Into the Egyptian Mind. Egyptian Art. The "Tree Goddess" offers sustenance and pours pitchers of water on the deceased and his wife on way to the Hall of Judgment for the Psychostasia.

Into the Egyptian Mind. Egyptian Art. Groups of people in differing attitudes.

Into the Egyptian Mind. Individuals offerings hands in the air in adoration.

Into the Egyptian Mind. Cairo Museum of Egyptian Antiquities. Deceased female stands before enthroned Osiris (Ausar) with Isis (Auset) at his rear.

14. THE EGYPTIAN MYSTERIES
BY
Dr. Fred Monderson

While delivering a speech at Tuskegee Institute and featured on U-Tube, Dr. ben-Jochannan was asked about the "Egyptian Mystery System," There, the old master, at the peak of his vibrancy, explained this issue was only a mystery of Greeks and Romans. That early curiosity was more contemporary with the Egyptians as these foreigners wanted to breach the teachings to which initiates were instructed. Naturally, that mystique grew during the eighteen hundred years before Champollion broke the Hieroglyphic Code. Throughout the nineteenth and into the twentieth century it grew further as scholars investigated "The records of the ancient records." This curiosity has persisted as most modern men further seeks to unlock those "mysteries" as they remain fascinated with the Egyptian culture and mystique.

It also remained a mystery because ordinary mortals could not initially comprehend the teaching given in all societies and organizations have a system of "portals" or if you will, "Pylons" through which individuals are allowed entry to reach the innermost "sanctum" or level of teachings. It has been shown the duration of Egyptian education lasted for decades. In fact, Herodotus in the *Histories*, Book II, *Euterpe*, devoted to Egypt, tells of an Egyptian priest who remained studying underground for some 40 years. This type of commitment was rewarded with full mastery of certain knowledge the society had accumulated over the course of its history. Therefore, entry into such schools of thought and preparation with the requisite commitment for long study was indeed a monumental task and cursory visitors "could not pay the price." Therefore, the system of education may have seemed a mystery to many even though several individuals who made the journey and "paid the price" benefitted tremendously and returning home, educated and influenced their fellow citizens. In some situations, however, the established authority did not respond favorably to this "foreign teaching" and so oftentimes proscribed the proponents. However, Pythagoras studied in Egypt for 22 years, as he withered the most humiliating treatment and assignments before the Egyptians though him fit to become knowledgeable about their secrets, religious and otherwise.

Several of these classical learned men as mentioned in George G.M. James' *Stolen Legacy* (New York: Philosophical Library, 1954) 1976, including Aristotle, Democritus, Heraclitus, Parmenides, Plutarch, Pythagoras, and Socrates, among others. In the Introduction of his article entitled "Egyptian Mysteries" in Hasting's *Encyclopedia of Religion and Ethics*, Vol. 9, Edinburgh: T. and T. Clarke, 1917,

Alexander Moret quotes Herodotus and Plutarch in the following manner. He states, according to *Herodotus*, Book II, *Euterpe*, the following: "At Sais is the burial-place of one of whom I scruple to mention [Osiris] ... On the lake [of the temple] the Egyptians represent by night the sufferings undergone by him and this representation they call mysteries. All the proceeding in these mysteries are well-known to me; but my lips shall plainly refrain from mentioning them." In Plutarch's *Isis and Osiris* XVII he states: "Isis would not that her own woes and grievously journeys, that the deeds of his heroism should fall into oblivion and silence. She therefore instituted holy, sacred mysteries which would afford an image, a representation in mimic scenes of the sufferings he endured that they might serve as a pious teaching and a consolatory hope to the men and women who passed through the same hardships."

He then explains, regarding such mysteries: "From such statements we may infer the following definition: The mysteries are rites in which recitation and mimic action are associated, i.e., dramatic performances of mystical character. Such dramas enact the Osirian legend; they teach a lesson and holdout consolation to the men who view them; the latter being bound to observe secrecy upon these mysteries, are 'initiates.' It has been alleged that Herodotus and Plutarch influenced by the Orphic and Eleusinian rites, transposed them to Egypt, and applied the name of 'mysteries' to ceremonies having no kind of analogy with the rites of initiation...but the author of such an assertion makes light of Egyptian sources themselves, which, on the contrary confirm the statements of the Greek writers on every point."

In a summary of the "Osiris Legend," Alexander Moret again in *Kings and Gods of Egypt* (Eng. Trans.), London: 1912: 77ff, writes: "The good being [Unnefer] reigned over Egypt, and with the help of his sister and spouse, Isis. He taught his subjects agriculture and all the arts and crafts; he also conquered the rest of the world to civilize it. His brother Seth

(Typhon), however, murdered him, and launched the coffin containing the body into the Nile. It drifted away to Byblos, and was discovered there by Isis, who took it back to Buto in Egypt. Seth again found the corpse, and cut it into pieces which he cast into the Nile. Isis resumed her mournful quest, searched for and found the fragments and wherever she found a piece, she raised a tomb over it. Then Horus, the son of Osiris, Thoth and Anubis his friends, came to Isis' help in order to 'Avenge Osiris;' they justified him before the court of the gods, and restored his now unified body to life and immortality. Thus, could Osiris hand over his realm to his son Horus who became the patron and ancestor of the pharaohs."

Osiris' head was buried at Abydos and his heart at Philae. In time temples were built at these locations in which the "Passion of Osiris" was performed. Setting up the "Tet" or "Backbone" of Osiris was a renowned ceremony, much of which is graphically depicted on the walls of the inner Osiris Shrine in the temple built by Seti I of the 19th Dynasty. Two things can be noted here quickly. Perhaps the coffin floating downstream can be equated with the cultural flow down the Nile from the effluence of Africa. This important ceremony was equally performed at the important site in proximity to the archaic kings' burial location. Thus, this latter underscores the purpose of the temple as a memorial to these kings and equally their place of actual burial rather than Memphis, where in all probability cenotaphs or dummy tombs of these kings remain.

Then again, a number of factors can be argued regarding Osiris. (1) While he was regarded as a king of Egypt and together his family may extend into remote prehistory, he does not come into prominence as the "God of the Dead" at Abydos well into the Old Kingdom. (2) The Frenchman Amelineau claimed to have found the "Tomb of Osiris" at Abydos which he dated to the beginning of Dynastic rule. However, his fellow countryman Gaston Maspero more correctly dated the tomb to a third dynasty king on basis of "tomb furniture." (3) Osiris succeeded Khenti-Amenti as the god of the dead at

Abydos. This adds to the significance of the site as a place of holiness. As such, again it weighs heavily as the burial place of the Archaic kings. (4) Petrie discovered evidence of 10 successive levels of temples at Abydos dating back to the First Dynasty including a temple of Narmer the unifier and founder of the dynasty. He also found the only image, miniature statue, of Khufu, builder of the Great Pyramid at Ghizeh.

Into the Egyptian Mind. Egyptian Art. Sennutem stands with empty, raised, hands before the gods in his tomb.

Into the Egyptian Mind. Egyptian Art. As the King sits enthroned with his queen beside, a priest pours a libation and prepares to incense him.

Into the Egyptian Mind. As one hand holds an incenser, another reaches for the luscious "Table of Offerings" on display.

Into the Egyptian Mind. While the bow of this sailing boat features a head wearing the Red and White Double Crown, a nearby sphinx wears horns, disk and feathers and to the right an individual hoist a container to pour its contents over a kneeling figure.

Into the Egyptian Mind. Egyptian Art. Papyrus.
Hathor and Horus (Heru) make nice.

Into the Egyptian Mind. Cairo Museum of Egyptian Antiquities. Papyrus. An individual and wife stands with his empty hands raised in adoration before enthroned Osiris (Ausar) in his Shrine.

Most important, however, while the "Passion of Osiris," the "Setting up" of his "Tet" or "Backbone," the intricate details of the ceremony remained essentially "secret" since most of it was performed in the temple, in its most inner reaches. Hence, the mystery designation! Naturally, part of the ceremony was performed outdoors involving proponents and opponents of the god's movement along a route observed by spectators. That is, while proponents were assigned to move the procession in its back and forth journeys, opponents tried to impede its progress. Nevertheless, and despite the staged "mock battles" the god had to complete his task and return to his temple abode. However, while the outward panegyrics were publicly observed, the temple activities were restricted. Hence, very little was recorded and only portions alluded to, from the earliest times.

The earliest of such recorded reference relating to the "Osiris mystery" Moret identifies as inscribed on a XIIth Dynasty stela during the reign of Senusert III, c. 1875 B.C., belonging to a high official Igernefert, who tells how he "conducted a ceremony called 'The Ceremony of the Golden Chamber for the Mystery (sesta) of the Lord of Abydos (Osiris)." Accordingly, "Igernefert, to whom Senusert III has committed the preparations for the performance, attends first to the properties and requisites for scenery. He procures a barge which is to stand for the solar Bari, a statue of Osiris adorned with lapis-lazuli; electrum and precious stones, and also movable shrines in which to place the statue. In his capacity of 'head of the mystery,' Igernefert conducts the process of fabrication and appoints sets of 'hourly priests' to execute the rites. When the action begins he plays the part of Horus (*samer-f* the beloved son'); after him, the principal parts are Anubis and Thoth, played by other high officials."

The saga, according to A.M. Blackman in "Worship" in *Encyclopedia of Religion and Ethics*, Vol. 12 (Edinburgh: T. And T. Clarke, 1921: 277) occurs in several acts, the first three of which corresponds as follows:

(1) It opens with a procession (*perjt*) of Anubis (*Upuaut*) who comes to protect Osiris, and, with the help of Horus defeats the adversaries of the barge (*nemset*), and overthrows the foes of Osiris. Those adversaries are figured as supernumeraries who come to blows with the subjects of Osiris, and the fights are sometimes pictured (A. Moret, *Mysteries Egyptiens*, Paris, 1913, p. 15); Herodotus alludes to them (II, 61, 132). We may suppose that now Osiris was shown sailing out in his barge in order to conquer and civilize the world, after his triumph over his adversaries."

(2) The death of the god is treated next. No less reliant that Herodotus (II, 17) and Diodorus (I, 2), Igernefert only points to this second act with a periphrasis: 'I conducted the great outing and I followed the god upon his steps.' Now, the

expression 'great outing' (*perjt oat*) means the 'great mourning.'

(3) After the burial, we witness the resurrection and triumph of the god. Igernefert says: 'I have avenged Unnefer (Osiris) on this day of the great fight; I have smitten all his foes upon the river of *Nedit*.'

Amid the cheers of his people the god sailed back in his barge to his city of Abydos; he entered his palace as a king (II, 21-24), and received there his 'Purification,' i.e., though Igernefert seeks to be informative he only provides limited information beyond what is witnessed in public and recorded by both Herodotus and Plutarch. It is interesting that this "mystery," while observed in public is recognized by Western scholarship as keen observation on part of the "father of history" but when he describes the Egyptians as having "broad noses, thick lips, kinky (or wooly) hair and are burnt of skin," meaning black, they question the validity of this important observation because it threatens the whole notion of a Caucasian Egypt. The issue is more significant for, if in Herodotus' time this is what the Egyptians looked like then through the New, Middle and Old Kingdom, even Archaic Period and beyond into the Pre-dynastic times, then out goes the "Caucasian Egyptian" falsity. Let us not forget, the 1820 mummy article in The *Gentleman's Magazine* described the "Negro imprint of that Egyptian of Roman time," the question then becomes, 'If, after the Hyksos, particularly New Kingdom importation of Asiatics, then the later Persians, Assyrians, Greeks and Romans, how could "Caucasian Egyptians" of "late" Herodotus and Roman times look so "Negro?"

Nevertheless, despite Igernefert "hiding the ball" in not going into too detailed accounts, the writer still affirms "This is the most complete account that we possess of an Osiris 'mystery,' but other documents preserved descriptions of festivals, which include certain episodes of a mystery. Thus, the feast celebration, 1ˢᵗ Pachons, when the king is seen cutting a sheaf with his sickle and sacrificing a white bull, seems to actualize the death of Osiris, god of vegetation (Moret, *Mysteries*, [p. 7, f). Another ceremony, the erection of the dad, the Osirian pillar, symbolizes the resurrection of the god and is associated with fighting and shouting (ib. Pp. 12-15); the Sed festivities bring before our eyes the coronation and victory of the resuscitated Osiris (ib. p. 16). Still more valuable are the rituals in the temples which describe the secret ceremonies of the passion and resurrection of Osiris. They were celebrated in small temples or in chapels secreted for the special use of the god, such chapels being found in all large Egyptian temples. Of these ceremonies, some would take place daily, others only at certain festivals, doubtless their rites formed the secret part of the 'Mystery,' the part which Igernefert piously refrain from explaining and in which the death and resurrection of Osiris are acted."

Goethe wrote, "Wherever Germans go they corrupt that culture," but it is also interesting how non-Africans, that is, Asiatics and Europeans have impacted on the African continent and especially Egypt. First, the Hyksos destroyed much that they did not understand. Then a millennium later, Persian, Assyrians, later Greeks and Romans destroyed even more in their conquests, pillaging and took away much to adorn their cities. Even more important, the Greeks and Romans impacted on traditional building practices and art decoration. That is, while "Greek and Roman Temples" were generally constructed along Egyptian/Nubian traditional specifications they were done under foreign over-lordship. The temples became more prolifically illustrated now having the ancient ritual and mysteries depicted throughout the temple walls. That is, while some have argued such depictions do preserve ancient beliefs and practices; others hold the sacred nature of these esoteric beliefs, not intended for the mundane gaze are now exposed to such vulgarity. This latter view is consistent with Dr. Yosef ben-Jochannan's admonition that his students not enter the Sanctuary in respect for the culture because in ancient times only the pharaoh and a handful of high echelon priests could enter the "Holy of Holies." However, every day we see scantily clad European females especially traipsing about these sacred spaces. It is a fact, the commercialization of the tourist industry in Egypt permits the guides to so enter in their tours and thus the sanctity of the Sanctuary is no longer of prime importance. The Arabs came and conquered Egypt and dominated for more than 1500 years. Next came nationals from France, Britain, Italy, Turkey, Germany and America; many of whom committed what Brian Fagan described in his book entitled *The Rape of the Nile*! Next, they removed objects "scientifically" before such artifacts were later removed under "legal arrangements."

Into the Egyptian Mind. Karnak Temple of God Amon. Part of the southern Colonnade of columns in the Great Court, looking east towards the rear of Rameses III's perpendicular temple.

Into the Egyptian Mind. Egyptian Art. While Ra-Horakhty sits with Disk in coiled cobra, another god rides a spotted cow in Sennutem's tomb.

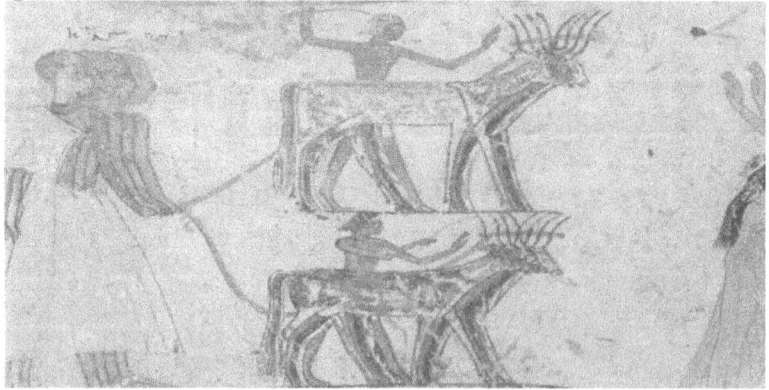

Into the Egyptian Mind. Egyptian Art. Two teams of 4-each oxen are led by four individuals while two others guide the beasts.

Into the Egyptian Mind. Luxor Temple of Amenhotep III and Rameses II. On a wall in the eastern rear of the "Ramessean Front," a priest pours a libation and burns incense before Ra-Horakhty and Anubis who hold hands and guide Pharaoh forward.

Into the Egyptian Mind. Luxor Temple of Amenhotep III and Rameses II. The waning sun casts its last beams upon the eastern colonnade with statues coming out from between the colonnade in the Court of the Ramessean Front.

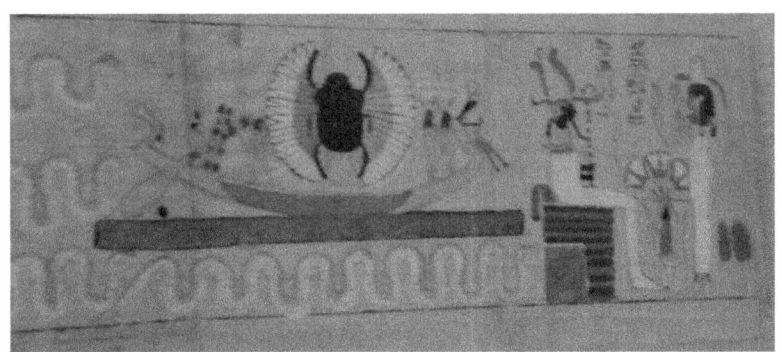

Into the Egyptian Mind. Cairo Museum of Egyptian Antiquities. Papyrus. A female with perfumed cone on her head and with raised hands stands before Osiris (Ausar), painted black, in his shrine with a winged beetle sailing in a boat on the Nile at his rear.

Nevertheless, the changes which the Greeks and Romans especially introduced, viz., decoration of temples, more revelation of the anatomy of female figures, the Mammisi or birth-house of the young god, now made public what Igernefert had served to preserve. In this regard, Moret writes: "The Ptolemaic temples have preserved in their Osirian chapels texts and pictures illustrating the rites which the hourly priests recited and acted during each of the twelve hours (*wnn-t*) of night and of day. It is a sacred drama played by priests who assume the different parts of the Osirian family; we see Shu and Geb, the father and grandfather of Osiris; Horus, his son; Anubis and Thoth, his brothers or relatives; the four children of Horus; the Goddesses Isis and Nephthys, wife and sister of Osiris; and, lastly, reciting and officiating priests. The scenery given by the reliefs consist of an image of Osiris swathed in the funeral shroud, a bed upon which the divine mummy is stretched, and several requisites, such as crowns, scepters, weapons, libation vases, pans and incense boxes."

Conjuring a conception of events on the big festival day, one sees: "The drama opens at 6 A.M. and closes twenty-four hours later; it falls into twelve hours of night (from six P.M. to six A.M.). Its subject is the passion and resurrection of Osiris. From the first to the last hour the rites lead, step by step, towards the triumph of the god; yet, this gradual advance is hardly felt because each hour is scenically treated as forming a complete drama in itself, in which the god passes from death to resurrection. At the beginning of each hour he is wretched irresistibly by the power of rites and formulae, only to be brought back anew at the close of the hour. (*Texts of Philae, Edfu, Dendera,* published by H. Junker) where 'The author makes a mistake in beginning with the hours of day,' as the rites, as in any other festival, begin at 6 P.M. The right order is twelve-night hours followed by twelve-day hours."

Into the Egyptian Mind. Karnak Temple of God Amon. S somber look at the full face of the Great Pylon with holes for flagstaves that flew flags of the temple, Nome and state. The left half of the Propylon has deteriorated but two levels of flagstaves are evident attesting to the height and breadth of the structure, imposing as it was.

15. CIRCUMCISION
By
Dr. Fred Monderson

The question of circumcision in ancient Egypt is an issue hotly debated by modern scholars but the results are not conclusively agreed to except that "Circumcision arose in Egypt from the idea of ceremonial purity of the people in the service of their god." All the other factors consider whether anteriority, consistency, general nature among the upper and lower classes, borrowings from nearby people and the reliability of classical commentators have led to divergent views expressed by moderns who examined the subject in the great age of reclamation of Egyptian knowledge through archaeology and analytic anthropology in almost a century from 1850-1950. Nonetheless, the question of circumcision as a health issue has not gotten the attention it deserved even though today in Brooklyn, New York, a sign outside a doctor's office reads: "Circumcision prevents AIDS!"

Notwithstanding, as it relates to ancient Egypt, George Foucart has written an interesting article on "Circumcision" (Egyptian) published in *Encyclopedia of Religion and Ethics* Vol. 3 (Edinburgh: T. and T. Clarke, 1910) in which he examines the "Documentary Evidence," "Representations and Phases of Circumcision," and "General Characteristics of the Practice" before concluding with the religious nature of the practice.

Thus, in his "Introduction" Foucart states: "The question of circumcision in Egypt has always been one of general interest, since it involves three questions of a general type. First, there is the investigation as to whether as has been affirmed at various times it can explain by a historical connection, circumcision as practiced by the Israelites. In the second place, it may, if carefully studied in its general bearing and in its details, help to elucidate the question of the Libyan, Asiatic or

Bantu origins of the primitive civilization of Egypt - a question much debated and still very obscure. Finally, from the more general view-point of the history of religion, we may allow that the great antiquity and long life of Egypt make Egyptian circumcision a good means of solving the problem of the original source and signification of this usage that is witnessed in so many religious civilizations."

Nevertheless, the subject of Egyptian circumcision, while not getting much attention, save a cursory mention in Biblical experiences, came to the forefront during and after the massive excavation expeditions by the end of the 19th Century and after. In the enormous ancient knowledge unearthed, as scholars began to examine this treasure, both illustrative and inscriptional, the questions, 'Where did their civilization begin, where did it come from, what did classical writers say about Egyptian circumcision, which other nations practiced this custom, for what purpose and so on,' have taken on new meaning.

The sources from which these questions were generated and to some extent answered, according to George Foucart are as follows: "The documentary evidence properly so called, is of the most varied kinds: (1) scenes representing the actual operation; (2) frescoes and bass reliefs showing nude figures circumcised; (3) statues of the same; (4) Egyptian texts of the classical period understood to refer to circumcision, from a religious or historical point of view; (5) papyrus-texts of the Roman epoch relating to the practice of circumcision; (6) evidence of classical writers; (7) the mummies of kings, chief priests, and a great number of Egyptians of noble rank or affluent condition." The wide diversity of evidence, nonetheless, he advised caution in viewing the data, notwithstanding.

Based on seemingly contradictory evidence from ancient through modern times, citing Garner Wilkinson in *Manners and Customs of the Ancient Egyptians*, I, 83 and ii, 385. Being a preeminent authority by mid-19th Century, it was "in his opinion that circumcision was of great antiquity in Egypt, he proved this from the evidence of the ancient writers and his personal observations, but he did not think circumcision had been compulsory, except for priests and initiates." It sprang, in his opinion, from motives of ceremonial purity, and only later became a distinguishing mark of the orthodox exception as opposed to the outsider."

Into the Egyptian Mind. Egyptian Art. Two adults and a youngster.

Into the Egyptian Mind. Egyptian Art. A sailing boat with a cabin, a Sem Priest in leopard skin and other individuals as they ply the Nile.

Into the Egyptian Mind. Luxor Temple of Amenhotep III and Rameses II. Just at the start of the Processional Colonnade, statues of Amon and other figures lay disfigured.

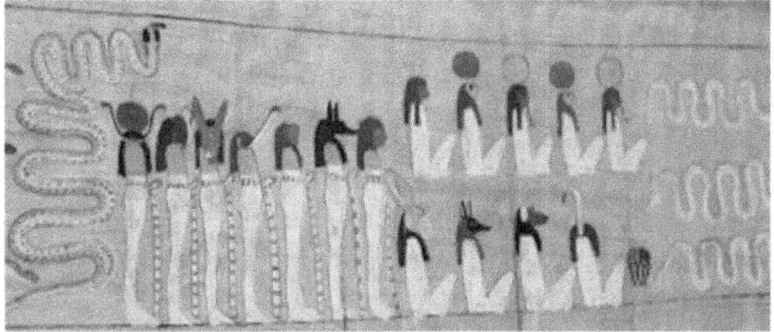

Into the Egyptian Mind. Cairo Museum of Egyptian Antiquities. Papyrus. The gods in tranquil repose.

Into the Egyptian Mind. Luxor Temple of Amenhotep III and Rameses II. Alabaster figures of Tutankhamon and his wife, badly disfigured.

However, while recognizing the importance of Wilkinson's penetrating deduction as early as the mid-19th Century in Egyptological thought, decades before one great avalanche of archaeological evidence when so much was revealed, Foucart continued, in his day, the data had not been subject to sufficient analytic scrutiny. Thus, critiquing the various kinds of data as enumerated above, he proposes a critical frame of reference approach as follows: "The variety of sources of information would appear to be an excellent basis for scientific study, but two facts detract greatly from their value: (1) Several of these classes of evidence reduce to a very small number of examples, either because we do not know any more about them at present (as in the case of the scenes of circumcision on the statues), or because the whole material at our disposal has not yet under gone methodological study (as in the case of the mummies). (2) Even in an apparently well-supported series, investigation leads us either to eliminate much of the information as of doubtful value (as in the case of most Egyptian texts of the Pharaonic period), or to draw conclusions that appear at first sight absolutely opposed to each other. Further, even supposing we are so-far agreed to-day as to the antiquity of this practice, the phases of actual operation, and, to a certain extent, the age to which it was carried out; still the two most important points are not settled: (a) Was circumcision general in Egypt, or was it confined to certain classes? Was it obligatory or optional in some cases, and in what cases, specially and in detail? (b) Can we, consequently, define the origin of circumcision, its nature and its religious and social significance?

As an example of the conflicting results of moderns who examined this subject, we seem to understand how diverse and opposed these scholarly views are. For example, Naville contests "both the generality of this practice and its religious importance by showing the scarcity and uncertainty of the texts, the paucity of the figures, and the lack of convincing results from the examination of the mummies." Equally, Wiedemann, having examined a great body of literature, negatively concludes as to general practice, contending: "Circumcision was never general, this frequency varied, it had no absolute religious value, it was not a privilege reserved to certain classes, and it was not even compulsory for the priests." On the contrary, Wileken believed "circumcision was practiced by the whole people: and his opinion based on the papyri of the Roman Period is corroborated by that of Bissing, which founded on the Egyptian evidence proper, and the words of Wendland on Graeco-Roman sources. This view seems also to be held by Elliot Smith, at least for the classes of society that practiced mummification."

Therefore, given all the skepticism and competing theories as Foucart argued, it's best to begin with an examination of the actual sources or representations though he acknowledges silence on part of both classical writers Herodotus and Strabo.

Nevertheless, regarding the primary evidence; spectacular in their own right, "The first is a bas-relief in the Theban temple of Khonsu (XXIst Dynasty), reproduced for the first time by Chabas in 1861 and mentioned in all works thereafter, it created a great sensation on its publication and was for many years the only specimen of its kind. A second representation was discovered by Loret at Sakkara (1899), and was briefly commented on by Bissing (1902). The discovery at Sakkara of an authentic representation of circumcision, dating from the Vth Dynasty, was at first met with doubts as to the actual existence of such evidence; but these doubts were dispelled by the evidence provided in 1904 and 1907, by the reproductions and commentaries of Max Muller and Capart."

This is further underscored by James Henry Breasted, who after the successes of his *History of Egypt* (1905); *Ancient Records of Egypt* (1906-07); *Ancient Times* (1916); and *Conquest of Civilization* (1928); *Dawn of Conscience* (1933) wrote: "The Egyptian background out of which Moses had developed into to a great national leader must in itself have contributed to his vision of Yahweh's place in the life of his people. Born in Egypt and bearing an Egyptian name, Moses enjoined his people to adopt an enormously ancient Egyptian custom, the rite of circumcision, which in his day had been practiced among the Nile-dwellers for at least three thousand years and more." This, adoption in Breasted considered judgment is further elaborated in a footnote indicating: "The bodies of Egyptians exhumed from the earliest prehistoric cemeteries back of 4000 B.C., have disclosed the evidence of circumcision, whenever the body is sufficiently well-preserved to make observation possible. The actual performance of the operation by the Egyptian surgeon is depicted in an Egyptian tomb relief of the twenty-seventh or twenty-eighth century B.C. in the cemetery of Memphis." Further emphasizing Egyptian cultural influence among the Hebrews, Breasted writes even more: "Hebrew tradition always attributed the origin of this rite to Moses, and that the fact that he adopted as a universal distinguishing mark of the

Israelite a sacred Egyptian practice, with which he had obviously been acquainted in Egypt from childhood days, is unequivocal contemporary evidence that he was consciously drawing upon his knowledge of Egyptian religion."

Nevertheless, pursuing the matter further, in both the Sakkara and Karnak examples, the circumcision operation is graphically described and not only does they represent evidence of the practice being performed in the Old and New Kingdom or thereafter, it also presupposes such in the intermediary period. After all, arguments from the lack of survivable evidence, especially in a culture such as Egypt that reveal new and pertinent ancient data, such a position is not especially tenable. Notwithstanding, a view, whatever the following is a graphic description of the circumcision operation generally practiced for much of dynastic rule.

"The operation seems to have comprised two essential parts - the circumcision itself and a dressing. Only the first part is represented in the Theban bas-relief. The child is placed before the operator, and its arms are securely held by an assistant (a woman at Karnak, a man at Sakkara; at Karnak, the hands are held behind the back, at Sakkara they are brought in front of the patient's eyes). There is no written explanation at Karnak; that of Sakkara is important. Short though it is, it follows the custom of the period by being divided into three sections - the title of the scene, words spoken by the principal actor, and the 'response' of the assistant, meant in these scenes to assure the magic success of the actions represented by euonymus words. The title is *sobit*, 'circumcision' - a fact which forever establishes this technical term for ancient Egyptian, and proves its connection with the Coptic word. The operator says, 'Hold him, that he may not faint away,' and the assistant replies in the usual formula, 'Do your best.' Leaving out of account the age of the child and considering only the operation itself, we see that the operator knelt to his task, and held the organ in his left hand while he operated with his right. The instrument itself is a sort of small blade pointed like a stiletto, in the Karnak bas-relief; and oval in shape with a medial line (an indication of relief [(?)]) in the Sakkara scene. There is nothing to indicate what material it is composed of. Wilkinson, judging by hypothesis only, hesitates between the 'sharp stone' spoken of in Exodus 4: 25 and the 'sharp knife' mentioned in Job 5: 2; Chabas (supposes, but doubtfully, that it was a stone knife, basing his opinion on the fact that the mummifiers used stone knives to open the bodies; and Max Muller thinks, but cannot prove, that the instrument in the Sakkara bas-relief is a flint. We may safely suppose that the ideogrammatic sign following the word *sobit* in the hieroglyphic title, which has the appearance of a sickle without a handle, is a survival of a primitive era and represents a stone instrument. In any case, we may admit that the use of the sharp stone instrument persisted long after the discovery of metal, because of the religious value of the custom, just as it persisted among the mummifiers for opening corpses, and as it has survived, in Africa itself, for numerous important sacerdotal ceremonies, and often, naturally, for circumcision itself. The question would be of exceptional interest for prehistoric antiquity, but at present we are reduced to mere hypothetical probability.

The Karnak bas-relief shows further that the operation was performed on several children on the same occasion. It shows a second child further back ready for the operation, and held by a second woman. This may offer a hint for comparing facts given very much later by the Graeco-Roman papyri. The second phase of the operation is shown at Sakkara. The title of the scene is *sunu*, 'anointing.' The operator says to the child, 'Here is something to make you feel comfortable (*nohimu*),' and the euonymus reply is, 'That is perfect.' The operator is seen rubbing the member operated on with a substance which is probably some kind of grease or balm. We have no details, in these scenes or in any texts, to show whether the excised organ was the object of any of the innumerable ceremonies mentioned as belonging to non-civilized nations (destroyed, burned, buried, hidden, placed in the temple, worn round the child's neck, etc.)."

However, the age of the child or children is not given and thus scholars have had to look to other sources for credible deductions. That is, while "the Karnak children appears to be between six and ten years old (in any case, they are beyond the 'first childhood' of the Egyptians, which ends at four years), and those of Sakkara look from ten to twelve. Zaborowski and Wilkinson oppose each other's view while the latter argues, "there was no fixed time in Egypt for circumcision.' Thus, the focus turned to a second century A.D. source that, in a way, supports Wilkinson's contention. That is, in the *Tebtunis Papyrus*, iv, 292, the child presented is 7 years of age, and a second child is 11; and quite recently the Geneva papyri, published by Nicole (1909), show a father presenting his three sons aged 2, 5, and 8. These facts, then, invalidate the conclusions of Reitzenstein and Walter Otto on the publication of the first papyri.

Into the Egyptian Mind. Deir el Medina. Native Egyptian Guides Mr. Sayeed and Mr. Shawki Abd Rady examine a pyramid zenith among the rubble at this important site of construction and art.

Into the Egyptian Mind. Egyptian Art. To stand before a god of such august power and majesty who wears the White Crown with feathers, says something of the individual deceased.

Into the Egyptian Mind. Egyptian Art. Carrying baskets of accoutrements.

Into the Egyptian Mind. Egyptian Art. "Traveling" Amon-Ra wearing feathers.

Into the Egyptian Mind. Kurneh Temple of Seti I. The entrance colonnade with "one band." Notice how evenly the Abacus fits the column zenith as it supports the architrave overhead.

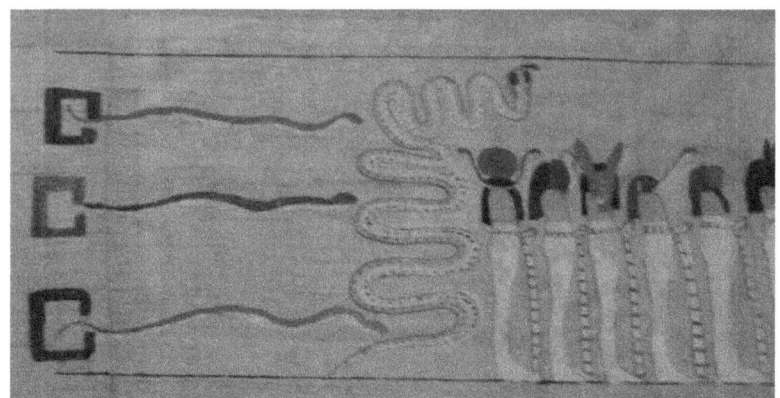

Into the Egyptian Mind. Cairo Museum of Egyptian Antiquities. Gods and snakes or vipers, among the powers that be!

The probability is - if we must assign a meaning to their number of 14 years - that this age was regarded, at least in the Roman period, as the extreme limit after which authority to circumcise could not be granted. It is most interesting to compare the fact established by Elliot Smith in his analysis of the mummy of a young prince of the XVIIIth dynasty, that 'this boy of eleven years of age, who still wears the Horus lock of hair, is not circumcised."

Looking at the texts to determine the nature of the general character of the practice, the author poses a number of questions that drove the inquiry. These involve, "to what extent circumcision was a general practice in Egypt, to which class it was limited, if limited at all, and, in the latter case, whether it was regarded as an obligation or as a privilege."

"The three texts most often quoted (the inscriptions of Merenptah at Karnak and Athribis, and the inscription of Piankhi, [cf. full reference in Breasted, *Ancient Records*, iii. 588, 601, iv. 443]) have no clear significance for our present subject. They make only incidental mention of circumcision in four or five words, and Egyptologists have never agreed as to the meaning of these words.; Although, in the Merenptah inscriptions, Brugsch, Breasted, Erman, Maspero, and Meyer have accepted the meanings 'circumcised' and 'uncircumcised' for the respective terms in the Egyptian inscription, these meanings are contested by Bissing, Max Muller, and Wiedemann, and recently inverted by Naville (*Sphinx*, xiv. [1910] 253). The terms in which Piankhi Grande *Inscr.* 106, 159) speaks of the 'uncircumcised' lords, and of *Nimroti*, 'who was circumcised and abstained from eating fish,' are capable of a much less precise translation, as Bissing has shown. And, finally, everything seems to justify the objection of Naville that all these terms are both vague and complicated, while the Egyptians had a technical term for 'circumcision' which has not been employed in any of these inscriptions."

The meaning of these historical documents has been a matter of debate for forty years, but by today's standards 150 years, with no decisive results.

"We must likewise pass over, as doubtful, texts like the passage in the Khumhotep inscription, in which some have seen an allusion to circumcision (cf. Wiedemann, OLZ vi. [1903] 7), and also a (unique) passage in the celebrated Texts of the Pyramids which speaks of a god *Tesebu*, translated 'circumciser' (cf. Maspero, *Pyramides de Sakkara*, p. 128, n. 1; Budge, *The Egyptian Sudan*, I (London: Kegan Paul, Trench, Trubner and co., 1907: 514), for there is no context to justify this purely etymological translation. All that finally remains is a very mystical text of the Book of the Dead (xvi. 23) and an Ostrakon found by Spiegelberg in the Ramesseum at Thebes. The former, described long ago by de Rouge speaks of 'the blood which fell from the phallus of Ra, when he accomplished his own mutilation.' The latter, of recent discovery, is dated the year 44 of the Reign of Rameses II and speaks of the day 'when men come to rid themselves of impurity before Amun.' Both these documents seem to denote the act of circumcision by their periphrasis, though the former appeared very mystical to Benedite, Naville, and several others."

Into the Egyptian Mind. Egyptian Art. Two images of the deceased greet Ptah (left) and Osiris (Ausar, right). Interesting how white is so predominant and red is miniscule, when we consider "red and white" as opposed to "white and red."

Into the Egyptian Mind. Egyptian Art. Professional mourners at a funeral.

Into the Egyptian Mind. Kurneh Temple of Seti I. Seti in White Crown, presents a platter to Amon-Ra with Khonsu and another at his rear. Notice the God's color.

Into the Egyptian Mind. Kurneh Temple of Seti I. Holding an incenser in his left hand, Seti gestures with the right hand before enthroned Amon-ra with Mut and Khonsu at the enthroned god's rear.

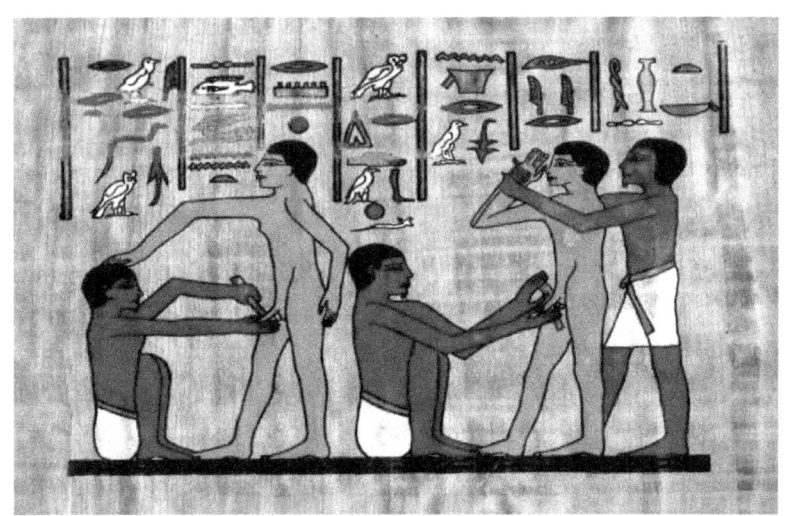

Into the Egyptian Mind. Egyptian Art. Papyrus. The Circumcision Operation.

Into the Egyptian Mind. Cairo Museum of Egyptian Antiquities. Another decorated personal chest of Tutankhamon.

Into the Egyptian Mind. Egyptian Art. Papyrus. A winged Ma'at kneels before enthroned Hathor while Horus (Heru) in Double Crown introduces Nefertari.

Into the Egyptian Mind. Egyptian Art. **Deir el Medina**. In his tomb, Iri-Nufer kneels before enthroned Ptah.

Into the Egyptian Mind. Egyptian Art. Deir el Medina. Hathor with horns and cows along with Horus (Heru) as a hawk, relaxes beside the Nile River in the Tomb of Iri-Nufer.

6. THE MUMMY MYSTIQUE
By
Dr. Fred Monderson

For a great period of his interaction with Egypt, Dr. Yosef ben-Jochannan has criticized how the authorities have treated the mummies of the ancient Egyptians. He has specifically singled out the Cairo Museum of Egyptian Antiquities for their disregard of the sanctity of the sacred and ancient relics. While some consideration can be given to ordinary mummies, the royal mummies are a special matter. While along with others, he advocated for returning the mummies to the sanctity of their tombs he insisted on providing for security in their resting places. Prior to his death, he was appalled that the Egyptian authorities now put on display with commercialize viewing these sacred and revered royal remains. While not a favorite of his, comparatively he explained, contemporary European royal families would certainly not allow public eyes to view their sacred dead.

The particular archaeological discoveries that shaped Dr. Ben's concern for the Egyptian mummies were essentially three in number. These were the discovery of the "Deir el Bahari Cache" in 1881-82; the mummies found in the tomb of Amenhotep II in 1898; and the discovery of the tomb of Tutankhamon by Howard Carter in 1922. This latter occurred one hundred years to the date of Champollion's deciphering the Hieroglyphic Code. However, while a great deal of sensationalism surrounded the recovery of these special relics, subjecting them to official, scholarly and public scrutiny for study and on display caused persons of concern to voice opposition to this form of treatment.

Another mummy of special significance, while not known at the time, would turn out to be that of Queen Hatshepsut who built her mortuary temple at Deir el Bahari. The queen's mummy, languishing in the byways of unidentified persons had one outstanding characteristic no one had paid much attention to. This was a missing tooth. As it turned out, there was a personal toilet cabinet of the queen that was well-regarded. Only recently opened for inspection, it was discovered to contain a missing tooth. Lo and behold, a bee-hive of activity emerged to determine whose tooth it was. Then someone remembered there was a female mummy, languishing in the realm of the unknown that also had a missing tooth. Fired-up interest assembled a scientific team who, through dental science, x-ray technology, a committed objective, and the scholars were able to determine the tooth fitted the missing space on the unidentified mummy.

Into the Egyptian Mind. Egyptian Art. Ra-Horakhty as Horus (Heru) performing the "Opening the Mouth Ceremony" on a mummy. Now you know what an adze looks like, very different from an axe.

Into the Egyptian Mind. Egyptian Art. Male and female in white, kneel with empty hands raised in adoration.

Into the Egyptian Mind. Kurneh Temple of Seti I. Holding two vessels for Libation, Pharaoh dances before enthroned Osiris (Ausar) with another divinity at his rear. All three figures were defaced seemingly in a systematic fashion.

Into the Egyptian Mind. Kurneh Temple of Seti I. Standing beneath an overhead flying vulture, pharaoh presents two bouquets of flowers to Amon as Min, seen balancing not holding the flail.

Into the Egyptian Mind. Cairo Museum of Egyptian Antiquities. Undergirded by an enormous snake under the mountain, this divinity, painted black stands erect.

Knowing whose tooth it was; that fit exactly where the missing tooth belonged; scholars were able to determine the mummy was actually that of Queen Hatshepsut. This was a remarkable scientific project that correctly identified the mummy as that of Queen Hatshepsut! Without a doubt, this was the second mummy scholars have been able to correctly identify. That is not to say, the other mummies identified are not who they are but theirs is through circumstantial evidence, a coffin, mummy wrappings, a tomb, etc. However, while that of the Queen is more uncontroverted.

While this is so, and coming after, Dr. Zahi Hawass had pointedly stated, "Tutankhamon is the only king of whom we are absolutely certain because we found him in a sealed tomb." Now the queen's identification makes this a second such realization.

However, in regards to the discoveries mentioned, the "Deir el Bahari Cache" in particular, upon discovery of the hiding place of this sacred depository and realization the Rasul Brothers, among others at Luxor, were looting the place and releasing valuable artifacts on the market; official scrutiny caught the culprits and had them reveal the location of the valuables. A whole host of mummies and royal paraphernalia were discovered, scattered throughout the floor of the hiding place, perhaps tumbled out as the thieves rummaged coffin after coffin to find marketable pieces. What the discoverers did realize; first, there was an enormous amount of wealth and some of the most important monarchs, particularly of the Eighteenth Dynasty. They seemed placed in this location for safe-keeping; perhaps, in some upheaval facing the nation and the authorities thought this a fitting resting place, even though the place was crowded with artifacts. There was evidence of confusion regarding whether this or that king was in his correct coffin. Even more important, there seemed to be confusion as to who each king really was, even though there was still sufficient markings, mummy cloth and otherwise, to determine the exact names.

In the flurry of sensationalism surrounding the discovery, authorities and scholars gathered and eventually unrolled the mummies, taking measurements, doing x-ray studies and examining the bandages and other body jewelry placed there in the wrapping. While the studies revealed much in terms of the physical make-up of the kings and others deposited in the hiding place, it seemed the interpretation of the racial identity of these great Africans actually did not properly reflect the true record. Given that much of this was not only being conducted during the emerging science of Egyptology and the attendant disciplines that would eventually be associated with it, there was the question of white supremacy ideology and practice then prevalent around the world and how this shaped interpretation of the data. Thus, this unfolding phenomenon was not without taint perpetuated by representatives who were colonizing the world, exterminating peoples even killing excavators, seizing cultural artifacts, and interpreting history that showed Europeans as morally, culturally and of course militarily superior to, especially non-white people. Thus, culminating much of the 19th Century's belief that Africans could not have built Egyptian civilization, the evidence seemed to point to solidifying that these were Caucasians. Naturally, closer inspection proved otherwise.

As discovery after discovery reclaimed much of the ancient Egyptian history, artifacts and personnel in the 19th Century, the tomb of the 18th Dynasty king Amenhotep II revealed another cache of important persons. This discovery therefore added to a great number of known kings and queens especially of the New Kingdom and later. Again, the same problem that attended the first find applied to this second. Of interest, however, another important revelation became manifest.

Brian Fagan's book *The Rape of the Nile* chronicled how much artifacts were removed from Egypt especially during the 19th Century, the skullduggery involved, who were the principal players and which museums, institutions and private collectors were beneficiary from the thievery. That is to say, practically every major European nation had been involved in collecting Egyptian artifacts. Though the Cairo museum was host it was not until the discovery of the "Deir el Bahari Cache" was it able "to be on par with the Turin Museum," as an example, that had been collecting for the longest. Thus, the "Amenhotep II Cache" added to Egyptian respectability in this regard as it struggled to compete with ill-gotten artificial gains as well as to institute controls on who, what, how, and when of archaeological and anthropological investigation, excavation and removal of artifacts unless sanctioned under official supervision. By the time of the Tutankhamon discovery in 1922, there were sufficient regulation in place as well as the prohibitive nature of sensationalism surrounding something as great as the discovery of an intact 18th Dynasty tomb. Therefore, skullduggery was played down and much of the treasure of the Tutankhamon trove remained accounted for.

Nevertheless, the contradiction associated with the question of 'Who were the ancient Egyptians?' has remained a point of contention to this day. To recap, individuals as John David Wortham in *The Genesis of British Egyptology 1549-1906* (Norman: University of Oklahoma Press, 1971: 9) has written: "Great progress was made during the nineteenth century in the study of Egyptian mummification. Augustus Bozzi Granville, a physician and student of Coptic, undertook the earliest nineteenth century dissection of a mummy at his London home in 1825. From his detailed dissection, he correctly concluded that the ancient Egyptians were Caucasian." This is interesting because the statement and publication came 146 years after the dissection, and as such, presented as rock solid, not giving credence to any contradictory evidence since that time. However, four "epoch changing developments," at least, erupted in proximity to Wortham's statement as reflective of the prevailing view that questions the objectivity of this position all such as articulated and held to be the standard today. These are, essentially, (1) The 1820 *Gentleman's Magazine* article; (2) The discovery of the "Deir el Bahari Cache" and the mummies of Amenhotep II's tomb as explained in G. Elliot Smith's *The Royal Mummies* (1905); (3) The 1965 Cairo Publication of H.S.K. Bakry's *A Brief Study of Mummies and Mummification*; and (4) William Arnett's statement in *Evidence for the Development of Evidence of Hieroglyphics in Southern Upper Egypt* (1982) in response to Cheikh Anta Diop's principal position in *The African Origins of Civilization: Myth or Reality* (1974) Unfortunately, Wortham's position is a conclusion in search of evidence for it ignores much of the above.

Into the Egyptian Mind. Egyptian Art. Roy and his wife, she sporting a perfumed cone stand with hands raised in adoration before Shu and Ma'at;' and, at right they also stand before a Table of sumptuous Offerings."

Into the Egyptian Mind. Egyptian Art. Coming face to face with one's own likeness as a "Ba-Bird" is awesome.

Into the Egyptian Mind. Egyptian Art. Roy and wife being introduced by Horus (Heru) without crown (left) and wearing Double Crown (right) as Osiris (Ausar) sits enthroned in his Shrine.

Into the Egyptian Mind. Egyptian Art. The image is subject to interpretation.

Into the Egyptian Mind. Egyptian Art. Anubis (Anpu) sits atop a bier and has that "Thousand-Yard stare."

Into the Egyptian Mind. Kurneh Temple of Seti I. Seti kneels to receive symbols for millions of Years" from enthroned Amon-Ra, with his wife Mut and son Khonsu beside him, forming the "Theban Triad."

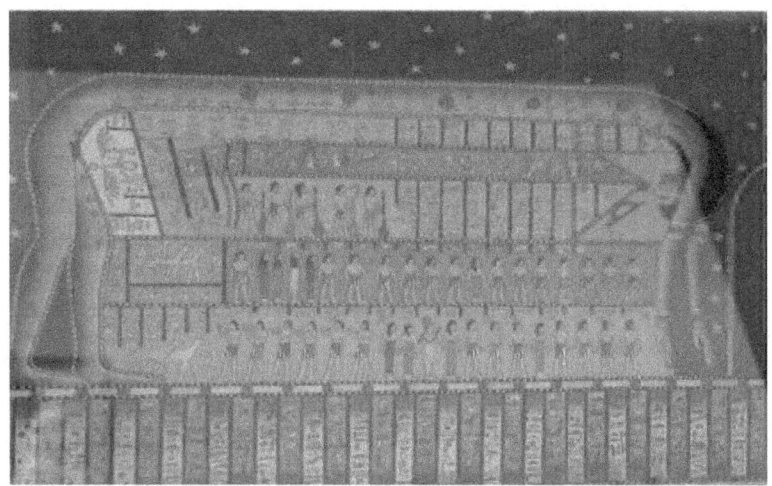

Into the Egyptian Mind. Egyptian Art. Papyrus. The Sky Goddess Nuit spans the heavens and accommodates the drama of the heavens.

Into the Egyptian Mind. Cairo Museum of Egyptian Antiquities. Female wearing perfumed cone on her head stands before a sumptuous "Table of Offerings" to colorful and enthroned Ra-Horakhty wearing horns, White Crown with feathers and uraei with horns and disks while Hathor stands behind the god.

17. LAND OF MANY WATERS
By
Dr. Fred Monderson

Strange that a desert country with one source of water, the powerful Nile River, yet could be considered "A Land of Many Waters," but all things considered, practical and philosophical ancient Egypt fits the category.

As a given, water is a life-giving source and no more practical manner in which this applies than in the process of the Inundation of the Nile. Egypt, a desert country straddles the Nile and both its banks receive bountiful benefits of the overflowing of the river that paves the way in wonderfully fertilizing of the land and depositing silt that helps contribute to bountiful harvests. Some years, depending on the behavior of the river, a second, sometimes a third crop is achieved in the agricultural cycle because of the Nile's bounty. At the end of this cycle when the water has evaporated and the land becomes parched, the rains of Central Africa initiate the phenomenon of the Inundation that begins all over again. For thousands of years this process, as part of the Nile and Sun duo, has enabled the Egyptians to develop and sustain a civilization very early in the human evolutionary cultural experience that created much of the utility mankind is today heir to, both practical and intellectual that set the stage for development in all fields of knowledge. First, W.J. Perry in *The Growth of Civilization* (1934) quotes G. Elliot Smith in *The Ancient Egyptians* (1911) who stated: "The Egyptian did a great deal more than merely invent agriculture and devise the earliest statecraft and religion. Not only did they devise the methods of working wood and stone and the art of architecture, they seem also to have been the inventors of linen and of the craft of weaving, of the use of gold and copper, and the making of metal tools and implements. They were the first people to measure the year and to devise a calendar, and later on to substitute for the rough calculation based upon the date the observation of the sun's movements. They also invented shipbuilding ad constructed the first sea-going ships. In a thousand and one of the details of our common civilization the originality of Egyptian civilization is revealed. The art of shaving, the use of wigs, the wearing of hats, the invention of the kilt and of the sandal and subsequently a variety of other articles of dress, many of our musical instruments, chairs and beds, cushions, jewelry and jewel-cases, lamps – these are merely a few of the items picked at random out of our ancient heritage from the Nile Valley."

Margaret Murray in *The Splendor that Was Egypt* (1949: 57) best characterized such creations in the following statement: "For every student of our modern civilization Egypt is the great storehouse from which to obtain information, for within the narrow limits of that country are preserved the origins of most (perhaps al) of our knowledge. In Egypt are found the first beginnings of material culture – building, agriculture, horticulture, clothing (even cooking as an art); the beginning of the sciences – physics, astronomy, medicine, engineering; the beginnings of the imponderables – law, government, and religion. In every aspect of life Egypt has influenced Europe., and though the centuries may have modified the custom or idea, the origin is clearly visible. Centuries before Ptolemy Philadelphus founded his great temple of the Muses at Alexandria, Egypt was to the Greeks the embodiment of all wisdom and knowledge. In their generous enthusiasm, the Greeks continually recorded that opinion, and by their writings they passed on to later generations that wisdom of the Egyptian which they had learnt orally from the learned men of the Nile Valley.

However, we must be careful in their attributing the "Our" to Europeans rather the Nile Valley Africans or humanity in general. Nevertheless, these accomplishments are attributable to the effervescent overflowing of the river that not simply watered the actual banks of the river but "Uplands" as well.

These latter benefitted from Nile water diverted by extensive canal systems creating checker board patterns of water distribution bringing even greater segments of the land under effective cultivation.

Thus, the ancient agricultural methods, under effective administration enabling bumper crop yields earned Egypt the description as "Breadbasket of the ancient world," enabling a significant percentage of the population to pursue the various cultural dynamics, we have come to recognize and appreciate as Egypt's to the forward progress of the human family.

The Nile River's influence on the desert country has been so profound, in the minds of its theologians it was elevated to the term "Hapi" the Nile God. The river was also associated with Osiris the god who rose from the dead and its return in the Inundation has been equated with that Resurrection. As such, the river for its part shared in the land's bounty and barrenness, life and death, because of its thousands of years of observed predictable behavior morphed into the philosophic esoteric and spiritual concept of resurrection and immortality underscored by religious practices that spoke through the guiding principle of Ma'at with its effective components of justice, balance, order, truth and righteousness.

Without question, the ancient Egyptians were a deeply religious people and this practice pervaded every walk of life flowing from the divine, through the king and onto the people. As such, worship ritual performed for the god in the heavens and in the Sanctuary on earth is the same for the king, both alive and dead. Thus, the benefit of one benefits the other and even the common folks share in the collective benefit granted these who live by the potent principles of Ma'at.

Cosmologically speaking, in the beginning, the ancient Egyptians believed divine forces emerged from the watery mass of nothingness, creating matter and material and ultimately sanctioned a moral and social contract with man, in a symbolic relationship, that of obligations and rewards. Very early in the relationship, the gods communicated with and instructed their servants or priests on the make-up of the earthly structures in which they were to be housed and what specifications were required to assure their safety on earth. They also made it known, in Egypt, malevolent spirits existed whose intent was simply to harm the divine spirit but also to sow disequilibrium that threatened the normal functioning of the state.

Suffice to say, the residence and treatment in praise of divinity was determined by the period of history and the ruling dynasty managing the society. In Egypt, the earliest god of significance was the Sun-god Ra resident in and having his temple in the northern city of Heliopolis or On. Of course, the god's manifestation was associated with one of the first two constants recognized in the sun and its companion, the river. As the society shifted the nucleus became Memphis and there the God of Prominence became Ptah. Much later, during the Middle and New Kingdoms again a shift occurred and this time Amon, later Amon-Ra was worshipped and housed at Thebes in Upper Egypt. By the 20th Dynasty, a further change occurred and the residence was now in the north under the functionality of the Goddess Neith. However, while the fortunes and residences of these principal divinities changed in status and location; Osiris, an early king who was murdered, resurrected and ruled the Underworld as Judge of the Dead appeared closer to the average citizen and remained a most potent divinity throughout dynastic rule, outlasting his premier counterparts and even migrating beyond his nation's border as a potent religious force along with his wife the Goddess Isis.

Into the Egyptian Mind. Egyptian Art. With Isis and Thoth and Hu and Sa, the deceased sails the boat on the Heavenly Nile.

Into the Egyptian Mind. Kurneh Temple of Seti I. The King, whose cartouches are to the right, offers two ointment jars to enthroned Khonsu.

Into the Egyptian Mind. Kurneh Temple of Seti I. The king offers a platter to enthroned Mut of the Theban Triad.

Into the Egyptian Mind. Cairo Museum of Egyptian Antiquities. The deceased and his wife, ploughs the land on both side of the Celestial Nile.

18. PUTTING THEM AWAY NICELY

By
Dr. Fred Monderson

Having attended the funerals of Sonny Carson, Jitu Weusi, Elombe Brathe, Major Owens, Mary Pinkett, Ollie McClean, Rev. Clarence Norman, Sr., and most of all, the spectacular "home-going" of Dr. Yosef ben-Jochannan; I'm reminded of when the question of burials of our loved and revered ones was put to Dr. John Henrik Clarke he simply responded, "We Put Them Away Nicely." In the African community, that final going home ceremony is most an affirmation of joy rather than an expression of sadness! Granted, we'll miss the loved one and so some sad remorse is expected, but the joy of having experienced their presence, witnessed their good works and in some instances been a part of their light illuminating the path of humanity as a part of their earthly existence is what constitutes the joyous moment. With that belief comes an even greater expectation that this earthly goodness so wonderfully created will continue to benefit those who shared in the magnanimous life experience.

While million-year old African fossils many not have revealed any evidence of the beauty of a well-orchestrated burial, this is not the case among Nile Valley dwellers who went to great lengths to dispose of their dead. In that case, the ancient Egyptians left extraordinary evidence of intricate preparation to make the Afterlife a truly wonderful and lasting experience. The building of pyramids and tombs, the development of the practice of mummification, the provisioning of the tomb, the religious beliefs and practices conducted, prior to and after depositing of the deceased into his "eternal home" are parts of the big picture that we vigorously discuss such experience today, millennia later, which means that immortality they sought was attained.

From as early as the Predynastic Period before 5000 B.C., evidence indicates a belief in an afterlife phenomenon that became formulated, crystallized, and imbedded in a religious practice subscribed to by high and low, that is from king to commoner.

As it came to be articulated in a philosophically enshrined belief system, these ancient Africans believed this earthly existence was a temporary sojourn but the world beyond death is of a more eternal nature. They held that a life guided by the principles of Ma'at, viz., justice, truth, righteousness, with adequate preparation one could attain that justification and immortality. As such, in the evolution of tracing such a belief, the period immediately before the dynasties is divided into three culture sequences labeled Badarian, Amratian, and Gerzean or Naqada I and II. From this early time, c. 4200-3200 B.C., evidence in graves point to an aspiration in an afterlife where individuals hoped to continue their lives, in spirit form that was essentially, similarly as they did on earth. The graves reveal the deceased equipped, for example, with tools of his profession; the words of philosophic religious and spiritual power; food, clothing and leisure devices; and even in the case of companionship males had miniature effigies of women and most importantly, where appropriate, to accompany them for purposes of pleasure and purity.

Narmer, a Theban from Upper Egypt, mobilized a military force c. 3200 B.C., sailed north to Lower Egypt and defeated a comparative force, as some have argued, because of the emerging and prevailing wealth of the Nile Valley, this early in time. Then this first king of the first dynasty unified the country under a single administration ushering in the Archaic Period of dynasties 1 and 2. He set in place the social, political and administrative structures that would shape the society for three millennia. By the time of the Old Kingdom,

Dynasties 3-6, with the society's fundamental institutions in place, the practices of art and architecture and religious beliefs began to define the manner of disposal of the dead. Whereas in the Predynastic Period burials were simply holes in the ground, by the third and fourth dynasties funeral architecture evolved through the Mastaba, "Step-Pyramid" and finally the "True Pyramid" forms. By the fifth and sixth dynasties, five pyramids were illustrated with the *Pyramid Texts* that by the Middle Kingdom became the *Coffin Texts* and in the New Kingdom, the *Book of the Dead*. Certainly, by the time of the New Kingdom the art of mummification had achieved a state of perfection today witnessed, especially in the preserved bodies in the royal and Noble Mummies in the Cairo Museum and elsewhere.

While in the Old Kingdom the *Pyramid Texts* of hieroglyphic symbols nearly a millennium in evolution, represented a collection of social commentary, primarily they represented the religious dogma that defined and regulated the process by which the king was received in the Afterlife and where he became a god. In this case, the "big dog" or king with the requisite resources at his disposal left ample evidence of the practical, philosophic and religious drama designed to create the immortality we have become so familiar with. However, all the trappings that go into the pyramids, tombs, the decoration and provisioning of the "eternal house" attracted a "criminal element" who would desecrate the sacred site, assault the blessed dead, and loot the treasures accompanying them into the next life. Thus, despite "lock and key;" "watch men;" in endowment responsibilities; traps and pitfalls; nothing really stopped the desecration and denial of the ultimate objective. Therefore, the deceased finally resorted to a belief in magic that would protect and transform his preparation for the final objective.

Into the Egyptian Mind. Egyptian Art. Thoth (Tehuti) hold ankh and another instrument before enthroned Osiris (Ausar) backed by Isis as Ma'at.

As such, a number of factors contributing to the end result can be enumerated as follows;

(1). Because the Egyptian believed this earthly existence was temporary and the future life more permanent, he built his domestic residence of perishable material and secured his "eternal home" for more lasting duration, with attendant protections. Conversely, and as an example, the king built his palace of perishable material, and his god's temple of the more permanent material, stone.

(2) The process of provisioning, that is, making his tomb comfortable for the spirit that would inhabit it, was provided with all manner of luxury items from graphic illustrations food to tools and leisurely and recreational items of games, musical instruments to furniture and religious paraphernalia,

to a place where relatives and priestly officials could come to offer food and drink to steles before the tomb that passers-by could read the magical formulas contained therein, he thought of everything.

Into the Egyptian Mind. Egyptian Art. Enthroned and aboard one's boat, is a refreshingly exhilarating experience.

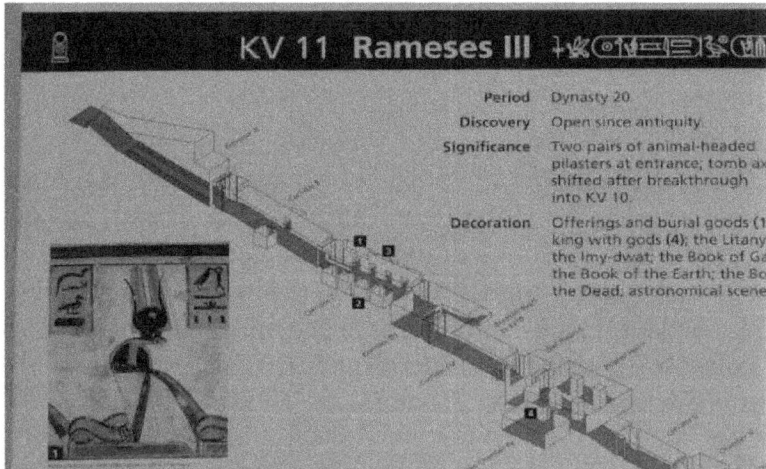

Into the Egyptian Mind. Valley of the Kings, Luxor Egypt. The Tomb of Rameses III showing how such structures descend into the earth or in this case, mountainous area.

Into the Egyptian Mind. Tomb of Rameses III. Valley of the Kings, Luxor Egypt. Image of Rameses escorted by Thoth (Tehuti) and Khenty-Khety.

Into the Egyptian Mind. Tomb of Rameses III. Valley of the Kings, Luxor Egypt. Deceased offers a vessel with cone to enthroned Osiris (Ausar) holding scepter and whip with a huge snake with legs at the god's rear. Notice Osiris (Ausar) is painted Black.

(3)All representations were symbolic and aesthetic conventions expanded and became refined domestic utensils, military equipment, industrial implements and other entertainment paraphernalia including evidence of the hunt, the banquet scene of music and joviality, working the fields, making grape juice and wine, even bakery, butchery and statuary to represent the deceased empowered with words of magic to partake of all preparation. The African thought of everything to be able to "Carry it all with him!"

To this we add, not simply "reserved' statues of the deceased in case the mummy was destroyed but also servant statues called "Ushabtis" or "answerers" who would do the manual things the deceased was required to do such as working the fields, to preparing his food and toilet, to providing joy, entertainment and protection.

Into the Egyptian Mind. Egyptian Art. Ceiling decoration in the Tomb of Djehutimose of the Eighteenth Dynasty.

19. THE ETERNAL HOUSE
By
Dr. Fred Monderson

Marcus Garvey looked at the Pyramids! Most people asked, "How were they built?" Garvey asked how were they paid for? He reasoned; they were paid for by the creation of a surplus economy. With a surplus, the society's leaders and thinkers were able to remove some people from the regular agricultural base of the society and encourage the development of skills - technical skills, building skills, artistic skills, scientific skills, medical skills, especially to treat those injured on work sites relative to preparation for the preparation for the dead, and most important, religious skills to provide for the needs of divinity.

1. CHRONOLOGY - There were two Chronologies, the *Long Chronology* and the *Short Chronology*. Lots of political dynamics involved in these which I will not go into except to say the Short Chronology is the more manageable one. We have 3000 years of Egyptian history divided into the Old Kingdom - Dynasties 1-6; the Middle Kingdom - Dynasties 11-13; and the New Kingdom, essentially dynasties 17-20. There is a late period of dynasties 21-30. Dynasties 1-2 is called the Archaic Period which follows the Predynastic Period; Dynasties 7-10 is the First Intermediate Period; Dynasties 14-16 is the second Intermediate Period. Dynasties 17-20 is the New Kingdom.

Dynasties 1-6 -   -   3200-2240 B.C.
Dynasties 11-13   -   2000-1785 B.C.
Dynasties 17-20   -   1785-900 B.C.

The Predynastic stretches anywhere down to 3000 B.C.

1. INTRODUCTION -

Very early the young Egyptian, African, especially was told two things.

Into the Egyptian Mind. Egyptian Art. Anubis (Anpu) sits atop the Sarcophagus holding scepter and flail and manifesting that "Thousand-Yard stare."

Into the Egyptian Mind. Egyptian Art. Twin Hathors offers twin ankhs to twin pharaohs.

Into the Egyptian Mind. Tomb of Thutmose IV. Valley of the Kings, Luxor Egypt. The beautifully decorated Sarcophagus of the King.

Into the Egyptian Mind. Tomb of Thutmose IV. Valley of the Kings, Luxor, Egypt. Isis (Auset) on the Sarcophagus with raised hands.

Into the Egyptian Mind. Cairo Museum of Egyptian Antiquities. Papyrus. A deceased female backed by divinities approach enthroned Osiris (Ausar) painted green with Isis (Isis) and Nephthys (Nepty) at his rear and further on a collection of deities sit enthroned before an enormous snake.

First, get a wife to have children who will eventually bury you. You must know, even down to our day, for the parent to bury the child is a heart-wrenching experience. More important, however, having a wife is to have an heir, a son, to carry forward your name and to inherit your property. In their day, the men ruled but the women carried the sacred genes. That is why, Hatshepsut had such a hard time as a woman trying to rule, thought she did for nearly two decades. Nevertheless, in this earthly existence, you must strive in life to be able to leave something. The Egyptian, however, loved children. They believed they were sweet. They bequeathed property to their offsprings but insisted property not be split up or sold.

The second thing the Egyptian was advised was to "Prepare your tomb," your place of final refuge. Prepare to meet your death. In essence, prepare to meet your god. Consider where you will be buried. No one knows when the Messenger of Death will come for you. You must be prepared. You just can't say, "I'm young, not ready to go and so on." As you stand before your god to be judged, you must show you have done something worthwhile on earth.

Prepare you tomb has a deeper meaning. It means live a life that has meaning. Live a life to bring good into the world. This probably means live a life that has worth. Do good things, do for others. Do Ma'at to other people! Make your mark so you can be remembered. For those of you who were here on Sunday, I made a comment, "To be remembered, you must write your name upon the minds and hearts of the people." This we recognized Forbes Burnham did and that is why, despite the character assassination he was subject to, the people loved and worshipped him so that in "After years" he is still a revered person.

Into the Egyptian Mind. Egyptian Art. Alabaster factory decoration on the West Bank at Luxor, Upper Egypt.

Into the Egyptian Mind. Egyptian Art. Papyrus. Horus in Double Crown introduces the deceased who then kneels before the Shrine of enthroned Osiris (Ausar) and Isis (Auset) and Nephthys (Nepty).

ETERNAL HOUSE THE EGYPTIAN TOMB
BY
DR. FRED MONDERSON

"Behold the dwellings of the dead. Their walls fall down; their place is no more: they are as though they had never existed. That which hath come into being must pass away again. The young men and maidens go to their places; the sun riseth at dawn, and setteth again in the hills of the west. Men beget and women conceive. The children, too, go to the place which is appointed for them. Oh, then, be happy! Come, scents and perfumes are set before thee: mahu-flowers and lilies for the arms and neck of thy beloved. Come, songs and music are before thee. Set behind thee all cares; think only upon gladness, until that day cometh whereon thou shall go down to the land which loveth silence." Is an old admonition.

Imhotep, who built the Step-Pyramid at Ghizeh for Pharaoh Zoser in the 3rd Dynasty was the world's first multi genius as mathematician, Prime Minister, architect, physician, priest and poet. He said, what is considered the saying of the ages: "Eat, drink and be merry for tomorrow you die." What is going to happen after that is what the Egyptian was concerned about.

The religion of Egypt is about preparation for the eternal, after, life.

The prominence of the gods rose and fell depending on the time and family that ruled Egypt. Nevertheless, two prevailing religious belief about the afterlife prevailed. These were the celestial heaven and the earthly abode. The celestial heaven fell under the domain of God Ra and the earthly abode under Osiris. Essentially, from the earliest period the king ascended to the heavenly abode to be judged,

naturally, but to dwell among the gods like a circumpolar star. The small man was consigned to essentially the earthly kingdom of Osiris.

Now, the theologians were able to reconcile these two beliefs and their dogmas by explaining, Ra the Sun God traversed the heavens in the day and traveled in the underworld at night. There were 12 hours of the day and 12 hours of the night. In each segment, a particular occurrence manifested and at a certain time, Ra traversed the Kingdom of Osiris. The two gods meet in the underworld, there for an hour, Ra shined his rays on the denizens who occupied Osiris' abode. He sorts of refreshed them! Then he departed to appear on the horizon in the early morn to repeat his daily functions.

Before he set out, he had to be lustrated or given his bath. That is, he had to be washed, roughed with sweet smelling unguents, put on his lipstick and you name it. His feet were massaged and then he was fed. This same washing and purification the Sun God undertook was same as that done to his earthly statue in the sanctuary and that done to the Pharaoh before he officiated in the temple. That is, the Washing of the King took place in the "House of the Morning." This purification of the Pharaoh was repeated when he arrived at the temple and the same as the Consecration or Purification of the temple where all parts had to be invoked to come alive before the ritual could commence. The same washing or purification of the king and the temple was the same washing the dead had to undergo so that he too was considered pure. After all, he was headed to the place where the gods were born. This was a place of purity and so he had to be pure.

Though the king was buried in an earthly sepulcher, he was not considered dead, consecrated in washing and after being justified at the Judgment, again purified, he now joined them and became a full-fledged god.

Interesting that in the time of the pyramids only the king could get to heaven. So, people wanted to be buried within the shadow of his pyramid. There were 5 pyramids decorated with the *Pyramid Texts* and these were those of Teti, Unas, Pepi I and Pepi II and Merenra. The first was of the Fifth Dynasty and the others of the Sixth Dynasty.

The *Coffin Texts* were inscriptions inside and outside the coffins and also on the Sarcophagus, above and below. This period is called the democratization of the afterlife because now other persons could get to heaven, essentially, however, it's really the rich who could so afford.

By the New Kingdom, everybody could get to heaven because now the doors were opened. The *Pyramid Texts* and the *Coffin Texts* were now transformed into the *Book of the Dead*, more appropriately the Book of Going Forth by Day or the Per-em-Hru. How much of the *Book of the Dead* one could afford depended upon one's wealth but all books had the most essential parts such as Chapter 125, the **Negative Confessions**.

Into the Egyptian Mind. Egyptian Art.
Raised relief of workers engaged as seen in a tomb in the Mountain of El Kab.

Into the Egyptian Mind. Egyptian Art. The Sem Priest in Leopard Skin raises an adze, a device used in the "Opening the Mouth Ceremony" and is followed by a procession of men and women.

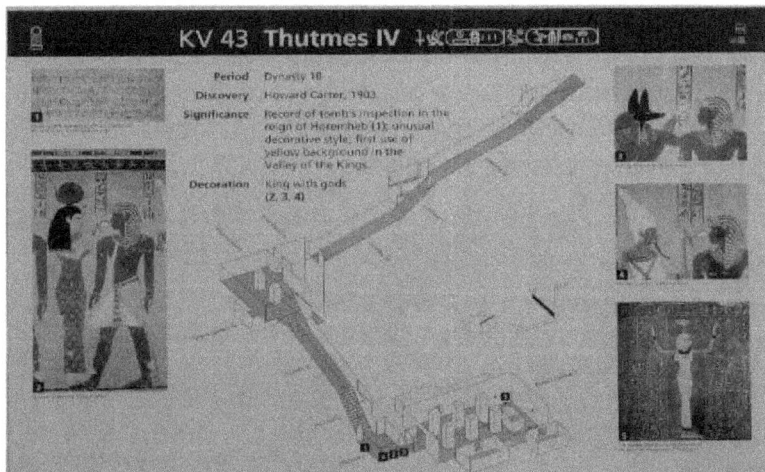

Into the Egyptian Mind. Tomb of Thutmose IV. Valley of the Kings, Luxor Egypt. Image showing the king with various gods.

Into the Egyptian Mind. Tomb of Thutmose IV. Valley of the Kings, Luxor, Egypt. Isis (Auset) kneels on golden Heb at the foot of the Sarcophagus.

This leads us to the practice that drove the Egyptian to prepare for his final internment, to "prepare thy tomb," that is best explained by Isaac Myer in *Account of the Ancient Egyptians* (Edwin W. Dayton, 1900: 136-138) where he examines some of the ancient sources and provides the following admonitions:

"Place before thyself as an aim, the attainment of an old age, as to which they (i.e., people) may be able to bear witness, to the end thou may be found having perfected thy house which is in the funeral valley, on the morning of the concealment of thy body. Place this before thyself in all the duties which thou hast to consider with thy eye. When thou wilt be also a very old man, thou wilt sleep in the midst of them; therein is no surprise for the one who acts well, he is prepared; act so that when thy messenger (of death) shall come for thee in order to take thee, he may find one who is ready. Certainly, thou wilt not (then) have time to speak, because in coming, he is suddenly before thee. Say not: I am a young man; wilt thou seize (me)? For thou knowest not the (time) of thy death. Death comes, he seizes the nursling who is in the arms of his mother, as well as he who has reached old age. Behold: I have said to thee these excellent things which (thou ought) to consider in thy heart; do them, thou wilt become a good man and all evils will be far from thee."

HERE's another admonition:

"Tread the way which the upright man follows: thou wilt find that it will well prepare thy place in the valley of the tombs, and thy body will remain concealed. Think thereof always in the works which thy hand directs ... Speak not of the youth in which thou rejoice, because thou knowest not when death will come. Death will come; it will seize the nursling on the bosom of its mother, as (well as) the old man advanced in age. Regard me and let me tell thee what is the advantage of virtue, which ought to be the path of thy heart. So, thou wilt become a worthy man and all evils will remain far from thee."

"Recall to thyself what thou hast been (and) know it (i.e., remember it). Place before thee as a way to follow, equitable conduct; thou wilt then be considered as having prepared thyself a proper sepulture in the funeral valley, which tomorrow will conceal thy body. Let that be before thee in all things which thou hast to decide. In the same way as the very old men, thou wilt sleep in the midst of them; there is not any remission (of this, even) for him who conducts himself well; he is (also) disposed of same. In a like manner to thee will come thy messenger of death so as to carry thee away; yes! He is found already prepared. Discourses will not serve thee, because he comes, he holds himself in readiness before thee. Say not: 'I am a young child, I, whom thou carriest away!' Thou knowest not how thou wilt die. Death comes; he goes before the nursling, the one who is at the breast of its mother, as well as (before) him who has reached old age. Behold! I have told thee salutary things which thou wilt decide in thy heart to perform; from (the performance of) them thou wilt find happiness and all evil will be diverted from thee."

So, this is the admonition and warning.

The Egyptian tomb, the "eternal house," therefore, was a special place not simply because of the function it served, but importantly because of its location as transitional sacred space between this world and the next. That is, while the home was "temporary" for his sojourn on earth, the Egyptian believed the tomb was more permanent and where he intended to spend heavenly eternity. So, he lived a life guided by the ethical principle of Ma'at with its righteous components of truth and justice, then structured his tomb in a manner in which he would enjoy the privileges and luxuries of this earthly life for the duration in the next. Therefore, in this effort to understand the tomb we must consider a number of factors relative to the concept and the involved process wherein no other people in ancient times had similarly devoted as much resources and time to make this process reality. We must also recognize the cornerstone of the funerary process was influenced by religious beliefs and practice; a process that remained unchanged for millennia. As such then, and first of all, we must consider the make-up of the outer structure of the tomb in the particular location in both time and space. The form of the inner structure must also be considered as well as the religious belief system and even depicted reliefs regarding disposal of the dead. Along with this we must consider the ceremonies performed, the purification of the deceased, whether during the mummification process or as it was before mummification, on the mummy, at the tomb publicly on the mummy itself where the grieving relatives were in attendance witnessing the "Opening of the Mouth Ceremony," and finally at the closure of the burial chamber. We must consider the size and function of the funeral procession and the role of the paid professional mourners. We must also consider the significance of the religious implication of the decoration as it related to the afterlife. To this must be added the actions of the deceased before death, through set-up endowments for the deceased to be symbolically and philosophically involved at the various feasts at which time he was prayed for during the celebratory festivities from which offerings were left at or inside the tomb's area prepared for this. That is, an area set aside for ceremonies, offerings, etc., before the sealed inner reaches of the tomb.

To this we may also consider the power and significance of libations family and friends will continue to make subsequent to the burial. However, in as much as this practice can be traced back through Old Kingdom dates; a variant was practiced in Nubia as late as the beginning of the twentieth century. Nonetheless, while modern day Nubians practiced a variant of the libation offering on Fridays, an Islamic "Holy Day," the practice is not actually Islamic and can be traced to at least the Third Dynasty mortuary rites of ancient Egypt.

To understand much of this, we can begin by agreeing with John Garstang in *The Burial Customs of Ancient Egypt* (London: Archibald, Constable and Co., Ltd., 1907: 1) who correctly argued: "The burial customs of ancient Egypt are the foundation of Egyptological studies." In this, among other things, he points to the physical character of the land, beyond the reaches of the Inundation, in the desert margins, for: "In the desert which bounds the cultivation on either side, the Egyptians sought for their tombs more permanent security than they deemed necessary for their dwelling house." That is, while the poor were buried in holes in the desert, the well-to-do sought refuge in rock-cut tombs in higher elevations. Equally, we must recognize the actual deposit of the dead is not the end of all things. However, addressing the notion of festivities and offerings that continued after the burial, Garstang (1907: 2) additionally provides insights as: "The periodical visitations to the tombs, the feasting and observances on these occasions, the prayers and invocations made almost directly to the dead, the belief in the presence near or in the tomb of the 'good spirit' or double of the deceased, and the provisioning of the tomb with food. Even a model of a boat or dahabiyeh is sometimes placed within the tomb-chapel for the pleasure of the deceased, as the custom was in the days 2000 B.C.... From such instances of direct survival, it must appear that the burial customs of Egypt and the religious impulses which prompted them are a product of the land itself

Into the Egyptian Mind. Cairo Museum of Egyptian Art. Papyrus. As a female deceased pours a libation, she is backed by four divinities.

Another important factor we must also consider is the placement of steles outside the tomb that describes the deceased and the concomitant magical/mystical invoking of divine favors for the deceased by passers-by. The Egyptian believed the simple reading of the inscriptions would symbolically and magically transform those words into substantive offerings infused with a metaphysical and spiritually potent receptive capability. Equally, and again, the decoration of the tomb's interior in graphic and art forms were designed to reflect his expected leisure dynamics, provide the wherewithal to magically overcome the challenges of the journey and the esoteric invoking of all within the tomb, food, art, inscriptions, to his benefit, all being readily at hand.

Thus, to understand the make-up of these facilities and the involved phenomenon, we get assistance from the *Dictionary of Art* (1996: 836) under the topic "Religious Architecture, 'Tombs'" that provide an enumerated description of these eternal dwellings from earliest Old Kingdom burials wherein this source tells us: "There were four principal tomb types: pit-graves, mastabas, pyramids and chapel tombs." There were, however, variations in these forms of burials and tombs overtime. The simplest and commonest of all such internments was the pit-grave in the ground at the desert edge, of sufficient size to house the corpse and basic funeral goods." Foremost were the Mastaba and later the Pyramid. Even further, Weeks (2001: 836) continued: "The Mastaba was the natural progression from the pit-grave, adding a superstructure; it was the characteristic tomb of the elite during the Old and Middle Kingdoms (c. 2575-1630 B.C). Pyramid tombs probably developed from mastabas, were used for royal burials in the Old and Middle Kingdoms; with its associate structures, the form was revived during the New Kingdom and later periods on a much smaller scale in mud-brick for private dwellings. A further development from the Mastaba was the chapel tomb, which took two forms: tomb chapels with the offering chambers hewn out of the rock and free-standing tomb chapels with the superstructure in the shape of a small shrine. In both cases the chapel has a subterranean room or rooms, reached by a shaft cut through bedrock, to accommodate the burial and grave goods. Some of these tombs occur contemporaneously in the same cemeteries."

Naturally, and beyond the security, human and structural, needed to protect the tomb, those expected privileges and luxuries, however, were contingent on a lived life by the principles enshrined in the philosophy of Ma'at as a tenet of social order in the cosmos. This powerful social and ethical philosophic standard molded the well-balanced individual who could stand confidently before his god when judged in the afterlife.

SIGNIFICANCE OF THE TOMB

The significance of the tomb in ancient Egypt has changed according to the period in question. That is, as events, circumstances and times changed religious beliefs and burial practices also changed through changes in the structure and construction of tombs. Even the provisioning decoration of the tomb changed as did ceremonies on the mummy and again at the tomb. In fact, Dieter Arnold reinforces this view in "Ancient Egypt: Tombs" in the *Encyclopedia of Religion* (2000: 836) with the statement: "The design and development of Egyptian tombs was inextricably linked with religious beliefs. The essential idea was to provide a suitable and enduring setting for eternal life after death. From the earliest periods, the tomb was thought of as a 'house of eternity,' a burial place where the corpse could be protected, the necessary funerary goods deposited and regular food offerings made for the sustenance of the deceased." However, the greatest improvements were made especially to royal tombs during the New Kingdom's "Golden Age" period. Notwithstanding, the two fundamental beliefs that the burial place is where the Egyptian would spend eternity and so it had to be secure, protected and provisioned meant that the ka of the individual, seemingly the most important part of the personality, would remain associated with the deceased in the tomb; thus, it had to have special consideration for its protection. Equally, the ceremonies performed and ensuring of consistent sustenance were important to ensure the next life would essentially be a mirror image of this life. As such, the sacred space from circular to oblong graves in the ground for the simplest people during the Predynastic Period, to tombs of monumental structures of pyramids with subsidiary mastabas during the Old Kingdom for society's upper class generally buried in kingly cemeteries consumed much resources, energy and time.

By the Old Kingdom the king had become entrenched as a god on earth, one who, upon death, gained immortality alongside his brother and sister gods. So much so, these kingly divinities on earth built and provisioned more elaborate tombs, mastabas, and finally pyramids and so, their subjects, the upper crust of society especially, considered it an honor to be buried in the shadow of their god king. To gain coattail immortality they vied for special locations within the cemetery of the respective king laid out systematically in areas surrounding the kingly place of internment; that is, whether in mastabas and finally pyramids, and where nobles built elaborate structures that displayed material wealth and intangibles that made the future life seem easier to countenance required much thought and resources. For those individuals who built larger Mastaba tombs, even their family members were afforded a place not simply to come and pay respect in terms of funerary offerings and so on, but they were also provided a place to rest beside their loved one.

All this notwithstanding, we therefore see the place of final internment and nature of the burial practice change dramatically in terms of location, structure, content, guiding philosophy and the significant role these developments played in painting a fuller picture of the nature of the society. Yet, seeming socially contradictory, while the methods of burial and final resting place of the king, nobles and other well-to-do persons changed with the society's fortunes, that of the poorest or peasant essentially remained the same throughout dynastic rule though there were some slight modifications in poor burials by the late Graeco-Roman periods. Nevertheless, the tomb, therefore, proved tremendously important especially by the time of the wealthy state of imperial New Kingdom. Thus, the tomb especially from this period has provided great storehouses of insights into religious practices, architectural and artistic knowledge for scholars, archaeologists, anthropologists, historians, art historians, linguists, etc., who came to unearth, study and write about the ancient Egyptian tomb. As such, whether it was a hole in the ground, a grave on a flat plain, a pyramid or a tomb dug into the side of the mountain, the shape and nature of this final resting place changed over time in terms of size and practice as the society matured. Equally, not only did the plan of the tomb change but also the ritual, ceremony, even the contents also changed as reflective of the deceased's status. This status, not only reflected in decoration of tomb walls but also in many respects particularly on biographic stela recounting a great deal of the individual's service to the society, his connection to the king, his praises of the king, how he acquired the site of his burial, whether he was a beneficiary of the king's largesse, and the nature of its contents as well as his instructions for cult officials if he could afford it. To this we might add that his family, even passers-by who, whether through thought or deed reading his engraved messages might assist in the belief of keeping his memory alive.

Let us not forget modern fascination with Egypt whether through books, videos, museum displays, or even actual viewing as tourists, the tomb has continued to be a favorite because it transports the viewer, actually and philosophically, back into the time of the Egyptians' existence. However, some visitors, whether ancient or modern, have had a tendency to desecrate the tomb, not in the manner the

Egyptian first believed but by leaving graffiti inscriptions, removing artifacts or even so far as living within and excreting body waste. However, only in recent times, as the Egyptian came to understand the economic value of the tomb in its attraction to visitors and lovers of antiquity who pay to come see its glory, have the authorities employed attendants that have, to some extent, halted any behaviors that assaulted the tomb in any way.

As such, then, the Egyptian tomb remains a subject of serious and revealing fascination. Keeping in mind, however, most of the tombs, particularly those viewed in the tourist circuit, have been open a long time; some since antiquity, and thus have been bruised, battered, graffitied and even sanitized. In that respect, the ethnicity question of the ancient Egyptian has been muddled at worst, cleaned-up at best and so raises more questions about this question. Nevertheless, the Egyptian tomb represented a mirror image of how this Nile Valley inhabitant behaved, thought, lived his many aspirations for the present and future life and in many respects, depicts many of the objects of industry and practices he invented that still impact modern humans' daily existence. If nothing else, this ancient African, molded from the cultural effluence of Africa along the banks of the Nile River, established two never to be forgotten hallmarks of human existence. That is, the belief and practice of religion and the practice of moral principles embodied in the philosophy of Ma'at, that if adhered to, was designed to cultivate the highest good in the human spirit. To this we can also add wisdom, for when the question of burial within the African tradition was asked of Prof. John Henrik Clarke, he simply responded, "We put them away nicely!" He himself as well as dr. Ben-Jochannan, Elombe Brathe, etc., were put away nicely at Abyssinian Baptist Church in Harlem, New York City. This essentially is why today we can learn so much about the ancient Egyptians as archaeology more and more often continue to unearth, paint and explain that fascinating picture we so love to study whether in books, museums or on a visit to Egypt, in North-East Africa.

Into the Egyptian Mind. Egyptian Art. Seated Noble holding scepter seated beside wife, both are showered with incense and libation by two servants.

Into the Egyptian Mind. Egyptian Art. Raised relief. A funeral scene carrying the body's bier, (above) and the River journey (below).

Into the Egyptian Mind. Egyptian Art. The King pours a libation before divinity.

Into the Egyptian Mind. Valley of the Kings, Luxor, Egypt. Mountain view of a no-longer affordable photograph of the burial region below. Now it is illegal to climb the mountain.

Into the Egyptian Mind. Cairo Museum of Egyptian Antiquities. Papyrus. Deceased and wife stand before enthroned Osiris (Ausar) in his shrine. Notice the God is painted green.

George G.M. James' penetrating revelation and exposure entitled *Stolen Legacy* (1954: 122) has indicated there were actually 9 parts to the human personality embodied in the soul. This the Egyptian hoped to reconstitute after death to make the person whole again. Quoting the Greek philosopher Aristotle whom he criticized, James wrote: "According to Aristotle the soul possesses the following attributes (1) Identity with body, as form with matter (2) The power which a living body possesses, i.e., the radical principle of life, manifesting itself in the following attributes that helped characterize the individual:

(a) **Sensitive** - acutely affected by external stimuli or mental impressions.

(b) **Rational** - of or based on reason.

(c) **Nutritive** - the need for food or nourishment.

(d) **Appetitive** - a natural desire to satisfy bodily needs.

(e) **Locomotive** - the power to move from one place to another.

Even further, (1954: 123) James continued: "In the Genesis story, it is asserted that God made man out of matter (i.e., the dust of the earth), and breathed into his nostrils, the breath of live, and 'man became a living soul.' Here we have a clear statement of the identity of 'body and soul,' taken from a document (*Genesis*) which antedates Aristotle by many centuries."

Even more, James (1954: 123-124) noted: "In the Egyptian Book of the Dead, we also find that the human soul is composed of the following nine inseparable parts:

The **Ka**, which is an abstract personality of the man to whom it belongs possessing the form and attributes of a man with power of locomotion, omnipresence and ability to receive nourishment like a man. It is equivalent to (*Eidolon*), i.e., image.

The **Khat**, i.e., the concrete personality, the physical body, which is mortal.

The **Ba**, i.e., the heart-soul, which dwells in the Ka and sometimes alongside it, in order to supply it with air and food. It has the power of metamorphosis and changes its form at will.

The **Ab**, i.e., the Heart, the animal life in man, that is rational, spiritual and ethical. It is associated with the Ba (heart-soul) and in the Egyptian Judgment Drama it undergoes examination in the presence of Osiris, the great Judge of the Unseen World.

The **Khaibit**, i.e., shadow. It is associated with Ba (heart-soul) from whom like the Ka, it receives its nourishment. It has the power of locomotion and omnipresence.

The **Khu**, i.e., spiritual soul, which is immortal. It is also closely associated with the Ba (heart-soul), and is an Ethereal Being.

The **Sahu**, i.e., spiritual body, in which the Khu or spiritual soul dwells. In it all the mental and spiritual attributes of the natural body are united to the new powers of its own nature.

The **Sekhem**, i.e., power or the spiritual personification of the vital force in a man. Its dwelling place is in the heavens with spirits or Khus.

The **Ren**, i.e., the name, or the essential attribute for the preservation of a Being. The Egyptians believed that in the absence of a name, an individual ceased to exist.

In explaining some of the above, in a "Note Below" James (1954: 124125) further writes: "It must be noted that according to the Egyptian concept, the soul has nine parts, whose unity is so complete, that even the Ren, i.e., the name, is an essential attribute, since without it, it cannot exist. The Ba (or heart-soul), is connected with the Ka, Khaibit, and Ab (Abstract personality or Shadow and Animal life) on the one hand, and also with Khu and Sekhem (spiritual Soul and spiritual personification of vital force) on the other hand, as the power of Nourishment."

The **Sahu** is a spiritual body which is used both by Khu and Sekhem.

The **Khat**, i.e., the physical body, is essential to the soul while manifesting itself upon the physical plane.

The **Soul** has the additional following attributes:

Omnipresence - the ability to be everywhere.

Metamorphosis - ability to change character condition.

Locomotion - the power to move from one place to another.

Nutritive - possessing the need for food or nutrition.

Mortality (in the case of the Khat) - being subject to death.

Immortality - living forever in spirit or memory.

Rationality - the ability to reason.

Spirituality - having to do with religion and the divine.

Morality - subject to conforming to accepted rules and standards of human behavior of right or wrong.

Ethereal - highly delicate in appearance, heavenly.

Shadowy - a body that can cast a shadow.

"It is clear from such a comparison as this, that the Aristotelian doctrine of the soul is identical and coincides with only a very small portion of the Egyptian philosophy of the soul, which therefore stands in relation to it as a whole to its part. Consequently, we must conclude that Aristotle obtained his doctrine of the soul from the Egyptian Book of the Dead, directly or indirectly."

Into the Egyptian Mind. Egyptian Art. With raised empty hands, the deceased stands before Ptah, holding is instrument of power.

Into the Egyptian Mind. Egyptian Art. Protected by the "Two Eyes of Horus."

Into the Egyptian Mind. Image of the rugged terrain that must be conquered to survive.

Into the Egyptian Mind. Deir el Bahari, Temple of Queen Hatshepsut. From the Mountain, view of the Second Court, First and Second Ramps and the Upper Court with remaining columns before the Sanctuary.

Into the Egyptian Mind. Cairo Museum of Egyptian Antiquities. Papyrus. Burial scene. Taking the deceased to the tomb. Osiris (Ausar) on guard. The boat sled, people in the procession, and the Sem Priest performing the "Opening the Mouth Ceremony" on the mummy.

Nevertheless, and in conjunction, James Henry Breasted in *The Dawn of Conscience*, (New York: Charles Scribner's Sons, 1934: 48) in attempting to explain the various efforts expended to restore functionality to the deceased before beginning the Afterlife existence, explained: "In harmony with these conceptions was the desire of the surviving relatives to insure physical restoration to the dead. Gathered with the relatives and friends of the deceased at the tomb, the mortuary priest stood over the silent body and addressed the departed in the "Opening of the Mouth Ceremony": 'Thy bones perish not, thy flesh sickens not, and thy members are not distant from thee.' However effective these injunctions may have been, they were not considered sufficient. The motionless body must be resuscitated and restored to the use of its members and senses. This resurrection might be the act of a favoring god or goddess, as when accompanied by Isis or Horus; or the priest addressed the dead and assured him that the Sky-goddess would raise him up: 'She sets on again for thee thy head, she gathers for thee thy bones, she unites for thee thy members, she brings for thee thy heart into thy body.' But even when so raised the dead was not in possession of his senses and faculties, nor had he the power to control and use his body and limbs. Several devices were necessary to make of this unresponsive mummy a living person, capable of carrying on the life hereafter. He had not become a ba, or a soul, merely by dying, and it was necessary to aid him to become one. Osiris when lying dead had become a soul by receiving from his son Horus the latter's eye, wrenched from the socket in his conflict with Set. Horus, recovering his eye, gave it to his father, and on receiving it Osiris at once became a soul. From that time, any offering to the dead was commonly called the 'Eye of Horus,' and might thus produce the same effect as on Osiris. 'Raise thee up,' says the priest, 'for this thy bread, which cannot dry up, and thy beer which cannot become stale, by which thus shall become a soul.' The food which the priest offered therefore possessed the mysterious power of effecting the transformation of the dead man into a soul, as the 'eye of Horus' had once transformed Osiris."

So, let me wind this down by saying the following:

1. First and foremost, the ancient African of Egypt believed in an Afterlife of great duration and prepared for it. He considered this life a temporary sojourn and the afterlife eternity. He sought to live a life of righteousness, truth and justice so as to prevail in the "Afterlife."

2. We recognize the tomb was a special place between this world and the next. However, it was not difficult to get in contact with the deceased. They believed he heard the prayers and smelled the incense they burned and partook of the food they presented. The tomb had a sort of entrance way, a hall in which the relatives and friends could visit, say prayers and leave offerings. To this was attached a shaft dug deep into the earth that reached the resting place of the deceased.

3. From the time of death to deposit of the body in its Eternal House, a number of developments took place, chief of which were:

a. Mummification of the body - its washing and consecration.

b. Preparation of a voyage to the Holy City of Abydos, where the realm of Osiris the God of the Dead was located. The price of the real estate at that site was expensive and only the wealthy could be buried there. However, to make the symbolic voyage to the City was important and the voyage became a principal feature of tomb decoration. Sort of to say, I was there.

c. Establishment of a stone stela outside the tomb as a sort of biographical reference about the life to the deceased. This was twofold. It recounted the life experiences of the deceased but it also contained magical expressions so that passers-by could simply read the saying and it would magically transform and provide the intent for the deceased as represented on the walls of the tomb. As he statue he could reach out and touch the food.

Keep in mind at the last lecture I mentioned before the Pharaoh entered the temple. Magically and spiritually he had to be purified and so too the temple. At the magical consecration and purification, the priest visited every room in the temple to make it came alive. So, this phenomenon transformed the words into deeds.

d. Depending on the time period in which he lived, the *Pyramid Texts*, *Coffin Texts* or *Book of the Dead* were designed to guide his voyage to the place where the gods held court. Along the way, there were devils, monsters or evil forces he met who were guardians of some 20 Gates he had to by-pass and tried to impede his passage. Along the journey, the "Tree goddess" poured four pitchers of cooling waters on him. Nevertheless, the *Book of the Dead* was the Compass that helped guide him along the way. It told him the name of each of the demons he would encounter and answering "What is my name?" He told them correctly.

4. A number of ceremonies had to be performed on the body, whether during and after mummification and also, more important at the gravesite.

The "Opening of the Mouth" ceremony had to be performed so that deceased could retain all his lively functions when he went to meet the gods. Among those ceremonies he had to be washed and when he arrived at the heavenly abode, he had also to be again purified by the gods to live among them.

There he had to undergo the judgment in what was called the **Psychostasia**. There he recited the **42 Negative Confessions**, in essence saying I did not commit these sins. There were also Positive Confessions where he admitted I did this, I did this, I did that, to help humanity!

Foucart believed there was a place at Deir el Bahari, a cavern, where the deceased entered to begin the journey to the Hall of Judgment.

Sometime after the burial and judgment, he was able to have the elements of his soul reconstituted and he returned to occupy the tomb. That is to say, having been "Justified" or proved "True of Voice," he took on godlike qualities and was able to re-emerge from the heavenly abode and inhabit the tomb. The decoration of the tomb walls with all the things he desired, were there for him to enjoy.

If he was wealthy, he could leave endowments with the temple priests so that when they celebrated certain festivals, his name would be called, they would burn a candle for him. In this way, he would be part of the festival. In essence, when all these things came together, he would re-live his earthly experience but within the Eternal House.

Into the Egyptian Mind. Egyptian Art. Thoth (Tehuti) feeds fluid to the deceased's mummy.

Into the Egyptian Mind. Egyptian Art. At a banquet, deceased and wife, being served from a decorated table, and pouring of libation by a Sem Priest who wears the Leopard Skin.

Into the Egyptian Mind. Deir el Bahari Temple of Hatshepsut. View from the mountain of the vehicles that come to the temple. Because of the fumes from such vehicles, this area has been moved further back.

Into the Egyptian Mind. View of the two Deir el Bahari Temples. Mentuhotep II (right) and Hatshepsut's (left). This view is no longer available for it is now illegal to climb the mountain.

Into the Egyptian Mind. Cairo Museum of Egyptian Antiquities. Papyrus. Scene of the weighing of the heart at Judgment; Osiris (Ausar) in his Shrine; the four baboons and the deceased before the Maati sisters.

20. "FESTIVAL"
By
Dr. Fred Monderson

Back in 1989, Dr. ben-Jochannan celebrated 50-years as a Tour Guide to Egypt. Then he promised to return the *next* year to celebrate "Festival" and he did. Then, with the Nubian Elders at Aswan, together with Nubian Groups from the village of Daboud, he launched the First Nubian Festival celebrating culture and history. This was personal celebration showcasing dress, music and dance. Interesting that, on many of his "Trips" or "Tours" there was one "Nubian Night" set aside where those accompanying him were requested to dress in Nubian/Egyptian gear and sing and dance with the Nubian singers and dancers invited to entertain and participate. There they played Nubian musical instruments, sang Nubian songs, did Nubian dances and all experienced the dynamics of Nubian/Egyptian culture as part of "Festival."

A few years later, the Aswan International Sculpture Symposium with its assembled craft pieces now housed in the Open-Air Sculpture Garden Museum was inaugurated and continued every year since with sculptural representations spread across a wide area. These wonderful pieces of stone sculpture in the Nubian Sculpture Museum represents works by artists from far and wide; yet, many Nubians in this city are unaware of this resource and its location, on the way towards entrance for motor boat to visit the Temple of Isis.

The contradiction is, today, enquire of most Nubians at Aswan, have you heard about the Nubian Sculpture Festival or Nubian Sculpture Museum and invariably they would say no! That is, despite the fact, every year since the Nubian Sculpture Festival is held at Aswan where Sculptors from as far away as Europe and America would join Egyptian counterparts to participate and donate their work to be displayed in the outdoor Open-Air Museum located on the road at Aswan on way to the pier from which motor boats embark for the Temple of Isis on Agilka Island.

The idea of "Festival" is so pervasive in Egypt, certainly ancient Egypt, ongoing all year long, making the Egyptian socially a happy-go-lucky sort. However, many of the Festivals celebrated in ancient Egypt were of a religious nature and there was also a mortuary connection to some festivals. This latter is underscored in Miriam Lichtheim's *Ancient Egyptian Literature*: *Old Kingdom (*University of California Press, (1973) (1975) where, in a mortuary engraving the "Little Ornament" Princess requests endowments of on the following festivals.

Nevertheless, while there may be local, even Nome social festivals, daily or monthly, the national festivals are generally religious whether in praise of a god or king, though sponsored with temples playing a significant role in sponsorship and participation. In addition, the notion of temple ritual, the daily ritual, that is, is certainly a festival. Though not as pronounced as the national festivals, the Opet Festival, the Min Festival, Sokar Festival, Feast of the Valley, etc., involve some travel, very often outside the walls of the principal venue of the celebration. In the case of the Opet Festival during the Middle and New Kingdoms when Amon became the national god, his principal temple at Karnak, "Throne of the Two Lands" it was not simply regarded as the center of all activity but the nucleus from which all such festivals originated.

Into the Egyptian Mind. Egyptian Art. Raised relief. Embraced by a beautiful companion while seated to enjoy the view. Both faces are defaced as if "purposeful," and this is because they demonstrate the "Negro mold."

Into the Egyptian Mind. Egyptian Art. Papyrus. Isis (Auset) with arms and wings outstretched.

21. ANCIENT FOUNDATIONS OF HEALTH
By
Dr. Fred Monderson

You probably wonder where the symbol for medicine comes from? Every temple had this symbol at its entrance. You may be surprised to know the birth chair was the first method used in child birth. On a back wall of Kom Ombo temple, Goddess Isis is depicted seated in the birth chair. Nearby the principal surgical instruments are pictured with a basin for washing the physician's hands after the operation. This medical evidence is what has survived the destructive nature of time and man. It is also clear, in the *Odyssey*, according Dawson (1930: 39), Homer wrote, "In Egypt men are more skilled in medicine than any of humankind."

As such, then, there is a tremendous body of evidence, sources, both ancient and modern, highlighting ancient African accomplishments in the gentle heart of healing. However, when we say ancient evidence we must distinguish between indigenous and that from Greek and then Roman sources. Equally, in modern times, from the end of the 19th Century into today, when we begin to assess the evidence of early medicine, we realize in their view the heart was extremely important, and equally significant, it played a principal role in the judgment, being weighed against a feather of truth.

In regards the accumulated ancient knowledge, the sources go beyond the part of healing for, as Shaw (2000: 11) notes: "Two Egyptian textual records of Sothic risings (dating to the reigns of Senusret III and Amenhotep I) form the basis of the conventional chronology of Egypt, which, in turn, influences that of the whole Mediterranean region. These two documents are a 12th Dynasty letter from the site of Lahun, written on day 16, month 2, of the second season in year 7 of the reign of Senusert III, and an 18th dynasty Theban medical papyrus (Papyrus Ebers), written on day 9, month 3, of the third season of year 9 in the reign of Amenhotep I. By assigning absolute dates to each of these documents (1872 B.C. for the Lahun rising in year 7 of Senusret III, and 1541 B.C. for the Ebers rising in regnal year 9 of Amenhotep I), Egyptologists have been able to extrapolate a set of absolute dates for the whole of the pharaonic period, on the bases of records of the lengths of reign of the other kings of the Middle and New Kingdoms."

First of two things, not only does medical knowledge provide evidence for chronology of Egypt and the Mediterranean but it also explains how the reign of the king was counted, not in the forward flowing sequential dating we are familiar with, but in day and season of years so and so regarding each reign. This was then begun anew when another king ascended the throne to receive his protocols.

Now and equally, as we begin to understand the vocabulary of medicine, we realize these early medical scientists had over one hundred anatomical terms for this shows they differentiated and understood functions of many of the organs. They studied not simply human but also animal parts to learn even more. Exploring this issue further we realize the Edwin Smith Papyrus is an extremely important document, a sort of "handbook of practical treatment applied to wounds. It deals, not with remedies but with cases." The cases are arranged in a practical manner of which the physician approaches a patient. That is, the steps are: "(1) Title, (2) examination, (3) diagnosis, (4) verdict, (5) treatment." Significantly, this studied method of approach lays to rest claims that Egyptian medicine was magic based, and establishes the Edwin Smith Papyrus as a true scientific book. According to Alexander Henry's *History of Medicine* (1860: 263) the Egyptians possessed a book called "Ambres" meaning "Rules of the

Medical Arts." Accordingly, the physicians are required to examine the patient lying down. If they follow the rules of the Ambres and the unfortunate patient dies, they are not held responsible. If, however, they do not follow the rules and the patient dies, then their lives were forfeited." James Finlayson "Ancient Egyptian Medicine" in *The British Medical Journal* (May 13, 1893: 1014-1016) equally holds according to Diodorus Siculus: "In Ancient Egypt, the practitioner was obliged to regulate his conduct not by his own views, but solely by what was written in the six sacred books of Tot (Thoth Hermes). Provided he followed these implicitly, no blame was incurred though the patient died; if he departed from them in the least, and at the same time the case ended fatally, his own life became the forfeit."

Into the Egyptian Mind. Egyptian Art. Kneeling before three images of Anubis, a God of the Dead.

Into the Egyptian Mind. Egyptian Art. Papyrus. Ma'at kneels before enthroned Hathor.

Into the Egyptian Mind. The Deir el Bahari Temples. View of Hatshepsut's Temple showing the First and Second Courts; First and Second Ramps; and the Upper Court with its remaining columns. The Shrine of Hathor is to the right.

Into the Egyptian Mind. The Deir el Bahari Temples. The platform Temple of Mentuhotep II of the 11th Dynasty (right) and partial view of Hatshepsut's Upper Court (left).

Into the Egyptian Mind. The Deir el Bahari Temples. From the "Bird's Eye View," the two temples with the Second Ramp, Upper Terrace and Upper Court entrancing the Holy of Holies mountain sanctuary.

Into the Egyptian Mind. Cairo Museum of Egyptian Antiquities. Bust of King Tutankhamon. He certainly does not look like alabaster!

Let me also add, while we associate medicine with the priesthood, a priestly association, there must be made a distinction between various factions which I will describe as such. First, the priests can be considered keepers of the books of medical knowledge. Physicians would be those trained who tended medicine, and thirdly, there is a distinction attended to embalmers who did the process of mummification. Comparatively, today we have the academic, even the priest, the physician and the embalmers or morticians.

All this notwithstanding and despite their medical successes, they had their problems, for as Dawson (1930: 41) has argued: "They entirely failed to understand the nerves, muscles, arteries and veins. They appear to have regarded them all as various parts of a single system of branching and radiating channels common to all parts of the body. The same word is used for the vessels communicating with the heart as is employed for the muscles in the prescriptions for stiff joints and rheumatoid complaints. It is only from the content that we can gather what was meant." They paid little attention to the brain which was removed but they emphasized the heart which was left in situ in the body. Both the *Ebers Papyrus* and the *Berlin Medical Papyrus* deals with the heart and a passage of the former is entitled, "The beginning of the science of the physician. To know the movements of the heart and to know the heart." This is reinforced in the view, they "recognized the relation of the heart to the pulse, and it is stated that the motion of the heart can be detected, not only in the region of the organ itself, but by placing the fingers on the head, the hands, the arms or the legs."

Even further, they understood, "the number of vessels which serve every part of the head, limbs and body. The 'vessels' for the nose, for instance, were four in number: two of these conveyed blood and two mucus. There are four vessels within the temples which convey blood to the eyes, and a gloss adds that when the eyes water, the moisture comes from the pupils or from the eyelids, e.g., the water is produced locally and is not conveyed by the vessels. Each part of the body including the internal organs is similarly dealt with, and further passages describe the abnormal behavior of the heart during illness and its effect upon various parts of the body." Even more: "Thus, the vessels of the nostrils conveyed air to the heart and to the lungs, those of the testicles conveyed semen, and those of the liver carried moisture and air. The ears being the organs of hearing, were thought to be part of the pulmonary system, for it is stated that 'there are four vessels for the two ears, two on the right and two on the left. The breath of life enters by the right ear and the breath of death enters the left ear."

So, we see, very early in their history the ancient Egyptians were concerned with their health and developed extraordinary measures to treat such. Two things we must bear in mind created tremendous challenges to the health of inhabitants along the river in the Nile Valley. The sun and the desert as well as the river itself posed challenges then and now. Second and most important, because these ancient Africans were among the first humans to become conscious of their intellectual, cultural and social capabilities, they went to great lengths to invent utilities to make their life experiences and expectancy easy and enjoyable. Even more significant, because this earliest society was isolated from other peoples, their greatest and most far-reaching intellectual and medical inventions were original in the truest sense. They had no one to emulate or copy and so writing on a clean slate of human knowledge or *tabula rasa*, they were the earliest creative geniuses. In such areas dealing with human health as experienced in medicine as obstetrics, surgery, dental surgery and anatomy and physiology, much of their advances were acquired through trial and error and developments in the art of mummification. This was of tremendous assistance in understanding the make-up of the human body. To this was added knowledge of the anatomy of cats, dogs and other animals. As such then, modern efforts of criticism are enabled because of an existing documented body of knowledge showing among other things, the ancient

Egyptians pioneered in important areas of health care. Because much of this was priestly and linked to religious belief and practice, it was therefore inter-linked with both the living and the dead.

The "Holy Men" or priests of Egypt were this culture's earliest intellectuals, a position developed from their responsibilities of administering principally to the gods and then the king and nobility, stewards of the state. Because the king was the son of god on earth and himself a god, his "handlers" were concerned and became guardians of his health since the belief his optimum health kept the state in equilibrium. This meant he had to procreate to have as many heirs and to be of equal mental, spiritual and physical virility. To accomplish this much, priests studied nature and developed a pharmacopeia based on herbs, minerals and animal fats, skins and sinews and even animal and human waste. Today some think human urine is considered a credible medicine, while others think it is toxic and harmful.

Magic was also an important priestly medical weapon; a small part; but only resorted to generally after the scientific method had taken its course and proved useless. Here we could also add circumcision, for though it was practiced, it was only considered a religious observance not a medical practice. Therefore, and important, just as the priests cared for the living, they ended up caring for the dead and even became involved in the drama of the Afterlife leading to religious doctrines and documentation that regulated the events of this phenomenon called the Judgment, even predicting events of the next world. Thus, very early in the evolution of priestly functions and responsibilities, they developed two practices that, for the rest of time would have the most profound impact on human health.

The first of these was the old adage, "cleanliness is next to godliness," and so practitioners did everything possible to maintain this state of social purity with its implications for a health-wise balance. Because priests administered to the god, they themselves had to be clean. They washed themselves sometimes at least three times or more per day, shaving much of their bodies and only wore linen clothing during their time of service in the temples. Also, in periods of service and since some priests only served for three months at a time, they abstained from certain foods such as the pig, fish and naturally remained free of any sexual contact to maintain that purity in mind and body. Most of the temples had a Sacred Lake which was fed by underground springs connected to the Nile River. In a rainless country, these individuals washed themselves just as they washed the god, even more so.

Into the Egyptian Mind. Egyptian Art.
Amenhotep I and his mother Queen Nefertari enthroned among the gods.

Into the Egyptian Mind. Egyptian Art. Raised relief. Squatting individuals wearing perfumed cones in the Mountains of El Kab. Evident is the signature and disfiguration of purposeful actions.

Into the Egyptian Mind. Hatshepsut's Temple at Deir el Bahari. View of the Second Court, Second Ramp and entrance into the Upper Court with the Sanctuary's entrance to the right against the mountain.

Into the Egyptian Mind. Hatshepsut's Temple at Deir el Bahari. Clear and classic "Bird's Yet View" of the Middle Colonnade and Upper Platform with remaining statues and colonnade and to the right the Upper Court and entrance to the Sanctuary.

Into the Egyptian Mind. Cairo Museum of Egyptian Antiquities. Heads of stone coffin statues.

The god resided in the Sanctuary, a place of utter darkness and the door to that chamber remained locked. Just as in heaven, where the chief god was awoken and given his ablutions by his bath attendants, then toweled, and anointed with sweet smelling unguents, perfumes, rouge and even lipstick before his meal, so too here on earth the same was done for the divinity, to make the mouth pretty. The priests gargled with salt (Natrum), even chewed it, to make their mouth fresh during the cleanliness process. All the while, rituals were conducted, songs sang, rattles and tambourines shook and the room incensed, all to create that holy, mystical, magically sacred environment in which to entertain the god in a duplicated heavenly environment. Interestingly, incense was never burned on the altar but in a corner in an incenser or in a held-held device. Incense was used to drive away evil and unclean forces.

We know the Egyptian priests were involved in all facets of the intellectual dynamics of the society, and so they were the principal practitioners of mental and physical health as well. Practicing medicine, within the concepts of specialization in every part of the human body, each one specialized in a different area. Whether in obstetrics, gynecology, surgery, ophthalmology, dental surgery, etc., and particularly anatomy and physiology, each played a direct role in their healthcare. The god Thoth was the inventor of knowledge, music, writing and even mathematics. He was the Chief Minister to Osiris; his lawyer; God of the Dead. Thoth was also chronographer involved in the construction of the heavens as an assistant to the god Ptah, God of the Artisans, often called the "Blue Collar God." Thoth is credited with writing "six books on medicine."

In the earliest period of priestly existence, one day, according to mythology, an ibis was observed washing itself by the waterside, as we know such creatures do. It was seen taking a beak full of water, turning its long neck and inserting the beak of water into its anus, then shaking itself before passing it out. This early feature of health care led priests to begin a regimen of what we would later call "colon cleanse."

During the Middle Ages, an English doctor outlived everyone, living to the ripe old age of 150 years. When he died the king ordered an autopsy to determine the secret of his long life. It was found he had the cleanest colon one could imagine. He probably cleansed once a week. That in itself is perhaps too frequent, some believe, but certainly once a month is adequate. We do know death begins in the colon and so this organ should get special attention.

To record various forms of knowledge, these Nile Valley Africans of Egypt invented papyrus, a plant they prepared through a process that enabled them to write and become the earliest literate culture in the world. Much of their medical knowledge was written on papyrus. So very early they began writing medical lore and we know the first physician to stand out from the mist of history was Imhotep, the world's first multi-genius. He was an architect as was his father and grandfather; because theirs like so many other crafts considered family secrets, were passed down from generation to generation through the family.

As a wise man Imhotep's idea were also taught from generation to generation. He was described as a "master of poetry" and "patron of the scribes." He is credited with the philosophy of the ages, "Eat, drink and be merry, for tomorrow we die." The *Westcar Papyrus*
contains some of his magical feats. However, the *Ebers*, *Oxyrchynchus* and *Edwin Smith Papyri* mention his cures for many illnesses.

Imhotep therefore made great contributions to the gentle art of healing. The Egyptians made him a demi-god and the Greeks made him their God of Medicine, Aesculapius. He should be considered the "father of ancient medicine" while Hippocrates must be considered the "father of modern medicine" but this is not so preached. Imhotep practiced medicine some 2300 years before Hippocrates. Without deviating, we must understand the power of naming. The Greeks and Romans named the gods, monuments and professions. They named the seven wonders of the world. All others have perished except the one in Africa, the Great Pyramid. Dr. Ben-Jochannan often wondered why the Temple of Hatshepsut at Deir el Bahari was never given this designation, for built by a woman, a three-story building when one was the norm and possessing all the art and architectural features of a magnificent structure, its beauty still radiates 3500 years later.

None the less, from the earliest times, temples were built to Imhotep at such places as Thebes, Philae, Edfu, and in Nubia. He was also worshipped in other gods' temples. Books were written about him and his profession. A cult grew up around his name and work as a doctor; a physician of note, whose fame traveled abroad.

There were many after Imhotep whose work as physician has come down to us perhaps by virtue of their work in other fields or survival in their tombs. We know that Hesire a contemporary of Imhotep, whose wooden relief in the Cairo Museum has been a source of numerous commentaries, was a physician, dentist and administrator.

Carole Reeves in *Egyptian Medicine* (1992: 22) point to another, "Iry was a chief of court physicians at Giza during the Fourth Dynasty. He was also 'master of scorpions,' 'eye doctor of the palace,' 'doctor of the abdomen,' and 'guardian of the royal bowel movement.' *Sekhet-n-Ankh* was 'nose doctor' to Pharaoh Sahure (Fifth Dynasty) and successfully cured him of a 'sickness of the upper air passages.' The only Egyptian lady doctor yet known was *Peseshet* (Fourth or early Fifth Dynasty), whose title, *imy-rt-swnt*, may be translated as 'lady director of lady physicians." So, there were women doctors in Africa this early in time.

Thus, we know, the level of medical practice reached by the Egyptians was higher than that of their neighbors in the ancient world. This has much to do as they combated the environmental challenges of their day. Regarding such, Dawson (1930: 44) informs: "Generally speaking, the maladies with which the papyri were concerned are those which attack the natives of today. Intestinal troubles due to bad water, to worms and other parasites, ophthalmia and a large number of affections of the eyes, boils, sores and bites of insects, skin diseases, bilharzia infection and mastoid disease figure among the many maladies for which the ancient physician had to find remedies. The actual evidence of many of these diseases has been found in Egyptian mummies."

Since the Egyptian doctors were famously skilled and specialized, to be treated by one psychologically and physically helped the patient to recover even quicker. Their medical men, considered excellent physicians, treated kings and queens of other lands. So much so, their services were sought later than the time of the famous Cyrus and Darius kings of Persia, c. 500 B.C. Thus, in their medical treatments they had compiled more than 2000 years of documented medical knowledge; though thousands more of actual trial and error learning the effectiveness of plants and minerals and even their combinations and concoctions of diverse materials.

A Christian writer, Alexandrinus Clemens, in Alexandria about 200 A.D., mentions the **42 Books of Thoth** (Tehuti), displayed in religious processions. Reeves (1992: 21) notes: "Six of these books were concerned totally with medicine and dealt with anatomy, diseases in general, surgery, remedies, diseases of the eye and diseases of women. No examples of these books survive nor of the anatomy books said to have been written by Athothis, second Pharaoh of the First Dynasty."

Reeves (1992: 21) confirmed further: "During the Old Kingdom the medical profession became highly organized, with doctors holding a variety of ranks and specialties. The ordinary doctor or *sinw* was outranked by the *imy-r sinw* (overseer of doctors) the *wr sinw* (chief of doctors), the *smsw sinw* (eldest of doctors) and the *shd sinw* (inspector of doctors). Above all these practitioners was the overseer of doctors of Upper and Lower Egypt. There is evidence that a distinction was made between physicians and surgeons, the latter being known as the 'priests of the goddess Sekhmet.' There were also healers who used purely magical remedies or exorcism."

As such, medicine had progressed much by time of the New Kingdom and priests were in full control of their profession. They were general doctors but many specialized on different parts of the body. J.A. Rogers' *World's Great Men of Color* Vol. I (1946) (1972), notes regarding specialization among doctors: "One ministered to the eye, another to the chest, another to the limbs. None trespassed on the anatomy of the other." In addition, Reeves (1992: 22-23) added: "Each specialization of medicine had a patron god or goddess and the physician worked directly under the auspices of his particular deity. Duaw was the god of eye diseases; Taurt was a goddess of childbirth, as was Hathor. Sekhmet, the lion-headed lady of pestilence, sent plagues all over the land and Horus had power over deadly stings and bites such as those of crocodiles, snakes and scorpions (the most common type of 'everyday' injury appears to have been from bites). The human body was divided into 36 parts and each came under the protection of a god or goddess. The goddess protecting the liver was Isis; that of the lungs was Nephthys; the stomach was the domain of Neith and the intestines belonged to the care of Selket. The "House of Life" (*Per Ankh*) was the medical study center where doctors were taught and these existed at major cult temples along with centers of healing." Overtime, Rogers noted, these skilled practitioners treated more than 250 diseases. These included, "15 of the abdomen,

11 of the bladder, 10 of the rectum, 29 of the eyes, and 18 of the skin.

These medical specialists knew how to tell a disease by the shape, color or condition of the visible parts of the body. Looking at the skin, hair, nails and tongue, showed how well a person was. They also treated illnesses, according to Rogers, such as "spinal tuberculosis, gall-stones, appendicitis, gout, arthritis, and dental caries." They treated body aches, various fevers, coughing, broken bones, cuts and other types of wounds.

These men of early science performed surgery, listened to the heart, and thought it the seat of all things. Imhotep, it is said knew of the circulation of the blood 4,000 years before it was known in Europe. Further, their doctors were familiar with the positions and functions of the stomach, lungs, and other vital organs. They knew the importance of hygiene in the recovery of illnesses. The brain's usefulness, however, was not fully understood; they placed more emphasis on the philosophical role the heart played in the judgment and the practical one in pumping the blood. Thus, the brain, was easily set aside during the mummification process, but the heart, it was said, remained in place. Since Egyptians emphatically believed in an Afterlife, the art of preserving the body was highly developed. In this, they learned much about anatomy and physiology in preparing for the burial through the process of mummification in hope the spirit would reanimate the corpse after the judgment.

Into the Egyptian Mind. Hatshepsut's Temple at Deir el Bahari. Erik Monderson on the Upper Terrace, before a statue of Hatshepsut.

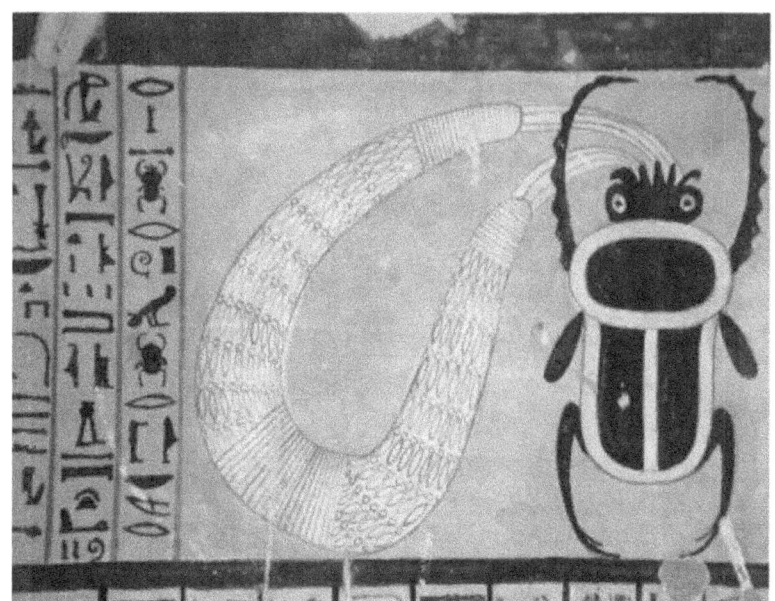

Into the Egyptian Mind. Egyptian Art. Khepra the beetle with huge Menat.

Into the Egyptian Mind. Deir el Bahari Temple of Hatshepsut. Again, a "Bird's Eye View" of the magnificent structure's Upper Terrace and Upper Court.

Into the Egyptian Mind. Hatshepsut's Temple at Deir el Bahari. Entering the First Court and First Ramp with associated ruined fragments found in the temple.

Into the Egyptian Mind. Egyptian Art. Photographic mock-up of the Tomb of King Tutankhamon.

Herbal remedies were an important part of the pharmacopeia, medicine being also made from minerals and other substances. Accordingly, one writer is quoted as saying: "Historically, African medicine was founded upon holistic intelligences that produced all of the sciences. This pre-Egyptian medical science is believed to be 20,000 and 10,000 years old." In that process of learning the process of nature, herbal or vegetable medicine listed in the records include castor oil, aloes, coriander, caraway, gentian, and turpentine. "It appears that as early as 6,000 B.C., meadow Saffron was given internally." Such sources also mention as medicine myrrh, juniper, fennel, herbane, linseed, and peppermint.... Iron, soda, lime, salts of lead, sulphate of copper, and magnesia." Other drugs used came from animal bodies including fats and blood from the ox, lion, and hippopotamus.

Regarding patient examination and treatment, *What Life Was Like on the Banks of the Nile* (1997: 40) indicates: "A physician's bedside manner included interviewing patients, palpitating abnormalities, examining secretions, and even smelling wounds. Along with aloe, garlic and honey, his medicine chest might contain such items as lead, sandal leather, soot, semen, cow bile, and excrement - both animal and human. Salves and poultices prepared with these distasteful ingredients were intended to make the patient's body so repugnant that the disease - or the demon - would be compelled to find a more suitable host."

Hilary Wilson (1993: 170) adds: "In medical papyri the ingredients of prescriptions are sometimes quantified, especially in the case of valuable substances such as spices or incense. The quantities suggested may be given in 10, a mouthful being the equivalent of a modern tablespoon, or by weight. It seems that very small amounts could be accurately weighed against wheat grains or the seeds of the carob tree, both of which are remarkably uniform in size and weight." It is also important that we know where the origins of our neighborhood pharmacy and pharmacists come from.

In regard medical preparation, Cyril Aldred (1961) (1987: 194) in *The Egyptians* says: "A training as a scribe was also a necessary preliminary to a career in such professions as medicine, the priesthood, and art and architecture. A medical student would be apprenticed to a practitioner, almost always his father or some near relative; but an ability to read was necessary for learning the various prescriptions, spells and diagnoses contained in medical papyri, whether the work in question were a quasi-scientific treatise on surgery and fractures such as the **Edwin Smith Papyrus**, or a specialist work on gynecology such as the **Kahun Papyrus**, or a mere collection of medico-magic recipes, nostrums, and incantations such as the **Ebers Papyrus**."

Paul Johnson in *The Civilization ofAncient Egypt* (1987) (1999: 120) writes: "Egyptians were the first to use certain well-known drugs which have come in use ever since. Their experience is reflected in Hebrew, Syrian and Persian medical texts, in such classical writers as Theophrastus, Pliny, Dioscorides, Galen and Hippocratus, and in Roman Imperial, Byzantine and Arabic medical handbooks, which were in use throughout the Middle Ages, the Renaissance and beyond. Egyptians had an enduring reputation as expert poisoners, springing from their skill with sleeping-potions." He goes on to note there are "eight medical papyri in the British Museum alone, including one on surgical treatment." This is part of what I call "a culture in captivity."

Among these sources of early medicine, one, found in a Theban tomb in 1860 and passed into the hands of Georg Ebers in 1873, this papyrus that bears his name, **Ebers Papyrus**. Within, Dawson identifies, "a long series of prescriptions for numerous named ailments and diseases, specifying the drugs to be used, the quantities of each, and the methods of administering them." Written about 1500 B.C., in almost perfect condition, it is the longest and most famous of these documents. Reeves (1992: 49) notes, the document contains "876 remedies and mentions 500 substances used in medical treatment." Among these are such remedies including sedatives, hypnotics, expectorants, tonics, astringents, purgatives, diuretics, disinfectants and antibodies.

Reeves says (1992: 49) further: "The **Ebers Papyrus** describes treatment of and prescriptions for stomach complaints, coughs, colds, bites, head ailments and diseases; liver complaints, burns and other kinds of wounds; itching, complaints in fingers and toes; salves for wounds and pains in the veins, muscles and nerves; diseases of the tongue, toothache, ear pains, women's diseases; beauty preparations, household remedies against vermin, the two books about the heart and veins, and diagnosis for tumors." Grimal's *The Oxford History of Ancient Egypt* (2005) informs of other meaningful ways the Ebers Papyrus has been useful to scholars.

In 1862, while in Luxor, the American Egyptologist Edwin Smith, acquired the papyrus that bears his name. Reeves (1992: 51) pinpoints the **Edwin Smith Surgical Papyrus**, is dated at about 1600 B.C. but Old Kingdom words in the text suggest that it was copied from a work written around 2500 B.C., when the pyramids were being built. It was published in 1930 with a translation and commentary by James Henry Breasted and is now housed in the New York Academy of Medicine." Based on this document, Bob Brier (1994: 62) in *Egyptian Mummies* discusses the Egyptian understanding of the relationship of the brain to the body. He states: "In the Edwin Smith Surgical Papyrus, three specific, traumatic head injuries, so serious that the brain is exposed, are discussed. It is clear that the author of this papyrus was aware of the meningeal membranes surrounding the brain, and of the brain's convolutions." He does add, however, their medical men believed "the heart managed the body." As we know, this is not so for this function belongs to the brain.

Petrie found the **Kahun Medical Papyrus**, with other Middle Kingdom Papyri, in the town of Kahun in 1889. Consisting of only three pages, it has been variously dated between 2100 and 1900 B.C., the oldest such document. It is preserved in the Petrie Museum of Egyptian Archaeology at University College, London. The papyrus is devoted to diseases of women and pregnancy and is possibly the oldest medical papyrus to be discovered. It was first published in 1898, as a hieroglyphic transcript with a translation by F. Ll. Griffith. It deals with gynecology, treatment of a woman's ruptured womb, possibly the first case of rape and prevention of conception. Heinrich Brugsch discovered the **Berlin Papyrus** in a jar during excavation at Saqqara in the early years of the twentieth century. It consists of 279 lines of prescription and has been dated around 13501200 B.C. Translated and published by Walter Wreszinski in 1909, it is housed in the Berlin Museum with a fifteen-column papyrus. It contains one of the earliest tests for pregnancy utilizing barley and ember in urine. Containing altogether 204 sections, it also has a passage on methods of ascertaining sterility and the sex of unborn children.

Into the Egyptian Mind. Egyptian Art. Raised and Sunk relief. As the couple sit and embrace, an individual in leopard skin stands before them and the "Table of Offerings."

Into the Egyptian Mind. Erik Monderson has time to relax in Mr. Ibrahim Soliman's garden on the West Bank.

Into the Egyptian Mind. Egyptian Art. While he raises his empty hands in adoration, she carries all the implements.

Into the Egyptian Mind. Egyptian Art. Mr. Ibrahim Soliman and Shawki Abd Rady on the West Bank.

Into the Egyptian Mind. Hatshepsut's Temple at Deir el Bahari. Another close-up of the Second Court, Second Ramp, Middle Colonnade, Upper Terrace and statues before colonnade and partial view of the Upper Court that entrances the Sanctuary.

Into the Egyptian Mind. Hatshepsut's Temple at Deir el Bahari. Descending the hill, another view of the temple.

The **Chester Beatty Papyrus VI**, housed in the British Museum, is dated around 1200 B.C. and consists of eight columns dealing solely with diseases of the anus. It was translated and annotated by F. Jonckeere in 1947.

Reeves explained: "The Hearst Papyrus, now in the University of California, dates from about 1550 B.C. and appears to be the formulary of a practicing physician. It is incomplete and contains eighteen columns. A Translation by Walter Wreszinski of the **Hearst Papyrus** and the **London Papyrus** (c. 1350 B.C.) were published in 1912. The **Hearst Papyrus** contains over 250 prescriptions and spells and has a section on bones and bites (notably the hippopotamus bite) and affections of the fingers. It also deals with tumors, burns and diseases of women, ears, eyes and teeth. The **London Papyrus** contains "61 recipes, only 25 of which are medical, the remaining being magical."

Finally, we could add the **Westcar Papyrus**, which, according to Dawson (1930: 35), "although not concerned with medicine at all, being a collection of popular stories, describes in graphic detail the birth of triplets, affording much interesting information on the Egyptian methods of accouchement."

Piotr O. Scholz in *Ancient Egypt: An Illustrative Historical Overview* (1977) wrote: "The Egyptians had some idea of hygiene: they practiced circumcision, and that can be considered a hygienic measure. Surgery was successful in the treatment of broken bones. The guidelines for treatment are instructive and the methods correct. Medical instruments, known from temple drawings, came later and corroborate the assertion that medicine was a science of the temples. Egyptian physicians dared to admit in a given case that they could do nothing for the patient. Examination of mummies indicates that Egyptian dentists filled teeth, built simple bridges using gold wire, and treated infected gums."

Reeves (1992: 54) further mentions the **Brooklyn Museum Papyrus**, translated in 1966-67 by Serge Sauernon, contains "a mixture of magical and rational medicine, particularly with relation to birth and post-partum care. Also included in these papyri is a book on snakebites, describing all the possible snakes to be found in Egypt with a compendium of treatments."

Reeves adds (1992: 54) even more: "The **Carlsberg Papyrus Number VIII**, translated by E. Iversen in 1939 and housed in the University of Copenhagen, deals with eye diseases almost identical to those described in the Ebers Papyrus and obstetrics very similar to that in the Kahun, Berlin and Ebers Papyri." Finally, of those important medical treatises, Reeves (1992: 54) again indicates: "The **Ramesseum IV** and **V Papyri** are of the same era as the **Kahun Papyrus**. A translation of both papyri by J.W.B. Barns was published in 1956. Papyrus IV is medico-religious and deals with obstetrics and gynecology. Papyrus V is purely medical and deals mainly with stiffened limbs. The series of obstetrics prescription and prognostications in the Carlsberg, Ebers, Berlin and Kahun Papyri are so similar that it is likely that they were all taken from the same source."

In summary, the ancient peoples in Egypt and elsewhere along the Nile River, made significant gains in medicine and treatment of the sick. This was done thousands of years ago. Many of these ideas never reached Europe until much later, and when they did, they proved very useful. In fact, Breasted's *History of Egypt* (1905) (1923: 101) notes many Egyptian medicines "passed with the Greeks to Europe, where they are still in use among the peasantry of the present day." As we know, Imhotep was the first physician to stand out in history. Later the Greeks made him their God of Medicine. Today, young African-American students especially should try to become doctors. When they are qualified, they will take the "Hippocratic Oath." It is named after the "Father of Medicine" Hippocrates, who practiced medicine 2300 years after Imhotep. They should know, however, that the God Aesculapius, praised in the oath is really Imhotep, an ancestor, from the land of Egypt in Northeast Africa.

The Egyptians held Imhotep in such high esteem because, in addition to his medical skills, he was one of them who became a god. Since the gods were so remote, the locals were glad to identify with someone they had experienced. However, beyond this he was also a sage or wise man, mathematician and architect. A combination of these talents helped him to build the Step-Pyramid at Sakkara for Pharaoh Zoser, of the Third Dynasty.

This was a major accomplishment as it set in motion stone construction and laid the foundation for building the pyramids. In *A Brief History of Science*, A. Rupert Hall and Marie Boas Hall treats this subject. Accordingly, early Egyptian architecture was significantly aided by a "surplus of labor, combined with an exceptionally complex cult of the dead, created the elaborate tombs and monuments familiar to us as pyramids and obelisks. The colossal size and careful workmanship of these great structures suggest to the modern eye a complex technology." Similarly, "they were built with wedges and stone hammers to split the rock, sledges and ropes to drag the stones to the building sites, ramps from one level to another up which successive courses were hauled, levers to propel the stones into place, and water used to check when all was level. The Egyptians had no wheels or pulleys in the Pyramid Age (from 2700 to 2000 B.C.), and the secret of their success was unlimited manpower, patience, and a strong artistic sense." Their medicine was an important adjunct to treating workers injured on national projects.

One last thing that particularly has to do with health and must be noted. We know the Egyptians and Ethiopians were some of the earliest people to practice circumcision. Despite the magico-religious reasons for this procedure, an even more important modern use is explained. Riding along Linden Boulevard, in Brooklyn, there is a sign outside a doctor's office that reads: "Circumcision prevents AIDS." Thus, we can associate the ancient Egyptians with a potent health care practice, that thousands of years later is an equally powerful antidote to a powerful threat to health care!

Into the Egyptian Mind. Egyptian Art. Oh, what a life, sailing solo on the Nile.

Into the Egyptian Mind. Egyptian Art. The Cartouche (Shennu) reads Men-Kheper-Ra, Thutmose III in a small temple desert temple in the El Kab Mountains.

Into the Egyptian Mind. Erik Monderson strolls in Mr. Ibrahim Soliman's Garden on the West Bank at Luxor.

Into the Egyptian Mind. Hatshepsut's Temple at Deir el Bahari. The mouth of Senmut's tomb and the temple in the rear.

Into the Egyptian Mind. Hatshepsut's Temple at Deir el Bahari. Another view of the inner reaches of the temple.

Into the Egyptian Mind. Native Egyptian Guide Showki Abd Rady and his Driver in the small temple in the Mountains of El Kab.

Into the Egyptian Mind. Erik Monderson relaxes in Mr. Ibrahim Soliman's garden at Luxor, on the west Bank.

22. WALLS IN ANCIENT EGYPTIAN TEMPLES AND TOMBS
By
Dr. Fed Monderson

Building walls in ancient Egypt is an art form that very early reached mastery level. As a result, a number of types of walls were executed and while some were decorated others were not. This particular feature spans the whole gamut of Egyptian architectural engineering and varied in size, placement, disposition, height, nature of the stone used and much more. The forms of this construction came to include the enclosure wall that surrounds any structure, whether religious, domestic or mortuary. While, however, not too many enclosure walls have remained intact in Egypt, there is equally a dearth of domestic buildings that have survived from ancient times simply because they were built of perishable materials. So, we are therefore left mostly with religious and mortuary structures that were essentially built of stone to last for eternity. In such constructions then, the utility determined the expansion relating to size of area covered, height, thickness as well as the prevailing decorative feature that enhanced the outward appearance and equally what was encompassed within any such structure.

The earliest surviving example of this Enclosure Wall variety is found at Sakkara where Imhotep built his Step-Pyramid for the Pharaoh Zoser. The Third Dynasty, 2600 B.C., was a time of architectural innovation, motivated by genius elevating monarchy to divinity status. In this age of experimentation, the wall, as a convention, established standards of layout, decoration, durability and utility as the art form seemed guided by divine inspiration.

Into the Egyptian Mind. Egyptian Art. Horus (Heru) as Ra-Horakhty leads and gestures before the deceased couple.

Into the Egyptian Mind. Egyptian Art. Driving cattle for inspection by female supervisor, Hathor with Horus (Heru) figure on her head.

Into the Egyptian Mind. Luxor, Egypt. From across the river, the Temple of Luxor, Great Pylon and Obelisk (Tekhen) to the left and the Processional Colonnade to the right.

Into the Egyptian Mind. Luxor Temple of Amenhotep III and Rameses II. Bust view of one of the still standing, of four, statues before the Great Pylon.

Into the Egyptian Mind. Egyptian Art. Teams of "druggers" in the Tomb of Amenemopet.

Into the Egyptian Mind. Cairo Museum of Egyptian Antiquities Deceased female stands before Osiris (Ausar) in his Shrine where he is depicted Black.

Praising his king, this multi-genius and architect built a wall, some of which still stands that enclosed the expansive parameters of the pyramid complex. Central to the mortuary complex was the pyramidal form of Mastaba that rose several stories above ground with a sub-structure that was very complex. In addition to his tomb, within the enclosure was found a Valley Temple along a Causeway, or roadway that led from the Nile River. Here the deceased was welcomed by priests who performed the ritual of reception. Along this path was found a Sacrificial Altar, and another, this time, Sun

Temple. A Sphinx stood guard as customary and beside was an Obelisk. In a united land, the monarch was King of the Upper and Lower Kingdoms. Therefore, two "dummy buildings" represented the Upper and Lower Kingdoms and in the Heb Sed Festival of rejuvenation he ran around them to signify encompassing the whole of Egypt over which he ruled. Of course, there was a Heb-Sed Festival Pavilion from which he began the race. Beside these were Magazines for Storage of necessaries the deceased hoped to utilize in the afterlife. On the other side of the King's Pyramid were smaller Pyramids for Queens and Princesses related to him. Beside these were Mastabas for Nobles who relished being buried in the shadow of their sovereign's final resting place. To be in close proximity of his immortality was beneficial to their everlastingness. In this vicinity there was another, this time, Temple for the God worshipped by the king. In a culture and nation served by a river, boats were the principal modes of transportation. Therefore, the king had a pit called a Solar Boat Pit dug to house his Solar Boat that would take him to the next world. By the time of the Great Pyramid's evolution, Zoser, its builder, had five such pits dug and equipped with Solar Boats. These then were the components Imhotep's Enclosure Wall encapsulated and as such it had to be extensive.

In the evolution of the building practice, religious worship and mortuary temples were not as varied in their components, though they were either single or multiple structures within the wall. Hence, from what we can tell, from the Middle Kingdom, down through the New Kingdom and into the Greek and Roman Periods, the Enclosure Wall came to serve a number of purposes. Sure, they kept the secrets of the temple safe from prying eyes. They also kept others out. However, in times of danger, they also served as a refuge for which inhabitants hid within their seemingly impregnable or imposing dimensions.

Within the Enclosure Wall the temple and ancillary buildings had walls that were decorated on the outside and within.

Within the enclosure itself there was an Open or Great Court where celebrants were permitted to congregate yet prohibited from venturing further into the deeper recesses of the structure. Just as the outer enclosure wall was sometimes decorated, so too the inner wall beyond the Pylon was also decorated. Next, the temple structure itself was decorated on the outside and also on the inside that even fewer individuals were privy to their contents. So, from historical events on the outside of the walls to more esoteric depictions of the temple ritual within, the walls were built to support the structure as well as to be a canvass on which a great deal of which we know today was inscribed.

Interestingly enough, from the earliest period of the Old Kingdom, temple and mortuary rituals were either handed down orally or reduced to scrolls as very little illustrations were found associated with the pyramids and early temples. This was not so with the Mastaba tombs of great nobles who went to extra-ordinary lengths to graphically depict social existence with hopes of such having impacts on their future existence. By the Middle and New Kingdoms, temples began to be decorated, more or less, illustratively, with little text. However, by the Graeco-Roman Period there was a great deluge of illustrative and textual depictions on the walls of temples. Since such decoration simply continued the traditions of old, they helped, in their new form, to provide a great deal of the knowledge we now possess of the most ancient beliefs and practices.

A typical temple such as Karnak may have several Enclosing or "Enclosure" walls. Here there was an "Encapsulating Wall" binding the Northern (Monthu); Central (Amon: and Southern (Mut) temples of the Theban divine company. Altogether, some 22 temples comprised this conglomeration including the temple of Khonsu, the third person of the Theban triad. Each temple had its own enclosure wall upon which some aspect of the temple ritual was inscribed as part of its decorative feature. In his time, Thutmose III built a "Binding Wall" and Rameses II erected his "Girdle Wall." Practically every room's wall was decorated, especially in the later Graeco-Roman Period. Within and on the outside of the Sanctuary aspects of the ritual was inscribed. Certainly, the Second, Third, Fourth and Seventh and Eighth Pylons, themselves walls, decorated. The Walls of the Annals and of the "Botanical Gardens" of Thutmose III were also canvases upon which history and other cultural factors helped cement the over-all purpose of the wall, in Egyptian society. To the temples we could also add tomb walls especially of the Old and New Kingdom in which Mastabas and then Tombs of the Valley of the Kings, alley of the Queens, Valley of the Nobles and Valley of the Artisans display some of the most picturesque art of the ancient culture. A such then, walls served the purposes of enclosing for protection, compartmentalization of the temple and tombs, not to exclude domestic structures, as decorative canvases upon domestic and religious themes were inscribed in a ritualistic and informative manner.

Into the Egyptian Mind. Egyptian Art. A beauty Parade offering a bouquet of flowers.

Into the Egyptian Mind. Luxor Temple of Amenhotep III and Rameses II. Rameses, in "Blue" or "War Crown" holds two unusual incense burners with flames rising from their contents.

Into the Egyptian Mind. Erik Monderson stands beside items on display for sale on the Plaza at Karnak Temple.

Into the Egyptian Mind. Luxor Temple of Amenhotep III and Rameses II. In the Court of Rameses, the "Ramessean Front," Nefertari holds a Hathor symbol, the sistrum as she stands behind the King.

23. BAPTISM
By
Dr. Fred Monderson

Some years ago, a friend discussed the idea of Baptism in which she spoke of Baptism by water and as if, jokingly, she ventured into the idea of Baptism by fire! Naturally, she had no idea of talk of "Baptism by fire" in the military since this is where young men go to fight on their nation's behalf and are shocked into the realization of the dangers of their new situation and suddenly they become experts at surviving or the dead subjects of body bags. Then again, as a religious person she probably meant in the spiritual sense, to be actively involved in this "high science" which meant participants must remain spiritually pure and not engage in unbecoming behaviors, as this is anathema to spirit science.

In ancient Egypt, on the other hand, the idea of baptism related to purification especially for the pharaoh who must enter the temple to perform his functions relative to the God. The God himself had to be baptized or lustrated in the heavens to acquire and retain the purity necessary for his functions and existence. The same done for him in the heavens was also done for his earthly manifestation, the statue, in the Sanctuary. Equally, this baptism or cleansing for purity also involved the king as chief priest who must daily ritualize his god. However, he the king had to undergo many such episodes of baptismal cleansing on an on-going basis once he became the god's representative on earth who sat on the Throne of Horus. Nonetheless, he had to also undergo that same baptism at various stages of his life. At birth, the youngster who will one day become pharaoh is baptized and purified in preparation for the task of becoming king. Upon his coronation the king, before he is invested with the full powers of being king, must again be baptized to attain the prerequisites of righteousness so that truth and justice remain hallmarks of his tenure on the throne. In addition, he must be handed the material instruments that represent his stature and power as king such as crown, whip and flail, scepter, tail, and naturally the jewelry that adorn his royal person, such as earrings, armbands, rings, necklace, anklets, golden slippers, etc. To this we may add is fighting implements as sword, dagger, mace and some kings chose the bow and arrow.

Now fully invested with all the powers of pharaoh, as the heir of Horus sitting on his golden throne, his principal function in addition to being head of state is to administer to the god in his temple. However, before entering into the temple, he must again be purified because to enter the god's presence, which is an abode of purification, the pharaoh himself must be pure to enter a zone of purity.

In the continuing saga, once the king's life has expired, he must be washed, again purified, before he takes his journey to be judged in the Psychostasia, and deemed victorious or "justified" to dwell among the gods in their heavenly abode, itself a place of purification. Even there, the gods were the dead pharaoh, now in spirit form.

It is interesting, this purification or washing of the pharaoh whether alive or dead is not unique. The sun-god, who was once king of Egypt, undergoes a daily lustration before he appears on the horizon to begin his travels across the heavens.

Aylward Blackman, in a number of articles has shown connections between ceremonies in the ritual such as that in the "House of the Morning" and events that ultimately involved the "Opening of the Mouth Ceremony" that are part of the lustration of the god and the king both alive and dead. That is to say, that daily lustration of the god as evidenced from texts and illustrations from Heliopolis that the sun-god undergoes as part of his purification process is similar to the washing of the pharaoh before he enters the temple and equally when he is prepared for burial. The "Opening of the Mouth" ceremony is designed to restore functionality to the entire body of the dead man and so it is a part of the purification process.

Depicted on the walls of several temples, the pharaoh is seen being baptized, generally Horus and Thoth though there are instances where other divinities also perform the function. Equally, it is not a males' only function. These gods pour streams of ankh or symbols of life over the king's head, symbolizing the baptism cleansing he must undergo upon entering the temple. Though of a late period, Horus and Thoth are shown baptizing the king at Kom Ombo temple, dedicated to Haroeis and Sobek the crocodile god. The same is seen at Dendera. However, while Hatshepsut is shown being baptized by Thoth and Horus in a compartment beside the Sanctuary at Karnak Temple, the image is methodically and systematically chiseled out as a reaction to the Queen's rule of Egypt.

We must consider many images of Egyptians involved in many of the culture's religious, mortuary and social festivities, have vanished and those that do survive are, in many instances, badly damaged. Nevertheless, in as much as baptism in service was an absolute prerequisite, every temple throughout the land probably had a similar scene depicting the king being purified. I suppose this was simply a reminder to the king and the priests this function had to be prepared. Thus, this evidence has disappeared from view but the idea of this meaning and significance has not. Then again, Blackman and Fairman have shown, the temple of Horus at Edfu, essentially intact in much of its architectural features and artistic renderings recount much of the most ancient practices of the ritual and liturgy of temple activities. Equally too, on the left screened wall on the outer face of the Pronaos at Dendera temple of Hathor, the gods baptize the king before he enters the sacred spaced of the goddess.

We are always reminded, Karnak is the quintessential temple where practically every Middle and New Kingdom onward pharaonic act or attribute can be found, baptism is no exception. The Hypostyle Hall, begun by Amenhotep in the

Processional Colonnade, conceived in the expansion by Horemheb, begun by Rameses I, finished by Seti I with the northern half decorated by this pharaoh and the southern half's decoration completed by Rameses II, evidence of both kings being baptized in their "respective halves" of the hall.

On the northernmost wall of the northern section of the Hypostyle Hall, Horus and Thoth are seen baptizing Seti I. On the other hand, these gods are again seen baptizing Rameses II on the southernmost wall of the southern portion of the hall.

In Hatshepsut's "Red Chapel" in the "Open Air Museum" Horus (Heru) and Thoth (Tehuti) are again shown baptizing the Queen, who ruled as King, "Her Majesty Himself."

Into the Egyptian Mind. Luxor Temple of Amenhotep III and Rameses II. Before a "Table of Offerings," Amenhotep pours libation from a triple-vase and offers incense. Notice four Obelisks (Tekhens) below his feet and also the boats.

Into the Egyptian Mind. Karnak Temple of Amon-Ra. From the Southwest, view of the First Pylon with the Avenue of Sphinxes in foreground.

24. INCENSE
By
Dr. Fred Monderson

For much of the duration of dynastic rule in ancient Egypt, incense played an important part among festivities involving both the living and the dead. For that matter, we can recognize its significant use in religious worship undergirding the belief such practice thwarts evil spirits down through history. Of course, it has a commercial significance for certainly in modern times business people, certainly in the west in Botanicals, religious stores and general merchants sell incense for every conceivable reason, whether as house blessing, bring my lover back, money, and negate nosy neighbors and much more. Don't get me going on its use in the church, mosque and synagogue. Whereas, in the homes and other domestic locations, incense is generally burnt on a stick; however, in the religious institutions just listed, incense is sometimes combined with Sulphur, frankincense and myrrh. Equally too, while incense is sometimes burned on a stick it is burned in a device set to stand someplace, oftentimes in a corner or elsewhere. But, in a Christian church, for sure, incense is burned in a metal device attached to a lengthy chain-like handle a priest or assistant holds and swings. Movement activates the fiery charcoal to produce the smoke with its potent sight and smell, any place so directed especially in the procession to produce the desired effect. The pharaoh was often seen using a hand-incenser when incensing the god to whom he also poured a libation.

The use of incense in ancient Egypt and along the Nile has a lengthy history; in fact, antedating the emergence of dynastic rule. Perhaps this recognition antedates any such evidence of incense use anywhere in the world. Oh, how I love telling this story!

In a desert country like Egypt and in the recognition that a great deal of Nile water is lost especially during and after the Inundation as it sails into the Mediterranean Sea, the authorities decided on building what became the "Low Dam" at Aswan in 1902, a period under British administration. By the 1960s, after the nation had grown, become independent and the need for electrical power escalated, land reclamation for farming and housing requirement, the then President Gamal Nasser embarked on a plan to construct the Aswan "High Dam." Among the many consequences of this action, the displacement of thousands of Nubians, their ancestral lands, cemeteries and temples, cultural institutions which saw their way of life and culture disrupted; so ultimately these natives nicknamed the enterprise the "Damn Dam." Every time I recount this aspect of the story I recall Farouk, Nubian-Egyptian Guide now with the ancestors who coined the term. Of particularly special interest were the Nubian temples to be submerged and lost once the project got underway.

Nevertheless, once the authorities realized the soon to be created Lake Nasser resulting from the dam would engulf and drown the Nubian temples and way of life which would be lost forever, they appealed through the auspices of **UNESCO** that nations with a history of Nile Valley excavation undertake a "Nubian Rescue." All the major nations provided expeditions including the United States through the University of Chicago, that famous "Breasted School!" The end result of the non-American nations' involvement, finds and "take home artifacts" were never fully brought to light. However, Chicago's expedition under Dr. Keith Seele's leadership also did not give a full and accurate report about its findings.

Subsequently a graduate student at the University, Bruce Williams, "mining the basement" of the Museum of the University of Chicago discovered artifacts which *The New York Times* newspaper published under the title "Evidence of World's Earliest Monarchy found at Qustol, Nubia." The iconic Ivan Van Sertima, in a lecture recounted "Keith Seele knew what he had discovered but he never revealed the significance, he simply secreted his findings in the University of Chicago's Museum's basement hoping to carry its secret with him to the grave. Thankfully, this did not happen." What Mr. Williams, who happens to be white, revealed were the image of an enthroned king wearing the white crown, a palace façade or serekh with a hawk perched atop, sailing boats, animals and an incense burner! These remains were dated to approximately 3400 B.C. that is more than two centuries before we see these features emerge as pharaonic iconography after the Unification of Egypt and finding of the first dynasty.

Now, it is reasonable to assume these cultural features sailed down the Nile as its effluence bequeathed so much from inner Africa rather than believe "for some unknown reason," Asians crossed the desert, brought "a superior mental attitude" that "gave a new impetus to the existing culture." Thus, a number of factors can be considered.

(1) Seldom is a single person in any land, doing very well, give up their privileged position to seek better fortunes in an unknown environment. Some scholars have argued from the first dynasty onward Egypt's kings projected power eastward to encourage trade and export of ideas but for the most part, this was a one-way experiment. As such, and still, the migrating Caucasians who, "for some unknown reason," left their homes to establish "a new fatherland," in Egypt is nothing but pure "defense of a myth."

Egyptian society was organized, they were projecting power abroad, they possessed a reasonable system of record keeping and were certainly prepared, in nationalistic fashion, to defend their culture, repulsing invaders who threatened their way of life. So, how could migrants, seeking their fortunes abroad, perhaps the dregs of their society, arrive on the shores of an established and powerful state, as the E.F. Hutton commercial often boasted of arriving, "slap you on the bottom and say, I'm here!" Consequently, as Dr. Clarke often extolled, "Europeans claim to Egypt uses no logic!"

It is interesting, that as excavations revealed "the ancient records of the ancient history," societies as the **British Association for Advancement of Science**, the **Royal Society of British Architects**, the **Egypt Exploration Fund** and the **Manchester University** organization and similar organizations in Germany, France, Spain, Italy, Belgium, Switzerland, even America, Universities and Museums throughout, presented learned papers, wherein ladies and gentlemen of intellectual substance listened to these presentation and in "Votes of Thanks" made lengthy comments, critiques and injections based on their knowledge of the subject under discussion, yet never questioned the logic and feasibility as outlined above.

Into the Egyptian Mind. Erik Monderson in the Plaza at Karnak Temple, beside the Bazaar.

Into the Egyptian Mind. Egyptian Art. A beautiful couple.

Into the Egyptian Mind. Luxor Temple of Amenhotep III and Rameses II. Rameses in fancy hairdo offers a bouquet of flowers.

Into the Egyptian Mind. Luxor Temple of Amenhotep III and Rameses II. Amenhotep III kneels to present two bouquets of flowers.

Into the Egyptian Mind. Cairo Museum of Egyptian Antiquities. While a deceased female with a perfumed cone on her head offers to the divinity in his shrine, her alter ego is shown twice paddling her own boat and working the fields.

25. THE APRON
By
Dr. Fred Monderson

Ask any Mason or "Lodge Man" about the Apron and he will tell you the decoration on its front indicated the power or standing of the individual wearing it. In ancient Egypt, the pharaoh is hardly ever seen without his apron. However, while he may not always be seen wearing the Gallibea, that long flowing dress, when he does wear it, the apron is worn above this garment. In all the temples, when the pharaoh is seen making a presentation to his god he generally wears the apron. It is as if the apron is a necessary requirement for his stately acts, chief of which is to perform the ritual for the god and to lead in processions. In this latter, as a visible symbol, this garment may seem an indispensable part of essential pharaonic regalia.

In the display as he wears the apron, the king can be shown in a great many attitudes of presentation. Certainly, by New Kingdom times the king is graphically seen making a number of different presentations. One of the most frequently shown is the presentation of one, sometimes two bouquets of flowers, certainly to the goddesses, even to the gods, generally enthroned. In another scene the king is shown pouring a libation with one hand and holding an incenser in the other. While this is generally done standing, there are instances when he kneels to deliver a blessing. At times standing he receives the ankh, symbol of life, even the symbol of a long reign, and especially during the New Kingdom imperial days, Amon gave the curved sword to go conquer and bring booty to Karnak. In all these instances, he is seen wearing the apron.

The make-up of this garment is sometimes simple, sometimes complex. That is from simply two uraei at each end of the garment to five or six across to a much more complicated design that bespeaks of the power previously mentioned. In the southern most wall of the Hypostyle Hall at Karnak temple, whether Rameses II is introduced by the gods as he meets Amon; when he kneels to have Thoth and Seshat write his name in the "Tree of Life;" to be baptized by Thoth and Horus; or to be crowned by Amon, the King's apron is visible in sometimes, simple, sometimes complex forms. Across the Processional Colonnade in the Northern section decorated by the King's father Seti I, in an impressive display of exquisite depictions the king is shown praising or presenting to his god, being baptized, kneeling to have his name also written in the "Tree of Life," or even leading the "four bulls," the apron is certainly visible. There he not only makes offerings to Amon but also to Mut, Sekhmet, Ptah; again, he is aproned for the occasion.

Beyond, on the "Girdle Wall of Rameses II" is an exceptional artistic depiction making a tremendous number of presentations to Amon, Mut, Khonsu, Ptah, Sekhmet, where flowers, girdles, aprons, necklaces, ointment jars, even a sphinx is presented to the gods as Rameses comes "Fully equipped" with apron and all. Strange but the apron or Gallibea does not seem to be a garment worn by the gods who seem to prefer the short kilt. Thus, it can be argued the Apron is a kingly requirement in religious matters but not when he is primed for action on the battlefield, where the outstanding feature is the "Blue Crown."

As kingly attire Hatshepsut is seen wearing the apron on the walls of the "Red Chapel" now reconstructed in the "Open Air Museum" at Karnak. However, one of the more striking examples of "apron power" is depicted on a headless, colossal figure on a back wall in the back corridor in the double temple of Kom Ombo dedicated to Haroeis, the Elder Horus, and Sobek the Crocodile God. Given the "power symbol of the apron," the individual depicted is the ultimate! One unmistaken fact is that the wearing of the apron and the symbolism it represents remained consistent down towards the Graeco-Roman period. It is interesting, that though the Greeks and Romans were considered conquerors who destroyed, repaired some, built others, yet they significantly sought to inculcate aspects of the pharaonic culture to be beneficiaries of the goodness of the gods. Thus, wearing the apron became an absolute necessity of him who would be king!

Into the Egyptian Mind. One example of the Apron from Kom Ombo Temple.

26. THE HANDS
By
Dr. Fred Monderson

In one of his greatest oration, the Harlem Congressman Adam Clayton Powell III asked "What's in Your hands?" and recounted from the Nails in Jesus' hands on the cross to the dollars, some estimate at this time, one trillion annually in the hands, as spending power of African Americans. In ancient Egypt, on the other hand, in every situation, whether it's the God, king or official the hands tell a fascinating story. That is to say, the hands are portrayed in the art, receiving, holding or carrying something. As such, the hands serve as a guide to determine what the individual is doing or holding as preparatory to some action.

If we begin with the god or goddess, he or she is either shown holding a scepter; if for example, Hathor or Isis as a symbol of their power. On the other hand, Amon of Karnak is generally depicted standing or striding or "traveling," and even enthroned. In all these attitudes, the god is shown foremost with his scepter as the most effective weapon for his defense or as an example of his power. Besides the scepter, the god is also shown offering ankh or sign of life to the nostrils of the pharaoh. He is also shown offering the symbol of millions of years to his beloved son. To the New Kingdom warrior pharaohs, the god is sometimes shown giving the king the curved sword with which to conquer and bring booty and tribute back to Karnak, the "Throne of the two lands."

Into the Egyptian Mind. Egyptian Art. A funeral scene of individuals carrying Anubis hoisted high on a bier, a kneeling female wailing and standing individuals holding staffs at the rear.

Into the Egyptian Mind. Luxor Temple of Amenhotep III and Rameses II. The 14-columns of the Processional Colonnade as the last light from the west shines back to illuminate this classic piece of architecture.

Into the Egyptian Mind. Luxor Temple of Amenhotep III and Rameses II. From the south west, view of the Ramessean Front's colonnade, the Great Pylon and Obelisk, the Mosque of Abu Haggag to the top right and pitifully small Roman columns in the foreground.

Into the Egyptian Mind. Egyptian Art. Papyrus. Fishing and fowling in the Marshes with the Missus.

Into the Egyptian Mind. Egyptian Art. Carmen Monderson stands in one of the most beautiful tombs of the Nobles, Sennutem, at Luxor, Thebes.

The king, male or female, is shown in a multitude of attitudes, all directed toward the gods. For the most part, he or she is shown making an offering of some sort, in which he gives a plant, two water vessels, a bouquet of flowers, two ointment vessels, sometimes a sphinx, even his name as symbolic in Ma'at, or even food, whether meats, fowl, cakes or even a platter. Sometimes much of this is represented on a table of offerings. He is also seen, sometimes, pouring a libation or incensing the god. Infrequently, he is shown with one or two empty hands as if expecting to receive some gift from the god. In most cases he kneels to present the offering or to receive the gift. The king is also seen incensing the barque of the god carried aloft by priests or even when it is at rest. He is also shown incensing the god in his shrine aboard a sailing boat or barge.

The dead king has to be purified and justified just as did the god Osiris had to undergo before he was deemed pure and justified. The king has to be judged and once "justified" or declared "true of voice" and purified; he is allowed to join the body of the blessed divinities and dead. In that spiritual existence in the Afterlife, the king is sometimes shown wailing his boat or even tilling the fields for his sustenance.

As a warrior pharaoh, the king is depicted in his encampment and consulting with his generals and advisers, as well as carrying the sword to his enemies. There he is shown fighting with the sword and shield, shooting his arrows and even charging the enemy in his chariot, either with a charioteer or alone. In the latter case, he is either shown shooting his arrows or fighting with sword, shield or lance as he tramples his foes, charges the enemy or orchestrating the scaling of a wall or its ramparts. He is even shown in the traditional position of holding Egypt's enemies by the hair and administering the death blow. Now, with the battle over, he is seen driving his car, leading the enemy tethered by a string as he presents them to Amen. In many instances, he sacrifices these captives before the god as he again administers the death blow. Oftentimes the depiction shows the captives with hands, in the air as they plead for mercy. The goddess, for her part, depending on who she is, is shown with a number of attributes. For instance, the "two ladies," Nekhbet and Wadjet are often shown on heb, while gods of the Amon circle are shown as in the Theban Triad with Amon and Khonsu or joined by another more often than not, she is shown patting the king's back or introducing him to the god. The gods in their own right are shown baptizing the king, before he enters the temple or in the god's vicinity. This ritual of purity shows the hands of Horus and Thoth administering the ceremony to the pharaoh who, as the object of the exercise, welcomes the feeling of purity that empowers him to perform the lustration and purification of his god.

Now, having seen the hands of the god and king employed in their various tasks, it is time to consider the role of the female partnership in the human and divine experience.

Into the Egyptian Mind. Rameses II's Temple at Abydos. A Bull being led in procession and a young one follows.

27. THE BULL
By
Dr. Fred Monderson

The idea of the Bull runs deep in the psyche and festive practices of ancient Egypt. Whether we see the king as a strong bull gorging an enemy or battering his gates, even being worshipped as a divinity, the Bull held a special place in the mind of the Egyptian. When the king is referred to as "The Bull of his Mother" he is shown as a bull!

At the Mortuary Temple of Rameses III where the Bull is depicted, an enormous penis is also shown. In this temple as well as in the Court of Rameses II at Luxor, fat bulls in procession are led by priests as part of a ceremony of the sons of the king on way to that temple. One particular image depicts a Nubian lady coming out of the head of one of the bulls. This particular scene takes us back to a number of scenarios in which religious worship of the "Cow Goddess," as Brophy and Bauval have argued, antedate the start of pharaonic rule.

The number four has a mystical significance in that Abu Simbel temple is dedicated to four gods, Ra-Horakhty, Amon, Ptah and Rameses II, himself. That is not to say other numbers in their own context are not as mystically potent, especially the notion of three as it refers to Triads and multiples of threes. Nonetheless, At Medinet Habu, Mortuary Temple of Rameses III, in a side chapel to the right of the Hypostyle Hall, two sets of four baboons greet the sun-god sailing across the sky. Even more important, here and at Karnak the King leads four bulls to Amon. However, there is more to the idea of the bull.

Among his many accomplishments, Mariette, acting on a tip from the classical writer Diodorus Siculus discovered the Serapeum, a temple and tomb of the Sacred Bull particularly favored by the Ramesside kings, especially Rameses II. As a "lover of the Bull" himself, he is shown in his father Scti I's temple at Abydos, dedicated to Osiris, Isis and Horus of the Osiris cycle; Ra-Horakhty, Amon and Ptah the three great gods of the Empire period; and Seti I deified. Here Rameses is seen teaching his son Merenptah, how to "throw" or lasso the bull.

The **Sallier Papyrus** is a veritable gold mine of statistical evidence of donations Rameses III made to the temple of Amon and other gods, though at a lesser amount. Bulls, either as donations or part of temple property are shown to be many for they feature prominently in the ritual and sacrifices made during the various festivals.

Into the Egyptian Mind. Egyptian Art. Certainly a funeral scene with male and female mourners.

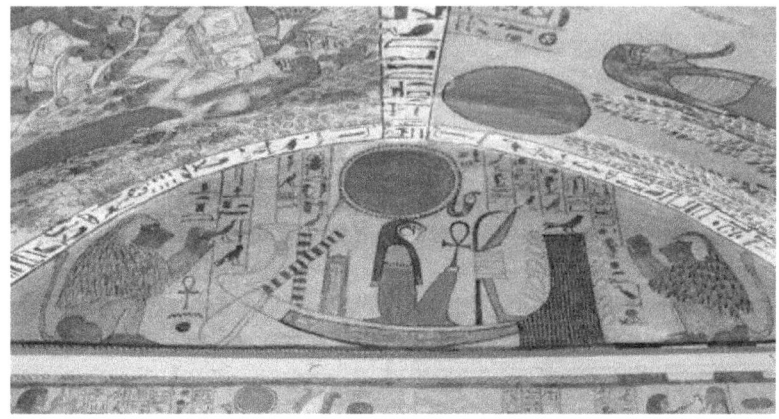

Into the Egyptian Mind. Egyptian Art. Ra-Horakhty sails the Celestial Nile while being greeted by Baboons in the Tomb of Sennutem.

Into the Egyptian Mind. Isis Temple at Philae. Standing at the head of the Dromos or walkway, the Kiosk of Nectanebo as one ascends to Isis' temple.

Into the Egyptian Mind. Egyptian Art. In the Tomb of Sennutem, Hawks guard the mummy's coffin while below a banquet is underway.

28. THE AVENUE OF SPHINXES
By
Dr. Fred Monderson

The Avenue of Sphinxes is essentially a New Kingdom decorative feature, or should I say, found its greatest display in this age, but was generally discontinued in later building practice. In actuality, it was a clever Egyptian strategy to utilize space as with the colonnade, to decorate the walkway to the temple and also to provide an esoteric and mystical form of protection to the temple. In as much as the temple was generally built some distance from the river, if there was no canal bridging the gap, the Sphinxes lined the walkway to the entrance pylon. Certainly, the surviving New Kingdom temples as Karnak, Khonsu, Luxor, and Mut had/has sphinxes lining their entrance. We can only speculate that Amenhotep III, Seti I at Kurneh, even Merenptah had sphinxes though none have survived. The record seems to indicate, the walkway from the Valley Temple to Hatshepsut's Deir el

Bahari temple was lined with sphinxes. The same can probably be surmised for Mentuhotep's nearby temple, though built five hundred years previous, it is not inconceivable they were obliterated through time.

Into the Egyptian Mind. The Avenue of Sphinxes leading out from Luxor Temple towards Karnak Temple, some three miles away.

Karnak temple has surviving Ram-headed sphinxes before the entrance pylon. Between the paws are miniature images of the king, Rameses II, and though most are disfigured, one survives with the face intact. Inside the Great Court, a full length of 19 sphinxes stand before the Northern Colonnade. Equally, to the south stand another set of Sphinxes before the Southern Colonnade, only this time they are interrupted by the miniature, north/south temple of Rameses III. Since there are columns and sphinxes beside this temple it stands to reason they were there before and thus, establishes the connection with Rameses II. In fact, it has been argued, in creating the Great Court, the sphinxes were removed from those fronting the Great Pylon and thus deposited before both the Northern and Southern Colonnades as well as the pylon were built.

The Temple of Khonsu the Moon-God son of Amon and Mut, within the Enclosure, also has an Avenue of Rams abbreviated within the Enclosure Wall. There is an Avenue of Ram-headed Sphinxes connecting Karnak with the Temple of Mut, the Earth goddess and wife of Amon, the Sun god. Thus, the temples of Amon at Karnak, that of Khonsu and Mut, the Theban Triad, all boast Avenues of Sphinxes and are the principal features of the Central and Southern complexes within the greater enclosure wall. It is interesting that each temple has its own enclosure wall but the Theban complex boast an even greater "wrap around" enclosure wall encompassing the northern, central and southern structures and all their appendages or ancillary structures. The now essentially destroyed temple of Monthu, the War-god, the principal feature of the northern complex of the greater whole, also boasted an Avenue of Sphinxes.

The temple of Luxor boasts an extensive Avenue of Human-headed Sphinxes erected by King Nectanebo of the 26th and last native Dynasty which links Luxor with Karnak over a three-mile area. It fell in disuse over the ages and with streets crisscrossing and with buildings being erected along the way. Like so much of antique Egypt that has become a lucrative economic commodity, repairs have begun on the "Sphinx

Road" to add it to the Tourist Circuit and encourage its economic viability, perhaps to benefit the surrounding communities.

Into the Egyptian Mind. Egyptian Art. As a Nobleman and wife sit with perfumed cones on their heads, a Sem Priest in leopard skin offers libation and incense. To the right two ladies sit on cushions before two "Table of Offerings."

Into the Egyptian Mind. Egyptian Art. Tomb of Sennutem. The deceased kneels with Anubis at his rear (standing) before a sumptuous "Table of Offerings" presented to Osiris (Ausar) in his Shrine.

Into the Egyptian Mind. Isis Temple at Philae.
Pharaoh offers a symbol of eternity to enthroned Amon-Ra in feathers and Mut, wearing the Red and White Double Crown.

Into the Egyptian Mind. Isis Temple at Philae.
Pharaoh offers two ointment jars to enthroned Isis in horns and Nephthys wearing the Red and White Double Crown.

Into the Egyptian Mind. Egyptian Art. Sennutem and wife stand in adoration before squatting gods.

29. THE COURT
By
Dr. Fred Monderson

The Court is an important element in the ancient Egyptian temple structure. Not as important as the Hypostyle hall or the "Holy of Holies" or even the Sacred Lake used for washing and festive displays but one cannot get to these much more significant locations without passing through this conduit. The Court is such an essential part of the structure, there are sometimes more than one, sometimes bearing the name "great" or "small," or even "succeeding."

The Court is generally the first space encountered once through the entrance pylon. It is where privileged visitors are allowed to observe or even participate in some temple festivities and important occasions. It is generally filled with all sorts of architectural features.

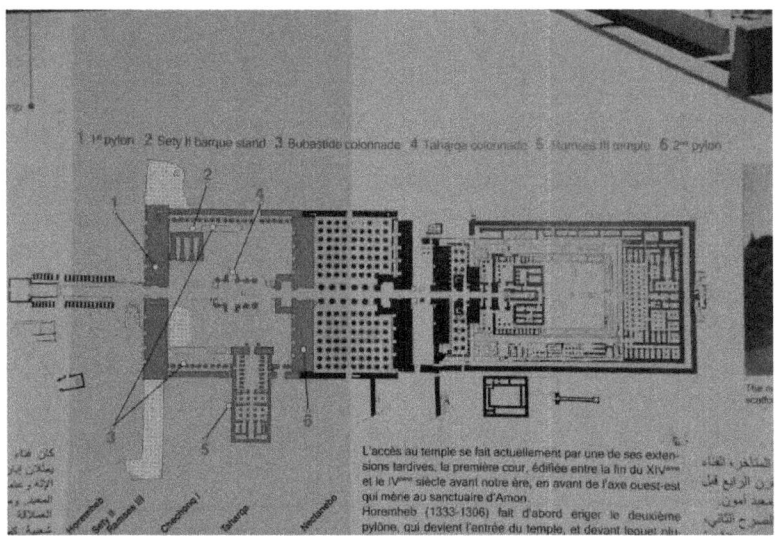

Into the Egyptian Mind. Karnak Temple of God Amon. The Great Court highlighted with its constituent parts.

The temple of Karnak is the most visible and best example in which to observe all forms of architectural detail, given that it took 2000 years to complete this temple considered a "Museum of Egyptian architectural history" and art in which succeeding pharaohs vied with each other to pleas the great god Amon. In addition, because this sanctuary of the Theban Triad in its north, central and southern capacities, served as residence of several gods; in fact, the Theban Ennead of 15 deities, it boasts a total of some 22 temples. Not only were there temples within this temple, but equally there were Courts upon Courts and this and more is what makes this "Select of Places" just that.

Architectural remains date Karnak temple to the Middle Kingdom but archaeological evidence pushes this back to, at least, the Second Dynasty. This writer was shown architectural remains at Tod, a nearby site in Upper Egypt with remains to the first and second dynasties. As such, as an Upper Egyptian shrine Karnak is in good company. Nevertheless, Karnak boasts Middle Kingdom, New Kingdom and Late Period Courts. The principal or Great Court at Karnak consists of a 20th Dynasty miniature temple of Rameses III that sits perpendicular to the main axis over which the Sun-god traverses. In its own Enclosure Wall, this small temple is equipped with a Court with Osiride Figures or pillars and the customary features of a complete temple, viz., Hypostyle Hall, "Holy of Holies," depicted illustrations of the king in various attitudes, etc.

Into the Egyptian Mind. Luxor Temple of Amenhotep III and Rameses II. Luis Casado stands in the Plaza at Luxor Temple in which the front entrance has been upgraded with all four standing statues now in place before the Great Pylon.

Into the Egyptian Mind. Egyptian Art. Man of noble stature holds two bouquets of flowers.

Into the Egyptian Mind. Egyptian Art. A Sem Priest in his leopard-skin get-up.

Into the Egyptian Mind. Isis Temple at Philae. The "Kiosk of Trajan" seen from the River as the visitor departs.

Into the Egyptian Mind. Isis Temple at Philae.
The Church of St. Stephens as seen from the River at Aswan.

30. THE COLONNADE
By
Dr. Fred Monderson

The Colonnade is one of the greatest inventions of the Egyptian mind, commencing about 2800 B.C., long before Babylonians or any other people could conceive of such a construct. This fascinating invention first appeared at Sakkara in Imhotep's Step-Pyramid for his Pharaoh Zoser in the Third Dynasty. Seldom has an invention been so instrumental and widespread, for it came to adorn religious, mortuary, domestic, civic and even military architecture for much of the 3000 years of dynastic building practice. Even more significant, this architectural feature migrated to many places but particularly influencing Greek and Roman architecture and with the clerestory became foundational in Western, Basilica church architecture. Even more far reaching, the idea of the colonnade migrated and significantly influenced construction techniques beyond the West where they came to adorn academic institutions, public building and even domestic structures. Unfortunately, with the exception of its later impact on basilica church architecture, nowhere else has its impact been more pronounced and multifaceted than in Egypt, especially during the New Kingdom and later.

Into the Egyptian Mind. The **Dromos to Isis Temple** at Philae (Now Agilka Island) is bounded by the Eastern Colonnade with 17 columns and the Western Colonnade with 32 columns.

This architectural innovation the "father of Egyptian" and "world" architecture encouraged the invention and development of a great many ancillary features of architecture considered "The great glory of Egypt." In fact, down through the ages of architectural trailblazing to have "one's name written in the colonnade" was considered one of the greatest honors the Egyptian society could bestow on a deserving individual.

What then was the colonnade and who was it employed are significant enquiries that evokes far-reaching answers?

The Colonnade can be a single but more generally a line of columns. A single or a number of lines, it can comprise as many as the author or builder desires, but generally four to twelve, or eleven is the most often chosen amount. Eleven is associated with Hathor and employed in Deir el Bahari colonnades, Lower, Middle and Upper. Like everything that man has created, that ultimately disappeared, not much evidence remains of the Old Kingdom but by the Middle Kingdom especially at Beni Hasan we begin to see columns used as roof support in tombs. These have alternated with pillars also as supports hews from quarrying in rock cut tombs. However, the magnificent Eleventh Dynasty Deir el Bahari temple of Mentuhotep II that served as transitional religious architecture from the Old to the New Kingdom, exceptionally utilized the colonnade twin feature, that is, column and pillar, to remarkable results. Some five hundred years later, and in as much as Hatshepsut, her reign and support personnel have been innovative in a number of cultural features that heavily impacted Egyptian culture down through time, Mentuhotep's use of the column influenced the Queen's architect Senmut in his choice for her mortuary temple and the significant influence columns would come to play in that architectural masterpiece.

As previously stated, the colonnade was an honorary place to have one's name reserved for kings and gods, as well as a few exceptional non-royal personnel. Perhaps such as exceptional person as Amenhotep, Son of Hapu, who had several statues placed in Karnak's hypostyle hall, would have been accorded such an honor. That is not to say there were no others who were just as gifted. However, in its utilization and decoration of space, the colonnade found its greatest fruition in the Peristyle Court and the Hypostyle Hall.

The Peristyle Colonnade is a roofless utilization of the colonnade generally with a covered or uncovered ambulatory running around its four sides most often in a court. The Hypostyle Hall, on the other hand, is a roofed enclosure where ritual and processions are generally held. In the Peristyle, the columns may or may not be decorated. At Philae Temple, the Western Colonnade's single row of 32 columns are decorated with images of gods and kings. The Eastern Colonnade's 17 single row columns are bare, perhaps unfinished. At Luxor Temple in the "Ramessean Front's" Peristyle Court, the double row of columns has statues that seem to strive from between. Further in, the magnificent Peristyle Court of Amenhotep III with its double row of columns are bare, being papyrus bundle columns, though the architrave contains cartouches and other illustrations of the king and Amon. In the Amarna Revolution, Amenhotep IV's adherents sought to erase every image of Amon among this and other temple locations. Lanny Bell has shown, atop the western colonnade's architrave, images of Amon escaped the wrath of these zealots, perhaps it's because they were tired of scaling such heights to seek vengeance on the god. The Hypostyle Hall with its four rows of papyrus bundle columns is not only undecorated but in their majestic deployment forms the southern section of the Peristyle Court.

The most famous Hypostyle Hall of columns is at Karnak where 134 are more exquisitely employed, decorated and representing the iconic thicket field or swamp "As at creation." The walls of this roofed enclosure are illustrated with scenes of the temple ritual and it is where the procession congregates for within performance or to begin a visit beyond the temple. A striking feature of the Karnak Hypostyle Hall is the "Processional Colonnade" consisting of two rows of six each, larger than the other 122 adjacent columns; though these latter are round, without a capital, while the Processional Colonnade boasts Open Papyrus floral capitals.

Into the Egyptian Mind. Egyptian Art. A kneeling beauty seems to be in a lamenting mood.

Into the Egyptian Mind. Isis Temple at Philae. The majestic "Kiosk of Trajan" with its elevated columns atop screened walls, varied capitals, elevated abacus supporting a wonderful architrave, essentially very much intact.

Into the Egyptian Mind. Egyptian Art. That Nobleman mentioned previously, now he carries a concoction.

Into the Egyptian Mind. Aswan. The Garden at Old Cataract Hotel, Aswan, Egypt.

Into the Egyptian Mind. Aswan. Another view of the Garden at Old Cataract Hotel.

Into the Egyptian Mind. Egyptian Art. Fred and Carmen Monderson in the Tomb of Sennutem, 2017.

31. THE PROCESSIONAL COLONNADE
By
Dr. Fred Monderson

The Processional Colonnade is an enormous compendium of stone, an architectural masterpiece, decorated with figures of the Gods, kings and queens topped by an equally exquisitely decorated lotus capital in bloom. Presently there are three at Thebes, one in the Luxor Temple of Amenhotep III; one at Karnak in the Hypostyle Hall; and one in the Ramesseum, mortuary temple of Rameses II. It is called the Processional Colonnade because it is centrally located in the ascent towards the Holy of Holies. At both Karnak and the Ramesseum, they stand between the two wings of the hall while at Luxor there is no hall accompanying the stand-alone colonnade. At Karnak its two rows of six, while at Luxor its two rows of seven. It is where the procession psses, and it is generally flanked on both sides by a Hall of Columns. These columns are equally decorated forms and in their enclosed hall are considered a Hypostyle Hall because of the accompanying roof. Conversely, an open court with columns set around its edges, but without a roof is called a Peristyle. Nevertheless, and again, not only does the columns support the Processional Colonnade but they often line the way for the processions demonstrated in the Hypostyle Hall but also when it ventures abroad. At other times the Procession of priest bearing the Ark of the God or king as a god on earth, ventures beyond the Hypostyle Hall, into the court and the entrance pylon on to some distant journey. In such a case as at Karnak, for example, once beyond the gate, though the procession may head to Luxor temple by boat with elements on foot to celebrate the Feast of the Opet. They then return to Karnak via a Sacred Canal and on land. Other times the procession may cross the Nile to the West Bank to visit the tombs of the dead kings and to celebrate the Feast of the Valley in the kings' mortuary temples.

Nonetheless, on the walls of the adjacent roofed columned hall, the temple ritual and the king with other gods are shown in adoration of the principal god, and again in the case of Karnak Temple, it is Amon, Amon-Ra assisted by other divinities. However, of the three processional colonnades mentioned Luxor, Karnak and Ramesseum; while the other two were finished, viz., the lateral appendages, the hall, Luxor appears unfinished and the colonnade stands devoid of this extension. Nevertheless, following the Amarna Revolution of Amenhotep III's son, Amenhotep IV, Ikhnaton, Tutankhamon effectuated the Restoration that helped Amon to re-emerge triumphant as king of the gods. Among the many efforts Tutankhamon instituted to appease Amon's adherents, he walled the two sides of the Luxor Processional Colonnade and depicted the events of the Open Festival's journey to and from Luxor back to Karnak.

There is another Processional Colonnade, or was at Soleb Temple in Nubia that James Henry Breasted, the American

Egyptologist attributed to Amenhotep III, crediting this king with experimenting to create and introduce a new form of architecture. This he did subsequently at Luxor and Karnak.

Into the Egyptian Mind. Garden entrance to the Old Cataract Hotel at Aswan.

This was a superhuman effort to have created 3 such stupendous undertakings for a single king who, in his own right, was building the Luxor Temple with its wonderful Peristyle Court, his Mortuary Temple on the West Bank, a Palace called Malcata for his beautiful wife Queen Tiy as well as constructing a lake for her to sail her wonderful barge. To this we may add Amenhotep's tomb in the Western Valley of the Kings and the embellishment of the Temple of Mut in which he placed hundreds of statues of the Goddess Sekhmet, his favorite. Naturally, the king would have been engaged in other constructions, for after all, he was dubbed "The Magnificent" and his empire was at the apogee of its "Golden Age."

Into the Egyptian Mind. Egyptian Art. A young man is held by the hand and led by Horus (Heru).

Into the Egyptian Mind. Another view of the front entrance Garden to the Old cataract Hotel in Aswan.

Into the Egyptian Mind. Egyptian Art. Osiris (Ausar) enthroned in his Shrine wearing the White Crown and holding the Crook and Flail, symbols of his power and authority.

Into the Egyptian Mind. Aswan. View from the Old Cataract Hotel of a nearby relaxing area.

Into the Egyptian Mind. Sakkara. The Step-Pyramid of Zoser built by Imhotep, 3rd Dynasty, 2600 B.C.

Into the Egyptian Mind. Egyptian Art. Below, "Two Eyes of Horus," two Anubi stand at the ready with that "Thousand-yard Stare."

32. SACRED LAKE
By
Dr. Fred Monderson

The Sacred Lake is an indispensable part of any temple for a number of reasons, principally because it is a source of water. It is generally connected to the Nile through an underground set of springs. The story is told of scholars at the 19th Century who sought to determine the sources of Karnak Temple's Sacred Lake's waters. They drained the lake but it soon filled again and so the underground source was not determined at first. Cleanliness was an indispensable part of temple life as a part of religious ritual, all embodied in the idea that the surroundings or abode of the gods must be one of purity.

Into the Egyptian Mind. Karnak Temple of God Amon. From the South-East view of the Sacred Lake with the 9th Pylon to the right and ruins of the 10th Pylon to the left.

In as much as there were at least three times in a given day the god's presence was invoked for meals and lustration, and then there was the need for water at these times. The god had to be washed, clothed, roughed, and fed three times on any given day. The priests administering the lustrations themselves had to be cleaned or purified before they could approach the divinity and then perform their services. However, while the king or high priest were the ones who directly administered to or laid hands on the god, because of the elaborate nature of the function a number of attendant priests were also involved. These included attendants who carried water, food, clothing, liquids, toiletries, and the books of the ritual, musical instruments, incense and incense holders, perhaps animals to be sacrificed and so on. As such, this whole retinue of attendants had to be washed and purified so as to enter or be in proximity of the purified space. All these particulars were necessary so that the administering ritual and ceremony would be successfully concluded and the divinity returned to his abode until the next occasion. In a desert country as Egypt and in temples sometimes distant from the Nile, the Sacred Lake is not only indispensable but takes on added significance.

Into the Egyptian Mind. Karnak Temple of God Amon. From just east of the Sacred lake, the two Obelisks and ruins of the Hypostyle Hall (center) and the First Pylon (left). Further on.

Nonetheless, the waters of the sacred Lake served more purposes than administering to the gods. It provided all the water for temple use. In addition, during certain ceremonies and festivals the boats or barques of divinities were placed to sail on the lake, sometimes for the full duration of the festivities.

Oftentimes the Sacred Lake has a "sister body of water" that provides similar or ancillary functions. From 1903 through 1907, Legrain, the French archaeologist in charge of restoration at Karnak Temple, began draining and searching the "Cachette Court," a body of water situated before the Seventh Pylon on the North-South axis on the temple. Lo and behold, as the pictures of men, chest-deep in water were able to retrieve thousands of statues placed in the water, all were in very good condition. Two theories have been propounded as to the source of this Cache. One is that there were so many statues of kings and gods donated to the temple and the excess were placed in the waters of the Cachette. The second idea is that in troubled times of an impending foreign invasion, the statues were deposited here for safe-keeping.

It is interesting, in one of the false statements in the grand scheme of falsity of a Caucasian origin of the Ancient Egyptians, the elaborate argument is made (1) in the mummification process of the deceased individual the brains were removed through the nostrils. Hence, the nose of the mummy was disfigured. Well, the statue of the deceased also had its nose broken in similar fashion and purpose. Such objects were always made in the image of the owner, the noses generally betray African mold of the art. The noses of statues discovered in the Cachette did not have their noses broken when originally placed in this location at Karnak. The "double statue of Neferhotep" was discovered intact below the obelisk of Hatshepsut near the Wadjet and its nose was not broken. Thus, the idea of the broken nose is not tenable.

Into the Egyptian Mind. Egyptian Art. Osiris (Ausar), painted green, sits enthroned among the gods with a hawk image of Horus (Heru) and an "Eye of Horus" offering candle-like flames to his reverence, as Sennutem kneels below.

Into the Egyptian Mind. Deir el Medina. Native Egyptian Guide Shawki Abd Rady at Deir el Medina.

Into the Egyptian Mind. Egyptian Art. Nakht and family hunt in the marshes.

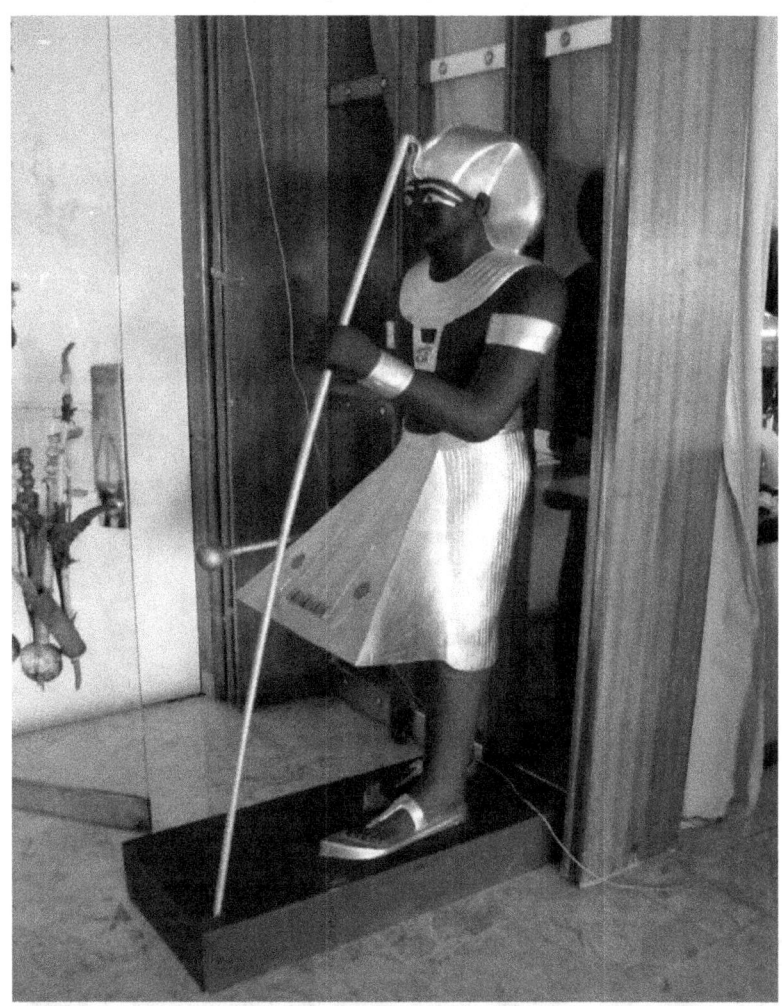

Into the Egyptian Mind. Aswan. Formerly the Oberoi Hotel Dining Room. Image of Tutankhamon bearing his real black-skin color as the modern Nubians of that region recognize him to be.

Into the Egyptian Mind. Aswan. Formerly the Oberoi Hotel Dining Room. Another ancient Egyptian king as the modern at Nubians at Aswan imagined him to be in his Black skin.

Into the Egyptian Mind. Egyptian Art. Nakht and wife sit before a "Table of Offerings" as they observe workers about their tasks.

33. THE CACHE
By
Dr. Fred Monderson

In one of those rare situations the term "Cache" proved significant in both ancient and modern times. Circumstances caused three significant precious ancient Egyptian artifacts to be deposited in three significant locations in ancient times and the persistent and inquisitive adventurous and archaeological sleuthing revealed three remarkable discoveries in the late 19th and early 20th Centuries. These finds essentially rewrote the thinking regarding the ancient Egyptian pharaohs, their mummification practices and the art and sculpture of their times. More important, the sensation generated in association with these discoveries highlighted the archaeological, anthropological and restoration and the men involved, encouraged a new impetus towards antiquities studies in the Universities, the curiosities posed in museum displays, a desire to visit and walk the land of such storied glory, all of which added to the acquisition and formation of collections of similar artifactual luxuries.

Into the Egyptian Mind. Egyptian Art. Raised relief. Couples sporting perfumed cones, sit and enjoy the ambience of the banquet.

Into the Egyptian Mind. Egyptian Art. Queen Nefertari stands before an enthroned Thoth (Tehuti) in her tomb.

Into the Egyptian Mind. Memnon. Two colossal seated statues that stand before the Temple of Amenhotep III destroyed in an earthquake.

Into the Egyptian Mind. Shawki Abd Rady and a friend pose for this photo with Memnon in the rear, standing before the Temple of Amenhotep III.

Into the Egyptian Mind. The Vulture and Uraeus, Nekhbet and Wajdyt on Heb, as they represent the "Two Ladies" title of the King.

Into the Egyptian Mind. Egyptian Art. Carmen Monderson in the Tomb of Sennutem.

The first such discovery occurred during the period of 1881-82 when the reclamation of Egyptian cultural history was in the throes of being systematically organized. Apparently, during some time of upheaval and uncertainty during the 21st or 22nd dynasties, Theban priest considered the guardians of the nation's mortuary repositories, decided to collect and safeguard the remains of some of its more famous rulers. Whether in fear of tomb robbers or invading forces who would probably violate the tombs of the revered dead, collected these historic persons' mummies and their wonderful funeral paraphernalia, viz., coffins, statues, various forms of art and artifacts, jewelry, garlands, canopic jars, etc., and secreted them in a gorge behind the temple of Deir el Bahari.

As time passed about early 1880 Egyptian authorities as Gaston Maspero and his assistant Herr Brugsch began to notice exceptionally rare pieces of artifacts appearing on the antiquities market and no significant tomb and its riches had been discovered. After investigative efforts and while Mr.

Maspero was away in France, Herr Brugsch had one of two Rasul Brothers arrested on suspicion of being involved in artifactual thievery and placed in prison. At first the culprit refused to talk, but knowing his brother, that is, while he was frying, the brother was flying. That is, he was looting the lucrative horde. Refusing to take the heat while his brother got the meat, he squealed and upon release revealed to authorities the source of their good fortune. Soon soldiers arrived to guard the treasure which was carefully collected and carted off to Cairo.

This discovery sent shockwaves around the world to know that persons of such prominence had been found and the media of the time enjoyed field-days publicizing the names of individuals who lived in biblical times and earlier.

The following persons' names were mentioned according to

The next significant discovery occurred in 1898 when the Frenchman Loret discovered the tomb of Amenhotep II, son of Thutmose III. In the sepulcher, another horde of kings' mummies was secreted and together with the Deir el Bahari cache, the Cairo Museum, at that time Bulaq, then considered on part with the great museums of the world, especially that of Turin, Italy.

While these two hoards of treasure were discovered in the land of the dead on the West Bank, another perhaps equally significant discovery was unearthed in the "land of the living." In fact, it was a temple, discovered in Karnak Temple, to be exact.

Into the Egyptian Mind. Egyptian Art. "Ladies in Waiting." One has grey hair.

Into the Egyptian Mind. Egyptian Art. In the Tomb of Nakht, two ladies surround a sumptuous "Table of Offerings" bounded by wonderful sized grapes.

Into the Egyptian Mind. Cairo Museum of Egyptian Antiquities. On the outside wall of the Museum, tribute to the great minds who helped establish the discipline of Egyptology.

Into the Egyptian Mind. Cairo Museum of Egyptian Antiquities. On the outside wall of the Museum, tribute to the great minds who helped establish the discipline of Egyptology.

Into the Egyptian Mind. Egyptian Art. The Gods and Nobles on display in the Tomb of Sennutem.

34. THE PRIESTHOOD
BY
DR. FRED MONDERSON

In ancient Kemet, now Egypt, along the banks of the Nile River, one of the earliest professional organizations came into being. This body, the Priesthood, combined a number of functions - religious, political, scientific, educational, administrative, economic, artistic and so came to exercise tremendous power for the duration of dynastic rule. In times of unity and division, prosperity and stagnation, this organization transmitted the ancient Egyptian, African, Nile Valley culture synthesizing, preserving and creating ideas and civil and politico-religious structures for the propagation of the gods in benefit to the Egyptian society. Thus, out of the religiosity of these ancient Africans, order in society emerged and helped to bequeath mankind a tremendous legacy of achievement in knowledge, social civility, art, construction, government, and science.

The land of Kemet is very dry, mysterious, cultural, and full of history. It is artistic, philosophical, spiritual and religious. Boasting the earliest sense of theological consciousness, these ancient Africans created a religious system and attendant intellectual, mortuary, spiritual and festive dynamics that helped to enshrine practices to influence peoples and cultures, far and wide, then and now. Owing to the significance of religion in the theocratic state, a bureaucracy very early grew up around kingly and divine worship at their principal centers of theological expression in Memphis, Heliopolis, Thebes, Hermopolis, Abydos, and in the Mortuary cults at Giza, Sakkara, Abu Sir, etc. Later in the Middle and especially New Kingdom the mortuary cults on the West Bank found full employment for the Priesthood. This unending and profound involvement earned these practitioners the professional designation of Priesthood. So much so, and among their literary and intellectual functions, Jill Kamil in *The Ancient Egyptians* (1984: 36) could write, "… the fabric of ancient Egyptian mythological tradition, which survived in embellished or mutilated form for thousands of years, was woven and rewoven, time and again, to justify new conditions to explain political trends; it was sometimes even entangled to promote a cause."

Into the Egyptian Mind. The Ghizeh Plateau.
The Great Pyramid of Khufu on the Ghizeh Plateau.

Into the Egyptian Mind. Sakkara, Home of the Step-Pyramid. "Dates in galore" only waiting to be picked and thus reflect the agricultural bounty of the land.

Into the Egyptian Mind. On the Road to Sakkara, a Carpet School.

Into the Egyptian Mind. Ceramic vases by the road on the West Bank at Luxor.

Into the Egyptian Mind. Egyptian Art. Nakht and his wife pour a libation while a smaller figure stands holding a vessel before them.

The Priesthood was thus a significant institution from the earliest times through its involvement in practically every aspect of the society's cultural development. This is underscored since, as early as the archaic first and second dynasties, institutions of religion were established to effectuate worship and mortuary practices, wherein essentially the major precepts of justice, honor, work, and art were practiced and prevailed until very late in Kemetic history.

Thus, by the beginning of the Old Kingdom, with the king considered a god and theocracy the form of government, this "elaborate officialdom bureaucracy" helped justify the king's divinity and thereby fuse civil and ecclesiastical offices in the Pharaoh and his high officials. Throughout this creative period producing abundant intellectual growth, artistic innovation, enshrined religious beliefs and practices, remarkable accomplishments were equally achieved in architecture, astronomy, engineering, and medicine.

Sadly, however, growth in the cultural wealth and political power of the nobles, not simply undermined the society's stability, but also led them to rival the monarch in elaborate funerary preparations to reflect their newly acquired social status. Later, as the Priesthood's power and influence increased during the ramifications of the imperial New Kingdom age, according to J.A. Wilson in *The Culture of Ancient Egypt* (1959: 171) regarding the principal administrators of the state: "The highest officials of the land under the Pharaoh were the High Priest of Amon at Karnak, the Vizier for Upper Egypt, the Vizier for Lower Egypt, and the 'King's Son of Kush' or Viceroy of Ethiopia. The last-named position included three responsibilities; the delegated rule of the African Empire; the responsibility for gold mines of Nubia; and the command of the army in Africa, pharaoh having the responsible leadership for pushing the Empire in Asia. This viceroy-ship was often a training ground for the Crown Prince." No less significant, these officials beneath the pharaoh were themselves members of the priesthood.

Within the dynamics of constructive growth under strong leadership, as all this unfolded, the state went to great lengths to propagate cultural, architectural, and artistic innovations, and the Priesthood was generally avant-garde in this effort. Still, while their earliest beginnings may be shrouded in the mysteries of time, it is safe to argue, the accepted date of invention of the calendar at 4241 B.C. Because of their profound utility in the society, this scientific innovation therefore places the Priesthood there, and speculation as to how many thousands of years earlier, may be still valid.

Their growing positions of power notwithstanding, the Pharaoh as the principal religiant in the land, assigned the religious organization responsibility for worshipping and ritualizing the gods and himself as a son of god on earth. In this role, the Priesthood became a powerful body and the king endowed them with lands, generally free from taxation. As a result, the body became self-reliant and in symbiotic harmony as a community were able to perpetuate the religious, spiritual and political symbolism the king represented in his efforts to bring order, justice and harmony as prerequisites to cultural success in the state.

Two of the earliest centers of religious and cultural rivalry were Memphis and Heliopolis. Near the borderline between the two lands we now have evidence of political rivalry. Heliopolis, founded by the Anu as indicated by Emile Amelineau and affirmed by Cheikh Anta Diop, was situated on the eastern bank of the Nile about 9 miles west of Cairo and Memphis on the western bank some 16 miles further south.

Such proximity enabled two theologies, the Heliopolitan Ennead and the Memphite Doctrine, to share many similarities and fused in practice.

Compare these with two other centers of Abydos, and the earliest dates for mention of Karnak, which may very well extend to the earliest period, though for the most part the latter holds remains from the Middle Kingdom.

Very early, priests in ancient Kemet were concerned about education and became "teachers and exponents of religious and moral duty." Significantly and additionally, as a powerfully organized body, they practiced hereditary succession creating their own systems of loyalty and practice. In this, the eldest son succeeded his father. That being the case, Wilson (1959: 171) further writes: "The retention of position within a few trusted families and the interlocking of the highest offices may be illustrated with two or three examples. Hatshepsut's Vizier for Upper Egypt, Hapu Seneb, had been preceded in that office by his grandfather; but Hapu Seneb was also High Priest of Amon, as his great grandfather in that office. A certain Thutmose held the Vizierate for Lower Egypt, and his son Ptah-Mose became High Priest of Ptah at Memphis." Nevertheless, writes Sauernon in *Dictionary of Egyptian Civilization* (1962: 224) though lacking the powerful social or family connections a man could equally well become a priest by co-option, without priestly forebears, either by buying his office or by royal favor. In this way the King was able to keep a check on the sometimes growing and alarming power of the Priesthood. This "power of the priesthood" is recognized in Wilson (1959: 272) where the effective grip of the High Priest of Amon upon the civil affairs and finances of the state, may again be shown by the distribution of offices within one family. "Ramses Nakht was the High Priest of Amon under Ramses IV. His father Meri Barset had been Chief Tax master and Ramses Nakht's sons were to hold two of the most potent offices in the land: Nes-Amon and Amen-Hotep successively as High Priest of Amon, and User Maat Re Nakht as Chief Tax master and Manager of Pharaoh's Lands. Thus, the priesthood of Amon could manage the finances of the state for its own benefit and withhold resources from the pharaoh as it desired."

Into the Egyptian Mind. On the road to Sakkara. The Oriental Carpet School.

Into the Egyptian Mind. Egyptian Art. Working the produce of the fields.

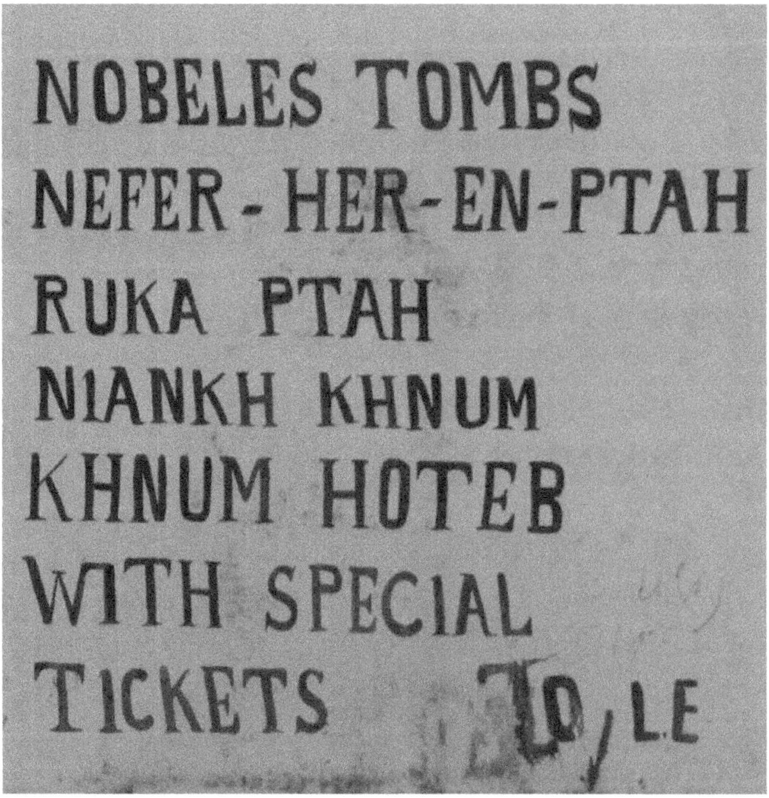

> NOBELES TOMBS
> NEFER-HER-EN-PTAH
> RUKA PTAH
> NIANKH KHNUM
> KHNUM HOTEB
> WITH SPECIAL
> TICKETS   TO/LE

Into the Egyptian Mind. Sakkara, Home of the Step Pyramid. Sign indicating Nobles Tombs nearby.

Into the Egyptian Mind. Sakkara, Home of the Step-Pyramid. Sign indicating some Monuments at this location.

Into the Egyptian Mind. Ceramic vases for sale by the side of the road.

Wilson (1959: 273) even further has tried to illustrate the power of this priestly head in that Rameses Nakht, for while not commander of the army, had acquired tremendous authority, resources and power concentrated in Upper Egypt making him someone to reckon with.

"His son Amen-Hotep, who held the High Priesthood of Amon from Rameses IV to Rameses XI, dared to sweep aside part of the pretense and violate one of the oldest canons of Egyptian art. The pharaoh had always been depicted in colossal size in proportion to all other Egyptians, who were only human and not divine as he was. In a scene in the Temple of Amon at Karnak, we see Ramses IX recognizing the services of the High Priest Amen-Hotep with decorations. Pharaoh is shown in his customary heroic size in proportion to the two bustling little officials who carry out his instructions, but Amen-Hotep had the arrogance to have his figure carved in the same scale as the king. Furthermore, the composition makes him the focus of attention instead of pharaoh. Nothing could illustrate more clearly that reality which the texts piously ignored: that the king was only an instrument of a ruling oligarchy."

Thus, we see, the Priesthood dramatically involved in the crucial arteries of the society, viz., politics, economics, art, transmitting from generation to generation, the skills and ideas necessary to serve the society, do justice, do Ma'at, and learn in the process. This represented and reinforced social stability from a moral responsibility of their religiosity.

The weather and climate has not changed significantly since ancient times. Dryness, humidity, ennui from the heat of the sun caused great concern about purification of the body, echoing an old admonition "cleanliness is next to godliness." The priests shaved their heads. They also shaved the entire body every third day. Strict rules of purity also dictated that priests be circumcised and abstain from sexual contact during time of service in the temples. They should also observe taboos of local gods. Sauernon (1962: 224) provide some insight into attire worn by priest how, "dress only in fine linen, wearing no wool nor leather which had been taken from a living animal."

Therefore, they wore linen clothing and papyrus shoes. Gold and silver shoes were used in religious ceremonies. Each priest had at least six pairs of papyrus and at least one pair of gold or silver shoes. They took baths in cold water twice per day and twice per night. Most priests abstained or did not use wine and animal foods. However, some did drink wine while the onion and pig were prohibited in their diets.

In the prehistoric period origins are difficult to trace. Still, in *Egyptian Religion* (1923), Flinders Petrie has explained, "the office of the priest was more often developed from civil than from religious functions." As such, the emergence and function of the priestly bureaucracy, representing millennia of cultural continuity, is reflected in the names or titles they bore. In prehistoric times they were the "Servant of the Crown." Later, they became professionals and blended priestly and civil functions as "Great One of Medicine," "Chief, Commander of Workmen," and "Inundation Man." In Defense, they were "Splendid," "General," "Warrior," and "Guardian who leads the Mesniu Troops of Horus." In religion, they were "Tongue of the God," "Lord of True Speech," "Opener of the Gates of Management," "Hider of Sins," "Servant of the Cow" (The Lady Isis), and "Guardian of the Guardian of the Pig." Many of these titles and even more honorific ones persisted throughout dynastic history.

Duration of service was easily worked out for the priestly institution. Accordingly, Sauernon (1962: 225) mentions times of service in the temples varied. "Each priesthood was divided into four classes of identical composition (the four phyles), which took turns to be in charge of the temple, its possessions and its ritual for a month. The same group would not be on duty again for another three months. During this time the priests returned to their villages to continue their lives as ordinary citizens."

Clearly, therefore, the civil experience of priests enabled them to become enmeshed in the social, economic, religious, political, cultural and intellectual lifeblood of the state, the essential prerequisites for the growth of civilization Africans are proud of today. This institution's contributions are thus seminal as think tanks. Positions as "Chief of the Palace," "Secretary," and "Chief of the Architects," "Keeper of Granaries," "Keeper of the Treasury," "Chief Justice and Keeper of the Armory," are additional examples of their civic power.

From the time of the Old Kingdom onwards, first Memphis then Heliopolis competed for primacy in politics and religion and in this rivalry, the intellectual wheels of ancient African civilization unfolded.

At Memphis, Kamil (1984: 37) writes further, the High Priest of Ptah, who was also the Chief artist, promoted his deity as the inspiration behind the metal worker, carpenter and sculptor. However, in the areas surrounding Memphis, two other deities were revered, these being: "Sekhmet the lion goddess and Nefertum a lotus god. As Memphis expanded it drew those into its orbit. The problem of having three deities in a single area was early resolved by explaining Ptah as chief deity, Sekhmet as his consort and Nefertum as his son. United they formed the Memphite Triad. Later, Imhotep would be adopted and the triad would then consist of Ptah, Sekhmet and Imhotep, their son." This then shows the Priesthood as theorists and also patrons of the arts. The end result was the enormous rise in the wealth and power of this thrifty and creative priestly body. By the Middle and New Kingdoms, their wealth increased from tribute and plunder of surrounding lands such as Nubia, Syria and Palestine. Imperial warrior Pharaohs made generous contributions and endowments in their worship and mortuary temples. In addition, tributes from foreign conquests that funded extensive architectural constructions were all part of the glorification of their father Amon, later Amon-Ra. In this they also sponsored and supported art and music and their domains equally became help centers, "Houses of Life," and colleges of scientific discourse and inquiry.

Endowments, tribute, and produce from priestly lands increased the wealth of the priestly body. This enabled them to play an active role in non-religious matters, providing teachers and technicians as in the military and in furthering astronomy, learning, building, mummification, farming, exploiting the Nile for irrigation, mathematics, and transport of quarried stone for greater building of secular and religious structures.

Sauernon (1962: 224) tells, in addition to the priests who were administrators of the economic organization of the sanctuaries; there were specialists who lived in these "Houses of Life." Here, Sauernon (1962: 224) has written: "They could, at the king's summons, represent the priests in a given temple. Among these specialists, mention must be made of the 'Scribes of the House of Life,' the 'Sages,' the 'Lector priests,' the 'Hour watchers' (astronomer priests, who decided when ceremonies should be performed) and astrologer priests, learned in hematology, who knew how to determine the lucky or unlucky character of the days of the year."

Into the Egyptian Mind. Sakkara, Home of the Step-Pyramid. Rubble of a Pyramid built at the location.

Into the Egyptian Mind. Sakkara, Home of the Step-Pyramid. Smelling the Lotus flower. This lady's facial image does seem to be in the "Negro mold."

Into the Egyptian Mind. Sakkara, Home of the Step-Pyramid. Search the land of Egypt, whenever the image of an ancient Egyptian official or person is shown with the face disfigured, it is because some sinister person did not like the "Negro face" of the individual.

Into the Egyptian Mind. Egyptian Art. While Nefertari salutes her husband Rameses II in Red and White Double Crown, Osiris sits at his rear in the next frame.

Into the Egyptian Mind. Ceramic vessels for sale on the road.

Into the Egyptian Mind. Egyptian Art. Two goddesses sit enthroned before a "Table of Offerings" in Nefertari's tomb.

Into the Egyptian Mind. Egyptian Art. With two smaller individuals at his rear, in their tomb, Menna and wife offer adoration to Osiris (Ausar) in his Shrine.

Having this skilled auxiliary at their disposal further increased priesthood power since their people were involved in management of the lands of the god, control over the collection of revenues, provisions for the altars and for the priests (who lived on the offerings placed on the altars) and negotiations with associated temples and with the royal administration.

The lowest of these was *Uab*, "the washed" or purified man. He had to examine the animals for sacrifice and perform the routine of the temple. Next was the *Kher Heb* or reciter of liturgy and spells. Then came the *Her*, who was over the temple. Above him was the *Kherp* or director of the temples. There was also the Sem priest who conducted the feasts and worship of the king. Above these was the High Priest or Chief Divine Servant or *Neter Hemtep*. This individual was actually the pharaoh.

There were also priestesses, women, in the temples. There was the *Neter Hemt*, or Divine Wife of Amen and High Priestess of Thebes. Next was *Urt Kheneru Ne Amen*, Great One of the Harem of Amen. Then the *Abyt* priestess, of various gods or goddesses. The *Sesheshet*, sistrum player and lastly, *Shemoyt*, musician of various gods, round out this lot. The role of the women, however, was limited even though they outnumbered the male priests in the temples. Still, on the level of the gods, females perennially accompanied the gods in triads just as Isis and Nephthys accompanied Osiris.

Herodotus, considered the "father of history," visited Egypt in 450 B.C. and wrote the Histories. Book II, Euterpe is devoted to Egypt. In this important historical and anthropological study, Herodotus recorded the thoughts of an Egyptian priest who had remained studying underground in a temple for many decades. Such devotion shows the great respect the people of ancient Kemet had for learning, "for its own sake and the respect it gave." The society crafted a practical and philosophical view of life that insisted students love learning like a mother. "Learn to write," admonished a wise sage, "there is no profession that is not governed. It is only the learned man who rules his-self." This seems an earlier version of an idea, Aristotle, the Greek philosopher (384-322 B.C.) called *Entelechy*. In this, he believed that knowledge should be pursued for its own sake and not for some practical purpose. Entelechy can thus become the reasoned mechanism that transforms the individual into a knowledgeable and useful member of society.

Education was high priority among the Priesthood. The priests of ancient Kemet taught justice and morals. They believed that justice should be the same for all. They also taught self-righteousness for the individual, self-restraint in one's doings and love and respect for the family. Equally too, the pharaoh, as the supreme father and judge, acted according to the philosophical beliefs of Ma'at, the goddess of justice, equality, balance, order, goodness. The monarch feared judgment in the afterlife if he did not adhere to fairness. So as an example, in legal matters he often admonished judges to be severe in their actions and not show any partiality to the rich. Treat them as you would treat the poor, he said. Thus, "leaning to one side in a cause is abomination to the gods," and this tenet became a philosophic pharaonic admonition.

The priests taught self-righteousness is sinful and mankind should seek to avoid it. Further, they believed persons should have honorable dealings with god and men. As a way of life, violence should be avoided and one should remember one's religious obligations. The strong should show respect for the rights of the weak. Merchants should practice commercial honesty and try not to hinder the affairs of others. They also taught the ancient Kemetic ideal was a man who should be strong, steadfast, and self-respecting. He should be active and straight forward, and quiet and discreet. He should also avoid covetousness and presumption.

Then, in a number of ways, Senmut can be considered an "Ideal man." For, according to Wilson (1959: 172), rising from humble beginnings, this nobleman achieved social status and titles as: "Hereditary Prince and Count, Seal-bearer of the King of Lower Egypt, Sole Companion, Steward of Amon; Overseer of the Fields, the Garden, the Cows, the Serfs, the Peasant Farmers, and the Granaries of Amon; Prophet of Amon; Prophet of Amon's Sacred Barque; Chief Prophet of Montu in Hermonthis."

Other titles of Senmut included, "Spokesman of the Shrine of Geb; Headman in the House of the White Crown; Controller of the Broad Hall in the House of the Official; Steward of the King; Overseer of the Royal Residence; Controller of Every Divine Craft; Steward of the Princess Nefru Re; Great Father Tutor of the Princess Nefru Re; Controller of All Construction Work of the King in Karnak, Hermonthis, Deir el Bahari, the Temple of Mut at Karnak, and Luxor; and 'a superior of superiors, an overseer of overseers of construction works.'" Significantly, Senmut could not have achieved such social prominence had he not been a member of some priesthood.

In family relations, priests taught that a man should not be rude to a woman in her house. In this ancient African Nile Valley culture of North-East Africa, the house belonged to the woman. That's even if the husband built or purchased it. She was the "Lady of the House" or "Mistress of the House." There was no "Master" of the house.

Though there was an occasional divorce, "marriage" or "unions" seems to always have been for life. "Children are sweet," is what they believed and taught. As such, the father did what he could for a dutiful son, who "should be regarded a true incarnation of the family spirit or Ka and treated with sympathy." The son, therefore, was taught "not to forget his mother and to remember all she had done for him." The daughter, however, was considered the heiress with property and lineage being passed down in the female line.

General associations with ancient Kemetic (Egyptian) culture emphasize pyramids, temples, tombs, art and mummification, as part of the effort to explain trans-human metaphysical existence. Mummification and the climate had an important role in this process, and it not only helped to preserve the remains of the wealthy and famous, but also became the catalyst for experimentation in science, anatomy, medicine and surgery. With overseas expansion and migration, preservation of the body spread far and wide, as Kemetic culture diffused, so that many of their secrets are being used today in morticians' never-ending work.

Into the Egyptian Mind. Sakkara, Home of the Step-Pyramid. The Enclosure Wall at the Step-Pyramid.

Into the Egyptian Mind. Sakkara, Home of the Step-Pyramid. A wall bounding the Great Court with steps (left) to exit. Notice the line of Uraei (Uraeus) at the top of the wall.

Into the Egyptian Mind. Sakkara, Home of the Step Pyramid. The Step-Pyramid while undergoing renovation.

Into the Egyptian Mind. More ceramic vases for sale by the roadside at Luxor, Egypt.

Into the Egyptian Mind. Egyptian Art. The Nobleman Menna sits holding a "staff of authority" before a sumptuous "Table of Offerings."

The priests were responsible for the mummification of the dead before burial for which a fee was paid. Herodotus mentions three types of mummification for the Pharaohs and nobles, middle class and the poor. While the wealthy was often entombed in elaborate preparation, fanfare and sepulchral structures, the dryness of the soil has helped to preserve some bodies of the poor in shallow graves. Still, the earliest mummified body using this process is now recognized as that of the Queen of King Zer of the first dynasty. However, the earliest fully resined body comes from Meydum in the third dynasty. Now, according to Herodotus, in preparing the body, it was opened by a long slit, usually on the left side from the hip to the ribs. The intestines were then removed and the body was washed with palm oil, aromatic spices, resin and perfume. It was then sewn up again. Next, it was soaked for up to 70 days in natron and then studded with jewelry and magical charms under the bandaged linen. The "Opening of the Mouth Ceremony" was performed and the body placed in its coffin and sarcophagus for burial. As if linking dynastic craft with prehistoric beliefs, the gods in the afterlife, used an adze to perform the opening of the mouth ceremony. In Tutankhamon's tomb, the High Priest Ayi is seen performing this function with adze and all. Generally made of iron, this tool's early existence poses important questions for the origins of iron. Therefore, throughout dynastic rule, the Priesthood provided an important service and played a significant role in the development and practice of the pharaonic system.

REFERENCES

Bierbrier, M. L. "Hrere, Wife of the High Priest Painkh." *Journal of Near Eastern Studies* (July 1973, 32: 311).
"Egyptian Tomb Endowments." *American Journal of Archaeology* VIL (1942: 342).
Herodotus. *The Histories*. Baltimore, MD: Penguin Books, (1954) 1973.
Kamil, J. *The Ancient Egyptians*. Cairo: The American University in Cairo Press, (1976) 1984.
Maspero, G. *Manual of Egyptian Archaeology*. New York: G.P. Putnam's Sons, 1926.
Mertz, B. *Black Land, Red Land*. New York: Dodd, Mead and Co., (1966) 1978.
"Occult Sciences in the Temples of Ancient Egypt." *Scientific American* I: 470, 496.

Oswald, M. "Egyptian Tomb Endowments." *American Journal of Archaeology* 44 (July 1940: 364).
Petrie, W.M.F. *Egyptian Religion*. London: Constable, 1923.
Piccine, P.A. "In Search of the Meaning of Senet." *Archaeology* 33 (July August 1980: 55-58).
Posner, Georges with Serge Sauernon and Jean Yoyotte. *A Dictionary of Egyptian Civilization*. London: Methuen and Co., Ltd., (1959) 1962.
"Priest Amidst Birds found in City of Dead." *Science News Letter* 36 (October 7, 1939: 231).
Wilson, J.A. *The Culture of Ancient Egypt*. Chicago: The University of Chicago Press, (1951) 1971.

Into the Egyptian Mind. Egyptian Art. Ma'at spreads her protective wings behind the throne of the seated goddesses.

35. PURITY AND PURIFICATION IN ANCIENT EGYPT BY DR. FRED MONDERSON

While righteousness is a hallmark of Ma'atian ethics manifesting in truth and justice, Purification is just as paramount in religious beliefs and practice, but equally in the social realm particularly as to how individuals, viz., royalty, priests, nobles, bureaucrats, laity and common-folk, behave but more especially how they relate to the king, the Son of God who is the principal dispenser of truth and justice. Notwithstanding, purity and purification are more pronounced in relationships of worship in temples through the methods and practices of ritual and liturgy; and equally secondarily in mortuary temple dynamics, whether in worship or in preparation for the journey into the Afterlife where the king as a deceased representative hoped to meet destiny in the final executed divine practice of justice.

Purity is a state of existence and a requirement in the place where the council of the gods are born, dwell and administer justice among themselves. It is where both king and commoner are subjected to the same standards divinity required of themselves. After all, when an individual is declared "true of Voice," or "Justified," he or she is therefore allowed to exist into eternity in that place of purity where the gods dwell. This place of heavenly bliss, solemnity and sacredness must be the epitome of purity since and those who dwell therein represents the essence of divinity as a force and fact everlasting. Still, no one mortal can conceptualize what heaven is like, a place of tranquil existence into eternity, until one gets there. That is why Egyptian belief held individuals must subject themselves to the most rigorous and resolute moral and spiritual preparation undergirded in practices of purity in thought, word and deed, in order to attain and manifest the prerequisites to guarantee immortality in such an existence of everlastingness.

In that sphere of the just where the gods dwell in spirit and truth, the good are rewarded for having lived a life of justice and service to humanity, while the evil, short-lived at judgment, are dispatched to the infernal regions for destruction, perhaps, penance. Nevertheless, they never share initially in the beatific vision and experience as examples of worthiness. Still, it is possible there is redemption. That is, probably only after an extensive period of rigorous cleansing to acquire that purity necessary for eternal life. For, having been given the sacred opportunity of life, yet never giving credit to standards of moral and spiritual purity, their lot ultimately becomes punishment in a lake of fire or similar experiences. Notwithstanding, we recognize in ancient Egypt there were two existing, not competing but complimenting belief systems, that of the Sky-Religion of the Sun-god Ra and the terrestrial religion of the Earth-god Osiris, judge of the Afterlife. Disparate yet together, they both laid down the law and requirements for membership into after-life eternal existence.

In exploring the potent ancient Egyptian conception of purity and purification we begin in the heavens with the rise of the Sun-god before he begins his trek across the heavens. We equally encounter the king, as Son of the Sun who undergoes his purification in the Per-dwet or "House of the Morning" in preparation for his visit to the temple. The same requirements of cleansing for the sun-god and the king is also required of the dead person in preparation for the next life experience. However, and notwithstanding, while the king does not generally reside in the God's temple, evidence indicates especially many of the New Kingdom kings' mortuary structure at Thebes, their "Temple of a million years," had an adjacent palace in which surviving illustrations of a few but specifically at Medinet Habu and Ramesseum, there "the king is depicted leaving the palace to enter the temple." In many instances and places, analogy is used to explain an act or fact at one place relative to another. In this respect, while there is an example on Rameses II's "Girdle Wall" at Karnak, at Dendera, Kom Ombo and Edfu, the king is seen on the outer portal being baptized by Horus and Thoth who bathe him in streams of ankh on the outside before he enters the temple. Given that though we know so much about ancient Egypt, in contradiction, so little has actually survived the passage of time and the destructive nature of man. As such, then, on the other hand, and while still reinforcing this idea of baptism, on a wall in a room adjacent to the Sanctuary within the temple of Karnak, on the northern side, Hatshepsut is depicted being baptized by Horus and Thoth but in this case, her image is systematically chiseled out of the baptism and purification act. This seemingly spiteful act is credited to Thutmose III and his adherents engaged in the reaction as retribution for the queen depriving him of kingly rule for some two decades.

Into the Egyptian Mind. Sakkara, Home of the Step-Pyramid. Image of two Nobles in similar attitudes with miniature females before them.

Into the Egyptian Mind. Egyptian Art. Ra-Horakhty sits enthroned while Hathor "got his back."

Into the Egyptian Mind. Egyptian Art. Men and Women as part of the work force in the field.

Into the Egyptian Mind. Sakkara, Home of the Step-Pyramid. Old Kingdom Nobleman holding staff and wearing extensive necklace.

Into the Egyptian Mind. Still more ceramic vases for sale by the roadside at Luxor, Egypt.

Into the Egyptian Mind. Egyptian Art. A decorated enclave in the Tomb of Menna.

Just as the Sun-god was lustrated upon his arising in the heavens on the morn, his earthly counterpart dwelling in the sanctuary's naos was subject to the same treatment. This time, however, while the Sun-god's lustration was theoretical in the minds of man, lustration of his earthly manifestation was more practical, constantly on a daily basis being performed by the king or high priest. Thus, and in order to perform that function both king and high priest had to also undergo purification. That is the same as was done for the king upon his arising in the palace, a cleansing he was subjected to in the "House of the Morning," that same cleansing was again rendered at the temple.

Blackman and Firman, using Edfu as an example, have shown the temple itself; not the initial consecration which was done at the completion of the holy place prior to being handed over to its owner, the resident god; this entity had to be baptized or purified in order to come alive daily, the whole temple so that the day's ritual could commence and be effective. In this perennial ritual, the god's servants, the priests and their helpers, had to be purified in order to successfully execute their functions in administering their responsibilities. Even the instruments employed in the execution of the ritual, viz., incense burner, vessels for water, ointments, freshly picked flowers, materials of clothing, even musical instruments and singers, the books and readers, and most certainly the other paraphernalia and support personnel engaged in assisting the day's events which generally occurred three times per day.

In1 similar fashion in all his earthly manifestations the king was subject to the rigorous and unending purification. As Crown Prince he was purified at birth; at his Coronation; on way to wage battle with Egypt's enemies; when visiting before he enters the temple; before he officiates in procession and temple ritual; at his death; in mummification preparation; at the tomb's entrance; on way to the Hall of Judgment in the Afterlife, the "Tree Goddess" pours four pitchers of water on him; before entering the Hall of Judgment; and once declared "true of Voice," having survived the Judgment, he had to be purified once more in order to live within the company of the gods in that place of purity.

Normally there was more to the whole purity and purification idea; for even in modern times, Dr. Yosef Ben-Jochannan instructed his students to not simply dress properly when entering the temple, demonstrate a temple decorum with respect for the culture of the holy place and don't enter the Sanctuary, for, in ancient times, only the king and his high priest designate could enter this inner sanctum where the god resided. "Cleanliness is next to godliness." Thus, Dr. Ben was big on the purity idea and so repeatedly stressed behavior therein. Heeding his admonition and painting a picture of temple restriction, we must remember, using Karnak Temple as an example, even nobles invited beyond the Pylon entrance were prescribed from proceeding beyond the Great Court. Only the priestly procession could assemble and proceed within and without the Hypostyle Hall. In a note of clarity, the temple procession, as part of some festivity within the temple or on a distant visit, for example, to celebrate the Opet festival at Luxor Temple or the Feast of the Valley across the river to the West Bank, were different to the Sanctuary procession to administer to the god. That is, while the Sanctuary Procession was more involved, the "visiting procession" traveled "light." Nevertheless, there was that rare yet solemn occasion, when in procession, the image of the god was bared and the faithful was rewarded with a quick view of the subject of their worship and veneration.

The area beyond the Hypostyle Hall that entrances the Sanctuary or "Holy of Holies," is called the Wadjit. Decorated with pylons, spacious halls filled with statues, obelisks, colonnades, the ritual depicted on the walls, and more, only the Sanctuary Procession enters this location. This location is sort of equated with a domestic "bedroom" where only the family members could enter. Important, while the support personnel carry the utensils, sing and play songs on musical instruments, read from the holy books, burn incense, fetch the food and flowers and water for sprinkling and washing, only the king and high priest among this purified body can "Open the doors of heaven." There they enter to awaken the god, bathe him, dress, rouge, serve his food and prepare him as part of the daily ritual. Upon completion of his task, done three times per day, serving a heavy breakfast and lunch, then a light snack at evening time, on those three occasions the servant, having fulfilled his mission, "brings the foot." That is, as the worshipper, king or high priest, withdraws facing, never backing, the god he uses a particular instrument, a branch of the hidn tree, to erase all footsteps from the sandy soil before the god. Then he closes and secures the door until the next occasion for awakening and disturbing the divinity's rest and to repeat the ritual again and again.

The use of sand is important in the area of the sanctuary before the god's naos.

In service of the ritual, therefore, we recognize use and involvement of:

1. Incense
2. Holy Water
3. Clothing of different colors, at least 4 or 5
4. Cosmetics and oils
5. Food, consisting of meat and vegetables
6. Sand sprinkled before the naos in which the god resides
7. Liturgy or words of praise read from a book
8. Hymns or songs sung by choristers
9. Musical instruments played by an accompanying choir
10. Utensils for various liquids are made of gold, silver or copper
11. The branch from the Hidn tree

Into the Egyptian Mind. Sakkara, Home of the Step-Pyramid. Seated statue, broken and defaced.

Into the Egyptian Mind. Sakkara, Home of the Step-Pyramid. Sunk-relief of Egyptian art.

Into the Egyptian Mind. Sakkara, Home of the Step-Pyramid. An embracing couple. Interesting how his hair seems to mirror that in the "Deir el Bahari Cache."

Into the Egyptian Mind. Ceramic jugs for sale by the roadside at Luxor, Egypt.

Into the Egyptian Mind. Egyptian Art. Sennutem and wife receive sustenance from the "Tree Goddess."

In a wonderful article entitled, "Purification (Egyptian)," Aylward Blackman in Hasting's *Encyclopedia of Religion and Ethics* Vol. X (Edinburgh: T. and T. Clarke, 1918: 476-482), details with succinct clarity the full panoply of events, individuals, materials and process in the experience of creating the divinely acceptable state of purity through purification in order to execute the responsibilities to protect the god and make him comfortable.

I. Purification Materials were:

1. Water –
2. Natron -
3. Incense -
4. Sand -
5. Food -
6. Fire -

Vessels for washing both hands and feet were made of gold and silver but more especially copper. Earthen pitchers were used for bathing or sprinkling purposes and even a metal vase was employed.

II. Purification of the Whole Person: This was accomplished through:

1. Bathing – In the Sacred Lake, sometime four times per day
2. Purification of the mouth – with natron or salts
3. Washing of the feet – To step onto holy ground
4. Cleansing of the nails – handling the god hands must be clean
5. Shaving of the – Removal of facial and head hair

    a. head – Priest shave every 2 or 3 days
    b. face – Generally shaved every day.

6. Depilation – Removal of body hair by pulling
7. Purification before a meal -
8. The altar must be purified before food can be placed on it

III. Purification to be part of a Community

1. Circumcision – Generally before the age of 11.
2. Purification at birth – He who would be king must be purified
3. Purification after sexual intercourse – Sex and temple service are incompatible
4. Purification for women – during the menstrual cycle

5. Sometimes the entire body -

a. During and after the menstruation cycle
b. After childbirth – a period of temple abstinence

IV. Religious Purity - is designed to purify the priest, even the Pharaoh before officiating in the temple in praise and ritualization of the god.

1. Purification of the living pharaoh -

a. In infancy -
b. Before coronation -
c. At Coronation -
d. Before officiating in the temple -
e. At a Sed-Festival –
f. Before he takes the field of battle

2. Purification after death - a. before and during mummification; b. on way to the tomb; c. at the tomb; d. completion of the ceremony; e. In the next life by the gods.

Thus, purity was the only guaranteed passport to posthumous happiness; that is, a purity upon which the welfare of the dead depended. Accordingly, "more than physical purity or cleanliness was expected of the pharaoh" and as time passed from the Sixth Dynasty onward, "the claims made by the dead to moral integrity and purity became more and more prominent where in the Books of the Dead's Negative Confessions the deceased declared he was not guilty, among other sins, of fornication, masturbation and adultery." Notwithstanding, the "confessions" he had to work and maintain the purity he would so finally boast of. In that respect, "There were several ways of attaining that purity upon which the welfare of the dead so entirely depended."

Into the Egyptian Mind. Sakkara, Home of the Step-Pyramid. Even more "dates in galore" only waiting to be picked.

Into the Egyptian Mind. Sakkara, Home of the Step-Pyramid. Still more "dates in galore" only waiting to be picked.

Into the Egyptian Mind. Sakkara, Home of the Step-Pyramid. This time the dates are red.

Into the Egyptian Mind. Still more ceramic vases for sale by the roadside at Luxor, Egypt.

Into the Egyptian Mind. Egyptian Art. Under the watchful eye of an overseer, doing work in the field (bottom) and preparing to load their produce on a ship (top).

    a.   Ceremonial acts performed by the deceased in his lifetime.

    i.   Bathing in Sacred waters or pools -
    ii.   Participating in the Osirian mysteries -

    b.   Spells asserting "that these acts had been performed" and "That all impurities had been avoided."

    c.   Ablutions performed after death by the deceased himself.

    d.   Ceremonies performed for him by the gods;

    e.   Ceremonies performed for him by the living at preparation of mummy and at the burial before the tomb.

3.   Significance of Posthumous Purification -

The funerary washing, sprinklings, fumigations, etc., possessed, therefore a secondary, what we might call sacramental, significance; they both helped to reconstitute the deceased and, together with the food and drink-offerings, supplied him with nutrient which enabled him to continue his existence and to maintain unimpaired all his reconstituted faculties and powers.

According to Blackman (1918: 479)

i. The water with which the corpse or statue was washed or sprinkled not merely cleansed the deceased from his impurities but brought together the head and bones and made the body complete (tm) in every particular. Accordingly, either stream of water that flows about the figure of the dead User terminates in a large symbol of life. With the offering of libation-water to the deceased is associated the giving to him of his spirit (ib) and his power (shm), and at the same time he is bidden to stand upon his feet and to gather together his bones.

ii. Incense-smoke had the same effect, cleansing the dead 'from all the evil appertaining to him,' and making him 'strong and powerful above all gods.'

iii. For the mysterious virtue of the food and drink-offerings

iv. The deceased was also, of course supposed to be similarly reconstituted by the purifications that he underwent to be reconstituted in the other world. After ablutions in the Field of Earu he received 'his bones of metal' and 'stretched out his indestructible limbs which are in the womb of the sky-goddess.' By the washings of Horus and Thoth and other divinities the dead was cleansed from all impurities, moral and physical, his body came together again or was entirely refashioned, and he was fit to enter heaven or the Tie, i.e., underworld.

V. Purity and Purification of Offerings to Gods and the Dead.

1. All offerings made to gods and the dead had to be purified. "The doorposts of temples often bear the following or a similar inscription: 'The offerings and all that enters the temple of such-and-such a divinity - it is pure.' The living pray that the mortuary equipment of the dead may consist of every good and pure thing.'"

2. **Purification of Offerings** - These were purified by pouring libations over them and by fumigating them with incense. The testing of all funerary victims was customary as far back as the Old Kingdom.

VI. Purification of Temples and building used for religious ceremonies.

1. Consecration of a new temple or shrine – That is, before it is handed over to the resident deity for whom it was built.

2. Renewal of purification -

3. Purification before the day's proceedings –

VII. Purity and Purification of the Priests

- The Web priest meant he was "the pure one." As such, a number of measures were taken to assure his purity.

1. In Graeco-Roman times a priest had to purify himself for several days before he performed his functions.

2. Priests had to always wash or sprinkle themselves before entering a temple. At its entrance, every temple had a pool or tank, maybe a basin set aside for this purpose. This is a carry-over in today's church practice with a basin of "Holy Water" at the entrance.

3. The priests also perhaps fumigated themselves with incense before they performed the daily ritual.

4. Great emphasis was laid on the purity of the priest's hands.

a. Pairing the nails -

b. Depilation -

c. Shaving -

d. Dress -

e. Circumcision -

VIII. Purity and Purification of the Laity.

1. They must undergo purity and purification before entering a temple or sacred place.

2. Purification in practiced or effectuated by "sacred water" or in pools. Near the Khercha stood a pool in which the Sun-god washed his face. This also benefitted humans who did the same. Perhaps this is where Piankhi washed his face on way to Heliopolis to be recognized by the Sun-god, to be blessed and declared Son of Ra. This was part of the ceremonial ritual in which the pharaoh received the protocols

and paraphernalia investing with full power and divinity status.

3. Two great pools stood at Herakleopolis manga, the "Pool of Natron" and the "Pool of Ma'at."

4. The waters of the First Cataract, the traditional source of the Nile, was believed to be endowed with special cleansing properties and therefore used (or supposed to be used) for all the lustrations and libations offered to the gods and the dead. The fact that, the dead go there to be bathed by the goddess Satis meant that the living also performed ablutions there.

In summary – Dr. Ben-Jochannan insisted on contemporary purity in clothing, behavior and insisted, "Don't enter the Temple Sanctuary." He also advised his students, adherents, pay attention to temple architecture and artistic ritual on the walls. Naturally, he loved Karnak's Hypostyle Hall and insisted students visit the magnificent wonder 5 or 6 times to fully comprehend its significance.

Into the Egyptian Mind. Ghizeh Plateau. A smaller structure beside a great pyramid at Ghizeh.

Into the Egyptian Mind. Ghizeh Plateau. Some of the surrounding structures and terrain beside the Second Great Pyramid.

Into the Egyptian Mind. Still even more ceramic vases for sale beside the road at Luxor, Egypt.

Into the Egyptian Mind. Egyptian Art. A Procession of individuals bringing produce of various sorts (above) and sailing boats with personnel (below).

36. TEMPLE ORIENTATION AND DIVINE WORSHIP
BY
DR. FRED MONDERSON

In 1894 Sir Norman Lockyer in *Dawn of Astronomy* indicated Egyptian temples were essentially oriented towards some solar bod0y; that is a star or planet. He even pointed to a temple to Hathor stood in the mountain vicinity of Deir el Bahari at 10,000 B.C.

We must be careful in our acceptance of the record as presented, for, as Dr. Leonard James taught regarding ancient Egypt especially, "The existential record contradicts the symbolic representation." Dr. Cheikh Anta Diop of *The African Origin of Civilization*: *Myth or Reality* fame, indicated in European hijacking of Egypt they made it so complicated, so confusing, we are forced to accept the white man's version as presented with its glaring falsity and contradictions. We must understand there was an Africa before the white man.

As we have come to understand, in Nile Valley religious beliefs, two religions emerged in Egypt, one celestial, one terrestrial. That is, one sky or heavenly and one earthly. In this we have the Ra religion which is sky and centered at Heliopolis, a city founded by the Black Anu race. Heliopolis, like so many other temple sites were founded by the Anu, and the religion they started remained paramount throughout dynastic rule. Some books teach the Egyptian mythology, its religion, came from the heavens and so in Hollywood distortion we have got **Battlestar Galactica**, the TV Series. Remember, then, from the deep blue beyond, these are people who came to get humans bringing religion and gods for black men to practice and worship.

We know and science has affirmed, *Zinjanthropus Boisie*, Lucy, Eve, all East African forms of humanity essentially gave birth to the human race who migrated to people the earth.

A popular aphorism has been, "Swim or Sink" and "walk or Ride" and in this case, even "Sail." So, in his dispersion one method of movement man descended the Nile River, the prominent highway at the time. He settled in Thebes and along the Nile in small communities. What we know as Upper Egypt extended from Aswan to the Delta in which 22 of 42 mini states or Nomes were demarcated. The other 20 to make 42 were later set. So, we have Upper Egypt with 22 Nomes and Lower Egypt with 20. There was no Middle Egypt in the earliest times of Dynastic beginnings. Middle Egypt essentially got prominence under the Amarna revolution.

We know evidence of stone tools were found at Thebes and dated to 300,000 years. So African craftsmen were working. Albert Churchward says equally these people were practicing their religion, having "Sweet communion with deity" as early as that 300,000-year mark.

What Norman Lockyer did say in the particular regard, there was a Temple of Hathor on the Mountain at Deir el Bahari vicinity dated at 10,000 and this may have had a connection to the chapel to the goddess in the Hatshepsut Deir el Bahari temple.

Now, Karnak Temple of God Amon of the Theban Triad of Amon, the Sun-god; his wife, Mut, the Earth Goddess; and their son, Khonsu, the Moon god was oriented East to West, the path of the sun. What is not stated, the temple of Hathor was oriented towards the Temple of Amon across the river. We know the Middle Kingdom, 2000 B.C. Temple of Mentuhotep II (11th Dynasty) and the Temple of Hatshepsut (18th Dynasty) some 500 years later, 1500 B.C., were both oriented in a line established survey towards the Karnak Temple. Such temple triangulation is consistent with the people of Nabta Playa studying the heavens and creating their star map.

The location of Luxor Temple, facing north, was also oriented towards Karnak. But more particular, Rameses II (19th Dynasty) added a Peristyle Court called the "Ramessean Front," the axis was turned towards Karnak. Some have said it was to avoid the river but more particularly it was toward the temple again, triangulation with the Sun-god Amon, home as the principal point.

Luxor Temple is unique, not only was it built to celebrate the Opet Festival, but it is the only temple with three axes, so states Schwaller de Lubicz in his Temple in Man. In this timeline

An invisible axis beneath the temple's floor; the axis of the original temple of Amenhotep III; and of course, the axis of Rameses II's court addition, the "Ramessean Front."

What does this have to do with Axis?

We know the people of Nabta Playa in the Western Desert of Upper Egypt were the predecessors of the pharaohs. They occupied tie region from about 15,000 B.C. to 3500 B.C.

1.   They were the first astronomers. They mapped the heavens and used the heavenly bodies as points of location moving their cattle back and forth. In this they were also pastoralists. Rainfall was plentiful in the region at this time. Hence, they practiced agriculture and kept cattle. They created the first calendar and began worship of the "Cow Goddess." Why a cow? The cow gave blood, milk, meat, leather and philosophically reinforced the "mother concept" of nurturing humanity. When the land began to dry-up from lack of rainfall, around 3500-3400B.C. or so, the Nabta Playa Africans migrated from the desert and settled on the banks of the Nile, perhaps in the Qustol area, south of Aswan towards Abu Simbel. They probably founded the *Kingdom of Ta-Seti,* in this vicinity where *The New York Times* newspaper has described "The world's earliest monarchy found in Nubia." There we see what later became pharaonic paraphernalia, viz., enthroned pharaoh, palace façade, white crown, sailing boats, incense burner, cows and other animals, etc., at c. 3400 B.C. that emerges in Egypt by Unification in 3200 -3100 B.C. according to the "Short Chronology." Remember the Hathor Temple at Thebes 10,000 B.C., well these people were worshipping her.

We also see the Goddess on Narmer's Palette. Hathor was the daughter of Ra, the principal deity of the sky religion throughout dynastic rule which places father and daughter at an early age. We must remember, soon after Ra created the world, he made Nubian People even before the made Egyptians. This is not surprising, since Ra, Ra worship and his center of worship at Heliopolis was founded by the Anu, a black African people.   The terrestrial religion, that of Osiris, centered at Abydos was also syncretized with Ra. Some have argued the Ra religion was for the intellectual, literate Egyptian, while Osiris worship was for common folk who understood the body was deposited in the earth, a process they would experience with hopes for justification and resurrection as did Osiris.

Into the Egyptian Mind. Tomb of Ramose. Columns in the unfinished hall of the tomb abandoned by Ramose in the move to Amarna during the reign of Akhenaten.

Into the Egyptian Mind. Egyptian Art. Tomb of Ramose. Mourning ladies and gents attending a funeral.

Into the Egyptian Mind. Egyptian Art. Tomb of Ramose. Procession of individuals sandwiched by kneeling and standing wailing women, often professional mourners, at a funeral as the bier is being dragged by animals.

Into the Egyptian Mind. Sakkara, Home of the Step-Pyramid. View of the Landscape with the Great Pyramids of Ghizeh off in the distance.

Into the Egyptian Mind. Even more ceramic vessels for sale by the roadside at Luxor, Upper Egypt.

Into the Egyptian Mind. Egyptian Art. Gangs of workmen with their supervisors.

A few things we know:

1.   Hathor is shown coming out of the mountains and she carried the deceased into the "Afterlife."

2. When the deceased began the journey into the Afterlife he entered a cavern in the Deir el Bahari area. Perhaps this is why the "Deir el-Bahari Cache of Mummies" were secreted in this area and discovered in 1881-82.

3. Brugsch-Bey argued the Egyptian painted himself red for illumination in the darkened journey into the Afterlife towards the Hall of Judgment presided over by Osiris.

Modern man prides himself with a unique ability that seems to know more than ancient man about his own culture and surroundings. Naturally, racist bigotry played an importance in this, oftentimes misguided arrogance. Nevertheless, at the temple of Luxor in the "Ramessean Front" Peristyle Court, on a back wall to the southwest there is an interesting scene. The façade of the temple is pictured with seated and standing statues, obelisks, etc., and the sons of Rameses II leading a procession of fat cows to be sacrificed for the ceremony. A fascinating depiction shows a Nubian lady coming out of the head of the lead cow. This is Hathor, a Black woman pictured in a leading position. Most books and even guides, even they take tourists to this particular feature show the temple but remain silent on the Nubian lady, the Cow and the Hathor connection. So, what is the message of all this?

1. Heliopolis was founded by the Anu, black people from Upper Egypt which was essentially Nubia, Ethiopia across the broad swathe of land down to the Apex of the Delta. In association, Ra worship was established.

2. Hathor was the daughter of Ra, and as a cow she was worshipped in long-standing.

3. The Black African people of Nabta Playa of the Upper Egyptian Western desert whom, in Natural genesis, Brophy and Bauval in *Black Genesis* (2011) describe as the "precursors of the pharaohs," initiated "cow-goddess" worship.

4. The first significant recorded historical document, the Narmer palette, depicts this "cow goddess" Hathor in a prominent position.

5. By the time of Thutmose III's 18th Dynasty rule, Amon, fused with Ra is depicted in the Luxor Museum with a Black face. In this period also, he is often fused in syncretism with Min, the Black or Nubian God, as Amon-Min.

6. This same Amon-Min is pictured in the 19th Dynasty temple of Rameses II as black-faced and the associated temple to his wife Nefertari, the Nubian, is dedicated to Hathor. Though both Abu Simbel temples are located in Nubia, "Hathor-land," perhaps it was a male thing, that his own temple was dedicated to Ra-Horakhty, Ptah, Amon and himself, deified, as was his father Seti I at Abydos.

7. There is this "Syrian thing" the racists trot out and propagate ever so often. The parents of Tiye, the 18th Dynasty Queen who wielded significant influence during her husband Amenhotep III's reign and her son Amenhotep IV, Akhenaton, reign, Yuya and Tuya were taught to be "Syrian" though this was proven to be false. Even Rameses II, the 19th Dynasty monarch was once described as Syrian. The interesting thing, at the Battle of Kadesh, battling Syrians, the king exclaimed in requesting assistance from God Amon in is time of challenge, in admonishing the god the king extolled, his ancestors had worshipped him from time immemorial. Consider that Rameses' father, Seti I who built the surviving Temple of Osiris at Abydos inscribed a significant feature, the **Tablet of Abydos**. This important document lists kings from Narmer to himself Seti I, deified, as ancestor kings. This is as potent evidence for Rameses' ancestors but nowhere are Syrians mentioned. Therefore, we have the falsity exposed wherein Dr. Leonard James' admonition, the "existential data contradicts the symbolic representation.' Explained. Rameses II "the Syrian" calls upon Amon-Ra, the African god in

blackface whom his ancestors had worshipped from time immemorial.

1.   Thus, we have Dr. Cheikh Anta Diop's charge, in their creation of the "true Negro," European scholars have reduced all the other negroes of the world to "fake Negroes."

2.   In their seizure of Egypt, Europeans have made the presentation of history tremendously confusing.

7.   Prof John Henrik Clarke pointed out, "European claims to Egypt is founded on no logic." But more important, "the people who preached racism colonized history" and "when Europe colonized the world, she colonized the World's knowledge." That is why, at the end of the 19th Century the prevailing intellectual imperialist view held, "for some unknown reason," Caucasians left South-west Asia and "seeking to found a new fatherland in the West," arrived in Egypt bringing "a superior mental attitude" that gave a particular "impetus to the existing culture." That is, after Narmer set out from Abydos and effectively reorganized the Southern Kingdom whose capital was Hierakonpolis, though Diop Says he was Theban.

Nevertheless, he unified the land, founded dynastic rule, built a temple and established Ptah rule at Memphis his chosen administrative capital, determined the nature of bureaucratic service, recognized and reinforced a viable nobility in support of the new dispensation, encouraged the furtherance of art and architectural developments, determined the nature of military hardware, even encouraged active internal and external trade in art, ideas and religious expression. Despite these indigenous creative accomplishments, the aliens arrived to "reinvent Narmer's wheel." Perhaps the new wheel was of a square type. Nonetheless, this end of the 19th Century view is consistent with and seeks to reinforce Dr. Jacob Carruthers' contention, "Hegel took Africans out of Egypt and Egypt out of Africa at the beginning of the 19th Century."

9. In his "Egyptian Religion" published in Hasting's *Encyclopedia of Religion and Ethics* Vol. 5 (Edinburgh: T. and T. Clarke, 1912), Flinders Petrie wrote, "The Seventeenth Dynasty, coming from Nubia, held Thebes as its capital...." Yet, no modern book, certainly not the *Cambridge Ancient History* (1970) has reported on this.

Into the Egyptian Mind. Ghizeh Plateau. Fred and Carmen "mug for the camera" with the Great Pyramid within the loving heart they formed.

Into the Egyptian Mind. Ghizeh Plateau. Another one of those spectacular beauties who proclaim, "I love Egypt."

Into the Egyptian Mind. Ghizeh Plateau. Before the crowds arrive, chairs for the "Sound and Light" show and the **Boat Museum** far-off before the Second Great Pyramid of Khafre.

Into the Egyptian Mind. Ceramic Vases for sale by the roadside at Luxor in Upper Egypt.

Into the Egyptian Mind. Egyptian Art. The Gods on parade with knives at the ready.

Into the Egyptian Mind. Egyptian Art. Men in various attitudes doing the natural things of daily existence with a supervisor sitting before a "Table of Offerings."

10. Now, contrast all of the above factual evidence with "for some unknown reason" and "a superior mental attitude" of the European (Caucasian) propensity to perpetuate the barbarity of slave trade and slavery; the exploitative nature of colonialism and imperialism; and in modern times, the harsh and practical aspects of political disfranchisement, systematic and horrendous prison incarceration; perpetuation of sub-standards in orchestrated ghetto enclosures and conditions; and concerted efforts in education shortcomings in order deny the intellectual autonomy of African people in a false and justifiable argument African people are inherently inferior in the natural and social orders. This state of affairs flies in the face of existential evidence Africans, particularly through Egypt, Nubia and Ethiopia have been in the forefront of lifting the veil of ignorance in humanity's development of consciousness and material accomplishments.

11. Despite the propagated inconsistency, contradictions, distortions and omissions of some of current historiography, G.H. Richardson in "The World's Debt to Egypt," in *Open Court*, 24 (1914: 303-317) provides:

1.   "Our modern civilization is the outgrowth of that of the Mediterranean, and this can be traced back to the Nile valley, where, if the antiquity of the monuments is a safe guide, we find an advanced civilization many centuries before we find it in Babylon. In fact, it is in the Nile valley that we find the first civilization."

2.   In a note on p. 303, he notes, "Dr. Naville, in a personal note to the writer, after reading this, writes: 'the relative antiquity of Egypt and Babylon is very much discussed between Egyptologists and Assyriologists. It is undeniable that the civilization of Babylon goes very fa back though I do not agree with Hommel and others who pretend that Babylon was the mother of Egypt. Still it seems to me that Babylon's birth is in a very remote past.'" The Predynastic discoveries made since this note was sent seem to justify the statement of the text. Mosso (*The Dawn of Mediterranean Civilization*) says: "Many still believe that our civilization comes from Asia, but anthropology has decided the controversy and we know that the Asiatic race never penetrated into Egypt or into the isles of the Aegean. Although the origin of man is wrapped in mystery, naturalists are agreed in admitting the preponderating influence of Africa upon the population of Europe."

Into the Egyptian Mind. Ghizeh Plateau. Fred and Carmen throwing caution to the wind with the Sphinx and Pyramids at their rear.

Into the Egyptian Mind. Ghizeh Plateau. View of the great Sphinx from its rear.

Into the Egyptian Mind. Ghizeh Plateau. The majestic Great Sphinx that has seen so much with the second Great Pyramid at its rear.

Into the Egyptian Mind. Ghizeh Plateau. "Well, can you tell me your story?" a visitor asks of the Sphinx of Ghizeh.

Into the Egyptian Mind. Egyptian Art. Thoth (Tehuti) a Moon God, introduces the deceased to enthroned Osiris (Ausar).

Into the Egyptian Mind. Egyptian Art. Sailing within a shrine with Khepre and his Menat below the ship.

Into the Egyptian Mind. Egyptian Art. Viewed from the left, Nefertari offers two ointment jars to enthroned Hathor and the sumptuous "Table of Offerings."

Into the Egyptian Mind. Egyptian Art. Viewed from the right, Nefertari offers two ointment jars to Hathor above the "Table of Offerings."

37. CONCLUDING POTPOURRI

In order to investigate this issue, the interrogative hypothesis "Is there substantive evidence that omissions and distortions, mis-statements and outright fabrication in ancient Egyptian studies has occurred?" is very much appropriate. Such a position, from a detached stance, allows a fair inquiry into the intent and purpose for which this falsity is perpetuated and objective scholarship has not effectively dealt with the problem. Perhaps the purpose of over-looking such unscholarly writing with their untenable propositions "under the glaring light of the living room" is more sinister and pernicious than generally thought. A principal prognostication regarding the events surrounding this issue is the intent of denying a meaningful role of Africans in ancient Egyptian civilization, to wit, as Afrocentrists have argued the German scholar Hegel took "Africans out of Egypt and Egypt out of Africa."

In ancient times, the term "Mysteries of Egypt" had to do with the esoteric and philosophic drama of temple ritual and all forms of knowledge developed particularly as they were controlled by the Priesthood. It's understandable that as man's consciousness developed in the emergence from the mist of antiquity, great bodies of knowledge accumulated in the fields of science, art and technology. Access to this life changing experience was restricted to organizational initiates or handed down practically from father to son.

This practice continued for more than two thousand years and as word leaked out about the wisdom of the Egyptians destructive invading hordes vented their wrath on Egypt when the state had ceased to be an imperial power. On the other hand, visitors with an inquisitive bent came to Egypt in search of knowledge, wisdom, enlightenment, and adventure, anything that would lift their consciousness above the ignorance of their countrymen at home. In the latter case, one of the earliest Greek visitors was Hecataeus of Abdera, who rightly called Egypt "The gift of the Nile." Then Herodotus came and got credit for the statement. We know Socrates, Plato and Aristotle visited Egypt.

There were many others. All visited Egypt, learned new ideas and even got credit for formulating new theories that had taken the Egyptian millennia to develop through trial and error testing. Thus, the tradition of the esoteric nature of Egyptian knowledge helped color the concept of the "Mysteries of Egypt." That is to say, those to whom bits of knowledge were given were to not only claim original authorship, but unintentionally spread the word about the "Mysteries of Egypt" that would resonate down through the ages.

For nearly two thousand years tales of the "Mysteries of Egypt" and the exploits of Africans as benefactors of goodness, moral quality, viz., Homer's "long lived Ethiopians," praises of other Greeks, all propelled the Africans to almost god-like stature, simply because Egypt could only be admired not possessed. In modern times, the key to hieroglyphics lay in the egg awaiting the great minds that would later decipher its secrets and unleash an avalanche of interest in ancient Egyptian, Nile Valley antiquities and history. Naturally, much of this came about because of an accident of history. The war in Europe, following the French Revolution, forced Napoleon to retreat to Egypt to "winter" and "lick his wounds." He took scholars and scientists with him who would impact the ancient culture in ways unimaginable.

The British followed him and there was fought the "Battle of the Nile" which was actually fought in the Mediterranean. From these encounters a number of subsequent developments took place that forever changed the face and landscape of ancient Egyptian history, perception, presentation, propagation and interpretation. The first of these developments was the French fascination with the art and architectural accomplishments of these early Africans whose influences had far-reaching implications for medieval and early Modern European cultural and artistic development. *The Description of Egypt* Napoleon's savants or scholars (wise men) produced remains a classic on Egypt two centuries later, for no other work has done as extensive and comprehensive an assessment as this classic. Concomitant with this publication, Count Volney wrote his *Ruins of Empire*.

Into the Egyptian Mind. Cairo Museum of Egyptian Antiquities. Sarcophagus and Lid, uncovered.

Into the Egyptian Mind. Cairo Museum of Egyptian Antiquities. A collection of Statues.

Into the Egyptian Mind. Cairo Museum of Egyptian Antiquities. Ceramic vases, underscoring the "sets of four."

Equally Count Denon was the first modern artist to paint a picture of the Sphinx of Ghizeh in its intact form. He would later write that elements from Napoleon's artillery regiment shot off the nose and disfigured the face of the Sphinx because of its Black African god-like facial features that had remained intact throughout the glorious achievements of the Old, Middle and New Kingdoms, the Late Period and beyond the Assyrians, Persians, Greeks, Romans, Arabs, Turks, etc. Perhaps they asked the Sphinx and he told them, all that he had seen as he looked out into eternity.

Everyone knows to change custom and tradition is a difficult aspect of human experience. Many scholars ascribe the Sphinx to Khafre, builder of the Second Great Pyramid at Ghizeh, during the Fourth Dynasty. Any cursory glance at the Sphinx will reveal its African facial features. Therefore, if we accept it's the likeness of Khafre, then it's easy to assign this king, his father Khufu and his son Menkaure to the African race. In as much, Cheikh Anta Diop has argued, the formative years and foundations of Egyptian Civilization, the Predynastic and Archaic periods and the Old Kingdom were of a people of African physiognomy. As such, this eruditely research and articulated view debunks the Caucasoid origins of Egyptian civilization for Diop has shown the first significant influx of foreigners only came with the Hyksos invaders, after the fall of the Middle Kingdom.

Into the Egyptian Mind. Cairo Museum of Egyptian Antiquities. One of King Tut's most prized pieces, the four ceramic figures together.

Into the Egyptian Mind. Cairo Museum of Egyptian Antiquities. Wonderfully artistic decorated stone coffin.

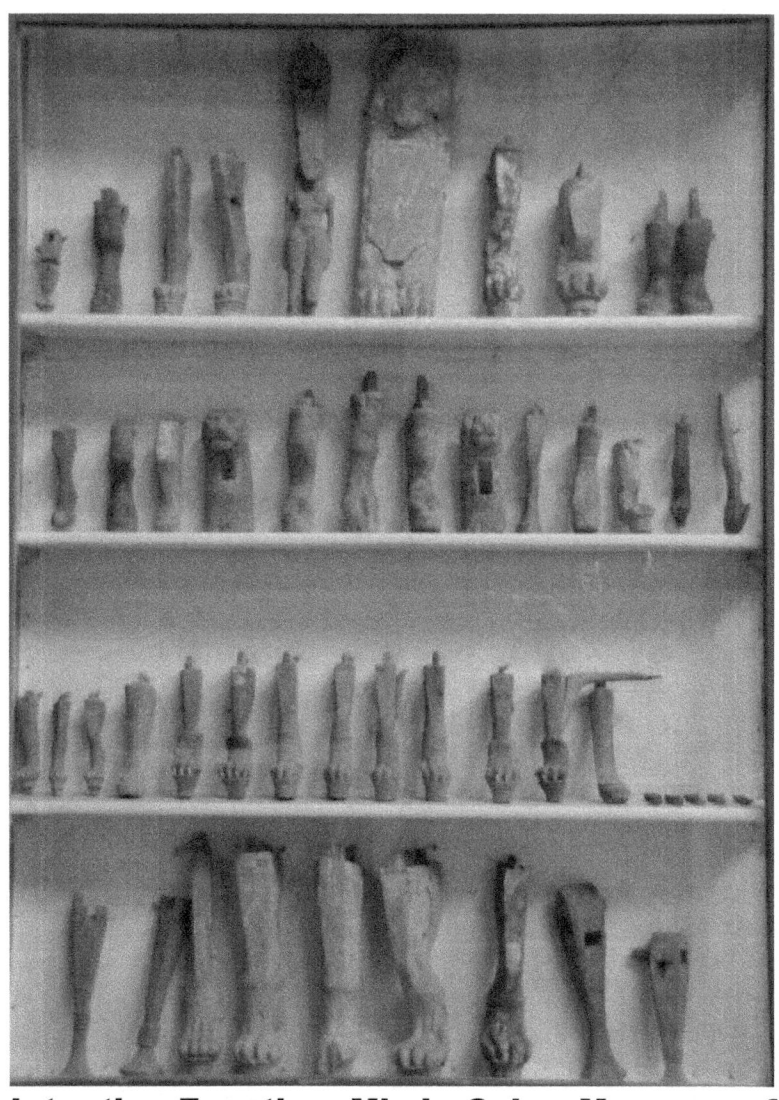

Into the Egyptian Mind. Cairo Museum of Egyptian Antiquities. Chair legs made of wood in the various styles.

Into the Egyptian Mind. Cairo Museum of Egyptian Antiquities. Stone bust of a King. The nose is smashed but the lips are "African." Notice his short beard.

Nevertheless, other scholars have attributed an age of almost 10,000 years to the Sphinx, arguing that while evidence links the Sphinx of Khafra, it's simply because he did repairs to the monument and so inscribed his name to it.

If we fast-forward to the New Kingdom, Hatshepsut built the Kiosk of Amon, Mut and Khonsu, the Theban Triad, at Luxor Temple in the "Ramessean Front." This was certainly before Amenhotep III built his temple there. This meant, there must certainly been a Middle Kingdom temple standing at Luxor when Senmut, the Queen's architect, erected the Kiosk. The temple standing there, Amenhotep III tore down to erect his classical masterpiece with its Processional Colonnade. As the colonnade was unfinished, Tutankhamon completed it and inscribed his name. Later Ay, Horemhab, Rameses I, Seti I and Rameses II did repairs and inscribed their names. Rameses II, in constructing the "Ramessean Front" addition to the Temple of Luxor, repaired Hatshepsut's Kiosk, which Thutmose III had appropriated, and inscribed his name to it. For anyone now knowing this, history would ascribe the Kiosk to Rameses II because his name is there.

Elsewhere, at Karnak, the Eighth Pylon has a unique history. Hatshepsut built this Pylon. Thutmose III appropriated it, erased her name and inscribed his. Later in the dynasty, during the Amarna Revolution, Akhnaton, Amenhotep IV, Amenhotep III and Queen Tiye's son, erased the name and image of Amon and inserted that of the Aton and his name. In the Ramesside Restoration, Seti I erased the Aton and reinserted the name of Amon alongside his name. Therefore, the name being there on a particular monument is simply not sufficient to ascribe ownership to that particular individual.

Fate is sometimes rather strange and perhaps it was the same artillery officers who shot at the Sphinx, probably made the discovery of the Rosetta stone. This single piece of rock has had the most far-reaching influence and implications in the history of human progress than any other inanimate object known to man. The Guides at the Cairo Museum boast the institution has 120,000 authentic pieces and one imitation, the Rosetta Stone. The original is in the British Museum whose agents wrested it from the French in the age of trial and error of decipherment following Lord Nelson's defeat of Napoleon.

The Rosetta Stone is a tri-lingual inscription of Greek, Demotic and Hieroglyphic, on black basalt in which pharaoh Ptolemy Epiphanes V, is praised by priests for his tax concessions and assistance to the temple during the second century B.C.

Once the matter of ownership was settled in the aftermath of the "Battle of the Nile" and it came into British Museum ownership, facsimiles were make and distributed among scholars in Europe. The third or ancient Green part was translated first and those with knowledge of Coptic, a derivative of ancient Egypt, began to do comparisons with the Greek.

Into the Egyptian Mind. Cairo Museum of Egyptian Antiquities. Princely hair discovered in the 1881 "Deir el Bahari Cache." Note, they are 'strongly curled" same as found at El-Amrah a feature of the prehistoric period.

Into the Egyptian Mind. Cairo Museum of Egyptian Antiquities. Seated official in Black marble. A "Naos for the God's image" sits at his rear.

Into the Egyptian Mind. Cairo Museum of Egyptian Antiquities. Thutmose IV's Chariot frame and other stuff.

Akerblad, Young and Champollion made the most progress and by 1822 the latter announced to the world his success in deciphering Hieroglyphics. Recent revelations have indicated contrary to ancient beliefs the Romans killed the last priest who understood the language; there were Egyptian priests as late as 1850 who lived underground and had kept alive the knowledge of how to read and write hieroglyphics. No one knows what pressures were brought to bear on these priests to divulge their knowledge to aid decipherment.

Nevertheless, because Champollion was a brilliant linguist, proficient in English, French, Ancient Greek, and Coptic, his efforts were the most successful and he got full credit for cracking the Code of Hieroglyphics. It's often commented on how proud and excited he was with his successes that he endeavored to decipher every inscription he could get his hand on. He worked so feverishly that within 10 years, from 1822 to 1832, he dropped dead from exhaustion, having bequeathed the world his priceless accomplishment. All this notwithstanding, and whereas, the world lauded Champollion for his cracking the Code of Hieroglyphic, not much attention has been paid to his writings on initial observations of the nature of the people of ancient Egypt and their neighbors. He certainly recognized the Black African nature of the ancient Egyptians and other Africans and the inferior position of their Caucasian neighbors in comparison.

Cheikh Anta Diop in *The African Origin of Civilization*: *Myth or Reality* has a chapter entitled **Recent Falsifications of History** in which he examines and analyses the original letters of Champollion to his younger brother. Equally, he has shown how the brother distorted Champollion's message as if he was a part of the cartel, a la Hegel, who had begun and were forcefully propagating the false foundations of a Caucasoid Egypt.

First the American, then the French Revolution produced an age of intellectual boldness that within a few decades, man's powers of reason expanded immensely. The idea of the *Encyclopedia* came into being and the French *Philosophes* and their British and German counterparts created all manner of philosophical paradigms based on the teaching of the Greeks, Romans, Medieval and even early Modern philosophers whose intellectual foundations were traceable to ancient Egypt and Africa.

However, by 1800 A.D., because the European trade in African bondsmen was at its height a new movement, grounded in prejudice, racism, and white supremacy emerged to deny the role of Africans in Egypt.

The German philosopher Wilhelm Hegel was a standard bearer of this movement that so stained the intellectual consciousness of Europeans and even some Africans that the idea of a "Caucasoid Egypt" began to take hold. So powerful has this line of thought been espoused, though false, even the masses of non-intellectual Europeans were emboldened and made proud in propagation of a white over Black mentality and to this day trumpet this false notion. This falsity existed, nevertheless, side by side with the works and revelations of scholars such as Volney, Denon, Godfrey Higgins and much later, Gerald Massey, Kersey Graves, Raymond Dart, Albert Churchward and even Patti and Greaves whose scholarship revealed the greatness and intellectual contributions of Africans in Egypt.

The decipherment of Egyptian hieroglyphics set in motion a number of things that developed and created significant spin-off throughout the Nineteenth Century. The first of these was an enormous interest in the study of the ancient monuments. This in turn had an equally enormous impact on later archaeological excavations and rapid print of reports that fed the emerging readership of the "Penny Press" in such places as England and elsewhere on the continent of Europe. By the end of the 19th Century, a whole slew of organizations especially from England, including The **Egypt Exploration Fund**, founded by Amelia Edwards and Stanley Lane-Poole; and the **Egyptian Research Account** spearheaded Nile Valley excavations with rapid publications of these reports on every conceivable site in Egypt. Much of this activity was matched by German, French and Swedish interests. Turkish, Polish and other nations' interests came later but equally held their own.

American institutions as the Metropolitan Museum of Art, Brooklyn Museum, Boston Museum of Fine Arts, Philadelphia Museum, and schools as the University of Chicago, Harvard, California, etc., sponsored excavations to Egypt and secured the beginnings of their collections. Each published a journal extolling the progress of their acquisition process as well as issued reports on their field work and any other interesting developments taking place at the time. Universities that did not sponsor excavation expeditions subscribed to books published on the subject so that old universities such as Columbia, etc., have all the books as they came out year after year.

Into the Egyptian Mind. Cairo Museum of Egyptian Antiquities. Oarsmen at work propelling a boat.

Into the Egyptian Mind. Cairo Museum of Egyptian Antiquities. One of the many halls with display cases. It would take days to examine the extensive collection of this museum numbering some 120,000 pieces.

Into the Egyptian Mind. Cairo Museum of Egyptian Antiquities. Decorated stone coffin and sarcophagus.

The phenomenon as Brian Fagan entitled "The Rape of the Nile" began to unfold following discovery of the Rosetta Stone and Champollion's decipherment. There were no rules governing antiquities in Egypt at its early time in the 19th Century.

This reminds me and is a sort of parallel. I was being chauffeured in Cairo on way to Sakkara. My driver's name was Gala. El Sawy. Trust me, there are a great many cars in Cairo! We came close to a collision and as a driver in the passenger seat; I instinctively moved my foot to "mash the brakes." He noticed! I said: "I'm a driver too." He replied: "Ah! You drive with the rules. There are no rules for driving in Cairo." Now to return to my topic!

The initial ring leaders in the "Rape of the Nile" were Salt and Belzoni, the "strongman Egyptologist;" As Sgt. Major once said: "If it's not tied down, I'll move it." These antiquities hunters stole everything they could get their hands on, large or small, to sell in Europe. Some things were purchased from native Egyptian dealers who were beginning to realize there's money to be made in Egyptian antiquities. Everyone got into the act to secure antiquities and to sell to institutions, governments, and private collectors. And so, it continued for more than a century as the "Rape of the Nile" ensued laying the foundations for the grand museum collections that would stun and entertain visitor today. All this before the Egyptian authorities decided to impose some rules for antiquities collection and export.

It's interesting how in 1881 with the discovery of the "Deir el Bahari cache of Royal Mummies" one report boasted how this find would now put the Boulak, today's Cairo Museum of Egyptian Antiquities, on par with such European Museums as Turin and the Louvre.

As all this madness unfolded, a few voices could be heard "crying in the wilderness" about the "Destruction of Ancient Monuments in Asia and Africa," specifically Egypt. Those antiquities removed from Egypt were never "gift wrapped" by some clerk in a Bazaar. The rascals, thieves and plunderers, who stole those objects, viz., statues, columns, stela, paintings, sarcophagi and their lids, obelisks, jewelry, mummies, coffins, etc., used all manner of tools and strategies to uproot and remove those objects from their positions in situ. In the process much damage was done to the monuments.

In my researches, I discovered in ancient times temples were destroyed in two different ways, other than by some natural disaster as an earthquake. In the first instance, whether internecine struggles between the adherents of rival deities and theologies, who attacked the other's temple out of spite; or, invading forces whose initial intent and target was the state's principal god's temple that they wrecked before retreating. A good example of the first is the conflict unleashed in the Amarna Revolution when Amenhotep IV, Akhenaton's god Aton decreed the name of his rival Amon should be erased and his temple attacked. When the Aton was overthrown by Amon's people, they in turn attacked and destroyed the Aten's temple, his city Amarna and wherever his name where it could be found.

On the other hand, invading forces, at first the Hyksos, who came after the Middle Kingdom, wreaked much destruction on temples and other infrastructure before they settled down to live in Egypt amidst the destruction they had unleashed. It's no wonder these invaders were expelled by the 17th and 18th Dynasty kings who later founded the New Kingdom glory days or "Golden Age" of Egypt. Equally too, with the efforts at expulsion, Egypt became a military and imperial power. In the second same instance of destruction of temples, the Assyrians and Persians destroyed much, hauled away a great deal and left a bad taste in Egypt. Many temples were destroyed by them, principally Karnak and Luxor, home of the Theban and Empire god Amon-Ra. One could well imagine "Their March through Egypt" or "spreading of locust" mentality as they scorched the earth from Delta to Luxor. If their actions at Karnak and Luxor were such one could well imagine the wake of destruction they left in their path up and down the Nile in their invasion and retreat.

Conversely, when the Ethiopians invaded Egypt and founded the 25th Dynasty, they respected the culture, according to Piankhi, "of the ancestors." The Ethiopians built and repaired structures, brought stability and prosperity to Egypt and defended her against foreign hordes. Alas, they were pushed back into Nubia or Ethiopia when the hordes returned with their evil intent to wreak further destruction. In their retreat, the Ethiopians did not destroy!

Into the Egyptian Mind. Cairo Museum of Egyptian Antiquities. A contingent of Nubian soldiers viewed from the rear.

Into the Egyptian Mind. Cairo Museum of Egyptian Antiquities. Anubis at work on the inside of a decorated coffin.

Into the Egyptian Mind. Cairo Museum of Egyptian Antiquities. Sarcophagus and lid with famous dwarf on the top.

To the Greeks and Romans, equally, can be attached the label or term "appreciative conquerors." First, the Greeks were amazed at the color of the Egyptians, as well as the high level of intellectual, religious, scientific, art and architectural and medical knowledge and social, philosophic and ethical standards the Egyptians had attained. The Greeks employed a two-pronged strategy of oppressing the people yet paying "lip service" to the religious establishment, the Priesthood, which played a significant role in the culture. Greek rulers who became Pharaohs of Egypt started and completed temples and also repaired structures throughout the land. Surviving temples are at Edfu, Kom Ombo, Esneh and Philae, among others.

Equally too, Greek travelers and scholars visited Egypt in search of adventure and knowledge and would write volumes later. Many gave credit for the sources of their knowledge. Nearing the end of the 20th Century, as critical Afrocentric scholarship developed and the truth about ancient Greece and

Africa unfolded, the many names of Greek visitors and philosophers who studied in Egypt became known.

The second type of temple destruction occurred in a more orderly manner. When a pharaoh wanted to build a great temple he generally chose a site already sacralized by an existing older temple so he systematically and orderly dismantled the older structure to make way for the new one. Oftentimes bricks or stone from the older temple would be reused as foundation fill for walls, beds of colonnades or as fill for pylons. Nevertheless, it was the Egyptians who willingly and in an orderly manner dismantled or destroyed their temples.

By mid-19th Century the intellectual assault on Egypt had begun to pick-up steam. As the museums of Europe and other academic institutions could now boast of having extensive collections, a sort of "possession is nine-tenths of the law" mentality emerged. This sort "cart before the horse" syndrome in essence argued "Since we Europeans have all these antiquities, then naturally the ancient Egyptians were Caucasians." Naturally, this did not go well with the visual images of the monuments given the "existential data contradicts the symbolic representation." So, the linguistic argument was put forward. A whole slew of arguments was proposed for the origins of the Egyptians and as a result, distortion and omission became the order of the day. The claim that Ancient Egyptian was a Semitic-Indo-European language was reinforced with a number of routes in which the Caucasoid Indo-European was thought to enter Egypt.

Into the Egyptian Mind. Cairo Museum of Egyptian Antiquities. Painting imitating Nefertari in her tomb.

Into the Egyptian Mind. Cairo Museum of Egyptian Antiquities. Bust of a king with straight beard and wearing Nemes headdress.

Into the Egyptian Mind. Cairo Museum of Egyptian Antiquities. King flanked by two goddesses. Notice how the faces are defaced, "Purposefully and systematic."

Pardon my digression but let me make this point. Today the racists mount a "bald-face" false claim that the ancient Egyptians were Caucasians. The argument shifted from being

Indo-European to Caucasoid to Caucasian. The Cairo Museum contains the Maherpra Papyrus, Number 142, which shows a very dark individual who stands before Osiris. In many instances Osiris is shown on papyrus as being black or even green as a symbol of fertility. In this case, while Maherpra's face is clearly evident, the Osiris before whom he stands has his face and arms erased or disfigured. This may appear purposeful, simply because if Maherpra's ethnicity is questioned, he stands before a Black image of Osiris, it does not take much to connect the dots. Are you following this line of argument? Nevertheless, the place or note-card attached to the display, done by Gaston Maspero, indicated that the tomb of Maherpra was discovered by Loret in 1899 at Thebes. He was described as the "Fan-bearer and child of the Nursery, Maherpra," of the 18th Dynasty, during the reign of Amenhotep II, son of Thutmose III. The card reads: Mahepra "may have been the son of Thutmose III and a Negress." Even further, it continued: "A detailed examination of his mummy which showed that he died at about 20 years of age, also showed that he was Negroid, but not actually a Negro."

How interesting, Caucasoid to Caucasian but Negroid not Negro. It can here be pointed out that the word Negro was a 16th Century AD invention by the Spanish and therefore any translation of ancient texts that inserts the name Negro is suspect. Let's face it, the name Negro, according to the book: *The Word Negro: Its Even Intent and Use*, is a racist term. In some translations, the Egyptian kings are made to say vile things about Negroes of Nubia. Dr. Ben Carruthers has argued these modern translators have put racist rhetoric in the minds and mouths of the ancient kings who never knew such things.

Another example can be made as part of the distortion and omission argument in the repertoire of the falsification of ancient Egyptian history. The famous American Egyptologist James Henry Breasted produced the classic *Records of Ancient Egypt* in 5 Volumes (1905-1907) by the University of Chicago.

Everyone knows the notion of "pick of the crop" means you choose the best in any lot, particularly if you intend to display it to the public with the intent of conveying a message, however false. Practically everyone is familiar with the idea of "The White Man's Burden."

During the Slave Trade perpetrated by Europeans on Africans from 1441 to the 1880s, European behavior has been described as "naked imperialism." With the abolition of the Slave Trade and the "second coming of Europe to Africa" the tactic changed to "Enlightened Imperialism." This meant the Africans shall pay the Europeans in land, raw materials and mineral resources for rescuing them and bringing the light of Christianity and civilization to Africa.

First and foremost, Christianity was not brought to Africa, as the *African Origin of Christianity* has been demonstrated by Gerald Massey, ben-Jochannan and John Jackson.

The Immaculate Conception has its origins at Abydos where this is clearly evident in Seti I's Mortuary Temple to God Osiris, the world's earliest site of pilgrimage. The death and resurrection of the savior is as old as the time when the gods ruled Egypt. Osiris was a good king, of divine origin, who taught his people love, compassion and industry. Out of jealousy, his evil brother Seth and his cohorts beguiled, entrapped, killed and mutilated Osiris. His faithful wife Isis and sister Nephthys (the two Marys?) with the help of divine messengers, Thoth and Anubis, found and reconstituted the god who became the judge of the dead and ruler of the underworld. The belief in the salvation, promised for the faithful permeated Egyptian civilization for the millennia of its existence. Because of the potency of the Osiris belief system, while the Egyptians, the first people to emerge from the mist of antiquity with a true sense of religious and spiritual consciousness, had many gods whose fortunes rose and fell, yet the Osiris cult remained consistent throughout.

Second, the first Christian Nation to exist was the African nation of Ethiopia, who has held steadfastly to Christianity despite the many challenges it faced from neighboring peoples who practiced other faiths.

Third, as Jesus the Christ anguished on that perilous march to be crucified at Calvary, it was an African Simon of Cyrene who came to his assistance and helped bear the cross. Just as Wortham's One mummy so its Caucasian" syndrome, Simon the Black may refer to Blacks over that North African land. Nevertheless, that humanistic concern has been at the foundation of African people's acceptance and practice of the principles and promise of Christianity, particularly the admonition to love thy neighbor as thy self. Unfortunately, the late comers who practiced and brought Christianity to Africa did not practice that fundamental tenet to love their neighbor as themselves.

Finally, if the Africans were rescued it was from an inhuman condition Europe had created called the Slave Trade and Slavery. If rescued from the frying pan of this condition, they were placed in the fire of colonialism that a century later the Africans are yet to recover to enjoy the "benefits Europe brought." Imperialism was replaced by Colonialism, and then independence was replaced by Neo-colonialism and the technological conundrum of challenges in the post-computer age.

All this notwithstanding, in Egypt specifically, "Enlightened Imperialism" took the form of a "quid pro quo" in the method of archaeological excavation to rescue the history of the past, resulting in "Intellectual imperialism." This new form of historical inquiry complemented linguistic studies well underway for decades. Significant archaeological excavation was undertaken from 1870 onwards by the Egypt Exploration Fund, the British School in Egypt, the British School in Athens, and the French, Italians, Germans, Americans, etc. The work of the British in Egypt was particularly interesting for one man, William Matthew Flinders Petrie spearheaded the approach that brought along an untold number of colleagues and their wives who produced the superabundant body of work credited to the above groups. As excavation followed excavation, rapid publication of reports fueled a developing frenzy for knowledge of antiquity as well as seeking artifacts of antiquity to hold and admire.

Into the Egyptian Mind. Cairo Museum of Egyptian Antiquities. Hatshepsut in a kneeling attitude offering two ointment jars. She wears the Nemes Headdress and sports a short beard.

Into the Egyptian Mind. Cairo Museum of Egyptian Antiquities. Royal couple put together after being broken up. Notice the Cartouche or Shennu at the feet.

Into the Egyptian Mind. Cairo Museum of Egyptian Antiquities. The Khepre beetle in stone.

The years 1870 to 1930 can be considered the "Golden Age" of British Archaeology in Egypt. Concessions to excavate were given freely since Egypt was under British Administration. Because a Frenchman, Champollion, had cracked the Code of Hieroglyphics, the tacit traditional acceptance held that the top antiquities position in Egypt should be held by a Frenchman. Rightly so, the French have maintained a distinguished tradition in Egypt from Champollion, through Mariette, Chabas, Maspero, Le Grain, Chevier, etc. While Mariette labored to excavate innumerable sites and establish a museum to house the recovered artifacts, Maspero emerged as a most prolific writer and authority on ancient Egypt, even though some of his calls were questionable.

Maspero collaborated well with the British Administrator Lord Cromer and this aided requests for British concessions to excavate. In addition, to organizational rights to dig, private individuals plied the Nile in their own boats and visited numerous sites and dispatched their observations to journals, newspapers, club meetings, and those therefore, supplemented the more extensive Memoirs published by such entities as the Egypt Exploration Fund and the British School in Egypt. Oftentimes, however, the observations of the private individuals though published in magazines, journals or newspapers never made it into the more established published works. As such then, these important tid-bits are now "lost" from history and only the most resolute research inquiry could ferret out these gems that are caveats to the racist juggernaut that's seeking to claim Egypt as Caucasian as opposed to African. This is why Dr. ben-Jochannan recommended "Find the earliest materials available and work from there." This advice may very well be useful because modern books are so sanitized they have followed Hegel's dictum by "removing Egypt from Africa and Africans from Egypt."

After the early ruthless methods of antiquities acquisition in the age of "Enlightened Imperialism" the cost to Egypt for systematic and scientific excavation was the right to pick some of the best pieces from recovered artifacts. Granted, much was recovered in excavation but when one views the displays mounted at museums throughout the world in Britain, France, Spain, Italy, Turkey, Australia, America, all with multiple cities housing Egyptian collections, one gets the idea of the great volume of the "Culture in Captivity." Fact is, only the best pieces were chosen for display in European public collections and with the suggestive nature of interior decoration enhanced by lighting, "Caucasian Egypt" has been achieved. However, it's sad that the general European and American public could be so misled by their own people, that all they know is based on a faulty foundation. This is not surprising since the Donation of Constantine, a forgery, remained undetected for nearly six centuries. What is, however, frightening, as critical Black scholarship such as the Afrocentrists unearth and expose the hypocrisy of "Race-based scholarship" they are attacked for seeking to set the record straight. I suppose people prefer the comfort of their ignorance rather than challenges of truth crushed to earth which shall rise to enlighten the ignorant and rightfully educate those searching for truth and meaning in historic scholarship.

Into the Egyptian Mind. Cairo Museum of Egyptian Antiquities. Golden vulture with wings outstretched and holding objects in its talons.

Into the Egyptian Mind. Cairo Museum of Egyptian Antiquities. Colossal statue of King Amenhotep III and his wife Queen Tiye.

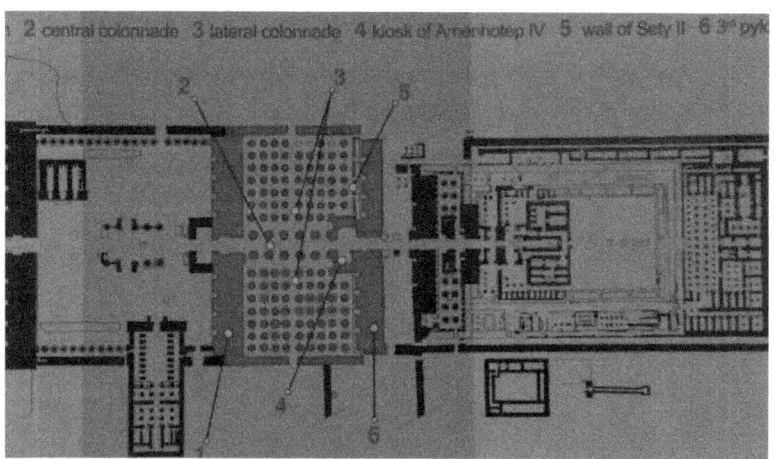

Into the Egyptian Mind. Plan of the Temple of Karnak showing the Hypostyle Hall highlighted.

Into the Egyptian Mind. Karnak Temple of God Amon. Erik Monderson stands in Taharka's Eastern Kiosk, beyond the *Akh Menu* (top); and columns of the Kiosk (bottom).

Into the Egyptian Mind. Egyptian Art. Papyrus. Celebration in which the King is among the gods in their astounding regalia.

www.ingramcontent.com/pod-product-compliance
Lightning Source LLC
Chambersburg PA
CBHW061948300426
44117CB00010B/1254